DON'T BE A TOURIST IN LONDON

THE MESSY NESSY GUIDE

A BOOK BY VANESSA GRALL

with writers and explorers

Molly Russell and Luke J Spencer

THIS BOOK BELONGS TO

____

*PLEASE RETURN WITH CARE**

QUESTIONABLY LEGITIMATE LIBRARY CARD NO. _______________

LOOKS COOL ANYWAY

LONDON BOOKMARKS	PAGE NO.
FOUND A TREASURE ON A VISIT TO...	
ATE LIKE A KING AT...	
GUILTY PLEASURE ALERT:	
THAT PECULIAR PLACE:	
GOOD TIMES AT...	

*IF LOST OR OVERDUE, PLEASE KINDLY CONTACT _______________

ye
Olde
Books

Good, we've found each other. I think we're going to make ideal companions in London. You've figured out that in an unpredictable world, time is far too precious to lose just scratching the surface on the tourist trail. You're looking for something personal and experimental; a different kind of road map that lets you follow your own instincts and emotions. Meanwhile, I've crossed out the "top-rated attractions" and major landmarks they said you had to see and instead, thought about how to switch our imaginations on again.

I'm Nessy by the way. I was born and bred in London and yet, I left the city that raised me, carrying with me childhood memories and a few ghosts from those very confusing years of young adulthood. The years passed, we had fleeting reunions, and in that time apart, I became an accidental travel writer and seeker of rabbit holes. You might have tumbled down one of them on MessyNessyChic.com, my long-running online cabinet of curiosities, or picked up my first book, *Don't be a Tourist in Paris*, and followed me onto New York for the second. To complete the 'Don't be a Tourist' trilogy, there was never any doubt that London was indeed calling. I always knew I'd come home again, one way or another, but how peculiar it was, to return to my hometown as a different person; as an outsider looking in. To help test my own formula on the city, I enlisted a small but trusted circle of Londonian writers and explorers who share an incurable curiosity; a desire to unlock the secrets of our urban environment. And so, as my whispers became words, shaped by the tides of change, heartbreak and healing, motherhood and milestones, cultural shifts and lest we forget, a pandemic, I came to know London all over again. Not as a tourist, but as an individual.

In case you're wondering, "tourist" isn't a dirty word here. Even the most experienced traveller should do something 'touristy' every now and again if the mood strikes. But mass tourism, now exacerbated by social media, has this funny way of making sure we all end up doing the same thing. This book inspires a different way to start your own journey, reminding us to check in with ourselves before hopping on the tour buses or making exhaustive bucket lists. What are you actually in the *mood* for? Each chapter is created for different mindsets, emotions, insecurities, niche interests and personalities, without worrying about the final destination. Use them to travel playfully, wandering freely in between points of interest and leaving room for chance. Break free of conformity and the impersonal nature of mass tourism by zig zagging around London soaking up the surroundings, collecting stories, asking questions, learning from unexpected characters. Learning about *ourselves*. Isn't that why we humans started travelling to begin with? The emphasis is less about ticking places off a list than it is about self-discovery. In this way, whether at home or abroad, in London or your local park, all destinations are rendered equal, and you can become the constant, artful traveller in a brave new world. Now, let our wild card adventure begin...

Nessy (aka Vanessa)
Founder, Editor and Janitor of Messy Nessy Chic

What's in this Book

MAP OF
LONDON
Scale of 1 Mile
KILBURN
CAMDEN TOWN
ISLINGTON
HOXTON
HAGGERSTONE
London Fields
Victoria Park
REGENTS PARK
CLERKENWELL
PADDINGTON
MARYLEBONE
BAYSWATER
OXFORD STREET
HOLBORN
CITY
STEPNEY
COMMERCIAL ROAD
HYDE PARK
Kensington Gardens
SERPENTINE
GREEN PARK
ST JAMES PARK
KENSINGTON
BROMPTON
WESTMINSTER
PIMLICO
LAMBETH
NEWINGTON
WALWORTH
KENNINGTON
BERMONDSEY
ROTHERHITHE
CHELSEA
BATTERSEA PARK
BATTERSEA
Water Works
RIVER THAMES
The Pool
DOCKS

Before You Start

In the spirit of rediscovering the personal joy and mystery of travel, remember to leave time to navigate the city spontaneously. See that map of London on the opposite page? It was found in a Thomas Cook guidebook published in 1894. With a pencil, draw a crooked line at random through its streets and take that line for a walk, noticing how the city's layout might have changed (or not) since. Find creative ways to use public transport: travel the entire length of a bus route that carries your lucky number, documenting what you see and find along the way (I've left you some space for scribbling notes at the back of the book). Think of the person who might find your notes in a hundred years time. And whether you keep this book on the coffee table or take it with you on your wanderings, don't be afraid to dog-ear your favourite parts, circle stuff and personalise it like your own scrapbook. These pages are yours now.

While I might not point you straight to them, some of London's most iconic landmarks and museums (which you won't need my help finding) can be very much worth the visit under the right circumstances; think quieter weekdays, during lunch hours or late night openings. And you'll often find this book hinting that you're "near the British Museum" or "around the corner from the Tower of London". Think of each address in this book as a clue, nudging you in the right direction to explore further at your own whim. You can always refer to the handy 'What's Near(ish) Me?' index at the end of the book.

London's main artery, the River Thames, an aquatic highway of activity and an iconic site in its own right, runs west to east bisecting the city into the North and South Banks – a reliable point of reference to get your bearings. Along its northern banks is the first City of London (always with a capital 'C') dating back to Roman times and now the financial capital of the world. This independent square(ish)-mile City *within* the city has its own government, Lord Mayor and separate police force, as well as some of its ancient border walls still visible near the Tower of London. Weird, right? In that sense, London is a tale of two cities – or is it three?! If we count the City of Westminster; the "second" London (founded two miles upstream by a medieval monarch who wanted to eclipse the more powerful Roman-born City); plus Greater London (all the smaller surrounding towns and urban pockets that expanded and merged over the centuries to become "London" as we know it), well, things can get a tad confusing. So let's just keep it simple: London's historical towns and villages

Hillgate Village, W8

within are now grouped into boroughs, which you'll find neatly sorted at the back of the book. Truthfully, one might hardly notice when crossing from one borough to the next, unless you're keeping an eye on the smallprint of the street name signs, which always indicate the borough (or City!) in which you are currently standing.

That vintage map, by the way, while it is lovely to look at (and travel playfully with), it probably won't cut it for pinpointing specific locations in a pinch. You can always pick up a recent map from any tourist office and most hotels, or, if you have a smartphone and you're coming from abroad, make sure your cellular plan includes data in the UK, or buy an eSIM (for roughly £10-£20 you can get more than enough data to cover your tracks). Do yourself a favour too, and procure a Visitor Oyster Card for riding the Tube, buses and even the Thames Clippers River Bus, a particularly enjoyable way to sail through rush hour between East and West London.

Running into unexpected diversions and closures is inevitable in a constantly evolving city, so double checking on locations online or calling ahead is always a good idea. And keep in mind that from the moment the ink dried on this book to the moment you've opened it, some places may not be exactly the same as they were when we wrote about them. If you discover a drastic change in one of our recommendations, slip us a note at contact@messynessychic.com or via Instagram @messynessychic.

Questions? Feel like you need just a little more guidance on something specific? Discover the Messy Nessy Chic Keyholder program, where you'll find direct access to my personal email hotline and travel concierge, an eBook library, an A-Z global directory of travel tips, as well as every location in this book digitally mapped. (MessyNessyChic.com/Unlock-The-Vault)

Northington Street, WC1

Shortcuts!

Could you just fire off some restaurant suggestions at me?

Sure thing. Pick the perfect restaurant for date night from pg 55 to 71. See where the cool kids are dining on pg 237 or go undercover with our secret restaurants on pg 269. My favourite Mediterranean gems are on pg 281. Eating on a tight budget? Try the best of British comfort food from pg 204 and don't forget London's most charming pubs, found throughout this book, with a good chunk of them waiting at the start of chapter 1.

Okay but it has to be really special...

Do a pull-out-all-the-stops kind of dinner at Sessions Arts Club on pg 66. Plot a surprise party, from intimate birthdays to extravants bashes on pg 318. How about a secret supper club? There's one on a Tube carriage on pg 327, one with a 'Dolce Vita' cinema night on pg 281 and one in an idealist's village deli on pg 271.

It's raining. What do you recommend I do today?

Take cover and go exploring below ground on pg 325. Linger at an underrated museum or kill time snooping through other people's houses in chapter 3. Stage a scavenger hunt at Harrods on p g295 or hang out in a revived Art Deco playground at Battersea Power Station on pg 103. Call it a movie day and enjoy one of London's wonderful independent cinemas on pg 230 or spend the day at an unusual spa on pg 227.

Where do Londoners actually go shopping?

Hit the flea markets on pg 149 and find the little black book of a thriftaholic on pg 251. Join Dame Westwood down the King's Road or at Liberty of London on pg 122. Wander the car-free shopping village at Coal Drops Yard on pg 68. Splash some cash in Notting Hill's chic boutiques on Westbourne Grove or follow Mr. Bond to get suited and booted on pg 81.

I'm in London for a 10 hour layover, what should I do?

Decompress with a dose of London village life in Hampstead on pg 30. Sample all the things at Borough Market on pg 201. Phone home from London's original phone box on pg 357.

Where should I take my friends who are visiting from out of town?

Do afternoon tea, but do it right on pg 291. Get dressed up for dinner on pg 43. Revisit a few of the classics like an expert guide on pg 295.

The kids are coming too...

Your Mary Poppins playbook is on pg 303, but also check out all that London's green spaces have to offer on pg 388

Where should we go on a night out?

Hit the dancefloor on pg 244. Catch a show at the pub on pg 177. A few of my favourite cocktail bars: Cahoots pg 43, Lounge Bohemia pg 273, WC Bloomsbury pg 331, Midnight Apothecary pg 59, The Last Tuesday Society pg 340, The Bridge pg 285 and Evans & Peel pg 278.

I'm thinking of getting out of town for the day, but I can't go too far...

Fake a vacation without leaving the city on pg 385, make it a tropical getaway at Kew Gardens on pg 299 and find inspiration for a fairytale weekend without driving more than 2 hours out of town on pg 397.

I have a meeting in London. Where should I suggest we meet?

For sophisticated client drinks in beautiful surroundings, try the NoMad Hotel on pg 380. To sit together with your laptops and plan world domination, set up basecamp in East London at Mare Street Maret on pg 48 or book a quiet and cosy alcove at the Windsor Castle pub in Notting Hill on pg 279.

I'd like to go on an interesting walk through the city. Can you set me on the right path?

Find my suggestions for an experimental walk through the city on pg 11. Discover one of London's lesser-known radical pockets of recent past in Vauxhall's leafy village on pg 270. Wander into London's Narnia on pg 30 and be pleasantly surprised by the place Charles Dickens hated most on pg 37. Look for dragons on pg 369 or vampires on pg 346. Start a conversation with concrete around the Barbican on pg 158 or take a skywalk with London's forgotten pedway system on pg 365. Soak up the river views in Hammersmith pg 21 or in charming Chiswick on pg 147.

Watch On The Thames, Upper Mall, Hammersmith

01
Lost in London

Where do you even begin with London? World-class culture, iconic landmarks and nearly 2,000 years of history to cover in a city twice the size of New York – the options are endless and expectations are high for the megalopolis often hailed as the greatest city on earth. Here's a thought: try the local pub. Our weary traveller needs a welcome drink, but also, a place to contemplate your next move; perhaps spurred by a chance encounter, a conversation overheard, or even a clue hiding amongst the mahogany. Remember to follow your own serendipitous path whenever you can. You're only ever a few unopened doors away from a truly unforgettable experience. Let the adventure begin...

A Pub Away from Home

Unlike a glitzy hotel lobby or a swanky cocktail bar, the pub is where you'll find a true British welcome. Warm and convivial, a place for the people to unwind after a hard day's grind; every Londoner has a local (pub, that is). The word 'pub', by the way, is shortened from 'public house', first coming into use in the late 17th century to indicate an establishment that was, quite literally, open to the public, at a time when alehouses looked much like any other house in the village. There's something irresistible about mixing history, battered fish with chunky chips and a good ale. If you love the idea of English pubs and everything they stand for, pick one that matches your mood and make it your first port of call in London...

The Dove

A Pint-Sized Ancient River Pub with an Arts & Crafts Afternoon

The Dove is one of those cherished pubs that'll stay etched in your memory of London; that perfect little hideaway you find one afternoon ambling along the river Thames. With wonky timber beams and an open fireplace, this tiny tavern tucked away down a leafy alley in Hammersmith has it all. Don't tell everyone, but the suntrap terrace overlooking the river is not only a superb secret beer garden but also a prime viewing location for the annual Oxford vs Cambridge boat race. The fish & chips and the warm hospitality never disappoint. But if walls could talk at this old-world pub, they sure would have some juicy stories to tell. It's been the haunt of a whole host of big names over the years. Legend has it that as the patriotism and pints started flowing one evening in 1740, poet James Thomson penned the lyrics to 'Rule Britannia'. Known to have the smallest bar room in England, with a certificate on the wall to prove it, this small but sturdy bar has propped up heavyweight writers (and drinkers) Ernest Hemingway, Dylan Thomas and Graham Greene. Textile designer William Morris also lived next door, so he likely stopped in for a pint on his way home too. *(19 Upper Mall, Hammersmith, W6, 020 8748 9474; Mon-Sat 11am-11pm & Sun 12pm-10.30pm; Dovehammersmith.co.uk)*

The Dove

Morris' Georgian brick mansion with idyllic views of the Thames is every bit as beautiful as you would expect from the giant of Victorian society. Kelmscott House is still a private residence, but the basement and coach house are home to the **William Morris Society**, where you can see his personal printing press, the place where he wove carpets and held meetings of the Socialist League. It's an unexpected little museum that makes a perfect post-pub lunch discovery. *(Kelmscott House, 26 Upper Mall, Hammersmith, W6; +44 020 8741 3735; open*

Thursday, Saturday and Sunday afternoons, 12pm-5pm; Williammorrissociety.org). At the forefront of the Arts & Crafts movement, colourful fabric designs and printed textiles of Mr. Morris were the height of fashion, found in most well-to-do Victorian drawing rooms and artistic circles. To step back in time and see them *in situ*, take a five-minute walk further downriver to the preserved home of printer Sir Emery Walker, who was a great friend and mentor to the designer. A treasure trove of Morris fabric, wall coverings and furniture, **Emery Walker Trust** is open on Thursdays and Saturdays and guided visits are hosted by passionate volunteers who bring the house and the history to life (booking required). Finish up your afternoon wandering this idyllic slice of Hammersmith with an "Arts & Crafts Riverside Walk", highlighting some of the movement's history and stories of the area, which can be downloaded from the house museum's website. *(7 Hammersmith Terrace, London W6; open Thurs & Sat 11am-3pm; +44 020 8741 4104; Emerywalker.org.uk/plan-your-day).*

Gandalf's London Pub that Launched a Thousand Ships

There are some pubs that are particularly special; that have outlasted the eras, withstood wars and in one case, launched a thousand ships. **The Grapes** is a riverside pub that's stood on the pebbled banks of the Thames in London's Docklands area for nearly 500 years. And guess who owns it today: none other than Lord of the Rings' wizard himself –Gandalf, a.k.a, Sir Ian Mckellen. On a Monday night, when he's not off making movies, McKellen will usually host the pub's quiz night. His cosy establishment is part of a terrace of Georgian houses called Limehouse Reach that survived the Nazi Blitz which pulverised most of the Docklands during WWII. During the reign of the first Queen Elizabeth, this patch of dry land among the riverside marshes became the centre of world trade in the 16th century, and when the tide goes out, you can still see the pebbly beach below from which famed explorer Sir Walter Raleigh set sail on his third voyage to the New World. Charles Dickens knew the area well and in the opening chapter of his novel, *Our Mutual Friend*, he described a pub which is widely believed to be The Grapes. "A tavern of dropsical appearance... long settled down into a state of hale infirmity. It had outlasted many a sprucer public house, indeed the whole house impended over the water but seemed to have got into the condition of a faint-hearted diver, who has paused so long on the brink that he will never go in at all."

The Grapes in the 19th century

The Grapes retains the welcoming atmosphere of a true 'local' for the Limehouse residents, counting among them Sir Ian McKellen, who lives a few doors down. Behind the bar is a stuffed fluffy cat given to him by his old friend Patrick Stewart. By the window there's a bronze sculpture of Gandalf, naturally. The house favourite – fish & chips, of course –won't set you back more than a tenner, or you can opt for the fancier dining room upstairs. McKellen's co-owner of The Grapes is newspaper magnate Evgeny Lebedev who also owns *The Evening Standard* and *The Independent* newspapers. Before the Winter 2014 Olympics in Sochi, Lebedev organised a meeting in the upstairs dining room between Prime Minister David Cameron and activist comedian Stephen Fry to discuss gay rights in Russia. History is still being made in this improbable little pub, so take a venture to London's Docklands, where the tang of the Thames constantly assails your nostrils and a terrific, historical pub lunch awaits –and maybe, just maybe, a pint with Gandalf.
(76 Narrow St, Limehouse, E14; +44 20 7987 4396; open everyday from 12pm-11pm; Thegrapes.co.uk)

A Cockney Knees-Up & Old Fashioned Sing-a-long

Amongst the tall glassy buildings shooting up in Mile End lies **The Palm Tree**, a relic of a pub, keeping the records of East London's past. Walking through the doors of this small but mighty boozer is like going back in time to a Friday night in the 1950s. Just like old photographs, The Palm Tree lives in a different colour palette. Everything inside is soaked in a crimson hue. Legendary cockney couple Val and Alf have presided over the joint since the war and little has changed since then, including their fully-functioning vintage cash register. Be sure to drop by on a Friday for an intimate jazz house. The house band of local East End crooners rarely disappoint, and they're happy to share their piano with emerging young talent too (Amy Winehouse played some gigs here early in her career). It's a true cockney experience no modern bar can compete with.
(127 Grove Rd, Mile End, E3; +44 020 8980 2918; Everyday 12-11.30pm)

A Pint with the Pilgrim Fathers at the Old Post Office Pub

The catalyst of American settlement can be traced to a tiny, old fashioned pub along the banks of the Thames. Tucked away down in Rotherhithe, once a bustling sea port dating back to Elizabethan times, is the **Mayflower pub**. Today it's dwarfed by surrounding factories, renovated warehouses and new builds, but it was from the jetty just outside the pub that the Pilgrim fathers set sail in 1620, bound for the New World. The Mayflower claims to be the oldest pub on the River Thames, and has been around under different names–"The Shippe" and "The Spread Eagle and Crown"–since 1550, until an enterprising landlord three centuries later renamed the pub in honour of the Mayflower's crew. The docks may no longer throng with masts and sail, but the surrounding old cobbled streets and candlelit interior of the Mayflower evoke a bygone era when Britain was the world's greatest seapower. An old sailor's tradition still lives on in the Mayflower: back in the 1800s, when sailors arrived in port with little time to find a post office, they could buy a stamp at the bar along with their beer, allowing them to swiftly write their farewells to loved ones without ever having to leave the pub. It's still the only pub licensed to sell US & UK postage stamps, just ask at the bar and get to work on those letters home. A recent addition to the pub is a guest book signed by visitors who can prove they are descended from the original travellers on the Mayflower. And there's arguably no place more appropriate to celebrate Thanksgiving on British soil than this historic pub, which hosts decadent 3 course dinners around the American holiday, serving roast turkey, stuffing, cranberry sauce and the all-important pumpkin pie.

The actual Mayflower eventually returned to Rotherhithe where it was scrapped – pub legend has it that some of the ships' illustrious timbers found their way back to bar and were used in a later renovation. Find a seat on the rear terrace overlooking the port where Captain Jones likely once sat, looking out at his ship over a quiet drink, anticipating the perilous journey to come.
(117 Rotherhithe Street, Rotherhithe, SE16; +44 207 237 4088; Mon-Sat 11am-11pm, Sun 12pm-10.30pm; mayflower pub.co.uk)

The Mayflower pub

London's Poshest Pub

Cheyne Walk is one of those fabled London addresses that writers like Roald Dahl and Virginia Woolf chose for the homes of their protagonists. Famous residents include Sylvia Plath, the Gettys, Keith Richards, Mick Jagger and Marianne Faithful as well as Elizabeth Taylor, but if we never get to live in any of the majestic townhouses along Cheyne Walk, at least we can lunch there. **No. Fifty Cheyne** is a Victorian pub turned Michelin-starred secret that the Royal Borough holds close to its chest. Possibly the smartest pub in England today (although they pride themselves on being dog-friendly), it's owned by Sally Greene, the powerhouse restaurateur and philanthropist who also runs the legendary Ronnie Scott's jazz club (see pg 315). Look for the eggshell blue pub on the corner with its explosive floral arrangements climbing up the facade. Inside, the sumptuous dining rooms echo the grand interiors of those who live next door. An ideal address for celebrating something special with family over brunch (with bottomless prosecco) or an award-winning Sunday roast by the fire, with views of the Thames from upstairs. Take a post-roast stroll down Cheyne Walk, spotting the blue plaques together –there are ten in total for find.
(50 Cheyne Walk, SW3; +44 20 7376 8787; open Tues & Wed for dinner, Thurs – Sun for lunch, afternoon tea & dinner and Sunday lunch & afternoon tea; Fiftycheyne.com)

The Only Pub Left on London's Glitziest Street

If Sloane Street had a square on the Monopoly board, it would be one of the most expensive plots. Home to Harvey Nichols and all the French and Italian luxury brands luring a seemingly endless parade of supercars –the fact that one little British pub has managed to stand its ground here, sandwiched between Miu Miu and designer shoe guru, Roger Vivier, feels like a "David and Goliath" kind of victory (and a bit of an "up yours"). Licensed in 1835, **The Gloucester** is officially "the only public haven left on Sloane Street", an improbable slice of English comfort where you can definitely enjoy a hearty sausage & mash for a tenner or a fish finger sandwich for a fiver. Pop in for a pint, look around and ask yourself this: Do you really need those designer shoes when you've got hold-outs like this to restore the soul?
(187 Sloane St, Belgravia, SW1X; +44 207 235 0298; open Mon-Thurs 11am-11pm, Fri-Sat 11am-12am & Sun 12pm-11pm; Greeneking-pubs.co.uk/pubs/greater-london/gloucester)

A Rockabilly Social Club

The folks at **The Boogaloo** love music, so much so that they've got their own radio station broadcasting old school tunes to the world. This North London institution became part of celebrity folklore when Coldplay played an iconic gig here with Simon Pegg on the harmonica in the noughties. You can rely on a good time any night of the week at this unassuming corner pub with a 1950s rockabilly twist. You've got a games night on Monday, quiz night on Tuesday, poetry & film club on Wednesday, comedy club on Thursday, disco DJ sets until 2am on Friday & Saturday (dancefloor at your disposal) and for the cherry on the cake, Sunday afternoon is host to a gospel brunch and live country & blues band from 3pm. Both the staff and the Highgate locals are friendly and the buttermilk chicken burger and Tennessee ribs will go down a treat. *(312 Archway Rd, Highgate, N6; +44 20 8340 2928; open Mon–Fri from 12pm and from 10am on weekends; IG: @theboogaloopub)*

Beers at the Old Bowling Club

Victorian and Edwardian Balham has come a long way from its reputation some 30 years ago. Having spent a good part of the 20th century as a haven for crime, drugs and prostitution, it now has a Soho House, hip boutiques, farmers

markets and fiercely sought after real estate. A little piece of Balham's pre-gentrified spirit however, can be found just off busy Balham High Road at the **Balham Bowls Club**, a no-longer abandoned bowling club house dating to 1893, now a neighbourhood pub. The outside resembles a standard Victorian semi-detached house, but inside is a sprawling warren of cosy rooms and nooks, filled with old scoreboards, bowling trophies and other sporting reminders of the club's genteel past as a lawn bowls social club. To clarify, we're talking about the English outdoor version of the game played on grass, which dates back to the 13th century. Have a go! The bowling greens out back have been restored, while also doubling as a beer garden. Inside, wood panelling, low slung sofas, mismatched easy chairs and vintage trinkets give the BBC (as locals call it) a charming, old world atmosphere. From quiz nights to live music, there's always something exciting happening that lets you feel like a part of the community. The Bowls Club is run by Antic Pubs, who've carved out a niche in finding forlorn buildings, mostly in South London and turning them into thriving pubs: old Conservative Clubs, a Victorian tram shed, town hall, jobcentre and shuttered high street shops have all been lovingly restored to celebrate their past lives.
(7-9, Ramsden Road, Balham, SW12; +44 020 8673 4700; Mon-Wed 4pm-11pm, Thurs 4pm-12am, Fri 4pm-1am, Sat 11am-1am, Sun 12pm-11pm; balhambowlsclub.com

> ***"No, Sir, there is nothing which has yet been contrived by man by which so much happiness is produced, as by a good tavern or inn."***
>
> **– Doctor (Samuel) Johnson**

Continue your London pub crawl at these fine establishments:

- The Hollybush in enchanting Hampstead on pg 30
- A Georgian gastropub for date night on pg 58
- Some time-travelling Victorian gems on pg 89
- A secret medieval one on pg 77
- Pubs with theatres hiding inside them on pg 177
- Good places to strike up a conversation over a pint on pg 213
- A blooming marvellous one with a secret Thai restaurant inside on pg 275
- Secret beer gardens on pg 279

Start here (Where the tourists don't)

With a pint and some grub down the hatch, let's go for a wander, far from the madding crowd...

London's Narnia

Heaven is in Hampstead, a charming village on a hill in the north of London and one of the gentler ways to get acquainted (or reacquainted) with the city. It might feel like a hellish ascent up the spiral staircase from Hampstead tube station –the deepest station below ground on the city's entire network –but if you don't fancy a climb of 320 steps (the equivalent of a 15 storey building), there's a handy elevator to said heaven.

For hundreds of years, Hampstead was a Saxon village originally called *Hamstede*, meaning "homestead", where cows and sheep grazed and villagers grew crops. The wealthy elite began moving in to flee the plague that swept across the city in the 17th century. Medicinal springs were discovered in the 18th century, attracting an ever larger crop of London society to "take the waters"at their conveniently-close spa town. Naturally, 20th-century Hampstead became a haven for the intelligentsia, wealthy bohemian artists, writers, musicians, liberals; a real who's who of European eccentrics. Familiar names from a long list of famous residents include: Daphne du Maurier, Sigmund Freud (whose house you can visit, see pg 134) Peter O'Toole, Ringo Starr, Judy Dench, Sting, Boy George, Emma Thompson, George Michael, Helena Bonham Carter –you get the point. Despite its quaint architecture and bucolic charm, Hampstead has some of the most expensive houses in the city and more millionaires than any other neighbourhood in the country. But back to that quaint English charm... We'll begin with a taste of Hampstead's secret gems and curious streets a few minutes from the station where Holly Walk meets Church Row. Enter the gates of an enchanting historic graveyard lost in time and head up the slope, passing the tombstones of notable artists, writers, and poets being swallowed by nature and sinking into the earth. A site of worship has existed on the plot of land occupied by **St John-at-Hampstead Church** for as long as England was called England. You'll find a gate to leave the cemetery at the north-west corner. *(Church Row, London NW3; open 9.30am-4pm Mon-Sat, all day on Sunday)*

Continue heading up the hill admiring the pretty houses on your way to **The Holly Bush** pub, an achingly quaint 18th-century ale house tucked away on a tiny and impossibly picturesque curving street on the mount. You can get a perfect fish and chips in the rustic dining room or sit peacefully with a pint and a newspaper by the fireplace, enjoying the quiet chatter of locals coming and going. *(22 Holly Mount, London NW3; open everyday from midday to 11pm; +44 20 7435 2892; booking advised for dining; Hollybushhampstead.co.uk).*

Holly Walk, Hampstead

On your way to our next stop, take a small detour via nearby street, The Mount, keeping a keen eye out for a particularly charming enclave of cottages at number 12 (look for the white house with blue shutters). Carry on to **Fenton House**, where you'll be rewarded with a panoramic view from their attic balcony –one of the highest points in London –overlooking a stunning walled garden with meticulously trimmed hedges, trickling fountains, cheerful daffodil flower beds, an orchard and a greenhouse. Stay awhile and find a bench, making notes on your travels so far or starting a conversation with the friendly gardeners. The house itself is a 17th-century merchant's home bequeathed to the National Trust in 1952 by its last owner and resident, Lady Binning. It houses an unexpected collection of historical keyboard instruments (including one of the oldest harpsichords in the world), some of which are often played by a resident musician during visiting hours. Hopefully you'll find yourself wandering around looking at the paintings and porcelain while listening to some of Bach's greatest hits. *(Fenton House, Hampstead Grove, Hampstead, NW3 ; open Fridays, Sundays and bank holiday Mondays, 11am-4pm, pre-booking for house visits required while the garden-only tickets are available at the gate; Nationaltrust.org.uk/visit/london/fenton-house-and-garden)*

Let's now take a fifteen minute wander into the woods, the same woods that inspired C.S. Lewis to write *The Chronicles of Narnia*. Hampstead Heath is an enchanting 800-acre piece of countryside in the city which can't possibly be explored with a single visit, but a good place to start is the **Hill Garden and Pergola**.

Hollybush Pub

The faded splendour of this hidden Edwardian gem feels a little bit like stumbling upon London's lost garden of Babylon. Its tranquil terraces of ivy-covered pillars and arches were put here by a wealthy Lord to host extravagant summer parties from his mansion on the Heath. The garden fell into decline after World War II until the city began taking better care of it in the late 1980s, but the romance of a lost Edwardian Eden lingers. If you're ever in need of one, file it under 'places worthy of a marriage proposal'. *(The Pergola, Inverforth Close, Hampstead, NW3; open everyday from 8.30am-6pm)*

Before returning back to the depths of the London Underground at Hampstead station, zip around the corner to visit the charming shops of **Flask Walk**, starting with the Keith Fawkes antiques shop, filled to the brim with curious English bric-a-brac. Hampstead High Street is dotted with similar alleys. Wandering through the quiet backstreets, go on the hunt for **Mansfield Place**, a narrow enclave of brick houses behind their picket fences, pocket-sized lawns

The gardens at Fenton House, Hampstead

and uniquely decorated porches. Like a peaceful countryside hamlet, they're just about the most enviable homes you'll find in the city. When you can't make it to the Cotswolds for a weekend in the English countryside, Hampstead really is the next best thing.

Back to the pub? This time, a 30 year-old watering hole, complete with a beer garden and a jazz club. Behind the suntrap terrace of the **Duke of Hamilton** awaits **The Hampstead Jazz Club**, a well-loved music venue that hosts intimate performances most nights of the week.
(*Duke of Hamilton, 23-25 New End, Hampstead, London NW3; Mon-Sun, midday to 11pm; see the program at Hampsteadjazzclub.com/whats-on*).

The Mount, Hampstead

That's only scratching the surface with Hampstead of course, and you'll need more than an afternoon to enjoy its bounties. On the Northern edge of Hampstead Heath is the unmissable **Kenwood House** (see pg 172), a very worthy alternative if you don't have enough time to travel to one of the great English countryside estates. There are other wonderful house museums to add onto your Hampstead itinerary too, such as Goldfinger's modernist time capsule at **2 Willow Road** (see pg 79) and **The Freud Museum** (p134). Perhaps save another day to discover the rest of Hampstead Heath and its untamed pastures for winter walks with panoramic views or refreshing summer dips in the swimming ponds (see pg 387). You'll find no major landmarks or world-famous museums in this North London village, just a few of London's best-kept secrets.

Flask Walk, Hampstead

Opposite: Mansfield Place

PLACE

No. 70 Bermondsey Street

London's Not-so-Ugly Duckling

Charles Dickens detested Bermondsey. Immortalising it as the last refuge of the villainous Bill Sikes in *Oliver Twist*, he painted a grisly picture of the riverside area as a rookery of "every repulsive lineament of poverty, every loathsome indication of filth, rot, and garbage". The habitable ground amidst the marshes was once home to some French monks before it became known as the 'land of leather' in the 18th century; an industrial slum south of the river devoted to tanneries and skinners. One 19th-century social researcher described the water in Bermondsey as being "as red as blood" and Dickens remarked that the "air reeks with evil smells". If only he could see it today. Time has been very kind to Bermondsey and as you're probably aware by now, some of the most interesting places in cities used to be notorious slums.

We'll start with breakfast at the top end of Bermondsey Street, which used to be a causeway through the marshes for the monks to reach their monastery. At the entrance of an old mediaeval graveyard is **The Watch House**, a tiny café that was originally a posting for guards entrusted to protect the graves of St Mary Magdalen churchyard from body-snatchers. There was a time when the trade of stolen bodies was a thriving and lucrative business. Body snatchers, or resurrectionists, as they were also known, were commonly employed by medical schools and anatomists to advance their knowledge. Bodies were snatched regularly and without consideration and the epidemic resulted in "a harvest" of about 500 bodies per school year in some cities. It was such a problem that a necessity to guard the city's graveyards became commonplace across Britain. The Watch House today, restored to its former glory after years of neglect, retains the octagonal 19th-century structure with bare brick walls, but now serves up fresh artisanal baguettes and crumbly tarts on marble tabletops. In winter you can sip their creamy butternut squash and lentil soup by a roaring fire. *(199 Bermondsey Street, SE1, +44 20 7407; Mon-Fri 7am – 6pm, Sat – Sun 7.30am – 6pm; Watchhouse.com/blogs/locations/bermondsey-street)*

Is it Friday? You're in luck, there's the **Bermondsey Antique Market** just around the corner. Until the mid-1990s, this one used to get started at 4am as a *marché ouvert*, referring to a mediaeval French legal loophole that allowed for stolen goods to be sold openly (and shamelessly) between the hours of sunset and sunrise. The dodgy dealings were over in 1995 when some stolen paintings from the Inns of Court (where all of London's lawyers hang out, see pg 152) were caught being sold for £100 each at the market. Britain's best lawyers took swift revenge and saw to it that the *marché ouvert* was outlawed. These days, between the less shadowy hours of 7am-2pm you can still pick up some bargains; from traditional French antiques to vintage collectables, but leave with a clear conscience. *(11 Bermondsey Sq, SE1; Fridays 7am-2pm; Bermondseyantiquemarket.co.uk)*

Above: Bermondsey Antiques Market
Below: B Street Deli

Head back down Bermondsey Street to explore its old London charm. Look out for ghost signs on the old Victorian converted warehouse buildings pointing to the area's history as a hub of leather production. Stop in at the famous **White Cube** galleries for some cutting edge contemporary art. The minimalist space has some vast gallery rooms filled with large scale and breathtaking installations. Entrance is free too.
(144-152, Bermondsey St, SE1; +44 20 7930 5373; Mon-Sat 10am-6pm, Sun 12am-6pm; Whitecube.com)
Further up the street is the **Fashion and Textile Museum**, founded in 2003 by an icon of British design, Dame Zandra Rhodes. Their exhibitions always unveil some fascinating hidden fashion history and the workshop program is a wonderful resource open to all. If you have a staple item on your wardrobe you wished you had in another colour or a dress that's falling apart, sign up for one of their 'Copy Your Clothes' workshops. A museum tutor will share the skills used by couture fashion houses to copy elements of historical garments without the need to pull them apart. From pattern cutting and fabric painting classes to fashion drawing, there may very well be a class for you.
(83 Bermondsey St, SE1; +44 20 7407 8664; Tues-Sat 11am-6pm; Fashiontextilemuseum.org)
Hungry? Bermondsey Street has become a destination in itself for eating, with an abundance of excellent international restaurants such as the charming **Casse-Croûte** serving up authentic classics and plenty of French nostalgia *(109 Bermondsey St, SE1; +44 20 7407 2140; open for lunch & dinner everyday; Cassecroute.co.uk)* and drool-worthy bakeries like the **B Street Deli** across the street from the fashion museum
(88 Bermondsey St, London SE1; +44 7769 326455; open everyday 8am-11pm; Bstreetdeli.co.uk).

Casse-Croûte

Bermondsey Antiques Market

Try to save some room for Bermondsey's food markets later in the afternoon. The famous Borough Market is nearby (see pg 201) but on this occasion, turn your attention to a smaller alternative foodie haven nestled beneath a stretch of Victorian railway arches. **Maltby Street Market** feels a little bit like you're on the set of a *Peaky Blinders* episode, except instead of the industrial misery, you'll find a jolly street food feast for the eyes under string lights and British bunting. A stroll through the market by night, creating your own banquet as you go, makes for a pretty memorable evening in old London town. Bermondsey – *repulsive?* What in the dickens was Dickens on about?
(37 Maltby Street; open Friday 5.30pm–9pm; Sat 10am–5pm, Sun 11am–4pm; IG: @ maltbystmarket)

Maltby Street Market

Cahoots

All Dressed up & Nowhere to Go?

An Unforgettable Evening in a Wartime Tube Station

Cahoots is no ordinary vintage-themed speakeasy. Inside a veritable decommissioned underground Tube station that was once used as a WWII shelter, Soho's time travelling experience comes with cocktails and live jazz – and a full-sized replica of a 1940s Tube car. Wearing your vintage best, sip on period-accurate drinks from rationing tins and milk bottles, peering out of the carriage windows onto Northbound and Southbound train platforms, complete with wartime advertising posters on the walls. Hollywood's best set decorators would be floored by the amount of thought and detail that has gone into bringing the abandoned Kingly Court station back to life. And don't assume it's all just props and vintage replicas. When the disused station was discovered, a bounty of bric-a-brac was found and salvaged by the Cahoots creative team; crockery, furniture, lampshades and children's toys that had been dragged in by sheltering wartime Londoners to make their shelter feel more like home. Over the years, Cahoots has been slowly reviving the entirety of the station, from the underground train area (accessible by an old wooden escalator) to the old ground-level ticket hall for drop-in cocktails and most-recently, the cavernous signal station (the old control room) still covered in old switchboards, offering ideal acoustics for the live band that plays there every Friday and Saturday evening until the early hours. You can also catch live jazz and swing performances in the underground station area on Sunday evenings from 8.30pm to 11.30pm. Tables can be reserved online for all three areas, each offering unique, memorable experiences and reasons to come back again and again.

(13 Kingly Court, Soho, W1B; +44 20 7352 6200; Mon – Wed 4pm-1am, Thurs 3pm-1am, Fri 3pm-2am, Sat 1pm-2am, Sun 4pm-midnight; private hire available; more info & bookings at cahoots-london.com)

Find more underground ghost stations and wartime bunkers on pg 325 or for more live music, turn to pg 315.

Cahoots

Strictly Come Dancing at the Last of London's Lost Ballrooms

Let's twist again like we did last summer. And by last summer, we mean a balmy British summer of yesteryear, a trip back to the rockin' n' rollin' 1950s. Dust off your dancing shoes, grab your Teddy Boy or Girl and waltz on down to the **Rivoli Ballroom**. It may look like the love child of an English social club and an exuberant Art Deco boudoir, but here lies the last of London's lost ballrooms. After a stint as a cinema in 1913, a sprung maple dancefloor was laid in the late 50s, putting a much-needed spring in the quickstep of the post-war generation. As history comes full circle and many of the city's dance hall auditoriums are now transformed back into modern movie theatres, the Rivoli ballroom remains intact with its original vintage décor keeping it faithfully and forever 50s. It's a Grade II-listed vision of crimson, with Chinese lanterns, French chandeliers and kitsch glitter balls hanging from the ceiling. In between the regular retro party programme of jive and disco nights, you might spot a few famous faces hanging around. Elton John, Lana del Rey and the White Stripes all have music videos which feature Rivoli's signature red velvet backdrop. And you too can hire the venue for your own events of any kind –no rhythm required. A key date for the diary is the world-famous UK International Same-sex Ballroom and Latin

Rivoli Ballroom

Competition which has taken place here every year since 1997. You can practise your moves, build your confidence or simply suss out your competition on the first Saturday of every month, no judges, just jiving. See you on the dancefloor. *(350 Brockley Rd, Brockley, SE4; +44 020 0892 5130; Opening times dependant on events; Rivoliballroom.com)*

Treat Yourself to Crab, Cuvée and Chorus Lines

London is still a city where people dress up to go to the theatre, and there are some pretty spectacular Victorian venues to match your sartorial mood. Next to Broadway, the West End is one of the most famous and vibrant theatre districts in the world, home to around 40 theatres with something to suit all tastes (Westendtheatre.com). Before the show, take yourself to **Dalloway Terrace**. The restaurant's extravagant terrace is an overgrown greenhouse, draped in cascading flora that transform from a spectacular rose garden in spring and summer to a tunnel of auburn foliage in Autumn and a romantic winter wonderland during the holiday season. Accommodating early diners, the West End's theatre strip is close enough that you can feast on crab from the south coast and savour a bottle of Bloomsbury Cuvée before the curtain goes up.
(16-22 Great Russell St, Fitzrovia, WC1B, +44 207 347 1221; Mon-Sun 8am-10pm; afternoon tea 2pm-5pm; dallowayterrace.com)

Petit Paris in Piccadilly

Beneath the bright lights of Piccadilly Circus, a Parisian underworld of Art Deco elegance awaits. Descend the stairs of a perfectly pleasant street level café to enter the glorious golden age of fancy French dining. **Brasserie Zédel** is a sprawling arcadia of magnificent marble columns, gilded ceilings, and velvet rouge banquettes. To the soundtrack of tinkling jazz piano and a lively hum of chatter amidst clinking glasses, indulge in decadent dishes such as steak tartare and île flottante. It's glamourous gorging at its finest while being extraordinarily good value. If you opt for the prix fixe menu which is available all day every day, a slap up 3-course meal is yours for £16.00, or take 2-courses for just £12.25. Savings made, now go and splurge on post-dinner cocktails in the adjacent **Bar Américain**. Knock back Zédel juleps and French 75's surrounded by 1920s striped wood panelled walls and Josephine Baker artworks. It's Picadilly's Paris in all its beaux-arts beauty, without the passport checks.
(20 Sherwood St, Soho, W1F; +44 020 7734 4888; Mon-Sat 12-11pm & Sun 12-10pm; Brasseriezedel.com)

Press for Champagne

Did you know the Orient Express secretly stops in Soho? Climb aboard through the Art Deco doors and into one of the plush royal blue booths for a celebration of the golden age of travel, without the motion sickness. Put on your fancy pants for an evening of opulence and old-school glamour at **Bob Bob Ricard**. With polished marble counters, ornate metal fittings and waiting staff dressed in pastel pink waistcoats, this high-class establishment doesn't do things by halves. Welcome to the antithesis of minimalism. Wet your whistle and amuse your bouche the traditional way at this Anglo-Franco-Russian restaurant, with vodka shots served at −18 °C, jersey oysters and so. much. caviar. The *pièce de*

Brasserie Zedel

resistance, and most Instagrammable feature, is the addictively decadent 'Press for Champagne' golden buzzers at every table. With champagne practically mandatory, it's hardly surprising that BBR serves more bubbly than any other restaurant in the UK. What a boozy and blingy affair it is to live like Russian billionaires, even if just for a night.
(1 Upper James St, Soho, London W1F; +44 020 3145 1000; Open for lunch & dinner Fri-Sun, Mon-Thurs dinner only; Bobbobricard.com)

Bob Bob Ricard

A Clubhouse (For You and Your Laptop)

Easily-Distracted Entrepreneur

Don't worry about being booted off the wi-fi at **Mare Street Market**, it's tailor-made for laptop lurkers. Open everyday from 9am until late in the heart of East London, the sprawling and light-filled space is home to an all-day coffee bar and open kitchen, with a few extra amenities to indulge in the art of procrastination. In between emails, have a nose around the in-house antiques shop, browse the vinyl store, book an appointment with the barber shop for a close shave, a fringe trim, a blow dry (ladies welcome) or even a facial, and if you're feeling a little reckless, there's a tattoo parlour too.
(117 Mare St, London E8; +44 20 3745 2470; open Sun & Mon 9am-11pm, Tues-Thurs 9am-12am, Friday & Sat 9am-1am; Marestreetmarket.com)

A Free Museum, Library & Living Room

The **Wellcome Collection** is a grossly overlooked destination. Built to accommodate the research activities of American pharmaceutical entrepreneur Sir Henry Wellcome, today it's an open house of fascinating objects. The always-unusual (and free) exhibitions range from fine art to medical curiosities of eras past to thoroughly explore the history of human health. But that's only half of it. The Wellcome library and its spacious reading room upstairs might be one of the best places to hide out in London, furnished with comfy bean bags and couches for reading or sitting with a laptop, surrounded by beautiful art. Lounge as long as you like (also for free) but there is a great café with friendly staff and very reasonable prices. Conveniently located next to St. Pancras Station, if your train is delayed, go and make the most of it at the Wellcome building. Worthy of being more than just a place to kill an hour, it might turn out to be your second living room.
(183 Euston Rd, London NW1; +44 20 7611 2222; open Tues-Sun from 10am-6pm, until 8pm on Thursday; Wellcomecollection.org)

Mare Street Market

I Know a Wheelie Good Place

Searching for *la dolce vita* in London? Or perhaps just an excellent espresso and a cosy corner where you can park yourself (and your laptop) for a few hours? Originally a vintage scooter boutique and repair shop, **Scootercaffe** is now a quirky Italophile daytime café and cocktail bar. Take a seat in the charming red window where Bob, the resident cat, likes to doze off to Italian folk music and the aroma of freshly roasted coffee beans. It's easy to forget that you won't be walking out into a sundrenched, Neapolitan side street when you leave, so why not stay a little longer? Disappear downstairs when it gets dark and enjoy an *aperitivo* before it's time to take your vespa home.
(132 Lower Marsh, Lambeth, SE1; +44 207 620 1421; Mon-Thurs 8.30am-11pm, Fri 8.30am-12am, Sat 10am-12am & Sun 10am-11pm; Facebook.com/scootercaffe)

Take on the World from a Tube Carriage

Sitting high up on the remains of a disused railway viaduct in Shoreditch are four retired Jubilee Tube trains. **Village Underground** is a well-known gig venue in a restored Victorian warehouse (see pg 247), but most Londoners would have no idea those tube carriages sitting on its rooftop are available as co-working spaces for creatives and start-ups. You can apply for a space via the website (*villageunderground.co.uk/about*) and find yourself at the water cooler with a diverse pool of talented colleagues from artists and architects to filmmakers and producers. The views aren't bad and it sure beats a bog-standard beige office. Also good to know: Village Underground has two additional carriages from the 1960s Victoria Line that can be hired out for events, be it a pop-up, film shoot, fashion showroom, wedding, product launch or whatever you might be cooking up.They'll even deliver the 10 tonne trains to your event's location.
(54 Holywell Lane, Hackney, EC2A; +44 020 7422 7505; spaces available Mon-Fri 9am-6pm, music venue opens till late depending on events; Villageunderground.co.uk/hire)

Things to Do in London with
£10 in Your Pocket
£10
& Under
CASH THIS COUPON
£7
Three course meal
in a bookshop
p269
VALUABLE OFFER
CASH THIS COUPON
£9
Jazz concert
in a crypt
p316
VALUABLE OFFER
CASH THIS COUPON
FREE
to eavesdrop on
Parliament
p212
VALUABLE OFFER
CASH THIS COUPON
£8.40
Afternoon tea
& cakes
p292
VALUABLE OFFER
CASH THIS COUPON
£2
Philosophical
group therapy
p212
VALUABLE OFFER
CASH THIS COUPON
£10
Shopping spree
challenge
p251
VALUABLE OFFER
CASH THIS COUPON
£5
Cheapest movie
tickets in London
p232
VALUABLE OFFER
CASH THIS COUPON
FREE
Friday night at
the museum
p119
VALUABLE OFFER
CASH THIS COUPON
Pay what you can
Self- service breakfast
p428
VALUABLE OFFER
CASH THIS COUPON
FREE
To wander around
a Queen's house
p377
VALUABLE OFFER
CASH THIS COUPON
£4
To fake a vacation
in Provence
p385
VALUABLE OFFER
CASH THIS COUPON
Under £10
Two Pies
with mash
p208
VALUABLE OFFER
CASH THIS COUPON
Pay what you can
for an evening
at the theatre
p180
VALUABLE OFFER
CASH THIS COUPON
£8
All you can eat
curry lunch
p418
VALUABLE OFFER
CASH THIS COUPON
FREE
The best "nanny"
in the city
p314
VALUABLE OFFER

Campania & Jones

02

London, Just Like It Is in The Movies

(AND ON INSTAGRAM)

Here's the part where you get to live out your own 90s British romcom or your favourite period dramas, maybe even indulge in a few clichés. This is a chapter for the most charming and imaginative date spots, cinematic streets and dramatic diversions. London can be any 'genre' you choose; romantic, eccentric, gritty, iconic, but if you want to see the city like it is in the movies, it's time to start thinking like a location scout, or at least like a professional instagrammer.

Date Night: Cool & Casual

Window on the Water

You could "grab a drink" at any table, or you could suggest one that sits at water level, where the local ducks swim past your plates of fresh oysters and hand-cut chips. **The London Shell Co** has two barge boats in central London –the more romantic or formal option would be "The Prince Regent" which cruises down the Regent's canal, but for something more casual, but still highly original as far as date spots go, there's "The Grand Duchess", which remains static, moored on the Grand Union Canal in central Paddington and welcomes walk-ins for the ideal weekend rendez-vous. "Oysters on the canal at 5pm?" Somehow it just sounds nonchalant and sexy at the same time. Between 4-6pm, they're shucking oysters for £2 a piece and drinks are at happy hour prices too. Ask for a canalside counter table for two facing the windows. Enjoy the view and hopefully the company.

(The Grand Duchess, Sheldon Square, Paddington Central, W2; +44 7553 033 636; closed Sunday eve & Mondays; Londonshellco.com)

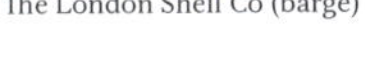

The London Shell Co (barge)

Wine & Cheese in a Historic London Nook

It's unlikely your date will know about **Tap & Bottle**, the hidden wine bar on the upper floors of an historic Grade II listed Georgian townhouse next to London Bridge. It's the kind of place that could probably land you a second and third date just so they could see what other London secrets you have up your sleeve. Situated in the old stomping ground of the notorious Kray Twins, it's got buckets of character and palatable history; nooks and crannies abound, exposed brick and old fireplaces where you can imagine the life of the family of 10 who once lived here. The outdoor terrace is a real hideaway underneath the railway arches and on the top floor, you can hire out "the snug" for intimate parties. As for the wine, with staff genuinely devoted to the grape, they'll really go out of their way to find the wine you think you're craving –and give generous pours to boot. When enough wine has worked its magic, wander into **Omeara** (Omearalondon.com) to catch some quality indie acts playing at the live music venue headed by Mumford & Sons' Ben Lovett, which can be conveniently reached via the mezzanine level of the bar.
(64 Union St, SE1; +44 20 3179 2906; Tues- Sat 4pm-11pm; Tapandbottlelondon.co.uk)

The terrace at Tap & Bottle

Gordon's Wine Bar

Mr. Kipling's Drinking Den

Gordon's Wine Bar is a crumbling candlelit warren of a drinking den and it also happens to be the oldest wine bar in London. Rudyard Kipling lived upstairs and wrote his novel *The Light that Failed* in the parlour above the bar. Located in the cellars beneath Charing Cross, this wine bar really is as old and unchanged as it looks. The building itself is from the 1680s and a drinking establishment opened in the 1860s. Now run by the same family since 1972, they kept the original décor as they found it, adorned with ghostly portraits of Victorians and the wrinkles of time. Guide your date to a rickety candlelit table and whisper sweet nothings over an excellent cheese board served with freshly baked French bread, pear chutney & quince jelly. Don't know your Chablis from your Chardonnay? Give the house's cheekily-named "Fat Bastard" wines a try, available as a light red Pinot Noir or a white Chardonnay. On a summer's day, you can opt for a table in the leafy back alley where they host regular al fresco wine tastings.

(47 Villiers St, Charing Cross, London WC2; +44 20 7930 1408; Mon-Sat 11am-10.30pm; Gordonswinebar.com)

Hidden Wine Rooms

Behind the Mediterranean blue shopfront of **Passione Vino**, past the shelves of 300+ Italian natural wines displayed against some enviable floral wallpaper, is a secret townhouse for wine lovers. Hiding beyond the shop are a number of cosy rooms over three floors where you can order fresh, homemade antipasti and exceptional wine. Eccentric and Italian-born Luca Dusi will welcome you with warmth and familiarity. He and his team will start sussing out your mood to match you with a wine you've never tried before. This is no place for your average Pinot and there is no 'wine by the glass'. It's all-natural, it's all very European; just go with their suggestions and let them show you a good time. *(85 Leonard St, Shoreditch, EC2A; +44 20 3487 0600; passionevino.co.uk; Mon-Fri, 12pm-9pm)*

A Reliable Rendez-vous at a Georgian Gastropub

For a casual and complication-free first date in London, you can't go wrong with a pub, but **The Thomas Cubitt** serves up just the right dose of sophistication, along with an outdoor terrace option for people-watching in warmer weather. No need to commit to a full dinner date, just order a few nibbles from the snack menu (try the lamb scrumpets with aïoli or crispy spiced squid), or if things go well, stay for a sirloin. End things with a stroll around Belgravia's elegant Eaton Square, developed by the Georgian master builder himself, Thomas Cubitt. *(44 Elizabeth St, London SW1W; +44 20 7730 6060; open everyday from midday to 11pm; cubitthouse.co.uk)*

Changing the Routine

Londoners are quite stubborn when it comes to leaving their own postcode. So here's a challenge for date night: step out of your comfort zone and try a good neighbourhood restaurant on the other side of town. Head to the northernmost quarter of Hackney in East London –unless you live in Stoke Newington, or "Stokey" as the locals call it, you've probably never spent any time there, which is exactly why we've choosing it. **Rubedo** is the perfect little understated neighbourhood restaurant that would absolutely be your local if you lived here. A warm welcome, natural wines, simple but beautifully prepared seasonal Italian-inspired dishes to share; it's a real home away from home and the true definition of a neighbourhood gem.
(35 Stoke Newington Church St, N16; +44 20 7254 0364; Tue – Thurs, 6pm – 11pm, Fri & Sat: 5pm – 12am; Rubedolondon.com)

Rubedo

Date Night: Creative

Campfire Cocktails in the City

If the secret world of foot tunnels beneath the river Thames (see pg 336) doesn't catch your attention, how about a fairy-lit rooftop cocktail garden above one of the forgotten entrances of said tunnels? Throw in an endless supply of marshmallows and s'mores to be roasted over your personal fire-pit with botanical cocktails, and you've pretty much got the perfect al fresco evening in London town. **The Midnight Apothecary** is without doubt, the city's best-kept secret south of the river, situated a mile downstream from Tower Bridge. The neglected space atop the little-known Brunel Museum was transformed by the very talented Lottie Muir (aka the Cocktail Gardener) into a whimsical secret garden in 2011. Ever since, she's been overseeing the foraging of ingredients straight from the rooftop herb garden that surrounds the campfire setting, to serve up some seriously aromatic beverages. While you might feel a million miles from the city, take full advantage of urban comforts and feel free to order in a meal with your marshmallows using a delivery app before settling in for an intimate bonfire date night.

Beneath you by the way, is the historical entryway to the subterranean Thames tunnel, the world's first tunnel built beneath a navigable river, courtesy of Victorian engineer, Marc Brunel, in the early 19th century. The unexpectedly vast entrance hall has since been moonlighting as a secret theatre, accessed by spiral staircases, host to clandestine concerts by **DEBUT** (another excuse to visit this underrated spot; Debut.org.uk). Take a break from roasting your marshmallows and ask the team for a quick subterranean tour before the night's over.
(Brunel Museum Rooftop Garden, Railway Avenue, Rotherhithe, SE16; open we-ekends; booking essential & available for private hire; Themidnightapothecary.co.uk)

A Secret Bohemian Rendez-Vous at the Old Theatre

Hugh Grant took Julia Roberts on a date to the **Coronet Theatre** in the loveable scene from *Notting Hill* that sees the Hollywood actress falling for the floppy-haired bookseller sporting his prescription scuba goggles. Back then, the Victorian theatre was functioning as a local cinema, but today, the Coronet has returned to its roots, offering a diverse performing arts programme, while also hiding one of Notting Hill's best-kept date night secrets in the basement.

Built in 1898, the playhouse once hosted royalty and welcomed stars like Sarah Bernhardt to its stage, but the Coronet couldn't keep up with the fierce competition of the lucrative West End theatre district and was converted to a full-time cinema by the 1920s. The Grade II listed building and its auditorium have been in need of some TLC over the years, narrowly avoiding demolition in the 1970s, but one could argue the faded grandeur only makes this place all the more nostalgic. Before (or instead of) the show, impress your date with

The Midnight Apothecary

cocktails in the candlelit bar hiding below ground, an eccentric bijou of a space decorated like a Belle Epoque salon, laden with Persian carpets, rustic mahogany furniture, curiosities and old stage props. Purchase your drinks from the grand piano and get snug on a velvet Victorian conversation chair. Time it well, and you might catch one of their monthly poetry nights when the theatre's bar becomes an intimate stage. The romance of a bygone era also awaits in the stunning main auditorium upstairs, under the original gilded arches and balconies. From avant-garde dance productions to revivals of forgotten T.S. Eliot plays, the company's eclectic Off West End programme is consistently high quality. By curtain fall, your love interest will surely be convinced of the prospect of a second date, if only for your exquisite knowledge of London's romantic hidden treasures.
(103 Notting Hill Gate, Notting Hill, W11; +44 20 3642 6606; the theatre bar opens one hour before every performance until 11pm; find the programme at Thecoronettheatre.com)

Coronet Theatre bar

First Date in a Cottage

Perched at the top of a hill in Richmond is a secret hideaway plucked straight from a storybook. Think a Brothers Grimm brainstorm brought to life (minus the wicked witches) and you won't be far off from the **Hollyhock Café**. Cosy up under the twinkle-lit terrace of this charmingly wonky "Hansel and Gretel" style house with the flower beds at your feet and a view of the Thames. Share some healthy and hearty vegetarian plates or homemade cakes and if it starts to get chilly, hot water bottles and blankets are provided. It's the perfect setting to spark your own happily ever after.
(146 Petersham Rd, Richmond, TW10; +44 020 8948 6555; Mon-Fri 8.30am-5pm, Sat-Sun 8.30am-5.30pm)

Hollyhock Café

Crown Works Pottery

Moulding Memories

Patrick Swayze, Demi Moore and a pottery wheel –you know where this is going. Re-enact one of the most romantic date nights in cinematic history for a tactile and intimate experience with some clay between your fingers. London's growing pottery class culture has seen multiple studios open up across the city, offering beginners workshops any day of the week. Have a laugh over your creative mishaps to break the ice at **Crown Works Pottery** (*crownworkspottery.com*) tucked away in an old Victorian mews or the cosy studios of **Columbia Road Clay** (*columbiaroadclay.com*), both in Bethnal Green. They offer one-off taster classes as well as multi-week courses or private classes for two. Tip: go for a quick drink at the pub before-hand and browse pottery on Pinterest together to find inspiration for a miniature masterpiece –smaller works are more manageable to finish and eventually take home with you. Have a dinner reservation at Campania (see pg 98) after class in case all goes well.

Sailing with the Royal Swans

The futuristic **Serpentine Solar Shuttle** is the UK's first boat to be entirely powered by the sun; gliding ever so peacefully among the King's swans of Hyde Park throughout the summer. Impress your date with the history of the royal park which was established by the hedonistic Henry VIII for his hunting expeditions. It was *the* place for duelling in the 18th century and suffragette debates at the turn of the 19th century. If you really want to push the boat out for an extra special occasion, you can even book the shuttle all for yourself on a twilight cruise. Back on dry land, take a walk through the rose garden, pass through the Serpentine Galleries (free entry), and to catch the last of the day's sun, take your pick of the waterside terraces at the Lido Bar or the Serpentine Bar & Kitchen.
(Board at the Boat House on the north side near the Serpentine Bar & Kitchen, W2; running every day throughout summer and on weekends for the rest of the year; call +44 207 2621989 or email enquiry@theboathouselondon.co.uk for specific information, requests and times; Solarshuttle.co.uk/solarshuttle.htm)

Dating in the Jazz Age

Knock on the inconspicuous wooden door with a nightjar engraved on a gold plaque. Await the nod of approval from the gatekeeper, head downstairs and slip into **Nightjar**, an underground speakeasy celebrating the golden age of cocktails and jazz. Travel through time as you make your way through the menu, divided up into drinks from pre-Prohibition, Prohibition and the post-war era. The cocktails are bright, bold and served in crazy drinking vessels; a gift for the 'gram if you wish to jump from the 1920s to the 2020s for a moment. Live jazz, swing and blues will soundtrack your evening as you sink into the early hours and the darkened corner of your red velvet booth. Like its namesake bird, this Shoreditch cocktail bar is mysterious, elusive and nocturnal and yet reliably good for a sophisticated first date.
(129 City Rd, Old Street, EC1V; +44 020 7253 4101; Sun-Wed 6pm-1am, Thurs 6pm-2am & Fri-Sat 6pm-3am; Barnightjar.com)

Find more secret bars on pg 269 or for more jazz, turn to pg 315.

Satirical Slot Machines

A bizarre funhouse museum to break the ice, **Novelty Automation** is an eccentric collection of around 20 handmade coin-operated machines brought to life by nutty cartoonist and mechanical mastermind, Tim Hunkins. The scientific playfulness of the Enlightenment period and the tongue-in-cheek social commentary provided by cartoons from the era have inspired Hunkins for over 30 years. He has been reinventing and engineering arcade games in the same spirit; delightfully analog with no fancy software in sight. His signature

gizmos include a spin-the-arrow game called "pet or meat" which decides and details the fate of a lamb, a money grabber machine based on the illegal activities of city bankers, an expressive photobooth and the two-player divorce race in which the winner (or loser depending on how you look at it) gets the kids and the cat. Luckily, Barry White's love line phone booth is there to provide some post-break up romantic advice. It's a trip to the amusements which is way more amusing and unconventional than winning a stuffed toy. Entry is free but you will need to buy £1 tokens to operate the machine; get a discounted bundle if you intend to try everything.
(1A Princeton St, Bloomsbury, WC1R; Tues-Wed 11am-6pm, Thurs 12-8pm & Fri-Sat 11am-6pm; Novelty-automation.com)

Novelty Automation

Date Night: Classic Casanova

Bring Someone You Want to Impress

You're going to want to put on something decadent (and book ahead) for a dinner date at **Sessions Arts Club**. Behind a very smart red door of a very smart Palladian-style building in Clerkenwell, awaits one of London's most surprising restaurants. Sessions House, a Grade II listed landmark has had several lives, starting as the nation's largest courthouse then a manufacturer of weighing machines and later as a Masonic lodge. Ring the doorbell and take the elevator to the 4th floor (or climb the spiral staircase for dramatic effect). Prepare for your jaw to drop as you enter the Dickensian vaulted space that used to be the old judges' dining room. You could've stumbled upon a secret society dinner in a decaying mansion in Victorian London or old Havana. Candlelit, even at lunchtime, the beautifully distressed walls, lunette windows and bohemian decor lure you into another place and time. The contemporary art on the walls curated by the Sessions team is all for sale, making it partly a gallery that "moves and shifts with the seasons". The food is just as interesting as the space; chickpea pancakes and lovely fishy things to share. Order more heavily from the starter courses which are the standout dishes. Don't forget to check out the lush roof terrace after dessert.
(24 Clerkenwell Grn, London EC1R; open Tues-Sat lunch & dinner, +44 203 793 4025; Sessionsartsclub.com)

Sessions Arts Club

Rendez-vous in Venice

London's 200-year-old royal waterways have a lot to offer a couple in search of a romantic escape. Meet in Venice –*Little* Venice, that is, at the heart of London's canal network. This charming neighbourhood became popular among artists and bohemian personalities in the mid-19th century, who lived and worked in the charming houseboats along the canal. Start with a cream tea from the **Waterside Café** serving breakfast, light meals and snacks from a charming narrowboat with tables outside on the towpath (*Warwick Crescent, W2; open everyday 10am-5pm & from 9am on weekends; waterside-cafe.co.uk).*

Across the basin is Rembrandt Gardens, one of London's tiny Victorian parks which really likes to show off in Spring. Take a few muffins to go from the café and set sail on the royal waterways. If you've got the budget, you could opt for your own self-driving electric boat. From £85, **GoBoat** lets you play pirates down the canals at a speed of about 3 knots –no licence required –and they even have boats with heated seats
(Merchant Square, Paddington, W21AS; +44 203 887 6955; open everyday from 9.30am-sunset; Goboat.co.uk/paddington).

If you'd rather not risk making a tit out of yourself at the captain's wheel, climb aboard as a guest of one of the historic narrowboats of the **London Waterbus Company**. Built around the 1930s and 40s, one of the vessels (the Perseus) was even built by Harland & Wolff, who also built the Titanic – a fun fact that will either impress your date or make them slightly nervous. Alas, while you won't be spotting any icebergs, admire the Georgian and Victorian homes and look out for the rare Egyptian geese along the leafy waterways. The 45-minute route travels hourly between picturesque Little Venice and vibrant Camden Town (*£15 a head, Booking essential via Londonwaterbus.com).*
If the date is going well, once you disembark at Camden Lock, continue following the canal by foot towards King's Cross. Have an eye out for the indentations in the walls and the marks on the wooden railings of the footbridge – these are left over from the ropes that were used to tow the canal boats by horse. Stop for a drink at **Coal Drops Yard**, an old industrial hub of Victorian London that was recently revived as a car-free village of restaurants, bars and shops. A little further down, stop in at the floating bookshop, **Word on the Water** (see pg 187) a delightful floating library to end your storybook date in London.

Rooftop Romance in Shoreditch

City rooftop venues tend to have a reputation for being impossible places to find a seat, let alone a decent drink, but Sir Terence Conran's rooftop bar & grill at the **Boundary** is a semi-well-kept Shoreditch secret that feels like a

Waterside Cafè in Little Venice

London Waterbus Company

holiday from all that. Whisk a date up to the boutique hotel's intimate terrace where olive and lemon trees and wicker lounge chairs will have you swapping stories about your summers in the Mediterranean. Book a table by the outdoor fireplace and bond over burrata. With panoramic views over East London, it's a pretty perfect first-date destination.
(2-4 Boundary St, Shoreditch, E2; +44 20 7729 1051; open everyday from 12pm-11pm; Boundary.london/rooftop)

Boundary (rooftop bar & grill)

The Rise and Fall and Renaissance of an A-List Hideaway

When interior designer Julie Hodgess founded her restaurant in 1969, Clarendon Cross was not the picturesque pastel-hued micro village it is today. It's hard to believe that this part of West London was ever considered to be on the "wrong side of the tracks", but the area had been witness to some of the worst fighting of the 1958 race riots. Being that it was once so cheap to live there however, it was a magnet for artists, writers and designers. Over the next few decades, **Julie's** became a bohemian dining institution, luring them in with an eccentric decor of thrifted bric-a-brac and a quirky layout of intimate alcoves and private rooms. Mick Jagger, The Beatles and Notting Hill music industry types made it their lunch canteen, while members of the Kensington Palace household also made under-the-radar weeknight reservations. Princess Diana became a regular. Kate Moss hosted birthday parties and Madonna, Hugh Grant, Annie Lennox and Liam Gallagher all had their preferred tables in the 80s and 90s. Hidden away from the paparazzi, it became a discreet dining club where British pop culture royalty could let their hair down and dance on tabletops. But after a bit of a rut in the naughties and the restaurant-wrecking pandemic, Julie's closed its doors on New Year's Eve in 2022 after more than 50 years in business.

Longtime regular, local resident and Cordon Bleu-trained chef, Tara MacBain, couldn't bear to see it go. She is probably Julie's last chance at bringing this iconic Holland Park secret back to life. Opening up that charming terrace once more (an unbeatable al fresco lunch location), putting a British spin on an all-day French brasserie menu, and breathing warmth back into Hodges' eclectic interiors; hopefully Julie's is now here to stay. Clarendon Cross just wouldn't be the same without somewhere to sit under the trees with a cold glass of sauvignon and the whisper of Holland Park's glory days.
(135 Portland Road, London W11; +44 20 7229 8331; Juliesrestaurant.com)

You'll find more date spots throughout the book, but for more restaurants ideas, turn to pg 269 for secret bars & restaurants and pg 237 for dining with the cool kids.

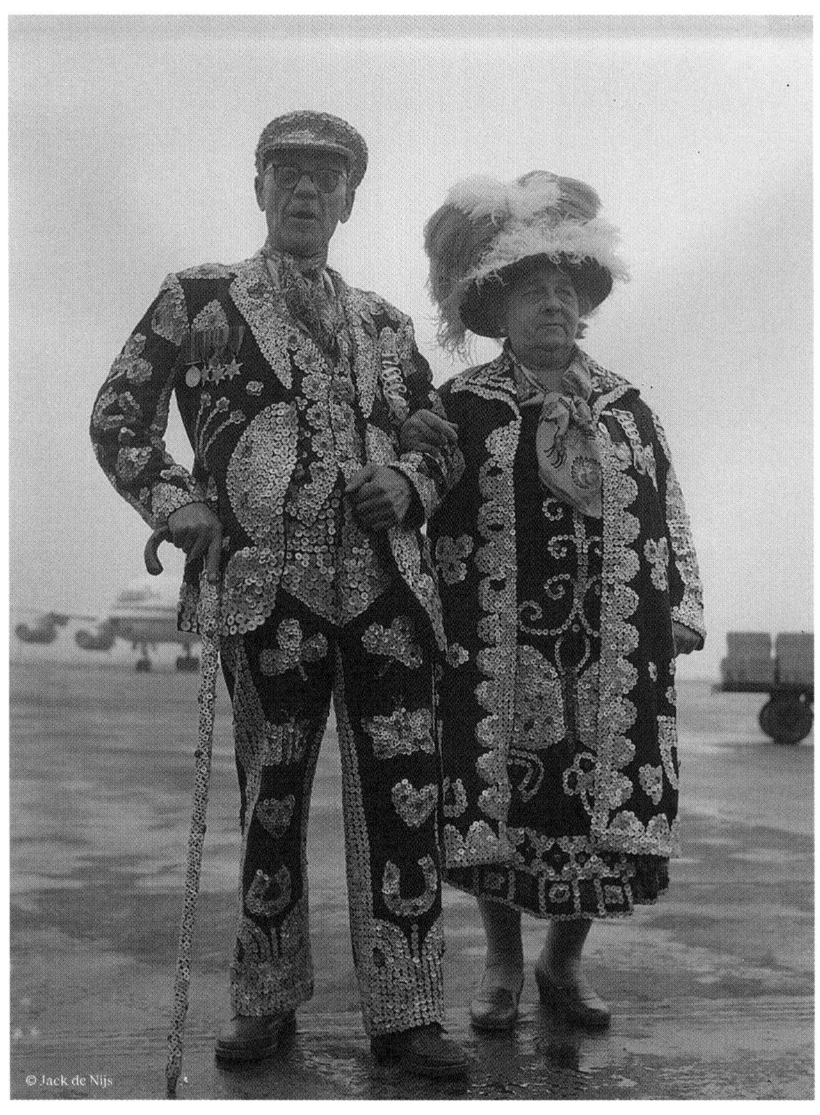

Pearlies of London

God Save The Crown

The royal family, like any other folk, have their issues, but whatever we may think of them, they are as much part of the idea of Britain and its culture as afternoon tea (we'll get to that in chapter 7). This book was still being written when Elizabeth II died after 70 years on the throne, marking the end of an era for many, ushering in new uncertainty for the future of the monarchy and begging the question: will England ever be the same again without its queen? Short of binge-watching Netflix's *The Crown* or waiting in the rain outside Buckingham Palace for the Changing of the Guard ceremony, consider some of these alternative and unofficial ways to get your fix of royal treatment with a dash of pomp & pageantry.

The Other English Royals

Britain is punk just as much as it is prim. Britain is cockney as much as it is conservative, and it loves the monarchy as much as it does a bit of anarchy. Ever heard of the Pearly Kings and Queens of London? Veterans of the East End, famous for their iconic buttoned outfits and charitable endeavours, the Pearlies are the unsung monarchs of Britain with a story worth telling. Dressed in fabulously kitsch and eye-catching suits that wouldn't look out of place at a David Bowie costume party, the sartorial subculture is a cherished part of London's heritage.

It all started in the poorest streets of Victorian London, with an orphan named Henry Croft, who was taken under the wing of the fruit sellers of Spitalfields market. Croft learned from their way of life and their role in the community as caretakers of the poor. They were a proud breed of Eastenders, known for their unique smoked pearl buttons sewn onto the seams of their tattered clothes to imitate the pearly fashions of the wealthy. As the story goes, Henry was wandering down the muddy banks of the Thames one day when he came across thousands of pearl buttons washed up from a big shipwreck. Keen to emulate his local heroes, he took the style to an extreme and covered an old dress suit and top hat with 60,000 pearl buttons, sewing them in artful patterns that spelt out Robin Hood-esque slogans like, "All for charity and pity the poor". You couldn't miss him in his pearl-covered suit, which helped draw attention to himself and raise money for charities and orphanages like the one he grew up in. Henry Croft became a legendary character of the East End, encouraging Londoners to be more charitable. In 1911, an official Pearly Society was formed and soon enough, every borough in the city had its own Pearly King and Queen. The organised charitable tradition of working-class culture in London continues to this day. You can find the Pearly Monarchy collecting charity twice a month in Covent Garden or at the corner of Cheshire Street and Brick Lane on the first

Pearlies of London

Sunday of every month. Sometimes you can join them for a knees-up at The Carpenters' Arms, an historic pub around the corner, once owned by the Kray Twins. St George's Day is a big day in the calendar at Trafalgar Square, where a statue of Henry Croft, the original Pearly himself, stands in the crypt of the church at the northeast corner. But the biggest event of the year is the Pearly annual harvest festival every September. If you're lucky, you'll catch a new coronation as the younger generation tries to keep the tradition alive. *(Find more details on Pearlysociety.co.uk)*

The Crown Jewels You Can Eat

The English know very well that bringing a box of **Charbonnel et Walker** chocolates as a gift to your dinner party host is a bit like offering the sweet tooth equivalent of a tin of Beluga caviar. The 150-year-old chocolatier holds a Royal Warrant, which was awarded by the late Queen Elizabeth II, who for many years was the company's most important customer. Princess Diana, Princess Margaret, and Wallis Simpson were also loyal patrons and even Oscar Wilde sang the chocolate shop's praises in 1890 as editor of a women's journal. Inside that beautiful and iconic packaging (the kind you keep to store jewellery on your dresser), it's all about their divine truffles. The sea-salted caramel, the pink champagne or the gin-soaked truffles are among the classics. The flagship boutique is located inside The Royal Arcade, a perfectly preserved indoor Victorian shopping arcade, well worth a visit in its own right, lined with historic shops and retaining all its original features.

(One, 28 The Royal Arcade, Old Bond St, Mayfair, W1S; +442073182075; Mon-Sat 10am-6.30pm, Sun 12-5pm; charbonnel.co.uk)

The Royal Family's Favourite Kensington Kitchen

Neighbour to the royal palace, **Maggie Jones's Restaurant** has been around since the 1960s, but was renamed from its original "Nan's Kitchen" in the seventies after a certain Princess began booking her tables at the Kensington eatery under the pseudonym, "Maggie Jones". It was none other than Princess Margaret, Queen Elizabeth's feisty little sister who became a loyal customer at this rustic country-style kitchen in the city. Serving the best pies around, and what one might call "posh comfort food", reserve yourself a large farm table with friends for Sunday lunch or a cosy candle-lit booth for two on a weeknight rendezvous. Theatrically decorated with floor-to-ceiling bric-a-brac, run by warm and welcoming staff, Maggie Jones still remains a firm favourite with the royal residents of Kensington Palace. A little birdie told us Harry took Meghan here on a few secret dates before they officially became an item.
(6 Old Ct Pl, Kensington, W8; +44 20 7937 6462; open everyday for lunch & dinner, Maggie-jones.co.uk)

Maggie Jones

God Save Pat Butcher, the Kitsch Queen of British Soap

Have you ever been to a Royal Wedding street party? At **Little Nan's Bar**, there's no need to wait for a prince to get hitched. A royal knees-up is hosted here every day. Inspired by the owner's fun-loving grandmother, this quirky and kitsch-tastic venue under Deptford's disused railway arches reflects Nan's eccentric style and patriotic spirit, adorned with union jack flags, plastic pink flamingos and glitzy party streamers. Heirlooms from every decade of Little Nan's life decorate the space, from Princess Diana memorabilia plates to a garish shrine for Pat Butcher, the queen of the beloved British soap, *EastEnders*. Indulge in Blighty's comfort food recipes plucked from the family scrapbooks and scribbled onto the handwritten menus. Book in advance for a birthday celebration and they'll design and name one of their signature teapot cocktails in your honour. Jump to the bit about party venues on p320 for more information on booking a larger private bash here for 65 –110 guests. Nan's also seasonally hosts a "Carless Caboot", where you can rent a table to sell your wares at their street flea market, information and schedule on their website. *(Deptford Rail Station, London SE8; +44 7792 205375; Mon-Fri 4pm-11pm, Sat & Sun 12am-11pm; Littlenans.co.uk)*

Little Nan's bar

The World's Most Beautiful Retirement Home

Walking around Chelsea, particularly near the King's Road, you might encounter the occasional elderly person wearing a smart and distinctive scarlet uniform. That's a Chelsea Pensioner, who is lucky enough to hang up their hat at the **Royal Hospital Chelsea**, one of the borough's most spectacular pieces of real estate. Any former soldier of the British Army, man or woman, over the age of 65, who faces spending their advanced years alone, can apply for residence at

Royal Hospital Chelsea

this glorious 17th century veteran's retreat designed by Sir Christopher Wren (the guy behind St. Paul's Cathedral) and founded by King Charles II. The site can be visited by the public with a friendly Chelsea Pensioner, who will share a personal account of everyday life at the royal estate, point out all its masterpieces, let you have a wander around their 300-year-old pleasure garden and even show you where they dine in a very Harry Potter-esque Great Hall. *(Royal Hospital Chelsea, Royal Hospital Road, London, SW3 4SR; Tours at 10am Mon – Fri or 2pm Mon – Fri excluding Thurs; Chelsea-pensioners.co.uk/guided-tours)*

Queen Elizabeth (the Tudor one) Was Here

Going strong since 1546, **Ye Olde Mitre** quite convincingly claims to be London's oldest-standing pub and still houses an ancient natural relic, older than the watering hole itself. In the corner of the front bar is the preserved trunk of a cherry tree that Queen Elizabeth supposedly once used as a maypole to dance around with her old chum, Sir Christopher Hatton. A warren of cosy rooms and alcoves to discover, the pub is only accessible via covered and narrow alleyways (the blink-and-you'll-miss-it passageway from the main street is wedged between two pawn shops) offering a glimpse of the higgledy-piggledy 16th-century city that was, before the Great Fire of London. If it's not busy, strike up a conversation with the friendly bar staff who can share plenty of anecdotes to make medieval history interesting over a refreshing pint. *(1 Ely Court, Ely Place, Holborn EC1N; +44 20 7405 4751; open Monday-Friday, 12pm-11pm; Yeoldemitreholborn.co.uk)*

Milroy's of Soho

Mr. Bond's Day Off

What would 007 do with some downtime in London town?

Meet on Greek Street, Behind the Bookcase of the Old Whiskey Shop

A sophisticated drinker takes pleasure in choosing precisely the right spirits and certainly doesn't settle for just any old bar in Soho. **Milroy's of Soho** was opened by the Milroy brothers in 1964 and quickly became known for selling the largest selection of whisky in London. The charming, compact shop offers an unparalleled selection of single malts, small batch bourbons and everything in between. But there's an added twist: step behind a swinging door disguised as a bookcase to discover a secret bar in the basement, **The Vault**. Whether you enjoy delicate, rare whiskies from the Highlands, or peatier Islay Scotches, Milroy's friendly, knowledgeable staff cater to everything the discerning whisky sipper and cocktail lover can imagine. The "Pickled Strawberry", with Champagne, sherry, and pickled green strawberries, is strongly recommended. With this chic but snug space, advance bookings are never a bad idea (*Thevaultsoho.co.uk*). And if you're interested in becoming even more of a sophisticated drinker, Milroy's offers a superb tasting class every Monday evening at 6.30pm-8pm, or private tastings based around your preferences are available to book.
(3 Greek Street, W1D; +44 020 7734 2277; Mon 10am-11pm, Tues-Sat 10am-11.30pm, closed Sundays. Milroys.co.uk)

Find more secret bars on pg 269

At Home with Goldfinger

No one would give number **2 Willow Road** a second look unless you were, well ... looking for it. But that's partly what makes it one of London's most intriguing house museums. Despite its underwhelming exterior, the former Hampstead home of Ernő Goldfinger is a pleasantly surprising look inside the mind of one of England's most controversial architects. Best known for his dystopian, Brutalist tower blocks like the notorious Trellick Tower in Notting Hill (now a listed building, see pg 299), Goldfinger was once so hated by preservationists that he was even immortalised as a Bond villain by Ian Fleming. The James Bond author also lived in Hampstead and strongly opposed Goldfinger's trio of Modernist terraced houses which were completed in 1939 after bulldozing a number of cottages to make way for the new "no-frills" housing. At the time, no one could have predicted it would one day be among the first Modernist buildings acquired by the National Trust. Once inside, there's a lot less to hate. Minimalist yet eclectic. Functional yet elegant. Sparse yet so much attention to detail. This is very much a home to prove the haters wrong. When it comes to style and taste, there's no doubt that he saw into the future. The house museum

is every bit the time capsule as if Ernő just stepped away from his typewriter to stock up on coffee filters, but these smart interiors wouldn't look out of place in today's *Architectural Digest*. Most of the furniture was designed by Goldfinger himself and his immaculate collection of 20th-century art includes pieces by Marcel Duchamp, Max Ernst and Henry Moore. Despite being a compact little house museum, you can easily spend an hour here making mental notes and interior design goals.
(2 Willow Road, Hampstead, NW3; +44 20 7435 6166; open Thurs & Sat for pre-booked independent or guided visits via Nationaltrust.org.uk/visit/london/2-willow-road)

2 Willow Road, former home of Ernő Goldfinger

How to Dress like an English Gentleman

The art of dressing up, they claimed, was dead. As the global pandemic took hold and sports & leisurewear became a mainstay, formal attire felt certain to become a frivolous indulgence of the past. They, whoever that is, were wrong. What every modern man deserves in fact, is a visual masterclass in the art of men's style by taking an enlightening journey down **Jermyn Street**, London's veritable HQ for the elegant gentleman. For if we had to demonstrate good grooming to aliens, it would probably be best achieved here. Created by Henry Jermyn, the King's courtier in the 1660s, this one-way street is the place to outfit any discerning gentleman's wardrobe, filled with shops selling handmade shoes, fitted shirts, colourful ties, traditional shaving brushes, delicate colognes and everything in-between; not for nothing is Jermyn graced with a statue of celebrated Regency dandy, Beau Brummel. Prices on Jermyn Street are pleasantly varied; from bespoke cobbler Foster & Son, whose shoes are still made by hand upstairs at No. 83, and the sumptuous Turnbull and Asser, who dressed Sean Connery in each of his appearances as James Bond, to the slightly more affordable flagship shops for elegant shirt & tie sellers as Thomas Pink, Charles Tyrwhitt, Hawes & Curtis, Harvie & Hudson and the like. Stroll down Jermyn Street and marvel at the rows of old-fashioned badger hair shaving brushes, and luxurious grooming goods from Taylor of Bond Street, who offer hot-towel shaves at the back of the shop. Or perhaps wander into Floris at No. 89, the oldest independent perfumers in London, where it's still possible to pick up the scent Lord Nelson picked out for his mistress, Lady Hamilton. Pop into Wiltons at No.55, serving delectable oysters and champagne since 1742. These are just a handful of the houses on Jermyn Street, where virtually every shop is a treasure trove for the elegant gent. Make a final stop at No. 93, where you will find the oldest cheesemonger in the UK, Paxton & Whitfield, whose wares and expertise are second to none, and who've held a Royal Warrant since Queen Victoria in 1850. "A gentleman only buys his cheese at Paxton & Whitfield", said Winston Churchill. *(Jermyn Street keeps mostly regular shop hours; details can be found at jermynstreet.net)*

A hop and a skip across Piccadilly, it's time for a sartorial rite of passage on Savile Row. Ian Fleming would often list James Bonds' clothes in fine detail; tropical worsted suits for abroad, paired with luxurious sea island cotton shirts and black silk-knitted ties. But at the cornerstone of his wardrobe was the well fitted dinner jacket. To find the finest, bespoke coats today, one need look no further than **Henry Poole & Co** of Savile Row, the very place where the dinner jacket was invented. In 1865, the Prince of Wales, and future King Edward VII, asked his friend and tailor, Henry Poole, to come up with a shorter coat in 'celestial blue' that he could wear to informal dinners. Poole took his scissors to the stiff, traditional tailcoat, creating what has become the standard evening dinner suit we know today. Legend has it that one dinner guest at Sandringham, American financier James Brown Potter, ordered a matching dinner jacket, returned to New York, unveiling the fashionable new suit at his swish sporting resort, the Tuxedo Club, where its popularity gave it a new name, "the Tux". In the archives at the back of the shop, you can find Winston Churchill's or Charles Dickens' measurements; both were good customers. You might be following in the footsteps of kings and heads of state, but rest assured that when you step inside Henry Poole's shop with its elegant mahogany cabinets and clubroom hues, you'll always be met with a warm and courteous welcome. You might not be in the market for a bespoke suit, but one can still shop here if you're simply after a good tie or a smart pair of cufflinks. Then again, a bespoke suit is one of life's greatest pleasures, and getting one made at Henry Poole is very much the cinematic experience you'd imagine it to be. If current funds permit (call it a wise investment), a two-piece bespoke suit starts at around £4,000, which takes an average of three months to perfect, all handmade on the premises at Savile Row. The nine step process with multiple fittings (don't worry, Gin & Tonics are on the house) uses tailoring secrets passed down through two centuries as a family business, to ensure you too can look as debonair and sophisticated as 007 himself.

(15 Savile Row, W1S; +44 020 7734 5985; Mon-Fri 9am-5:15pm; henrypoole.com)

A School of Wine in Napoleon III's Cellar

Supplying the royal family with its booze since the 1800s, **Berry Brothers and Rudd** is a three-hundred-something-year-old family business that started as a coffee merchant before marrying into the wine trade. They found the vine to be a much more lucrative business, particularly once the kings and queens of the neighbouring St James's Palace became regular customers. Beneath this old-world shop lies two acres of cellars storing some of the oldest and finest wines

Berry Brothers & Rudd underground cellars

on British soil. Napoleon Bonaparte's nephew, Napoleon III spent much of his exile from France down there, holding secret meetings and plotting political coups. Today, the labyrinthine cellars host supper clubs and wine tastings, as well as evening or one-day wine courses which can all be easily booked online. Look out for a bricked-up archway that faces in the direction of the palace. Rumour has it that they were built so Charles II could nip in and out of the high-class brothels that once lined this side of the street. *(63 Pall Mall, St. James's, London SW1Y; +44 800 280 2440; Mon-Fri 10am-7pm, Sat until 5pm; Bbr.com).*

Just outside, seek out a small forgotten plaque that is a remnant of an equally peculiar chapter of history. It reads that the "*Texas Legation in this building was the legation for the ministers from the Republic of Texas to the Court of St. James 1842 – 1845*". As it turns out, the rooms above the wine merchants were once the home of the official Embassy of the Republic of Texas. It is little known that for just a few short years, Texas was its own country, and in a bid to raise their international standing, the then President of Texas, Sam Houston, opened embassies in London and Paris. Texas finally joined the Union in 1845, and the short-lived delegation was closed, leaving only an unpaid bill of £160 with Berry Bros & Rudd. The Republic of Texas may be consigned to history but it still lives on in the hearts of many Texans. In 1986, members of the Anglo-Texan society visited the venerable wine shop on the occasion of the Texas sesquicentennial, and finally settled the outstanding debt still owed by the long gone Republic of Texas.
(Pickering Place, 3 St. James' St, SW1A; the plaque can be found on the inside corner of the tiny alleyway next to the side entrance of Berry Bros & Rudd)

Coffee and Cubans at Mayfair's Oldest Cigar Merchant

Lighting up in London is a no-go in indoor spaces, except for one lawless lounge in the poshest part of town. Just up the road from Berry Brother and Rudd, **James J Fox** has been selling cigars since 1787, supplying cigar aficionados with their favourite accessory. Former customers most notably include the biggest walking advert of them all; Winston Churchill. After you've sniffed out your favourite fine cigar from the walk-in humidor, puff on your pick in the comfort of the sampling lounge; a sophisticated state of the art smoking suite with comfy armchairs and complimentary tea and coffee on tap. It's a relaxing room to meet like-minded patrons or have a moment to yourself and let your mind drift away in the clouds. Extend your visit with a trip to the basement where lies a museum open to the public, though its petite quarters and secret entrance make it feel more like a private collector's den. **The Freddie Fox Museum** is dedicated to smoking history and memorabilia, including antique artefacts, Churchill's chair and Oscar Wilde's unpaid cigar bill.
(19 St James's St, St. James, SW1A; 020 7930 3787; Mon-Sun 11am-7pm; Jjfox.co.uk)

WILTONS
WILTONS

Victorian Time Traveller

Curtain's Up on a Secret Victorian Stage

There's a portal to another century waiting down a back alley, just around the corner from the much-more famous Tower of London. **Wilton's** could tell a thousand stories from behind its battered old door and crumbling facade. For much of the 20th century, having barely survived demolition as part of the slum clearance schemes of East London, the city's oldest music hall remained silent and derelict. After decades of post-war neglect, music once again rang from its halls in the late 1990s. In the hauntingly beautiful space that still feels as if it's only just awoken from a century-long slumber, guests today are invited for a tipple and a good old-fashioned knees up, while the ongoing but ever-so-delicate campaign to preserve the landmark continues. It began as an alehouse in the early 18th century, serving sea captains and merchants. In the 19th century, businessman John Wilton came into the picture and expanded the public house into an entertainment venue for the working folks of the East End, decorating it lavishly with gilded mirrors and chandeliers.

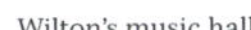

Wilton's music hall

What remains of that faded grandeur is a privilege to discover. Under the twinkling lights of Wilton's historic Victorian hall, the evening's entertainment ranges from the very popular cockney sing-a-longs to swing nights to post-punk cabarets. In cosy alcoves of peeling paint and 200-year-old exposed brick, drink in the atmosphere as ghosts of evenings past hover in the wings. You can also join backstage tours of the venue every month, which would be of particular interest to anyone restoring an historic property.
(1 Graces Alley, Whitechapel, E1; +44 20 7702 2789; the bar is open to all from 5.30pm on days with performances in the music hall and from 1pm on days with matinees; see the website for bookings, upcoming events and private hire; Wiltons.org.uk)

Wilton's music hall

The Most Elegant Way to Brighten up a Rainy Day

A rainy day is never far away in London, so what better way to keep the drizzle at bay than by skipping the £5 umbrellas sellers outside the Tube stations, and heading to England's oldest brolly shop. **James Smith & Sons** has such a distinctive Victorian shop window, that if you were to ask a London cab driver to take you to the 'umbrella shop near the British Museum', they'd surely drop you at 53, New Oxford Street. The exquisite plate glass windows advertise what's inside: the long lost days when gentlemen carried dagger canes, sword sticks and riding crops; and ladies, brightly coloured tropical sun shades lined with lace. James Smith & Sons has been around since 1830, moving into their New Oxford Street premises in 1857, where not much has changed inside since. Wooden display cases and wicker baskets are filled as far as the eye can see, under the watchful eye of a portrait of Jonas Hanway (thought to be the first Londoner to carry an umbrella –and briefly ridiculed for it). Umbrellas are given dignified names such as the Solid Stick and Fit-Up for gents, the Pencil and Birdcage for ladies, and ornate walking canes are topped with silver ducks, foxes and the like. Much of the work is still done below the shop, from umbrella repair to adjustments on canes, precisely finished according to the owner's height. James Smith & Sons' longevity stems from making an everyday item exceptionally well, with the craftsmanship and expertise that comes from nearly two hundred years in the business; a true London treasure.
(Hazelwood House, 53, New Oxford Street, WC1A; +44 020 7836 4731; Mon-Fri 10am-5.45pm, Sat 10am-5.15pm, closed Sun & Bank Holidays; James-smith.co.uk)

James Smith & Sons

The Victorian Surgery Found Hiding in a Church Attic

In the horrifying days before anaesthesia, Victorian doctors such as Robert Liston, known as the "fastest knife in England", would call out "Time me, gentlemen!" before amputating a limb in under 30 seconds. With less blood and gore, today you can ascend a narrow, 52-step spiral staircase into the upper reaches of a church and find a dramatic window into the world of 19th-century medical practice. Boarded up and forgotten about until it was rediscovered in the 1950s, the **Old Operating Theatre** was once part of St Thomas' Hospital, and in the small, steep amphitheatre, all eyes are naturally drawn down to the main surgery table at centre stage, resembling a large, well-worn butcher's block. Now an excellent museum, complete with sawdust on the floor, it's filled with surgical saws, trepanning tools, leech jars and scarification instruments that are not for the faint-hearted. Look out for the teeth marks on the sticks they used for patients to bite down on. Along with the discovery of the surgical theatre, a centuries-old apothecary was also found in the attic, where dried herbs and plants were stored amongst the rafters to make medicines using such ingredients as poppy heads, bloodroot, and "snail water". Alongside the historical demonstrations and medical based talks, the museum puts on musical evenings, films and art classes, as well as more unusual events, such as workshops for making your own Victorian medicines in one of the most fascinating time capsules hidden amongst the rooftops of London.
(9a, St.Thomas Street, SE1; +44 020 718 82679; Mon 2pm-5pm, Tues-Fri 10.30am – 5pm, Sat & Sun 12pm-4pm; oldoperatingtheatre.com for details on upcoming events).

Old Operating Theatre

Dickens-approved Pubs

It only seems right to begin a Dickens-themed pub crawl in the area where London's first printing press was built. Once you've found the tiny alleyway off Fleet Street, stoop under the low lintel and enter into **Ye Olde Cheshire Cheese**. You can get a sense of how ancient the place is by the sign outside the door: it lists all the monarchs who've been ruling since the pub started serving pints. As steeped in history as the wooden floorboards are soaked with five centuries of beer, it hasn't changed much since Charles Dickens included it in *A Tale of Two Cities*. Low ceilings, dark wood panelling, high-backed Victorian benches and little by way of natural light, the Cheshire Cheese is a labyrinth of rooms, lit mostly by lanterns, and in the winter, crackling wood fires. The pub must have been loved long before Dickens' time: it was one of the first to be rebuilt after the Great Fire, reopening a year later in 1667. There had been another tavern on this site back in the 1530s, and if you descend down the pub's uneven stone steps, you'll find traces of the monastery that stood on this site in the 13th century. Dickens' favourite chair is easy to spot: a small brass plaque to the right of the fire in the main dining room marks his regular table. Enjoy a true taste of old London under the watchful eye of the house parrot, Polly. Long departed, the stuffed parrot was said to have mimicked the sound of champagne corks and was so cherished, every Fleet Street newspaper ran her obituary.
(145 Fleet Street, EC4A; +44 20 7353 6170; Mon-Sat 12pm-11am, closed Sundays)

Ye Olde Cheshire Cheese

South of the river, near Borough Market, by the time Charles Dickens talked about **The George Inn** in *Little Dorrit* in 1855, the storied tavern was already centuries old. Located on the stagecoach route from London to the Channel Ports, the George was a galleried inn, well known as far back as medieval times to travellers looking for a hearty meal, tankards of ale and somewhere to sleep.

'Galleried taverns' were so named after the long balconies that overlooked the street and courtyard, where the coaches and horses would pull in. Today it's the last of its kind and a National Trust-owned property. The George has splendid long, white crooked galleries dating to 1677, where you'll find the best seats in the house, especially on Thursday evenings, overlooking the live houseband in the courtyard. Inside, explore an enchanting time capsule of uneven wooden floors, low beamed ceilings, fireplaces and a warren of ancient stairways, rooms and long corridors: the perfect place to sit back with an ale surrounded by the ghosts of London's past.
(75 Borough High Street, SE1; +44 20 7407 2056; open everyday, kitchen open from 12-10pm; Nationaltrust.org.uk/george-inn)

The George Inn

The Real Diagon Alley

Step inside an impressive Victorian entrance to discover one of London's most cinematic treasures, the covered **Leadenhall Market**. Exquisitely decorated in burgundy, cream and gold, under a celestial ceiling of wrought iron and glass, Leadenhall was the height of Victorian grandeur when it opened in 1881. Lovingly preserved, with cobblestones still under foot, you half expect to pass by ladies in bustle skirts and gentlemen in silk hats and frock coats. Leadenhall was once the centre of Roman *Londinium*, before becoming a market known for its game, meat, fish and poultry. Look closely and you'll see the original wrought iron hooks for hanging meat and produce. Today the butcher's shops have been replaced with boutiques, but Leadenhall remains one of the most magical shopping interiors in London (particularly at Christmas), most-notably used as a backdrop for Diagon Alley in *Harry Potter and the Philosopher's Stone.*

You might not find the Leaky Cauldron pub (currently the Glass House opticians at No. 2-4 down Bull's Head Passage), but the elegant Lamb Tavern pub is a charming alternative in which to savour the Victorian elegance of Leadenhall Market.
(Gracechurch Street EC3V; the public areas of Leadenhall Market are generally open 24 hours every day; shops, restaurants and bars keep their own hours, visit leadenhallmarket.co.uk for details)

Leadenhall Market

On the trail of Sherlock Holmes

Steps away from Trafalgar Square, the **Sherlock Holmes** pub looks much like any other in London, until you venture upstairs. There you'll find an incredible life-sized recreation of the fictional rooms shared by Sherlock Holmes and Dr Watson. This amazing rendition of Conan Doyle's 221b Baker Street comes complete with Holmes' famous pipe, deer stalker and violin, whilst the shelves are lined with scientific equipment and mementos from some of their most famous cases, such as a plaster cast of a great bloodhound's footprint, and a gold snuff box from the King of Bohemia. The collection had once been an exhibit at the 1951 Festival of Britain, and after the exhibition ended, the owners of the pub bought the entire display and installed it upstairs. The downstairs of the pub is decorated with memorabilia from the many stage and screen depictions of the famous detective, including the recent BBC reboot, *Sherlock.* Sample both Watson's Golden Ale and the Sherlock House Ale before wandering upstairs, where, as the pub owners themselves put it: "Mr Holmes and Dr Watson have just gone out, but they will be back at any moment..." *(10 Northumberland Street, Charing Cross, WC2N; +44 20 7930 2644; Mon-Fri 12pm-11pm, Sat-Sun 12pm-12am; greeneking-pubs.co.uk)*

The Sherlock Holmes Museum

Continuing on the trail of Holmes' London, hop on the Bakerloo line straight to **The Sherlock Holmes Museum** at 221b Baker Street. This address is somewhat of an oddity. When Conan Doyle was writing the adventures of his bohemian detective, Baker Street didn't run as far as number 221b. But when the street was lengthened in the 1930s, the council created an actual 221b, that was home to the branch of the Abbey National bank. Many readers of the popular detective were convinced he was a real person, and would write to the bank's address seeking help with a case. So many letters were delivered, they actually hired a specific secretary just to deal with the correspondence. When the Sherlock Holmes museum opened in 1990, it was located a few doors down, at numbers 237-241, but when the Abbey National left their building in 2005, the museum was given special dispensation to acquire the coveted number of 221b, making it the only address in London to have a house number out of sequence with the rest of the street. Imaginatively recreating the same living quarters found above the Sherlock Holmes pub, the museum is wonderfully decorated, giving the impression that perhaps Holmes and Watson were real people, even down to the brass plaque outside one of the world's most famous addresses, inscribed "Sherlock Holmes, Consulting Detective, 1881-1904".
(221b Baker Street, NW1; +44 20 7224 3688; open daily 9.30am-6pm; sherlock-holmes.co.uk)

A Victorian's Secret Pantry

Queen Victoria was still sitting on the throne when the North London grocers **W Martyn** opened its doors, and stepping inside here, you wouldn't think time ever moved on. Specialists of tea, coffee (they roast their own in the shop), biscuits, dips, chutneys and pantry goods, it's remarkably still owned and run by the Martyn Family over a century and a quarter later. A perfect time capsule of the British high street, complete with antique mahogany cabinets, weighing scales, sacks of grain by the counter and shelves lined with glass mason jars of English delicacies, the shop, quite rightly, has a historically listed interior. *(135 Muswell Hill Broadway N10, +44 208-883 5642; Open Mon-Sat 9.30am-5.30pm, Sun noon-4pm; Wmartyn.co.uk)*

A Photographer's Field Guide to London

Even if you've sworn off social media forever, or, at least until the end of the week, you never know when a list of Insta-ready locations might come in handy...

Picturesque & Cinematic Streets

Chester Terrace: See how the 1% live on one of the magnificent Georgian streets that encircle Regent's Park, showcasing John Nash architecture at its very finest. After falling into a serious state of neglect during WWII, the restored houses with their fluted Corinthian columns are now all Grade 1 Listed, and mostly still owned by the Crown estate. *(NW1, Regent's Park)*

Church Walk & Gordon Place: Turn off busy Kensington High Street down Church Walk, a blink-and-you'll-miss-it leafy passageway that leads to a micro village of charming boutiques and the heavenly Gordon Place, overtaken by wisteria in Spring. Pause for a pint at the Elephant & Castle, the corner pub with a delightful view of the blooms. *(W8, Kensington)*

Clarendon Cross: This charming pastel-hued micro village hiding in Holland Park is one of London's best-kept secrets. You'll find a cluster of chic homeware shops and Julie's (see pg 71), a restaurant loved by celebrities since the 1960s. There may not be a more pleasant place to sit on this side of the city than on one of those benches under the trees. *(W11, Holland Park)*

Goodwin's Court: Blink and you'll miss it, but that adds to the charm of stumbling across this Dickensian 18th century time capsule hidden away in the middle of Covent Garden. And "stumble" really is the operative word here; Goodwin's Court is dark, narrow and lined with crooked Georgian buildings and bulging bow-fronted windows. The tiny alley dates back to 1690, home to London's last gas fuelled streetlamps and is thought to have inspired Harry Potter's Diagon Alley. *(WC2, Covent Garden)*

Hornsey Road Baths & Laundry neon sign: The ghost sign for the once-famous Hornsey Road baths and swimming pools must be one of the most striking neon signs in the world. The baths, said to be the biggest in Europe, were built in Victorian times, partly destroyed in the Blitz and given a facelift in the 70s before closing down in the 90s. They eventually met the wrecking ball in 2006 but the original boiler chimney, clock tower and its evocative Art Deco neon still stands. Once you've photographed it from every possible angle (best snapped at twilight), head around the corner down Seven Sisters Road to **The Swimmer at the Grafton Arms**, the kind of pub you wish was your local, filled with vintage

HOLLAND PARK
MEWS

Chester Terrace

Kelly Street

Gordon's Place

Shad Thames

Alice's on Portobello Road

Neal's Yard

Goodwins Court

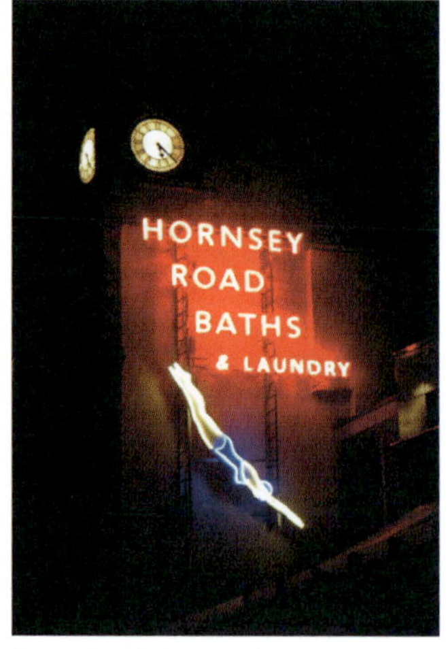

Hornsey Road Baths & Laundry

Warren Mews

swimming memorabilia collected by the owner, a jukebox, a fireplace and a friendly cat. *(Find the original sign at 179 Hornsey Road, find the pub at 13 Eburne Road, NY, Islington)*

Kelly Street: Find the end of the rainbow in Kentish town, on this curving technicolour tree-lined street. According to locals, the houses were painted for free by Dulux when the British paint brand shot an advertisement on the street in the 1970s. *(NW1, Kentish Town)*

Neal's Yard: Once a dark and dingy back alley used by the former Covent Garden fruit and vegetable market, today it's the cheeriest hidden enclave in London. In the 1970s, a nomadic activist and author of a series of guidebooks called *Alternative London* transformed the courtyard's derelict warehouses into a colourful micro-village of "caring capitalist businesses". These included a wholefood shop, an apothecary, a dairy and a coffee house. New shops and restaurants have made their home here since, but the quaint village atmosphere and rainbow palette are unchanged. *(Neal's Yard, London WC2H)*

Roupell Street: Nothing short of a 19th-century time capsule, a hidden historic gem in London's Waterloo and a treat for architectural enthusiasts and photographers. The perfect snapshot of old England, this street is known for its perfectly-preserved rows of Georgian workers' cottages that somehow survived the Blitz *and* the expansion of Waterloo Station. Halfway up the street, you'll find the Grade II listed pub, **The King's Arms**, where they host an excellent pub quiz on Sunday nights from 7pm. *(SE1, Waterloo)*

Shad Thames: It's one of the most dramatic cobblestoned streets in the city, with its old Victorian warehouses on either side, connected by what appear to be small bridges overhead. Those are called gantries and were once used for rolling barrels between warehouses. *(SE1, Tower Bridge)*

Warren Mews: A distinctive all-black tunnel entrance to one of London's more unusual cobbled cul-de-sacs. *(W1, Fitzrovia)*

Postcard-ready Shopfronts

Alice's: Possibly the most photographed shopfront on Portobello Road (discover less-crowded parts of the iconic market on pg 296), this antique cornershop has been in business for over a century, filled to the brim with British tchotchkes (some authentic, others not so much). It's a veritable rabbit hole of "vintage" stuff, just don't try to take pictures inside, they don't take kindly to it.
(86 Portobello Rd, Notting Hill W11, +44 20 7229 8187; Tuesday to Friday 9am-5pm, Sat 8am-3pm)

Algerian Coffee Stores: This Soho holdout painted in bright royal postbox red, topped with a candy stripe awning, is London's oldest coffee shop. The business has been in the same family since WWII when they bought it from Mr Hassan, an Algerian merchant who opened its doors in 1887. You can sample the best coffees from around the world –an espresso will set you back just £1, or you can create your own bespoke blend. If coffee doesn't do it for you, go for the nostalgic selection of 19th-century confections.
(52 Old Compton St, London W1D; +44 20 7437 2480; Mon-Wed 9am-6pm, Thurs-Sat 10am-7pm; Algeriancoffeestores.com)

Biscuiteers: With its illustrated façade and smart monochrome awning, is this the chicest biscuit shop in the world? Behind the façade, it even has its own "School of Icing" (see pg 313) where cookie monsters of all ages can master the art of biscuit design.
(194 Kensington Park Road, original Notting Hill branch, London, W11; +44 2077 278 096; Mon- Sat 10am -6pm, Sun 11am - 5pm; Biscuiteers.com)

Campania & Jones: In what is surely the East End's most charming corner, a southern Italian kitchen serves up some of the most delicious pasta in the city inside this former cowshed off Columbia Road Flower Market.
(23 Ezra St, London, E2; +44 207 613 0015; open for lunch & dinner Tues-Sat and 12-5pm Sunday; Campaniaandjones.com)

K & J Libretto & Daughters: You can't miss it, with the old red telephone booth and odd vintage cars out front, one of which is a yellow New York taxi cab. A place out of time, this locally-loved butcher is everything an old-fashioned family business should be. But why would you go out of your way unless you were in need of a roast dinner? Well, there just aren't many places like this left in the world - and who knows, by the time you're reading this it might already be gone.
(122 Wood Vale, SE23, near Forest Hill Tube & Rail Station; +44 20 8693 3175; check Google for updated opening hours)

Algerian Coffee Stores

Lily Vanilli: Careful not to walk past and miss this hidden bakery tucked away in a charming courtyard just a few feet away from Campania & Jones (pg98). It doesn't take much convincing to linger at their welcoming café terrace under string lights and sample the divine cakes and cupcakes fresh out of the oven. *(The Courtyard, 18 Ezra St, London E2; Thurs & Fri 11am-5pm, Sat 10am-5pm, Sun 9am-4.30pm; Lilyvanilli.com/the-bakery)*

Lina Stores: You can't help but stop and admire the beautiful mint green tiled façade of this delicatessen in the heart of Soho. Founded 75 years ago by Lina, an Italian immigrant from Genoa, her homemade spinach & ricotta ravioli recipe has been sold here since 1944. Oversized salumi hangs from the ceiling and the glass display cases are packed with little-known specialty cheeses. Head over just a few blocks to 51 Greek Street to find the restaurant serving up Lina's beloved classic pasta dishes in a 1940s-inspired diner.
(18 Brewer St, W1F; +44 20 7437 6482; Mon-Sat 10am-7pm, Sun 11am-6pm; Linastores.co.uk)

The Old Curiosity Shop: Wander south from Lincoln's Inn Fields (a secret village of law, pg 152) and you'll find a curiously out-of-place cottage, dwarfed by the surrounding modern buildings. Across its uneven, overhanging upper story is painted 'The Old Curiosity Shop – Immortalised by Charles Dickens', leading one to deduce that this relic of old London inspired his 1840 novel. But whilst the shop itself dates back to the 16th century and is thought to be one of the oldest in London, it was actually thirty years after the popular tale of Little Nell that the owner, an enterprising bookseller and binder called Tesseyman, decided to rename his business 'The Old Curiosity Shop' in a bid to draw in customers. It survived the Great Fire, and today it has been restored by the London School of Economics which rents out the ground floor to one of the luckiest shopkeepers in London. *(13-14, Portsmouth Street, WC2A; upon publishing this book, the retail space was not yet occupied following the completion of restoration works)*

The Old Curiosity Shop

Lina Stores

Location Scouting with Wes Anderson

Do you have another part-time job in the movie industry that nobody knows about? Same! Of course, it doesn't exactly pay well because ... well, technically our "boss" doesn't actually know we hired ourselves to do the job. But whenever he decides he needs us, conveniently, we'll have that compendium of Wes Anderson movie locations on file just for the occasion...

The Royal Tenenbaums' Eccentric Scottish Cousins

You might not have any genuine interest in military history, but the **London Scottish Regimental Museum** is a Wes Anderson location scout's dream discovery. A secret museum by appointment, London's most whimsical Scottish outpost is home to a beautiful Victorian drill hall hiding inside a fairly routine looking branch of the Territorial Army in Westminster. With its idiosyncratic collections and symmetrical wrought iron balconies painted a vibrant red, white and blue, it has all the nostalgia, boy scout aesthetics and colour palettes that Wes Anderson could possibly need to dream up a London-based film. Founded in 1859 by Scots, it's continuously used as a military base, and the regiment still drills here in the evenings; a stirring sight in their traditional Hodden Grey kilts, often accompanied by the oldest volunteer pipe band in the world. The museum and its artefacts tell the story of the regiment's history from the Boer War to Afghanistan; memorials, paintings, weapons, flags, three Victoria Crosses, and even part of the tail fin from a shot down Luftwaffe Junkers. Just picture it –Ralph Fiennes as the charismatic but slightly absurd Major-General and Tilda Swinton, as a long-suffering Queen of England who tries to fake her own assassination, only for it to be thwarted by the unlikely kilt-wearing regiment on duty. Light-hearted conspiracy and chaos ensues.

You can only visit the museum by booking an appointment with the curator, but that means a personal and intimate look around this little-known Victorian Scottish treasure, through its club rooms, libraries and bar.

(95, Horseferry Road, Westminster, SW1P; +44 020 7630 1639; check Londonscottishregt.org for details on booking a visit which lasts around 90 minutes)

The Quintessential British Bistro

As the clock strikes midday, suited and booted City boys flock to this long-standing nostalgic seafood restaurant like a seagull to a bag of chips. **Sweetings** sits smack bang in the centre of the Square Mile and runs off the same ethos that it established back in 1830. With original mosaic floors, dark wood panelling, marble countertops, and old pictures hung wonkily on the walls, this is a timeless but unpretentious landmark of British gastronomy. Famous for its fish dishes and traditional puddings such as spotted dick and treacle tart, people love this busy City institution for its traditions as well as taste. The bill is always handwritten no matter the size of the order, with a category for cigars at the bottom. White wine may be a seafood staple but their signature tipple, Black Velvet, is a must-try. The wonderful concoction of champagne and Guinness was created in 1861 to mourn Prince Albert's death and is still served in a tankard, as it always has been. As skyscrapers and stocks rise and fall around you in the beating heart of banking, tuck into a to-die-for fish pie and relish in the things that stubbornly stay the same.

(39 Queen Victoria St, EC4N; +44 020 7248 3062; Mon-Fri 11.30am-3pm; Sweetingsrestaurant.co.uk)

For Electric Art Deco Glamour, report to the Control Room

There aren't many Londoners who expected the **Battersea Power Station**, a brooding, crumbling eyesore on London's skyline, to become one of the city's most desirable properties. Today you can ride in a glass elevator right up to the top of one of its iconic white chimneys to reach a 360° viewing platform sitting

Battersea Power Station Control Room

atop the old smoke hole (Lift109.co.uk/tickets). This 1920s coal-fired power station, once described as a "Temple of Power", is the largest brick building in Europe, but you may know it better as the dystopian factory on the cover art of Pink Floyd's *Animals* album. Once in a while, you'd come across someone at the local pub claiming to have snuck inside the station during those decades of abandonment when it was sliding further and further into disrepair. The 20th century, giving way to a rise in gas and nuclear power, had sealed its fate -or so we thought. The industrial relic was only recently brought back to life by property developers, who appreciatively, opted to spare its most intriguing historic feature; the rare jewel at the very heart of the brick behemoth: **Control Room A**. Power plants and glamour aren't two things you'd normally put together in a sentence, but this is a glimpse back to the glorious "new age" of electricity, where great hulking industrial power met with the glamour, elegance and delicacy of art deco design. With its archaic dials, vintage signage and fonts worthy of a Wes Anderson title card, you can almost imagine it humming with the buzz of workers in white coats in a world where bulky buttons and switches once ruled the earth. For exclusive access, official guided tours of the space are offered once a week (tickets are typically released four weeks in advance via Batterseapowerstation.co.uk/official-guided-tours). Designed with the lavish decadence of a palace ballroom, it's only fitting that this space and its preserved 1930s equipment can also be hired out for events, dinners, exhibitions, film shoots or even weddings. If you're just up for a casual drink, head down to

Battersea Power Station Control Room

Control Room B, an all-day bar overlooking the power station's turbine hall. Surrounded by the original control desks, switch gears and synchroscopes, your high voltage cocktails are served. *(Upper Ground Turbine Hall B, 270 The Power Station, Circus Road South, Battersea SW1; +44 20 7590 360; open Mon, Tues 12pm-11pm, Wed 10am-11pm, Thurs 10am-12am, Fri, Sat 10am-1am, Sun 10am-10pm; Controlroomb.com)*

A Cult Classic 'Caff'

Established in 1946, as it says above the entrance, **Regency Café** has seen it all. This no-frills greasy spoon, with its Art Deco tiled exterior and bistro curtains, is a refuelling station serving unbeatable full English breakfasts and builder's brews. Marco, the owner, shouts orders to the kitchen at the top of his voice above the clatter of cutlery. Shuffle in next to Westminster politicians and burly builders seated around the formica-topped tables on bucket chairs nailed to the floor. It's easy to let your mind drift and create character storylines for the customers. This cinematic setting hasn't gone unnoticed by creative types. Daniel Craig and Tom Hardy both dined here for a scene in *Layer Cake*. It was also featured in Elton John's biopic, *Rocketman* and has graced the pages of *Vogue*. Cuttings from the magazine are framed on the walls, next to black and white portraits of Marco's favourite footballers and old boxing posters. *(17-19 Regency St, Westminster, SW1P; +44 020 7821 6596; Mon-Fri 7am-2.30pm, 4pm-7.15pm, Sat 7am-12pm & Closed Sun; Regencycafe.has.restaurant)*

Regency Café

Colour Paletting at the Grand Baroque Town Hall

In the depths of South East London, off the main tourist trail, lies the architectural wonder, **Woolwich Town Hall**, a rare example of an Edwardian Baroque building in London. The colour palette with this one is strong. For Woolwich locals, voting in an election, registering a birth, death or marriage has never been so aesthetic. The pastel pink ceiling with symmetrical white lines is like the exterior of the Grand Budapest Hotel turned upside down. A marble statue of Queen Victoria stands at the top of a white column staircase, dominating the main hall, laid with a handsome black and white marble tile. Behind her is a huge stained-glass window set against a teal backdrop. Scout it out by attending one of the council's committee meetings, which are held almost daily in the hall and free for the public to attend. If you wish to have the room to yourself, it's available to hire. And if your head isn't already in the clouds, look up for the real treat. The photographs will be so worth the neck-ache. *(Wellington Street, Woolwich SE18; +44 020 8854 8888; Mon-Fri 9am-5pm & Sat-Sun Closed; Royalgreenwich.gov.uk)*

Smithfield Market

Early Morning Adventures at the Victorian Meat Market

To get a real feel for **Smithfield Market** (and an early morning bargain) curious carnivores should try to arrive by 7am or earlier to snag a mighty ribeye for under £10. Discover *working* London, under grade-two-listed Victorian domes, with a bold palette of purples and greens, fancy wrought iron flourishes, a maze of underground tunnels and meat –lots of it –being pedalled to all the city's restaurants and butchers in the wee hours of the morning. As early as 1174, live animals were sold at **Smithfield Market**. Once described as "a smooth field where every Friday there is a celebrated rendezvous of fine horses to be sold, and in another corner are placed vendibles of the peasant, swine with their deep

Woolwich Town Hall

flanks and cows and oxen of immense bulk". Smithfield covers an area of almost 10 acres and many parts of it on Charterhouse Street still connect to the former railway tunnels via secret passages, where produce was once carried from the trains. It almost burned to the ground in a fire in the 1950s and took 1,700 firefighters three whole days to save it. Over the years, several of these Victorian buildings have been left empty and unused, falling into a total state of disrepair. In 1999, the old Metropolitan Cold Stores were turned into the iconic Fabric nightclub (see pg 247), and a much-debated decision was recently made to redevelop and restore what remains of the derelict market areas. The Museum of London is set to take over the old general and fish market, while other plans will include new public spaces, shops, restaurants and a food hall as part of the city's "Culture Mile" in the years to come. Despite rumours of its looming disappearance, the historic meat market will continue to operate on site in three of the remaining buildings. *(Grand Ave, Farringdon, EC1A, +44 207 248 3151; Mon-Fri from 2am, closed weekends; Smithfieldmarket.com)*

Stepping into the Ring with the Kray Twins

Scan the faded photos of old fighters that line the walls of the legendary **Repton Boxing Club**, and you might recognise two familiar faces. For long before the sharp suits, swinging nightclubs and lives of violent, organised crime, the Kray twins (Britain's most infamous 1960s gangsters) were passionate, aspiring boxers. Housed in an atmospheric Victorian bath house just off Brick Lane, the Repton is the oldest boxing club in London. It was set up in 1884 as a boys club in one of London's poorest communities, offering what was often the only alternative to a life of crime. "There are two things for a working class kid to do," explained the late and legendary head coach Tony Burns, "steal or box." The Krays, who lived a short walk away, spent many of their formative years here learning the sweet science; Ronnie winning four of his six fights by knockout, Reggie, unbeaten in seven. Whilst the Krays would eventually leave the ring in favour of a more ruthless path, the Repton still flourishes today under its motto of "No Guts, No Glory". The unchanging and cinematic setting makes it an attractive location for the film industry, having most notably featured in a few of Guy Ritchie's glamorous gangster flicks. Meanwhile, the gym remains all about its principles, discipline and determination, living up to its rough and tough reputation. There are no box-to-keep-fit classes on offer –Repton leaves that to the luxury gyms. Young amateur boxers with potential are encouraged to come down to the club and have a chat with one of the coaches on a Monday, Wednesday or Friday between 5pm & 7.30pm. Women can now join training on Saturday afternoons from 1.30pm and juniors between the age of 10 and 16 can come along on a Tuesday or a Thursday between 4.30-7.30pm to meet the head junior coach, but there are no one-off lessons. Membership at any level requires a commitment to the club, where all resources go towards training serious and competitive boxers. The Repton has produced over 500 champions over the years, and is still offering a vital service to the heart of the old East End. *(116, Cheshire Street, E2; +44 020 7739 3595; reptonboxingclub.com)*

Repton Boxing Club

Cosmic House

03
Desperately Seeking Inspiration

Love the arts but hate the crowds? Away from the selfie sticks and umbrella-led tour groups, find beauty, treasure and untapped knowledge by looking where others don't. Channel your cultural heroes, look for questions and answers in the architecture, lift the curtain on hidden places that need our attention most. From unofficial museums and overlooked artists' homes to flea markets and dusty old bookshops, seek inspiration where there's room for human emotion (and for that light bulb moment). Go forth like an artist in search of their muse.

Bohemians Welcome

Candlelight Jam Sessions from Jimi Hendrix's Bedroom

Number 23 Brook Street in Mayfair of London, is the only officially recognised Jimi Hendrix residence in the world. And coincidentally, located next door to the 1st floor flat where the rock & roll legend composed some of his most famous guitar riffs, is the former residence of Baroque composer George Frideric Handel, at number 25. "Separated by a wall and 200 years" as the **Handel Hendrix House** eloquently puts it, it was originally a museum dedicated solely to the classical musician, run by a charitable trust, whose staff used Jimi's old flat next door as an administrative office for over a decade. But we'll forgive them, because in 2016, after earning a £1.2 million grant, they permanently restored Mr. Hendrix's 1960s London home away from home to its former bohemian glory and opened it up to the public. Hendrix was frequently photographed at his lair in Mayfair, where in 1968, the musician paid £30 a week in rent. Using pieces owned and collected by the musician, original works and instruments belonging to him, as well as historically accurate furnishings, curators have done a very groovy job of recreating the psychedelic rock'n'roll den, once described by Jimi as the only home he ever had. He set up in the

Handel Hendrix House

Brook Street flat with his then-girlfriend Kath Etichingham, where he'd give interviews, write new songs and rehearse for concerts. As soon as Hendrix had learned that Handel would have been his neighbour once upon a time, he and Kathy made a bee line for the One Stop Record Shop on nearby South Molton Street (no longer) and stocked up on classical albums, which strongly influenced many of the symphonic qualities in Hendrix's music.

It seems only fitting that the memory of these musical housemates separated by time be upheld by the same museum. On Handel's side of the wall, you've got a four-storey period-accurate house to explore, imagining his homelife in Georgian London, from bedroom to kitchen. But the real magic begins after dark on Fridays when the museum stays open late to host intimate concerts by candlelight. Talented musicians of all genres –rock, soul, jazz, folk, classical – are invited to perform for a small audience on both sides of the wall, in Hendrix's bedroom and in Handel's dining room (6-8pm, student tickets £15, adult £20). You're also invited to help fill the Handel Hendrix House with music once a month on Saturday afternoons (1-3pm), when a resident guitarist hosts jam sessions from Jimi's bed. Bring your guitar or borrow one from the museum and rock out to the bohemian rhapsody. *(25 Brook Street, Mayfair W1K +44 20 7495 1685; Handelhendrix.org)*

A Real Jazz Den with a Fireplace

Down the alley of an old coaching inn, look for the door on the left. Follow the sounds of New Orleans down a flight of stairs, your destination is to the right. **Oliver's Jazz Bar** may have only opened in 2003, but it feels straight out of a film noir. It's dark, it's musty, the wine is cheap and the musicians play for love. You don't even need to know all that much about jazz to be humbled by the raw and undiscovered talent that comes through here. Offering live music most nights of the week, the Monday singer's jam is highly recommended, but the Sunday jams are also a treat. Oliver is a real person by the way, a delightful beatnik, most often present, and he lets you bring your own food to eat at your candlelight table by a coal grate fire. It's well worth the journey to this unexpected intimate basement gem out in Greenwich, which also happens to be one of the most beautiful areas of London (turn to pg 375 to fill up your day). After a long day exploring the rich, naval history of Greenwich, a stop in Oliver's is the perfect last port of call.

(9 Nevada Street, Greenwich Peninsula, SE10; +44 20 8858 3693; Mon-Sun 4pm-midnight, music most nights at 9pm, Sunday at 12pm & 5pm; Reservations recommended, check Oliversjazzbar.com for more details)

Find more live music, turn to pg 315.

Inside the Mind of Grayson Perry

Back before pop-ups were popping up everywhere, Tony Hornecker accidentally invented the concept behind a dilapidated pale blue door down a darkened alley in East London. As a skint artist in downtown Dalston in the noughties, Tony combined his chef training and set design skills to transform his humble home into an underground art installation and surreal gypsy dining experience. Knock three times to enter his dimly-lit den of disco balls, canopies and canapés. Shrouded in sweet-smelling smoke and whiffs of moonshine to stimulate the senses, you will be guided through scattered props to your table by Tony's mates: dressed-to-the-nines drag queens. In between multiple bottles of house wine and a 3-course banquet, the evening's gender-bending hosts provide entertainment in the form of an anything-goes, raucous cabaret. Although it was intended to last just one weekend, the door to Tony's secret party palace remains ajar after all these years. As more people have cottoned on to the cosy and camp carnage that occurs in this secreted-away abode, the **Pale Blue Door** has had to take on a life of its own to retain its back-alley secrecy. Giving Tony a bit of peace and privacy, the illusive dining club now lives up to its vagabond spirit by popping up in secret locations around London several times a year. To keep tabs on where it will be next and what colour door you will be knocking on, join the Pale Blue Door's mailing list via Tony's website. Tickets get snapped up quickly but luckily its success has launched the **Hornecker Centre** around the corner from the original location, where you can join 3 course dinner & drag shows and book your own parties.
(412 Kingsland Rd, Dalston, E8; +44 074 7681 8141; Learn more and review the events on offer at Tonyhornecker.com and Thehorneckercentre.com)

The Hornecker Centre

Woolcrest Textiles

What would Vivienne Westwood Do?

"There's nowhere else like London. Nothing at all, anywhere."
–*Vivienne Westwood*

A French Jewel Box in the Heart of London

The dearly departed queen of punk herself, Vivienne Westwood, called it "the greatest art school in this country" and one of the first things she did with her apprentices was send them off to the **Wallace Collection**. In this spectacular historic mansion tucked away in central London just behind Selfridges, is a treasure trove of French fine and decorative arts amassed in the 18th and 19th centuries by five generations of a British aristocratic family, one of the wealthiest in Europe. We're talking about a collection so rich that it rivals some of the greatest museums in Paris, boasting works like Fragonard's *The Swing*, five Rembrandts, nine Rubens's, four Van Dycks', two Delacroix, original Sèvres porcelain pieces and treasures from Versailles. Many of the pieces in the collection actually ended up here following the French Revolution after being seized from French aristocratic, royal and Catholic properties. England is particularly rich in the works of the *ancien régime* thanks to its wealthy families who attended the revolutionary sales, or *biens nationaux*, which were held to resolve the French financial crisis. Allow yourself to be deeply impressed by the collection, while at the same time, deeply perplexed at how this museum is not better known or packed with visitors, particularly since it's free to enter. Take your time getting acquainted with the art at a leisurely pace. Make yourself comfortable in the plush conversation chairs and marinate in the grandeur, admiring the palatial wallpaper and gilded details. The courtyard houses one of the most impressive settings for lunch or cream tea anywhere in London, among the sculptures and trees. The Wallace Collection is a place to come back to time and again; a place to spend an hour or a day, where the paintings and antiques will become old friends.
(Hertford House, Manchester Square, Marylebone, W1U; +44 207 563 9500; open every day from 10am to 5pm; free entry; Wallacecollection.org)

Dressmaking on a Dime

Whether you're finally fixing that elbow hole in your favourite sweater or giving your bed's outdated headboard a chic new velvet makeover, **Woolcrest Textiles** has got you covered. From pinstripe to PVC, this wonderful warehouse stocks endless reams of high-quality fabric in every colour imaginable and sells them to the public for wholesale prices. Material is sold by the metre, cutting cost and waste, making it a popular starting point for fashion students. If you're struggling to find the perfect pattern for a new pair of drapes, the cutting crew can source it for you and offer some priceless nuggets of wisdom for your project. After all, they've been on the receiving end of heaps of design dilemmas during their four decades in business. *(6 Well St, Hackney, E9; +44 020 8985 3686; Mon-Fri 9am-6pm, Sat 10am-5pm & Sun 10.30am-4.30pm; Woolcresttextiles.co.uk).* Just down the road is Mare Street Market, a hip Hackney hangout spot to spread out and review your purchases over coffee and a snack (pg 48).

Woolcrest Textiles

A Secret Archive of Pop Culture & Fashion

When wandering the streets of Bloomsbury, history is inescapable. There are blue plaques around every corner, reminding you of where some literary great once called home. In this part of town, you'd think that you're far more likely to feel the presence of Virginia Woolf rather than Vivienne Westwood.
But hidden in a quaint mews is a three-story alternative arts centre, celebrating the counter-cultural histories of London's subcultural class. **The Horse Hospital** has been putting on underground film screenings and avant-garde exhibitions celebrating the likes of Queen Viv since 1993. Head upstairs to the **Contemporary Wardrobe Collection**, a fashion archive set up in 1978 as a specialist hire company to supply rare vintage garms and couture items to the TV and film industries. It's where the best dressed get dressed, from The Rolling Stones to Annie Lennox to Harry Styles. A go-to for in-the-know stylists and creatives, call or email to make an appointment and get access to this trophy cabinet of fashion history (all of it is for hire; Contemporarywardrobe.com). And yes, as the name suggests, there really used to be a horse hospital here, and as far back as the 18th century, cab drivers' would take their sick horses to these double-decker stables for some TLC. *(Colonnade, Bloomsbury, WC1N; +44 020 7833 3644; Mon-Sat 12-6pm, Sun closed; Thehorsehospital.com)*

The Original Night at the Museum

Late night openings at museums seems like a fairly recent idea, but the **Victoria & Albert Museum** in South Kensington has been inviting the public to wander around the museum by gas light as far back as 1858. These special "out of regular hours" evenings were designed by the museum's first director, Henry Cole, to be "most convenient to the working classes". You could also find something to drink, as the V&A was the first museum in the UK to offer refreshment rooms. Whether you're interested in furniture, glasswork, jewellery, illuminated manuscripts or fashion, the V&A still offers its late night evenings every week, with the *Friday Late* on the last Friday of the month set aside for special events, often involving a live performance and the opportunity to browse the collection with a drink in hand. Today, with a staggering collection of over two million beautiful artefacts stretching back 5,000 years, the V&A is rightly regarded as the greatest collection of art and design in the world, and is the perfect (and free) place to find inspiration for your next artistic endeavour. Vivienne Westood regularly raided the V&A fashion archives searching for historical garments to inspire her own tartan and tweed gowns. In turn, the V&A now holds many of the most iconic pieces Westwood ever made –as well as a few other bits & bobs. Their fashion and textiles collection, spanning a period of 5,000 years, just so happens to be the largest in the world.
(Cromwell Road, SW7; +44 020 7942 2000; Sat-Thurs 10am-5.45pm, Fri 10am-10pm; Vam.ac.uk/info/friday-late).

Liberty London

Oscar Wilde and Cruella De Vil's Boatload of Treasure

Liberty is not your average department store, and not just because it's one of London's oldest, or because a young Cruella De Vil (looking a lot like Emma Stone) once worked there as a window dresser to nurture her career in fashion design. Disney characters aside, past patrons include William Morris and Oscar Wilde, who proclaimed "Liberty is the chosen resort of the artistic shopper." Both Yves Saint Laurent and Vivienne Westwood lent their talents to the in-house design studio, which still actively produces floral fabrics, print dresses, and silk scarves, drawing from an ever growing archive of more than 45,000 prints.

But can we talk about the building itself? From the mock Tudor exterior facade to the floorboards inside, all the original woodwork you see was harvested from timbers of old Royal Navy ships; the *HMS Impregnable* & *HMS Hindustan*. In the windows, spot the series of miniature glass paintings amongst the wood panelling that were taken straight from the captain's quarters. It's only fitting that Liberty's foundations would be fashioned from the old bones of maritime vessels since the store itself was founded on bringing goods from the East to the West via European-Asian sea routes. At the height of the British Empire, Arthur Lasenby Liberty had created an opulent emporium stocked with Indian silks and cashmere, Japanese ceramics, oriental rugs, ornaments and luxury goods sourced from around the world. Part Eastern Bazaar, part English stately home adorned with Europe's longest chandelier, the luxury West End store was designed around three sky-wells, each surrounded by cosier shopping rooms complete with tiled fireplaces.

Liberty also championed the burgeoning Art Nouveau and Arts & Craft movement, so much so that in Italy, Art Nouveau was first referred to as the "*Stile Liberty*" (Liberty style). Don't miss the carpet room; the oldest part of Liberty and a little museum in its own right, specialising in rare, old and antique pieces; where you can meet the carpet buyers themselves, who are only too happy to share their wealth of knowledge about the textile treasures they've brought back from Iran, Afghanistan, India, Nepal and Morocco and beyond. *(Regent Street, W1B; +44 020 3893 3062; Mon-Sat 10am-8pm, Sun 12pm-6pm; libertylondon.com)*

Liberty London

Going. Going. Gone to the Best-Dressed Buyer at the Back

Some of history's most iconic outfits were only worn once. A huge cultural moment is created, it's on the front pages of every newspaper, but what happens then? Surely Princess Diana's 'revenge dress' isn't stuffed in the back of a wardrobe somewhere, or Elizabeth Taylor's antique tiara, laying around gathering dust. The truth is that pieces like these often end up in the expert hands of one woman. Kerry Taylor is an esteemed British businesswoman who started out at Sotheby's as one of the youngest auctioneers in the company's history, rummaging through many a muse's closets. About five times a year, **Kerry Taylor Auctions** put on a one-of-a-kind mannequin catwalk of haute couture and museum-worthy jewellery and accessories as items go under the hammer and into the hands of the highest bidder. Once registered, you can attend an auction for yourself and witness fashion history, even if you don't intend to bid. Watch as the paddles go up for 17th-century ball gowns, a rare 1930s Madame Grès dress, a Vivenne Westwood showpiece or maybe a pair of Alexander McQueen 'Armadillo shoes'. It's certainly the place to hunt for vintage Westwood, Dior and Lagerfeld, as well as accessories fit for actual princesses, and if you keep an eye on upcoming auctions, you might just catch another Diana sale. *(249-253 Long Ln, Bermondsey, SE1; +44 020 8676 4600; See website for auction dates and viewing days; Kerrytaylorauctions.com)*

A Walk Down Vivienne Westwood's Memory Lane

Over the years, there has been one city street that styles London's innate swagger like no other. You don't walk down it, you strut. In the 1960s, the **King's Road** started swinging as a post-war playground for Mary Quant's mini-skirted poster girls. Come the '70s and the changing political climate, things got a little darker and more dangerous, with safety pins and the Sex Pistols setting the trend. At the turn of the 80s, punk went pop with the dawn of the New Romantics and their androgynous sound and style. Chelsea's 'village street' has seen it all, rousing rebellions and raising generations of subcultural icons for decades. It even homed Christian the Lion, yes, an actual lion cub bought from Harrods by a pair of young Australians in 1969. Talk about giving Mick Jagger a run for his money as the street's resident party animal.

Neighbouring Christian were a bunch of boutiques which paved the way for big name local designers and built the King's Road up to be a historic hotspot for groovy garms. Now selling chandeliers, 488 Kings Road once was the home of Granny Takes a Trip, the first psychedelic shop of the swinging sixties. As well as selling vintage clothes, the store was known for its mind-bending interiors and changing façade, which at one point featured a saloon car crashing through the window. Further down the road at No. 49 was Chelsea Drugstore, an open-all-hours, multi-layered extravaganza selling everything from records

Vivienne Westwood's Worlds End

to pharmaceuticals. On top of being a chic '70s hangout for the Rolling Stones and a film set for Stanley Kubrick, it was famed for its 'flying squad', a troop of Jane Birkin lookalike motorcyclists, (cat)suited and booted to deliver cherry soda from the store to your door. In the years after Christian the Lion's party days, the King's Road saw many more endangered species lose their patch. As is the way these days, Chelsea Drugstore is now sadly a McDonalds, albeit an architecturally attractive one. Thankfully, there is still one location that has retained its maverick power; a place to unlock the street's radical past and get to know a 'Chelsea Set' who were more rebellious than royal, more punk than posh.

430 Kings Road is an address engraved in the minds of fashion disciples like holy scripture. It was the epicentre of all the stylish and social revolutions that unfolded on its doorstep. After a stint as 'Mr Freedom', selling colourful satin pants to London's dolly birds and dandies, 1971 saw Malcolm Mclaren and Vivienne Westwood step into the shop, originally selling leather biker gear covered in studs and zips; a gateway of what was to come next. Each time a new collection of clothes were designed, the name and décor of the shop changed too. The rebrand as 'SEX' in 1974, with its tagline "rubberwear for the office" became the most iconic and outrageous era of them all. With the name spelled out in big pink letters, squeaky rubber curtains and the SCUM manifesto graffitied on the walls, it was hardly a surprise that stock centred on fetish and bondage gear. It attracted a clientele who wanted to shock, as well as shop. Regulars, and staff, included Sid Vicious, Siouxsie Sioux and Adam Ant. SEX wasn't simply a quick in and out, get what you need and leave the coins on the counter. It became the crucible for Vivienne's ideas, political and cultural. She created 'urban guerrillas' out of loitering punks, who would use the shop as a meeting place and a dressing up box full of tartan two-pieces and mohair jumpers.

In line with the street's spirit of reinvention, the shop was renamed again in 1980, and continues to be known as **Worlds End**, with a giant backwards-spinning clock face replacing the pink SEX sign. The King's Road has seen radical changes around No. 430 since the heyday of punk and its predecessors, but Vivienne Westwood's global fashion empire has kept its roots local. The Olde Curiosity Shoppe design serves as a reminder of the nostalgic history and creative future of this now high-end holy grail boutique. British fashion has a lot to thank Viv for, so go retrace her steps and see where it all started.
(430 Kings Rd, Chelsea SW10; +44 020 7352 6551; Mon-Sat 10am-6pm; Worldsend-shop.co.uk)

Continue shopping with Vivienne Westwood in 'The Little Black Book of a Thriftaholic' on pg 120.

Snooping Around Other People's Houses

When homes become museums, they might have smaller advertising budgets than the major museums, but they've got just as much to share...

She's Just a Cosmic House, from another Galaxy

A post-modern odyssey awaits on a sleepy boulevard in West London's Holland Park. **The Cosmic House** is an architectural masterpiece; a journey through time and space, conceived within the mind of the renowned visionary architect Charles Jencks who paved the way for other better-known architects like Zaha Hadid and Frank Gehry. The Victorian villa was his family home, which he transformed into a perfect collision of comfort and cosmology at the beginning of the 1980s. It's now a Grade I listed building (that's the highest level of protection), a museum, as well as an architectural and cultural salon. Dripping with symbolism and art, literature and pop culture references that unlock as you move deeper through the home, this is postmodernism like you've never seen it. There's a dome modelled off an Italian church that's been flipped upside down and turned into a jacuzzi. There's a sunken room facing the garden that doubles as a giant sundial. The library is a literal village of bookcases, and as the museum's guidebook puts it best, "the ceiling is disco mirrored in classical panels." It's humorous, it's kitsch, it's Dadaist and it's definitely cosmic. "I might have gone too far in designing certain rooms", said Jencks before he died, however, one can't help but be entirely grateful for every last detail in this very personal piece of his legacy. Do everything you can to get tickets and unlock the cosmos.
(19 Lansdowne Walk, W11; Jencksfoundation.org/cosmic-house/visit)

Cosmic House

Cosmic House

Cosmic House

Leighton House

A Painter's Bohemian Palace

Linger awhile in the neighbourhood known as Holland Park, home to some of the most incredible Victorian and Gothic mansions in the city. Among the most exquisite, **Leighton House** has been quietly open to visitors as a house museum since 1929. A feast for the eyes inside, marked only by its blue plaque outside, you would never know what treasures await behind that solemn red brick facade. Frederic Leighton was a well-travelled 19th-century painter who moved in all the right circles and made sure his lavish abode reflected that. Leighton House was his own bohemian palace of art, adorned with enviable wallpaper, the most precious china and exquisite carpets –and it's all just as he left it.

Leighton House

As soon as you enter, the sound of trickling water lures you to the home's *pièce de résistance*; a spectacular Arabian hall of intricate mosaics and Islamic tiles surrounding a luxurious indoor fountain under a great golden dome. It's entirely unexpected, and you may just recognise the room as a memorable filming location from the 1985 dystopian epic, *Brazil*. Upstairs in Leighton's former art studio, you can find his used paint palettes on a cluttered wooden desk, beneath those giant windows where the light floods in just so. Here, Leighton once entertained Queen Victoria herself, who bought his first major painting in 1885.

In this mini palace where he lived alone but welcomed many, we can imagine a day in the life of a successful artist of the late Victorian period (and all the wealth, status and taste that came with it). The museum regularly hosts out-of-hours events such as "drink & draw" classes, supper clubs and garden parties. You can even hire out the entire museum for your own event. Otherwise, it's simply the ideal museum to knock your socks off on a rainy morning in Kensington.
(12 Holland Park Rd, London W14; +44 20 7602 3316; open everyday except Tuesday, 10.30am-5pm; Rbkc.gov.uk/subsites/museums.aspx)

A Victorian Voyeur's Home Unlocked

Behind Kensington High Street, shoulder to shoulder with uniform townhouses, No. 18 Stafford Terrace appears to be just like the others. However, pushing the front door of **Sambourne House** unlocks a five-storey cabinet of curiosities plucked straight from the late-Victorian era. A hidden time capsule of bygone Victorian middle-class domesticity and style, the house also stands as a detailed personal archive, full of letters, sketches, and family photographs. The house was formerly lived in by satirical cartoonist, Edward Linley Sambourne. Take an atmospheric actor-led guided tour, performed by the Sambournes' housekeeper, Mrs Raffles, who peppers the walkabout with gossipy tales plucked directly from the Sambourne family diaries. Draw interior design inspiration from the *House Beautiful* aesthetic, characterised by dark earthy tones, Chinese ceramics, and William Morris wallpaper. The best part? Before you go, pay a visit to the smallest and most surprising room in the house: the bathroom, which doubled as a darkroom. Keen photographer and well-known voyeur, Mr Sambourne, would use the bathtub to develop his snaps, which he took with a hidden camera to capture unsuspecting Londoners (usually women) on the street, leaving behind a rare, unstaged glimpse of everyday life and fashion of the era. There's also a considerable collection of unknown models he photographed in the nude. You can now find these proudly pinned up on the surrounding walls. Enjoy, just don't stare for too long – she's old enough to be your great, great grandmother.
(18 Stafford Terrace, Kensington, W8; +44 020 7602 3316; Wed-Sun 10am-5.30pm; Rbkc.gov.uk/museums/sambourne-house)

Chasing Huguenot Ghosts

There's something about stepping inside **Dennis Severs' House** for the first time that makes the hairs stand up on the back of your neck. First, you can hear the age of the house; it creaks in the floorboards beneath you. Strange whispers and familiar odours seem to linger. A plate of freshly shucked oysters has been left by interrupted eaters in the dining room. Someone's timeworn laundry is hanging at the top of the stairs where an unmade bed lies empty; abandoned by

Dennis Severs' House

Dennis Severs' House

its sleepless occupant. A black cat brushes past your leg. You begin to feel as if you might have travelled through a frame into a still-life painting, and that all 10 rooms of this Georgian townhouse are inhabited by ghosts of the past. They always seem to be just out of sight, passing like shadows behind you as you enter every room looking for clues.

The house at 18 Folgate Street was once home to a family of 18th-century Huguenot silk weavers, but it was one man's dream to make you think they never left. The late Dennis Sever was the artist and eccentric creator of this immersive time machine, who lived in the townhouse himself for nearly 20 years, in much the same way as its original occupants would have done in the

Dennis Severs' House

18th century. There's still barely any electricity running through the house, save for a few power sockets installed after Sever's death, enabling a small and dedicated team to continue running his living museum. But this is no ordinary heritage house museum (those don't usually have their ceilings caving in). Today, immersive tours of the house invite visitors to time travel by daylight or candlelight. Sever called it "still-life drama"; a unique spectator sport that provides visitors with unexpected moments that stimulate all the senses. David Hockney once rated it as one of the world's great "opera experiences". Group and privatised visits are available from £16 per person. A special "Silent Night" visit includes fireside refreshments set up in a room of your choice where champagne is served, or mulled wine and mince pies in the winter. A visit to Dennis Severs' House will leave you feeling disorientated, dazzled and delighted all at once. Don't miss it for anything. *(18 Folgate St, E1; +44 20 7247 4013; open Sun & Mon, Wed & Fri Dennissevershouse.co.uk)*

Put yourself in Freud's Slippers

What they often forget to mention about Sigmund Freud is that in addition to his famous theories about the mind, he was also a very good collector. **The Freud Museum** is the last home of the founder of psychoanalysis after he escaped Nazi persecution in WWII. Though his home and practice were raided in Vienna, Freud was able to flee with most of his possessions, including his famous psychoanalytic couch draped in Persian carpets, as well as a surprising collection of ancient archeological objects. He spent the last year of his life in peaceful exile living amongst his personal things in this charming Hampstead abode, a smart North London cottage filled with several lifetimes of fascinating Freudian history. After Sigmund's died in 1939, his daughter Anna, the pioneering child psychoanalyst, continued to live and work here until her own death in 1982. Part of the museum is also dedicated to her life and work and there's always a thoughtful exhibition that dives into little-known perspectives of the Freud family legacy. The shop is worth a visit just for the fantastic selection of books (and the souvenir Freudian slippers). If you have the time, stay for a coffee in the beautiful and well-kept garden.
(20 Maresfield Gardens, London NW3; +44 20 7435 2002; open Wed-Sun 10.30am-5pm; Freud.org.uk)

Freud's couch at the Freud Museum

The Secret Behind 575 Wandsworth Road

On a seemingly ordinary street in South London, past the concrete tower blocks, the off-licences and chicken takeaway shops, is a strip of seemingly ordinary Victorian terrace houses. But one of these houses is not like the others. Hidden away behind the most unassuming facade, is a work of art and a place of possibilities; a small house that became the life's work of Lambeth resident and Kenyan-born artist, novelist and poet, Khadambi Asalache. This extraordinary man, who grew up reading Shakespeare while herding cattle in western Kenya, spent two decades hand-carving the interior of **575 Wandsworth Road** with lavish Moorish-inspired fretwork. The deceptively modest property is considered so unique, it is now managed by the National Trust and exhibited to the public as an artwork of national significance.

Asalache came to London in the early 1960s around the same time he published his first novel, *The Calabash of Life*, on the subject of Kenyan tribesmen. He had gained a degree in architecture in Nairobi and would earn another in mathematics at the University of London, all the while writing poetry for literary journals before becoming a civil servant. In 1981, he paid £31,000 for a "two-up two-down" Georgian terraced house that was in very bad shape and previously inhabited by squatters. Among many things, the kitchen needed some work to cover up the damp, so Khadambi headed off to the local skip to find some reclaimed wood. He fixed it against the wall, but looking a little too plain for his taste, he added another piece of wood on top and began carving a series of patterns as a fretwork. He didn't stop carving for the next 20 years.

Every day, he took the 77A bus home from his job in Whitehall and returned to his private paradise, a work forever in progress. Using a single tool, he covered every surface of the house. Khadambi Asalache was creating his own secret world behind the inconspicuous facade of 575 Wandsworth Road and the house is a testimony to his mindset. It speaks of Africa, Europe, Asia and the world. Asalache died of cancer in 2006, survived by his partner, Susie Thomson, a Scottish basket-maker who now welcomes visitors to the house, which functions as one of London's most intimate museums. To preserve the site, the number of visitors is limited to 2,000 per year. Asalache even hand-painted the floors, so shoes must be replaced by slippers to literally tip-toe around his work. You'll need to book well in advance, but visits can be pre-arranged by calling the booking office or via the National Trust website.
(575 Wandsworth Road, Lambeth, SW8; +4402076224109; open Thurs & Fri, tours at 11am, 1pm, 3pm; Nationaltrust.org.uk/visit/london/575-wandsworth-road)

There's No Place Like (Other People's) Homes

If your favourite part of shopping at IKEA is roaming through the model home display areas, you may enjoy a similar concept at the **Museum of the Home**, exploring British home life from the 17th century to the present day. Make your way through the historically accurate and immaculately dressed period rooms and gardens, housed in a row of restored Grade I-listed almshouses, where interior design lovers of all ages and eras are sure to find inspiration in the details. Full of personal touches, every household scene is just as enchanting as the last and at Christmas, each one is decorated for the holidays according to life during the time it's stuck in. Follow up your visit with an extra serving of nostalgia around the corner on Hoxton Street for some comfort food at F Cooke (see pg 208), London's iconic pie and mash shop. *(136 Kingsland Rd, Hoxton, E2; +44 020 7739 9893; Tue-Sun 10am-5pm; Museumofthehome.org.uk)*

The Many Delights of a Tudor Palace turned Art Deco Party Pad

The Courtaulds were no ordinary 1930s society couple. Virginia "Ginie" Courtauld came from Romanian nobility, claimed to be a direct descendant of Vlad the Impaler, and sported an exotic snake tattoo that ran the entire length of her leg. Her husband Stephen –brother of Samuel, who founded the prestigious

Eltham Palace

Courtauld Institute – was an explorer, mountain climber, heir to a vast textile fortune, and an early financier of the world's oldest film studio (Ealing Studios in West London). Together they hosted lavish parties for the Jazz Age glitterati at their opulent Greenwich mansion, a former royal residence surrounded by a Tudor moat. When they found it, **Eltham Palace** was suffering from centuries of neglect, but as the boyhood home of Henry VIII, it was rich with mediaeval and Tudor history. The eccentric Courtaulds not only restored the palace but added an Art Deco extension to create their own unique Tudor-Deco party house. Most rooms were hooked up to a gramophone sound system and fitted with built-in cocktail bars. The couple's pet lemur, Mah-Jongg, had his own heated jungle-themed living quarters and the basement contained the most luxurious private

Eltham Palace

bunker in London, which was only recently revealed to the public. Restorers also uncovered a map room where the couple employed a secretary to plan out all their extravagant voyages aboard the family yacht, and in Virginia's private quarters, her enviable walk-in wardrobe has been faithfully reconstructed and filled with beautiful vintage pieces. You're even invited to try on a few replicas of her most glamorous outfits. The centrepiece of the house is the breathtaking circular entrance hall of geometric splendour that wouldn't look out of place on an Art Deco ocean liner, as intended by the couple's architects, Seely & Paget. During the Blitz in 1944, the Courtaulds left town after German incendiary bombs damaged the estate, which seemed to quell their party spirit at Eltham Palace. They moved on to Scotland and later settled in Southern Rhodesia, leaving the Greenwich estate to the Army School of Education. Since English Heritage took over the property from the British army in the 90s, so much of Eltham's interior has been thoughtfully restored and well-preserved under their expert care, from the original wallpaper to the furniture and lighting fixtures. But don't forget to leave some time for the 19-acre historic garden, which deserves as much attention as the eccentric house. The stunning Arts and Crafts sanctuary includes a sunken rose garden, fantastic views of the London skyline and plenty of idyllic spots to sit and enjoy a picnic lunch.
(Court Yard, Eltham, Greenwich, SE9; +44 0370 333 1181; Sun-Fri 10am-5pm, Sat 10am-3pm; English-heritage.org.uk/visit/places/eltham-palace-and-gardens)

Eltham Palace

Meet the Man Who Lives Inside His Dreams

"I decided to go for the minimalist look", reads a sarcastic scribble pinned to the front door of a semi-detached house down a suburban South London street. On the inside, artist Stephen Wright's **House of Dreams** is a complex and colourful explosion of emotion. The project started out as purely decorative in 1998, but turned into a monumental response to grief after the loss of his partner and both parents. The visual mayhem of 45 Melbourne Grove is a shrine to the beauty and chaos of feeling all over the place; a museum dedicated to the fine line between laughing and crying. Ma and Pa's false teeth are cemented in the doorstep and poetic memory boards decorate the walls. As is the nature of outsider art, anything and everything can be made into a mosaic; broken toys, buttons and bottle tops bulge from every surface. Up until 2010, Stephen's curious creation was kept behind closed doors; it is the place that he eats and sleeps, after all. Fortunately for us, several days a year (until Stephen decides otherwise), you can join him and his patient partner Michael for a personal tour of his manmade museum. Keep an eye on the website for open day dates, entry for adults is £12 and pre-booking is advised, so they can put the kettle on. The House of Dreams will likely remain an unfinished masterpiece, constantly growing, while shrinking the couple's living space to just the loft upstairs. Who knows how long tours will continue so catch a glimpse of their symbolic and psychedelic grotto while you can.
(45 Melbourne Grove, East Dulwich, SE22; +44 020 8299 3164; Generally open once a month 10am-5pm; See stephenwrightartist.com/houseofdreams.php for dates)

House of Dreams

Collectors Secret Addresses

Seeking treasure in less obvious places...

The Restaurant that Rescues City Relics

If you find yourself eyeing up the furniture, the antique art prints or the collection of plaster castings in the hallway, the lamp fittings or even the fireplaces at **Brunswick House**, just bear in mind it's all for sale. This lone Georgian mansion in Vauxhall (an area that saw its historical architecture all but destroyed by railway construction, German WWII bombing and poor city planning) is ironically home to one of England's most important architectural salvage companies. LASSCO (London Architectural Salvage and Supply Co.) was born out of the building sites and skips of the late 70s and has been in the business of rescuing architectural relics from barns, attics, stables, out-houses of fusty institutions and country houses ever since. Previously inhabited by squatters after years of neglect, Brunswick House was arguably LASSCO's most important rescue when the company purchased it in 2004. Restored to its original Georgian splendour and then some, filled with architectural antiques, salvage and curiosities, today it's part showroom, part restaurant, café and events venue, or filming location for hire. LASSCO's larger showroom in Oxfordshire, Three Pigeons, is also packed with extraordinary salvaged finds and both sites now include hospitality as part of the shopping experience

Brunswick House

(which can be sampled online at Lassco.co.uk). Dining at Brunswick however, is anything but 'stuck in the past'; the ambience caters to a hip and informal new generation of antique lovers and the food and wine selection is just as impressive as the decor. Every Tuesday night, the hidden wine bar in the 17th-century brick vaulted basement is host to live "Jazz in the Cellars" gigs from 6pm (walk-ins only, unless closed for an event). Take a date, a group of friends, or the family; they'll all be dazzled by the wonders of this exquisite Georgian playhouse.
(30 Wandsworth Road, Vauxhall, London SW8; +44 20 7720 2926; open 12-9.45pm Wed-Sat, lunch on Sunday and for dinner on Tuesday; Brunswickhouse.london)

An Architectural Laboratory Frozen in Time

There is no place in the world quite like the **Sir John Soane Museum**, at least, not for a collector anyway, or a lover of sculpture, or an architect, or a decorator, or an historian –well, you get the point. This is an absolute must, for pretty much anyone who has a pair of eyes, to see at least once in their lives. Soane was a great 19th-century architect and the man who inspired Britain's iconic red telephone box (more about that on pg 357), but his most impressive legacy is without a doubt his own home. Filled with some 40,000 masterfully curated objects from around the world, this was his private architectural laboratory, a truly eccentric and extraordinary place that has been kept exactly as he left it upon his death nearly 200 years ago. A labyrinthine jewel box hiding behind what looks like a fairly austere facade of a Georgian townhouse, even the tiniest rooms are filled with treasure, whether it be his architectural

Sir John Soane Museum

Sir John Soane Museum

models, sculptures, paintings or an ancient Pharoah's sarcophagus. You can opt to walk around on your own (entry is free), but if you want to be able to take photographs, sign yourself up in advance for a candlelit tour after hours which gets you a glass of wine and access to some of Soane's secret archives, not normally open to the public (from £20). This is the only time photography is permitted to the public. The museum also hosts monthly evening design talks, listed via the website. Before you leave, the equally well-curated gift shop is well worth stopping into, particularly for the neoclassical jewellery and curiosities. *(13 Lincoln's Inn Fields, London WC2A; + 44 20 7405 2107; open Wed-Sun 10-5pm, Soane.org)*

Chelsea's Emerald Mini City of Antiques

A 30,000-square-foot antique emporium awaits at the quieter end of King's Road. **The Furniture and Arts Building**, or 'FAB' for short, lives up to its name. Everything about this spot is, well, pretty fabulous. The flashy emerald-green glazed-pediment building with its 120-year-old clock tower, is home to an Aladdin's cave of rare high-end furniture from times past. If you're in the market for an Art Deco dining table fit for hosting the Prime Minister, Victorian theodolites to add to your telescope collection or hunting down an authentic Chesterfield sofa sourced by the UK's most prestigious dealers, then this is your destination. Complete your visit with a Sunday stroll sizing up the sailboats around the Chelsea Harbour next door, before sitting down to a roast at The Chelsea Ram, a local's pub, well hidden in the residential back streets that hug the River Thames. *(533 King's Rd, Chelsea, SW10; +44 7780 773 204; Mon-Sat 10am-6pm, Sun 11am-5pm; furnitureandartsbuilding.com)*

A Hoarder's Paradise of Electric Antiques

Considering the direction in which humanity is headed, one man's remarkable private hoard of antique technology packed into a back garden shed in Dulwich, may just turn out to be one of the most significant historical collections of the future. For now, the **Vintage Wireless and Television Museum** is one of London's most under-the-radar and secret museums. If you ever wondered what happened to Britain's discarded vintage radios and TVs (remember the polished wood kind?) this is where they ended up. Born in 1929, Gerry Wells had been collecting them since WWII, when he began scavenging bomb sites as a child during the Blitz. After the war as an adult, he opened a radio and TV repair shop which eventually closed down in the '70s, at which point he decided to turn his house, full of electrical bits and bobs from the past, into a museum. Containing hundreds of radios, televisions, speakers and radiograms from wireless to the early transistor models, the collection is so vast that one day, the petrol magnate, John Paul Getty, got wind of it and called upon Gerry to help him repair a radiogram. The two met several times and Getty was so taken aback by the

collector's passion and talent that he paid the museum's utility bills for the rest of his life. Wells passed away in 2014, having dedicated his life to lovingly restoring and preserving his electric antiques. The museum is now set up in several small sheds at the back of his former Edwardian home in Dulwich with a team on hand to continue Gerry's legacy. Pre-arrange a visit that will blow your Netflix-fatigued mind.
(23 Rosendale Rd, Norwood, SE21; +44 208 670 3667; arrange an appointment via phone or email at info@bvwtm.org.uk; Bvwm.org.uk).

Vintage Wireless and Television Museum

Fan Girl Moment

You and your close friends likely have a secret language, maybe it's a knowing wink, a raised eyebrow or a simple codeword for 'come and meet me, this date is a disaster'. For centuries, these coded glances and unspoken sentiments, along with flirtatious gestures, were communicated through an accessory far more exquisite than a mobile phone or the flutter of a false eyelash. **The Fan Museum** on the cusp of gorgeous Greenwich Park (see pg 375) is dedicated to the long lost world, and contemporary incarnations, of fabulous fans. Housed in a Georgian townhouse, the museum holds over 5,000 specimens of handheld art from all over the world, including French propaganda pieces, modern camp creations and some dating as far back as the 11th century. The more you immerse yourself in the history and artistry of fan-making, the stronger the temptation is to get your hands on a fan of your own (theirs is not a gift shop you want to miss). The museum also hosts informative fan making workshops to gather and translate your secret language into fancy fan etiquette.
(12 Crooms Hill, Greenwich, SE10; +44 020 8305 1441; Wed-Sat 11am-4.30pm; The-fanmuseum.org.uk)

Fan Museum

Open South London's Secret Sewing Box

Wish you paid more attention in Home Economics class? Take a trip south of the river for the history of sewing machines through the ages. It might even be the push you need to finally men that hole in your trousers. The starting point of many textile projects can be a bit of a mess and likewise, **London Sewing Machine Museum** is sandwiched between a crusty car dealership and building supplier on a busy road in Tooting Bec. Don't let the suspicious location or elusive opening times (3 hours on the first Saturday of every month) put you off. Promise – this is the right place. Clamber up the stairs of the roadside warehouse and prepare to be amazed by the time travelling treasure trove which is scandalously locked up with the lights off for 353 days of the year. Admission is free, but it's appreciated if you pop a pound in the charity bucket. Looking like a ghost sweatshop from multiple bygone eras mashed together, the secreted-away museum charts the history of the sewing machine from 1830 to 1950. Over 600 unexpected vintage beauties are on display, including the first ever Singer machine, originally owned by Queen Victoria's daughter. There's also an unlikely connection between Charlie Chaplin and Boy George to be discovered; their mothers made their costumes on identical machines, both of which can be found here, and the latter is autographed. If you're inspired to take your foot to the pedal and make do and mend, a couple of doors down is Sewing & Craft Superstore, London's largest independent haberdashery haven to get you started. *(308 Balham High Rd, Tooting Bec, SW17; +44 020 8767 4724; First Sat of each month 2-5pm; Craftysewer.com)*

Antique Shopping Inside An Old Edwardian Picture House

The marquee of **The Old Cinema** went dark after its last screening in 1934 and then served as an unlikely storage depot for parachutes during World War II before sitting rather neglected on the Chiswick High Road for over a decade. It was converted into a three-storey antique department store in the 1950s selling Victorian furniture imported from the British colonies (just imagine all the wicker). But in 1979, it narrowly avoided demolition in favour of a supermarket chain when some local antique dealers rescued the neighbourhood relic. During some much-needed refurbishment, they uncovered the Edwardian cinema's original gilded dome ceiling, and you can still make out the frame of the screen's stage. As for the antiques on sale, you've still got some good Victorian cabinetry and battered old trunks, but the real stars of the show are the Art Deco and mid-

The Old Cinema

century Danish and Eastern European finds. And to bring it full circle, keep in mind that a lot of the most striking pieces often find their way onto Hollywood movie sets. If you have the cash, go splash but otherwise just go for the interior inspiration. *(160 Chiswick High Rd., Chiswick, W4; +44 20 8995 4166; open Mon-Sat 10-6pm, Sun until 5pm; Theoldcinema.co.uk)*

But hang on, when in Chiswick, don't pass up an opportunity to indulge in a decadent lunch at **Villa di Geggiano**. Step into an enchanting Tuscan playhouse, inspired by the original neoclassical-style rural palace in Siena. The family that owns both the villa in Tuscany and its Chiswick outpost claim to be direct descendants of a medieval Pope. You might bump into Sting and his wife (the restaurant also serves wine from their Tuscan estate) but that doesn't mean this address is a pretentious celebrity haunt. With the feel of a true family-run restaurant, staff are incredibly welcoming and the pasta is cooked with love in an open kitchen. The art and decor are pretty fabulous too, and there are several secret dining rooms that would be perfect for small private dinner parties. *(66-68 Chiswick High Rd., Chiswick, W4; +44 20 3384 9442; Tues-Sun 12-10.30pm; Villadigeggiano.co.uk)*

From Tuscany to the Thames, head down to the river to walk off some of that truffle tagliatelle in the direction of St Nicholas Church. Take a stroll admiring the quaint cottages, looking out for the old 15th-century Tudor pub at number 2 Church Street, and some spectacular listed mansions along Chiswick Mall. Continue on a very pleasant riverside walk into Hammersmith and finish with a well-deserved pint at The Dove (see pg 21), one of those cherished pubs that'll stay etched in your memory of London.

Catacombs of Subterranean Silver

Now where might one find hidden vaults of jewels in Central London that don't belong to the royal family? Behind an unassuming door on Chancery Lane lies an underground Victorian bunker no longer locked off to the public. Originally established as a safe depository for wealthy Brits to protect their valuables during the Blitz, these impenetrable vaults were then rented out by silver dealers and converted into family-run stores in the 1950s. **London Silver Vaults** is now home to the world's largest and finest retail collection of antique silverware. Here you can pick up beautiful inkstands, opulent goblets and even a cucumber slice which dates back to 1805. You'll soon realise that pretty much anything can be made from silver, including armchairs. Entry is free but there are rigorous security checks –it is a vault after all. Once you're down there, work your way through a prison-like corridor to find a warren of 40 shops tucked away behind sturdy steel doors. Underground spaces may feel off-limits, especially if they are filled with precious metal, but that's what makes it exciting. The silver merchants are happy to invite you in and offer a range of prices. You

don't have to be born with a silver spoon in your mouth in order to buy one. And what's the best way to get to London's silver catacombs? Taxi! London cab drivers have intel on the city's best-kept secrets as they have to pass "The Knowledge" to obtain their licence. The location of the Vaults is one of the test points in this famous exam, so you can bank on taking the quickest route and getting some insider information on the way.
(53-64 Chancery Ln, Holborn, WC2A; +44 020 7242 3844; Mon-Fri 9am-5.30pm, Sat 9am-1pm; Silvervaultslondon.com)

Cave of Curios in an Abandoned Railway Station

You will often find bits of furniture on the streets of suburban London, usually the odd chair or table up for grabs by whoever finds it first. True to its name, **Aladdin's Cave** is where all that stuff ends up. Scrapheap-chic furniture and fittings from all eras fill this otherwise unremarkable roadside. Leather sofas, Victorian fireplaces, wooden dressers, and gaudy life-size figurines pile high on the pavement, which is just the tip of the iceberg. Make your way through the organised chaos and into a makeshift grotto of thrifty finds, held together by a tarpaulin roof and walls structured by the salvaged stock for sale. Chairs dangle from the ceiling like chandeliers and ornate masquerade masks balance on toilet seats like an unshakeable Jenga tower. Space is at a premium all over the city, but nowhere more so than here. The building itself is a work of architectural reclamation. The site was previously home to Lewisham Road Railway Station, which closed in 1917 to save money during the war. The crumbling aesthetic of this local landmark suits the style of the shop. Much of the interior remains the same, though it is hidden by all the odds and ends. The deeper you dig, the more treasures will be revealed.
(72 Loampit Hill, Lewisham, SE13; +44 020 8320 2553; Mon-Sat 9am-5pm, Sun 10am-6pm; Facebook.com/AlladinsCave.London)

Aladdin's Cave

Finders Keepers Flea Markets

Junk in the Trunk

Going to a car boot sale, come rain or shine, is a British rite of passage. It brings back memories of Sundays being dragged around fields by your parents, as they root through the bar of cars in hope of a bargain. Attracting antique collectors and thrifty shoppers alike, **Chiswick Car Boot Sale** is one of the best "car boots" in the country. This serendipitous jumble sale on wheels is run by Chiswick School's (super cool) parent-teacher association and held on the school grounds. The first Sunday of every month, except January, loaded cars queue overnight to pitch up at the crack of dawn. As the sun rises, rummage through designer cast-offs from affluent locals, reminisce over retro toys and unearth vintage homeware finds. Every now and then, you strike gold and find a real jewel amongst the junk. Entry is £1, get there early as traders pack up around midday to go back to bed. *(Burlington Ln, Chiswick, W4; first Sun of every month excl. January, 7am-12.30pm; Chiswickcarbootsale.com)*

An Antique Hunter's Day at the Races

On the outskirts of the city, **Sunbury Antiques Market** is somewhat of a trade secret. Family-run for four decades and held on the second and last Tuesday of every month, this sprawling indoor-outdoor market is a visual feast of 700 stalls, scattered along the Kempton Park racecourse. Big-name interior designers, fashion stylists, and costume and set designers come here to find inspiration too. Arguably the best part is the people-watching; hang around

Sunbury Antiques

Sunbury Antiques Market

to watch other thrifters as they deliberate over an antique skeleton or a rare set of 70s armchairs. Many of the higher quality dealers set up inside the halls, particularly the French dealers, who bring over all sorts of treasures. Whether you're a pro or simply a curious flâneur, you won't regret getting there early (6.30am if you're really serious) to dip into the rush of frenzied collectors bargaining their way around the field.
(Kempton Park Racecourse, Staines Rd E, Shepperton, Sunbury-on-Thames TW16; +44 01932 230 946; second and last Tuesday of every month, 6.30am-2pm; Sunburyantiques.com/kempton)

Bric-à-Brac Bazaar

Presenting London's biggest lost and found box. Dive in and dig deep. At **Deptford Market**, you're sure to find anything and everything you never knew you needed. Head to Douglas Way, a side road off the main high street, where you will be met with tables and tubs of second-hand treasures. Deptford has become known as the new Shoreditch of South East London, full of quirky characters and creative types. So, when they clear out their attics and take the contents to the local market, some real vintage gems are waiting to be found. There's no limit to what's on offer; books, crockery, clothes, household goods and antique collectables, all on the cheap. Come for the bric-à-brac but stay for the chat. That vinyl record, or vacuum cleaner, is sure to spark a conversation with the traders, who are skilled at selling you everything but the kitchen sink, unless they have one of those to flog too. Handy tip: many stalls at this old school brocante don't accept card payment, so bring cash and don't be afraid to haggle. *(Douglas Way, Deptford, SE8; +44 020 8314 2050; Wed, Fri & Sat 9am-5.30pm; Lewisham.gov.uk/deptford-markets)*

Deptford Market

Architectural Digestifs

You might find your answers hiding in the architecture...

A Secret Village of Law

Criminally overlooked, one of London's most striking neighbourhoods couldn't be more central and under-our-noses. **Inns of Court** is a series of connected and sequestered enclaves that serves as an elite campus of sorts. 'Inns' refers to the lodging that has been historically provided for law students and professionals of the court system here for over 600 years. Spot London's wigged barristers, robed judges, solicitors and law students rushing through their network of

Lincoln's Inn

covered passageways, magnificent mediaeval courtyards and tranquil gardens. From Monday to Friday, their world is yours to wander with surprisingly very little restriction; particularly atmospheric at dusk when the old gas lamp posts light the way. There are four official courts –Inner Temple, Middle Temple, Lincoln's Inn and Gray's Inn –which function not all that differently to boarding school houses or collegiate fraternity houses, supporting both students and fully qualified barristers in a variety of ways. Anyone choosing to train for the Bar must join an Inn, where they will remain a member for life (perks included).

Inns of Court

Each Inn boasts various amenities, including grand dining halls, members bars, common areas, libraries, chapels, as well as private offices and apartments, often rent-free. Members of the public can get a literal taste of life at the Inns by booking a seat for lunch under the 16th century hammerbeam roof of **Middle Temple Hall**. Not only was Harry Potter filmed in this very dining hall, but William Shakespeare chose the site in 1602 to debut his play *The Twelfth Night* (make a booking via Middletemple.org.uk/lunch).

The Inns of Court gardens are some of the most beautiful in the city. Perch yourself on a teak bench beside perfectly manicured flower beds and admire the tapestry of architecture from different centuries to the soothing sound of trickling fountains and occasional passing sound bites of legal discussion. In the southernmost courtyards, notice the velvet lawns sloping downhill towards the river (previous page, top image). These were once the sandy banks of the Thames, where the tide reached before the Victoria Embankment was built in the 1860s. Drop by in the summer, and you might stumble upon a croquet tournament and witness some friendly competition between the Inns. Among the many architectural highlights, Temple Church was the English headquarters of the Knights Templar, who occupied the site before the court system (Tom Hanks came looking for secrets here in *The Da Vinci Code*).

Lincoln's Inn

Middle Temple Lane

Finding your way into the Inns of Court is half the fun too. There are multiple entrances to enter and leave from on Fleet Street (Old Mitre Court is an easy one), but the most dramatic way to start your visit is the riverside entrance, through an elaborate stone archway down the cobblestoned Middle Temple Lane.

In case you're left wondering where England's lawyers find all their wigs and robes and old world dress, you should probably go and have a look at where they shop. Luckily, their tailor, which happens to be the oldest in all of London, is just around the corner from Fleet Street at 93 Chancery Lane. In the windows of **Ede & Ravenscroft**, you'll find just about everything a judge or a barrister might need; britches, buckles, gowns and of course, those funny old wigs. Also known as perukes, they're made of horsehair and can cost up to £3,000. Speaking of funny old things, just a few feet away, there's one more curiosity to be found in this unique neighbourhood in the heart of London. Look to the left of the tailor and spot a mint green cast iron hut with a royal coat of arms jutting out from the brick wall of Lincoln's Inn. This peculiar little outbuilding was once a Victorian public toilet (or 'pissoir' as they were known); no doubt one of the more ornate public urinals that were introduced across the city in the 19th century; and now a Grade II listed private toilet, primarily being used as storage by the house across the street. Just an extra wee slice of history for you. *(Middle Temple Lane, London, EC4; closest tube station: Temple or Chancery Ln; open Monday-Friday)*

MENS CUJUSQUE
IS
EST QUISQUE

Michelin-Star Art Deco Dining in an old Tyre Depot

You wouldn't usually think to link Michelin tyres with Michelin tables, but the prestigious restaurant guide's beginnings were humbler than you'd imagine. So how did a company selling rubber tyres become the world's authority on restaurants? In order to increase demand for tyres, the Michelin Brothers needed to increase the demand for cars. And of course, to boost a demand for cars, you would need to convince people of a reason to travel further afield. Enter the Michelin Guide, offering useful information for travelling motorists,

Bibendum

including tourist tips, petrol stations as well as maps, instructions for changing tires, and eventually, restaurants and hotels listed by specific categories. Little did André and Edouard Michelin foresee the road to success they were paving. The tyre business boomed and in 1911, the company opened its London headquarters on the Fulham Road; one of the earliest examples of concrete buildings in the city, which later became the two-star restaurant it is today.

Sporting an Art Deco pastiche slightly before its time, castle-like cupolas and large stained-glass windows with original adverts featuring the Michelin Man himself, it would have made a fabulous casino for the French Riviera. The company mascot, officially known as "Bibendum", got its name from the Latin phrase you can still read at reception: *"Nunc Est Bibendum",* Latin for "Now is the time to drink". When it was snapped up by the late restaurant magnate Terence Conran in 1985, who turned it into Conran's Bibendum Restaurant & Oyster Bar and a Conran Shop, the landmark was given a second lease on life. But it wasn't until 2017, when French chef Claude Bosi took the helm, renaming it **Claude Bosi at Bibendum** and earning it two Michelin stars, that the icon became a proper fixture on the London dining scene; a table very much coveted by foodies who won't hesitate to race across town especially for it. *(Michelin House, 81 Fulham Rd, SW3, +44 207 581 5817; open for lunch Fri-Sun 12-2pm, dinner Tue-Sun 6-9pm, closed Mondays; Claudebosi.com)*

Conversations with Concrete

Brutalism is the marmite of architecture. Like it or loathe it, concrete buildings have made their mark on London with brute spirit. Dotted all over the city are controversial concrete structures, beautiful to some and beastly to others. After World War II, vast parts of London and the rest of Britain quite literally became a blank slate. Devastated by the Blitz, the country faced chronic housing

Alexandra & Ainsworth Estate

shortages, as well as the dilemma of how to rebuild politically after the trauma of war. In the period of social solidarity that followed, overcrowding was tackled with a modernist and utilitarian approach, which was radically concrete in mind and matter. Influenced by Brutalist architects like Le Corbusier and the Bauhaus movement, town planners came up with utopian experiments to build "new towns", "streets in the sky" and "garden cities". These post-war reconstructions took shape with low-cost raw materials and stark geometric blocks, a direct contrast to the lavish decoration of a nostalgic Beaux-Arts style. Perhaps the pinnacle of this radical project was one of the most ambitious housing estates anywhere in the world: **The Barbican**.

Built between 1965 and 1976, intended as a "city within The City", there was a desire to bring back a lively resident population to the Square Mile, which had gone from being a bustling market centre of warehouses full of trade and material commerce to an office district. But inner city living at the time was unfashionable, so to entice middle-class professionals, planners set out to introduce a rich cultural program within its perimeters, including a performing arts centre, a music school, a museum, a cinema, restaurants, local amenities, and a church; all connected by elevated walkways separating cars and pedestrians (explore those on pg 364). The Barbican has over 2000 residential flats, and in order to present the estate as a sheltered and safe sanctuary for its residents, architects were inspired by the idea of an impenetrable fortress or castle. This idea is echoed by parts of London's crumbling ancient city

The Barbican Estate

The Barbican Conservatory

walls that were left to run through the site. There are even references to the ramparts of Middle Age military defence; narrow slit windows in the concrete recall mediaeval balistraria through which arrows might be discharged. With its imposing walls and hidden entrances, it's not entirely obvious how to even enter or find your way around the Barbican either. The early days of the arts centre were infamously dogged by the difficulty people had in finding their way around the complex walkways. The first residents recall having to act like guides, pointing visitors in the right direction. Coloured lines were painted on the walkways, and there were three different redesigns of the signage system to help people find their way.

Despite the raw and unfinished aesthetic, the Barbican's distinctive raw concrete was actually very purposefully sculptured and crafted that way by Italian stonemasons, a style and technique pioneered by Le Corbusier, the master of *Beton Brut.* At the time, there was a growing rivalry between the young utopian architects who wanted to build Bauhaus-inspired steel and glass towers similar to what we see in New York City, and another camp that favoured solid concrete fortifications that were rooted to the ground, rather than connected to the skies. The glass towers that now crowd around the Barbican today, render it almost quaint and old-fashioned in comparison. Once inside our concrete castle in the city, its open spaces were designed to resemble miniature urban jungles, full of plant life, water features and wildlife to mimic an unlikely urban utopia, even in the midst of gloomy English winters. Go on a Sunday and discover the true meaning of a concrete jungle with free admission into the conservatory (the second largest in London). Exotic climbing plants wrap around exposed steel pipes and crawl over the concrete slab balconies. Some would argue it beats a visit to Kew Gardens. *(Silk St, Barbican, London EC2Y; Barbican.org.uk)*

Despite striving for the creation of a new worldview with tiny windows and socialist ideals, by the 1970s and 80s many of these Brutalist developments began to reveal social problems and came to symbolise an altogether dystopian future. Previously dubbed 'the town of tomorrow', **Thamesmead Estate** became the sinister backdrop for Stanley Kubrick's sci-fi crime *A Clockwork Orange* and you might still spot Erno Goldfinger's **Trellick Tower** (see pg 299) and the **Balfron Tower** in the music videos for gritty realist britpop and grime artists.

It's an unforeseen time for Brutalist architecture these days. Having spent the last three or four decades reviled in the public view, today's trends are seeing modernist buildings such as Trellick Tower or The Barbican, both now listed landmarks, finding renewed appreciation. They are now considered edgy, fashionable and in some cases, seriously sought-after real estate. Brutalist London is still used as a setting for film and fashion shoots –with less anti-

The Barbican Estate

establishmentarianism attached. One of the city's most frequently filmed examples is the **Alexandra and Ainsworth Estate** in Swiss Cottage, a Brutalist "boulevard" deemed by media as a "wildly expensive disaster" when it was built in 1978, but more recently lauded as an architectural gem, even compared to the Hanging Gardens of Babylon. Residents say there isn't a day that goes by that they don't see a film crew or some kind of fashion shoot or music video underway. However, the controversy of "cool concrete" looms when urban and working-class aesthetics are monetised by brands and celebrities for profit, breeding the fetishization of council estates. Should your interest in Brutalist architecture lead you to these places, it's important to be mindful of these underlying dilemmas and respectful of residents when visiting. The Alexandra and Ainsworth Estate was more than just a social housing complex. In the words of its progressive creator Neave Brown, who was awarded the UK's highest honour for architecture some 40 years after completion, it's "a piece of city". Shops, parks, schools, and stepped terrace flats are all tied together with a long 350m long curving Brutalist boulevard. The estate winds alongside a busy railway so the low-rise swooping walkway acts as a noise barrier but also stands as an example of Brown's people-focused design approach. In line with Brutalism's utopian vision, the openness of the route encourages the community to come together. Each home is connected by a network of streets opening out to the sky, with its own front door and private garden terrace. The overgrown greenery splayed on the concrete is the oxymoron of "urban jungle" exemplified, making it a desirable spot to live and play. Now impossible to define as public housing, the private flats of Alexandra Road occasionally find their way onto the market, often expected to sell for upwards of £500,000. Still curious about life on the inside? On occasion, Open House London (see pg 183) has been known to grant access to more private residential areas of the estate; an opportunity to meet the locals and discover an example of pioneering modern architecture of post-war Britain. *(90B Rowley Way, London NW8; Openhouselondon.open-city.org.uk)*

London treats its Brutalist buildings with a surprising amount of care, protecting many of them with heritage-listed status, but arguably, not all of Brutalist London is deserving of the same respect. In the race for post-war architects to create this new and exciting modern city, a mish-mash of buildings were hastily erected; some frightfully plain and barren, resulting in what many felt resembled Soviet Russia: Bauhaus without the artistry. Perhaps no one was more vocal about their disdain for Brutalism than one of classical architecture's greatest defenders, King Charles himself.

"Did modern planners and architects in London ever use their eyes?" he famously asked the audience in 1984 during a scolding speech to the Royal

Institute of British Architects. "Those planners swept away the lanes and alleys, hidden away squares and courtyards, which in most other European countries, would have been lovingly rebuilt after the war. You have to give this much to the Luftwaffe," he continued, "when it knocked down our buildings, it didn't replace them with anything more offensive than rubble. *We* did that."

If you're curious to know exactly which buildings he might have been referring to, head to the South Bank of the Thames, where you can kill two birds with one rough-hewn geometric stone and visit the **National Theatre** and the **Hayward Gallery**. Not only will you find a showcase of world-class artistic talent, but this area was also notoriously described by the King as "a nuclear power station in the middle of London" –and that alone, is arguably a reason to visit. We may not all be Brutalist superfans who go weak at the knees when peering up at a multi-storey monolith, but London is a place celebrated for its diversity. Why not make that architecturally so too?

Meet the Society Preserving the Past

Sitting pretty in Spital Square is a conspicuous red door resembling a traditional British letterbox. Hand-painted on the door of this 18th-century house are the words **Society for the Protection of Ancient Buildings** (SPAB). The Society which calls this place home is the oldest and largest pressure group fighting for the lost lives of run-down buildings facing demolition. True to its quest, this Georgian mansion was rescued and restored by SPAB, after discovering it was once a silk merchant's house, dating back to 1740. Digging even deeper, the site was also a mediaeval priory, established in the late 12th century. The history of SPAB is just as distinctive as its HQ. Revolutionary textile designer, William Morris founded the Society in 1877 after being appalled by half-hearted architectural restoration programs popping up around the country that destroyed or majorly altered beautiful features of historical buildings during renovations. This feeling is just as prevalent today as it was in Victorian times and the organisation is still run according to Morris' manifesto. Beyond simply admiring 37 Spital Square's façade, check out SPAB's website for courses, seminars, career advice in conservation and heritage and events which can grant you special entry inside. London's Open House days will also allow you to wander inside and take a peek at that gorgeous iron spiral staircase in the courtyard. *(37 Spital Square, Spitalfields, E1; +44 020 7377 1644; Mon-Fri 7am-12am, Sat-Sun Closed; Spab.org.uk)*

A Cathedral of Steam to Beat the Great Stink

If you're on the hunt for some of London's most photogenic spaces, let's hope you have the stomach for the backstory on this one. During the unusually hot summer of 1858, London endured what became known as "The Great Stink", a heatwave combined with an inadequate sewer system that made the smell of human waste coming from the River Thames so bad, it halted parliament. Some 250 tons of limes were needed to mask the odour and the unpleasant event led to a massive, much-needed overhaul of the sewer system, calling for the construction of pumping stations to drain the sewage beyond the metropolitan area. So let's call the **Crossness Pumping Station** what it is: a jaw-dropping shrine to the art of pumping poo. And despite its less-than-glamorous purpose, it's a breathtaking display of Victorian Gothic beauty; an industrial cathedral of intricate ironwork and dazzling colour that looks more like the Emerald City than a sewage processing centre. Today it's a museum, and one of the only surviving four stations built by Sir Joseph Bazalgette, the man tasked with ridding London of its stink, who some historians argue should be recognised as one of the city's greatest heroes. But why lavishly decorate something built

Crossness Pumping Station

to process sewage anyway? Home to some of the most impressive Victorian steam engines ever built, Crossness is a reminder of a time when steam had become a vital part of British power and economic prosperity. So mysterious were the powers of these great machines to most, they were practically afforded the same respect as royal palaces or places of religious worship. Even the engines themselves were regally named after Queen Victoria, Prince Consort, Albert Edward and Alexandra. Crossness is still a working sewage treatment facility, but after diesel engines began to replace steam in the late 1930s, the grand pumping station was decommissioned in the 1950s and abandoned for many years. Sterling work and restoration by the Crossness Engines Trust has since restored London's most beautiful secret to its former glory, and you can even catch the Prince Consort engine running once a month. There aren't many museums that require a hard hat, but this is a place that consistently exceeds visitor expectations with its surprising features and fabulous photo opportunities around every corner. Open for guided visits several times a month through advance booking, if you are in the least bit interested in engineering or history, make an afternoon of it. *(Bazalgette Way, Abbey Wood, SE2; 020 8311 3711; see crossness.org.uk for details about visiting and upcoming events)*

London's Secret "Downton Abbey", built by America's Richest Man

It was 1890 and William Waldorf Astor had just inherited the family fortune, making him the richest man in America. He built the 13-storey luxury Waldorf Hotel in Manhattan and was the toast of the town, but despite all the Gilded Age glamour, William disliked being in the public eye. So much so, that in 1892, he even went as far as faking his own death. Following a feud with his aunt, he packed up and moved to England with his family, where he built a mini mahogany palace in the heart of central London overlooking the Thames. No expense was spared in building **Two Temple Place**, which allegedly cost no less than $1.5 million to whip together. The grand oak staircase with its stained glass ceiling could have inspired the one aboard the Titanic, the ill-fated vessel that would later claim the life of Astor's own brother. John Jacob Astor IV was

Two Temple Place

honeymooning on the ship with his young and pregnant bride, who survived in a lifeboat. Walk the mansion's labyrinth of rooms, each one more opulent than the next, lit by dazzling crystal chandeliers. It's up for hire if you have the budget for a private Downton Abbey-esque party, but the building also welcomes group visits on weekdays, during exhibition periods and at other times by

arrangement. Keep an eye on the exhibition schedule and don't forget to stay for tea in the café on the ground floor of this Victorian gem.
(2 Temple Pl, Temple, WC2R; +44 207 836 3715; to make a booking go to Twotempleplace.org/visit-us/group-visits)

Hackney's Hidden Tudor Playground

Hackney is not where you might expect to find a Tudor house built in 1535, but wander down Homerton High Street and you'll notice something slightly different about the townhouse at No. 2-4. At first glance, typical Georgian features, yet upon looking closer, we see its Tudor-era gabled roof, handmade bricks, and diamond paned windows. You've stumbled across one of the last surviving remnants of Tudor London: **Sutton House and Breaker's Yard**. Built as the home of courtier Sir Ralph Sadleir, Secretary of State to King Henry VIII, Sutton House boasts a true Tudor interior featuring a warren of wood panelled rooms complete with ornately carved fireplaces and hidden cellars. Sutton House has lived a storied life since the days when Hackney was still mostly countryside, located outside the City of London. It has since been a school, a church, a men's club and a union headquarters before it was abandoned in the 1980s and became a squat, known locally as "the Blue House". Amidst the Tudor finery, you'll find one bedroom preserved to how it looked when squatters still lived here, from the makeshift bed to the painted murals. Adjacent to Sutton House sits Breaker's Yard, an award-winning garden with a clue to its own history in name; until 2011, this urban oasis was indeed a car-breaker's yard. Transformed by award-winning landscape designer Daniel Lobb, it went from scrapyard to community garden featuring artfully reused salvage. The eccentric installations include a two-storey 1970s caravan and bespoke gates crafted with over 1,000 toy cars. Lovingly restored and run by volunteers of the National Trust, parents will get the historic Tudor home visit and kids will get the quirky urban playground. A fine compromise.
(2-4, Homerton High Street, Hackney, E9; +44 020 8986 2264; generally open Fri-Sun 11am-4pm, see website for schedule; Nationaltrust.org.uk/sutton-house-and-breakers-yard)

Killing Time at the Old Railway Hotel

You've arrived a little ahead of schedule; perhaps your Eurostar to Paris is delayed. How fortunate for you, because this calls for an impromptu time travelling adventure –with cocktails. The imposing Gothic red brick and spires of Euston Road's Victoria railway hotel has long loomed large over King's Cross, but for nearly 30 years, it lay empty and abandoned, with no one able to see the gilded decor inside. Renovations saw the grand hotel finally reopen in 2011 as the **St Pancras Renaissance Hotel**, which now shares the building with the Eurostar terminal. Making a one-time exception for our feelings about luxury hotel chains, head inside to find refuge at the hotel's elegant cocktail bars and surround

St Pancras Renaissance Hotel

yourself with glimpses of old-world train travel. Choose between The Booking Office inside the old ticket hall, or The Hansom, equally atmospheric in the ground floor lobby, converted from the cobbled driveway of the original station. Relaxed and ready for your journey after a few cocktails, leave a little extra time to wander around in search of the most breathtaking staircase in London (hint: aim for the corridors to the left of reception). Three stories high, with arched stained glass windows that could grace any Gothic cathedral, and decorated with sumptuous crimson and gold wallpaper, the centrepiece staircase was built wide enough to allow ladies in their Victorian bustle dresses to comfortably pass each other. If you were a fan of the Spice Girls, they filmed their iconic debut video 'Wannabe' on these very steps before the hotel was renovated. And with that fun fact, your stay in London is now surely complete.
(Euston Road, King's Cross, NW1; +44 020 7841 3540; marriott.com/hotels)

Hidden Egyptian Façade in a Brixton Community Arcade

Paris gets credit for inventing the shopping mall with the introduction of its 19th-century covered passages. Designed like artificial indoor streets, lined with fashionable boutiques, society salons and boasting luxurious amenities like heating and gas lighting, the concept was borrowed by cities across Europe. These iron and glass-covered passages are a must-see for architecture hunters and modern-day flâneurs with a penchant for browsing small independent shops. Regency London flocked to the sumptuous Parisian-style Burlington Arcade (see pg 267) in Piccadilly, but south of the river, you'll find a cherished and rather more eclectic example of the city's time-worn covered passages, hidden away down in Brixton. **Reliance Arcade** is an art deco-covered market built into a 1920s Georgian house. The unconventional main entrance is fronted by a giant luminous rainbow. The pot of gold at the end of this rainbow is a popcorn stand, the wafting sweet smell adding to the theme park feel, but the real treasure is found upon exiting the arcade on Electric Lane. Look up at the façade behind you to see a rare surviving example of British Egyptian-inspired architecture. In 18th Century England, Egyptomania was en vogue following the discovery of Tutankhamun's tomb and European travellers became fascinated with Egyptian culture, bringing back tales of ancient remains to London. This hidden walkway is more than just architecturally different to Burlington Arcade and its Parisian counterparts. The stalls here don't sell exclusive brands or fine dining. Instead, you'll find tiny hair salons full of chatter, a Chinese herbalist, vinyl records shops blasting music and a ramshackle cobbler. It's a place for the Afro-Caribbean community to meet and hang out, a vibrant vein pumping blood to the heart of Brixton, all under one rainbow-glazed roof. *(455 Brixton Rd, Brixton, SW9; Mon 8am-6pm, Tues-Sun 8am-11.30pm)*

Discover more of Brixton in Chapter 10.

A Giant Gothic Chess Piece Hidden in the 'Burbs

Tucked away in Twickenham is a shockingly bright snow-white castle with dramatic towers, turrets, and battlements, a masterpiece in Gothic architecture and trendsetter for its style revival a whole century later. Extraordinary on the inside too, through the keyhole you'll find gilded gold ceilings, show-stopping medieval fireplaces, stained glass windows and a spectacular collection of Old Master paintings. Its 18th century owner referred to the pretty palace as his "little plaything house". Casual. It takes a certain kind of eccentric English gent to make such a trivial remark and build a holiday home so enchanting

Strawberry Hill House

and experimental for its time. **Strawberry Hill House** is the fanciful creation of Horace Walpole, man of letters, son of Britain's first ever prime minister and compulsive collector of curios. The neo-gothic rococo style, along with the scale of the renovation from two small cottages to a flamboyant fantasy villa began to attract nosy neighbours and visitors from further afield. This led Horace to put on daily tours, strictly limited to 4 people "and no children". Just as captivating today, the fairytale suburban chateau and its landscaped grounds are luckily open to explorers of all ages (with young'uns going free). It was here in 1764, inspired by a nightmare, that Walpole penned '*The Castle of Otranto*', the first ever gothic novel which laid down the blueprint for the spooky literary genre thereafter. You can read the novel for yourself in the study where it was written, or better yet, join the gothic book club which meets monthly to discuss the works of the Brontë sisters and beyond in the best room in the house: Walpole's magically macabre gallery.

(268 Waldegrave Road, Twickenham; TW1; +44 20 8744 1241; Sun-Wed 1am-4pm; Strawberryhillhouse.org.uk)

The City's Secret Society Townhouse

The financial centre of London is a jungle of imposing stone and glass buildings. Looking down from one of these skyscrapers you'll see ant colonies of tiny bankers rushing to meetings. All work and no play? The two are very much combined in the City. Squeezed in between tall glass towers is an exclusive club that looks like a charming doll's house. The **Walbrook Club** stands out as the smallest building in the Square Mile. This is where the elite Bullingdon Club –a secretive Oxford University dining society, notorious for partying too hard and leaving quite the mess behind them (members include former Prime Ministers David Cameron and Boris Johnson) –go to celebrate when they graduate. From one city of architectural grandeur to another, this tiny Queen Anne townhouse makes a stark statement in its modern surroundings. Property developer Rudolph Palumbo commissioned the red brick building in 1953 after making his livelihood and legacy, redeveloping WW2 bomb sites in London. Now managed by Palumbo's grandson, the Walbrook Club continues to promote old values in architecture and arts, while also making room for a new era of millennial City players and high-flying clientele who work just a stone's throw away. For its members, finance and fine things come together under absolute discretion. Deals are closed and negronis are sipped under the gaze of old paintings and family architectural sketches. Membership fees start at £375 a year but its spaces can be hired by non-members for hosting dining events, meetings or a very secret afternoon tea party. *(37A Walbrook, EC4N; +44 020 7623 6100; Mon-Fri 7am-12am, Sat-Sun Closed; Walbrook-club.co.uk)*

The Walbrook Club

Unexpected Art Galleries

A Real-life Bridgerton Mansion

Period dramas set in Europe were long devoid of diversity untilNetflix's *Bridgerton* burst on the scene with its multiethnic cast. But if you thought this was revisionist history of the Regency era, think again. What most people don't know is just how present Black people were in 18th and 19th century Europe – at literally every level of society. Now granted, *Bridgerton* sits in the steamy Harlequin fantasy romance genre, but the point Shonda Rimes' light-hearted series surreptitiously raises is that history has been largely written by its "winners"; from a White perspective; and that the full story is still in the process of bringing itself to light. Let's shine our spotlight on Dido Belle, one of Britain's little-known Black aristocrats who lived at **Kenwood House**, a neoclassical villa with the best views of Hampstead Heath. It also happens to be one of London's most stunning house museums today, with an art collection to rival the Tate's and a jaw-dropping library boasting a perfectly pastel colour palette.

Dido Elizabeth Belle was the daughter of a beautiful slave girl found chained to an enemy Spanish ship by Royal Navy officer, Sir John Lindsay. He brought their child to England in 1756 where her upbringing was entrusted to Lindsay's uncle, Earl William Murray. There, Dido grew up as the adoptive sister of Lady Elizabeth, an orphaned relative also raised by the childless Earl and his wife at Kenwood House. Educated as a free gentlewoman, Belle enjoyed semi-aristocratic status and was admired for her refined accomplishments. Historians believe that Dido helped influence the Earl in his abolitionist sympathies while doing secretarial work for him. The family commissioned a now-famous portrait of Dido and Elizabeth playfully posing on the terrace of Kenwood House, described as one of Britain's most unique paintings "depicting a Black woman and a White woman as near equals". A replica of the piece hangs on the villa's walls today (the original was moved to Scone Palace in Scotland). There is plenty to learn about Dido's life at Kenwood, which is staffed by a lovely team of volunteers stationed in every room offering softly-whispered anecdotes about the objects or paintings they might notice you admiring. The incredible art collection includes Rembrandt, Turner and Vermeer to mention a few and the 18th-century interiors will leave you agape. Make time for a long afternoon walk in the magnificent park with its meandering pathways and stay for lunch too. The café serves a selection of very tasty hot foods, cakes, drinks, nibbles and even a Sunday roast, with tables inside and outside. If you don't have enough time to travel to one of the great English countryside estates, Kenwood House is just the (free) ticket.
(Kenwood House, Hampstead Ln, London NW3; +44 370 333 1181; open everyday 10am-5pm; English-heritage.org.uk/visit/places/kenwood)

Above: Dido Belle and her cousin Lady Elizabeth Murray painted at Kenwood House in 1778 by David Martin

Kenwood House

Find the Narnia of Neon hidden on an Industrial Estate (and Cold Beers at the End of the Rainbow)

Up in Walthamstow on the northern end of the Victoria Line, there's an unassuming warehouse on an industrial estate. Look for the blue door amidst the parked cars and vans, and just before you give up, thinking you've been sent on a wild goose chase, you'll find **God's Own Junkyard**. East London's own mini Las Vegas, somewhere between a fairground arcade, a Soho sex shop and the set of Baz Luhrmann's *Romeo + Juliet*, this is seven decades of light, collected by three generations. Step inside the Bracey family's neon fantasyland of salvaged and reclaimed signs, old movie props, discarded circus lights, retro displays, and neon art made from found objects. Opened as a showroom-cum-workshop in 1978, Chris Bracey is the founder and neon magic-maker here, but it was his father who started collecting back in the 1950s when he worked for an East London lighting company, travelling up and down the country to carnivals and funfairs. Chris has been creating his own signs for 37 years, inspired by his father's mind-boggling collection. His clients included everyone from Kate Moss to Lady Gaga to Elton John, but don't let that intimidate you. The showroom doubles as a museum, open to all visitors to admire. You'll find everything from seventies sex shop signs to props made for the Hollywood sets of *Willy Wonka* and *Batman* –and everything has its price. Taking his father's business to new heights, cheeky chappy Matthew Bracey now runs the show and loves to see the reaction on visitors' faces when they first walk through his doors. Today, it's Europe's largest neon signage

God's Own Junkyard

business as well as a free museum. Matthew says his weekly electricity bill is around £700. It takes 5 minutes just to turn on all the switches and the circuit tends to blow several times a day. You can also stay for a drink at the family's "Rolling Scones" café which has a beer garden at the back –surely one the coolest and most unexpected of places to enjoy a pint.
(Unit 12, Ravenswood Industrial Estate, Shernhall St, Walthamstow, E17; +44 208 521 8066; Fri-Sat 11am-10pm and Sun 11am-6pm; Godsownjunkyard.co.uk)

The Peculiar Art of Over-Complicating Things

W. Heath Robinson was so good at imagining overly complicated and outlandish contraptions that his name became part of the English dictionary in the early 20th century to describe anything with an unnecessarily elaborate design. "That's a real Heath-Robinson!" one could say to describe an apparatus that performed very simple tasks in an eccentric but rather inefficient manner. The irony is that William Heath Robinson's most famous contraption evolved into a machine we use every day. Best known for his drawings of whimsical inventions to achieve

Heath Robinson Museum

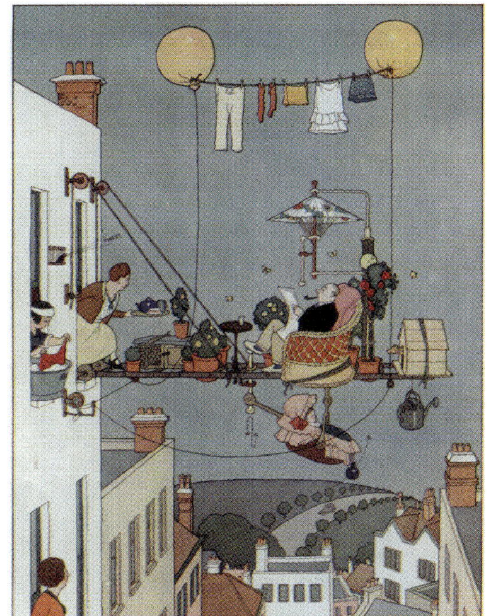

simple objectives, the English cartoonist, illustrator and artist inspired some of the greatest minds of his time –so much so that they named something else after him. During WWII, one of the code-breaking machines built to assist in the decryption of German message traffic (the predecessor to the world's first programmable computer), was named "Heath Robinson" in his honour. In the

1930s, he created a series called "An Ideal Home", to reflect the growing number of people living in flats in urban areas, lacking living space, and deprived of gardens and outdoor patios. In the wake of a pandemic and global lockdowns nearly a century later, much of his work still feels pretty relevant, offering humour and satire as a tonic for life's more unfortunate circumstances. It was only recently that the **Heath Robinson Museum** opened in a lovely North West London park, close to where the artist lived, housing a superbly curated collection of nearly 1,000 of his original artworks. Interactive, informative and amusing, the museum makes for a worthwhile Sunday out with the family, a mere 25 minutes from the centre on the Metropolitan tube line. Highly recommended, according to the museum itself, for "students of illustration, lovers of landscape paintings, advertising enthusiasts and academics, dads building contraptions in sheds, believers in fairies, children with time to dream, couples stuck in tiny flats [...] and anyone who's ever held something together with a bit of string". His name might be in the English dictionary, but you might be left wondering where the art of Heath Robinson has been all your life. *(50 W End Ln, Pinner HA5; +44 20 8866 8420; Thurs-Sun 11am-4pm; Heathrobinsonmuseum.org)*

Upstairs at the Gatehouse, a pub theatre in Highgate

A Night with Shakespeare... or Something like It

Plays and Pints Under One Roof

There is perhaps no finer & cheaper way to spend the evening in London than doing dinner in a pub downstairs, before heading up to a cosy, intimate theatre with an easy-to-order pint during the interval. Around the 1970s and 80s, a handful of pub-theatres started to spring up around the capital, drawing on the fine traditions of music halls, fringe & amateur dramatics, cabarets and comedy clubs. The **King's Head Theatre** in Islington is widely regarded as having started the pub theatre trend, converting their old boxing ring into an auditorium in the 1970s. Actors who've trodden the stage include Hugh Grant, Joanna Lumley and Kenneth Branagh, whilst many productions, such as *Trainspotting, La Bohème,* and premieres of plays by Tom Stoppard and Tennessee Williams all transferred to the West End to great success. The historic Tabard Pub and its charming fairy-lit beer garden is also home to the **Tabard Playhouse**, a small 96-seat theatre upstairs, where famous comedians have been known to try out new work prior to major tours. The **Finborough Theatre** has been combining vibrant new writing with revivals of forgotten 19th and 20th century plays for forty years above a charming horseshoe-shaped pub in Earl's Court. **Upstairs at The Gatehouse**, in the oldest pub in Highgate, a village auditorium has been in use since 1895, serving as a Victorian music hall, then a cinema, a Masonic lodge and a jazz club in the sixties before becoming one of the leading fringe theatres in London, offering a stellar line-up of small scale musicals. The **Old Red Lion Theatre**, is set inside another Islington pub that has been around since 1415, but the venue became better known in the early '80s for staging some of the most acclaimed "Off-West-End" productions. For some of the best new writing and directing, at a fraction of the cost of the West End, London's pub theatres are a delightful mix of pints and plays. *(Londonpubtheatres.com provides links to each pub theatre, and listings of upcoming productions which rotate fairly swiftly.)*

Tea House by Day and Theatre by Night

The Tea House Theatre is an old Victorian corner pub that was built the same year as London Bridge in 1886, but today the pint glasses have been replaced with dainty china teacups. Writers, artists and local entrepreneurs set themselves up with laptops by the fireplace for the day, surrounded by cosy leather armchairs (you may need to negotiate with the resident cats for your seat), mismatched vintage furniture, worn Persian rugs and strategically-placed electrical sockets. Hand-knitted tea cosies are on hand to keep your kettle warm at the table, as are board games for taking breaks over delicious homemade cakes. They also make a mean full English breakfast, a fine fish & chips, and a cracking Bubble & Squeak. Several evenings a week, the space turns into a makeshift theatre, with a noticeable preference for staging small-scale adaptations of Victorian thrillers, possibly a nod to the fact that this former pub, once known as the Queen Anne, stood slap-bang in the middle of Jack the Ripper's old hunting ground. But aside from Victorian horror, the theatre is frequently host to jazz and poetry nights, acting workshops, a regular debate club and an eclectic variety of unusual events such as lock-picking classes. The perfect remedy to chain coffee shops – in fact there is no coffee on offer, but rather the house's homemade loose teas. Places like this are rare to find these days, and you'd do well to venture over to Vauxhall to find it. After tea, continue your discovery of Vauxhall's little hideaways and some of London's best-kept secrets on page 270. *(139 Vauxhall Walk, Vauxhall, SE11, +44 207 207 4585; Mon-Fri 9.30am-10pm, Sat 9am-10pm, Sun 9.30am-8pm; Teahousetheatre.co.uk)*

The No-Frills Warehouse Theatre that Launched a Star

An off-the-radar theatre in a disused industrial space in Hackney Wick, **The Yard** marks the career debut of one of England's brightest young talents. It was here that British-Ghanaian writer, director, musician, poet and actress, Michaela Coel, produced her first play *Chewing Gum Dreams*, before catapulting her towards international success with hit television shows including HBO's *I May Destroy You*, landing her on *Time* magazine's list of most influential people in 2020. As the once-industrial neighbourhood evolves, The Yard remains unflashy, frills-free and committed to showing grassroots theatre while seeking out young local talent through creative workshops and community programs. If you're interested in discovering new British talent before Hollywood gets there first, pay attention to this theatre. Its impact on London's cultural scene isn't to be underestimated. *(Unit 2A, Queen's Yard, E9, +44 203 111 0570; check website regularly for updated schedule; Theyardtheatre.co.uk)*

To Be or Not to Be ... a Fan of Shakespeare

For many of us, our first encounter with Shakespeare took place in the school classroom, taught by a well-meaning English teacher who had us pick apart every word and dissect every sonnet until what felt like an early adolescent death by iambic pentameter. Fast forward a few decades, and you've probably now had the luxury of time and space to finally revisit and appreciate Shakespeare –and where better than **Shakespeare's Globe Theatre** itself. Rain or shine, there are performances of the classics throughout the year, and during the summer, one can attend special midnight matinées that start at 11.59pm under the stars. The audience is even given the choice of which play they want to see on the spot, by collectively stomping their feet to vote for the preferred title.

Adjacent to the main stage, modelled on the candlelit theatres of Shakespeare's London, is the enchanting **Sam Wanamaker Playhouse**, named in honour of the man who saw to it that the Globe Theatre rose again after 400 years. Here

Shakespeare's Globe Theatre

you can catch alternative and provocative new plays inspired by Shakespeare's work, as well as participate in workshops for directors and actors looking to develop their craft. Now, time to put to good use all those hours spent chewing your pencil while studying Shakespeare in school. *(21 New Globe Walk, Bankside, SE1; +44 207 401 9919; Shakespearesglobe.com/whats-on)*

The Little Victorian Playhouse That Could

It was a team of theatre historians that first rediscovered **The Normansfield Theatre** in the 1980s, shuttered up and unused since the 1910s, frozen in time and remarkably well-preserved. Some 100 original hand-painted theatrical sceneries were found abandoned backstage, depicting idyllic gardens, old English townhomes and historic interiors. Magnificent old fixtures, props and behind-the-scenes machinery were also discovered under layers of dust. Sequestered in southwest London between Wimbledon and Twickenham, the eponymous theatre was built by Dr John Landon Down on the site of an old hospital complex. It was here that he would give his name to Down Syndrome after the many years he spent researching the condition and caring for diagnosed patients. He founded the retreat to save as many as he could from the cruel fate of the asylums of the time and encouraged his patients to engage in the arts by learning music, dance and drama as part of their education. Along with the staff, patients would be treated to shows, which took place in the humble entertainment hall. Not long after his death at the turn of the century, Down's institution was absorbed into the national health system and the theatre was abandoned for generations. Fast-forward a century or so and the site's uniqueness has finally been recognised by the National Heritage list, and today, the Grade II listed treasure is privy to local spectacles ranging from "old time" music hall shows to classical concerts, opera and plays, as well as community events such as art classes, craft fairs and antique auctions. Join in on the bidding excitement every two months, when the theatre transforms into a mini Sotheby's for the day and plays host to Hanson Fine Art and Antiques Auction house. In the summer of 2018, two Fabergé flowers unknown to 21st-century

The Normansfield Theatre

aficionados were brought into the unassuming little Victorian playhouse on the Thames, wrapped in a tea towel, having been stored in a shoebox for over 40 years by the owner. You can also bring along some of your own potential treasure and take advantage of the free evaluations offered by onsite specialists *(*for auction details, see Hansonsauctioneers.co.uk/location/london*)*. The theatre's general program is available online for planning your future visit to the Langdon Down Centre, but if you're just curious to look around, the theatre is also open the first Saturday of each month, and an onsite museum was recently created to share the work of the archivists who continue to preserve the theatre and its history. *(Langdon Down Centre, 2a Langdon Park, Teddington, TW11; +44 333 121 2300; Langdondowncentre.org.uk)*

What We Saw from the Cheap Seats

"You *must* see a show in London" is a common recommendation, which is for some, easier said than done – those West End tickets can be expensive! So swap the West End for the East End; the tourists for the artists; the bright lights for tealights. The **Arcola Theatre** in Dalston is an intimate fringe theatre in a former paint factory. It promotes emerging and experimental artists through its programme of new and classic operas, plays and musicals. Best of all, in line with its socially engaged ethos, their "pay what you can" scheme ensures there's no financial barrier to accessing top theatre. Turn up a little before 6pm on Tuesday evenings and there will be a limited number of tickets up for grabs at a price of your choice. Catching a show when it's just hit the stage, before the reviews are in, will also help your chances of snagging the golden tickets. *(24 Ashwin St, Dalston, E8; +44 020 7503 1646; See website for calendar, Arcolatheatre.com)*

Backstage Pass

A Silver Screen Treasure Trove

In the golden olden days of cinema-going, you would be greeted at the picture house door by a *commissionaire*. Think of them as well-informed and well-dressed bouncers, in charge of welcoming customers and settling any rowdiness. As the movies moved on, commissionaires became a lost profession, and many artefacts deemed out of date disappeared along with the profession. Luckily for us, these timeless treasures found a loving home in a former South London Victorian workhouse, which rather aptly once housed a destitute little lad called Charlie Chaplin. The **Cinema Museum** is devoted to celebrating and protecting cinematic history. The story of filmmaking from the 1890s to now is told through an idiosyncratic collection of forgotten memorabilia including machinery, velour cinema seats, ashtrays, and popcorn cartons. All of this is brought to life by your personal tour guide, 'the last remaining cinema commissionaire in the world'! Meet Maurice, dressed head to toe in the classic

The Cinema Museum

1940s gold-trimmed uniform and a brown peaked cap, for an unforgettable time-travelling trip to the flicks. After you've worked your way through 17 million feet of film reel, you'll have a chance to see it in action, with a screening of short films and a trip to the cinema bar. If you're not ready for the curtain to drop on your visit, stick around for some evening entertainment. There's a regular and eclectic programme of events, including director talks, live music and bazaars, all taking place under a striking sculpture of Charlie Chaplin's silhouette.

(2 Dugard Way, Kennington, SE11; +44 020 7840 2200; Visits must be booked in advance; cinemamuseum.org.uk)

All the World's (Back)stage

Lift the velvet curtain and see what really goes on behind the scenes in one of the world's most iconic art venues. For the **National Theatre's Backstage Tours** you'll need to get into character yourself. This means donning a dashing high visibility neon vest marking you out as part of the AAA crew. Not all character

transformations are this easy as you'll soon discover in the costume, props and wig departments. Absolutely everything is made in-house. Good to know: at the end of a run, if the show isn't moving on to another theatre, the set and props often end up on eBay. The enthusiastic guides are founts of knowledge and share these secrets throughout the tour. No two visits are the same and can be tailored as you like it, based on your interests (and accessibility needs). Go and find out all the backstage drama before it hits the main stage.
(Upper Ground, Lambeth, SE1; +44 020 7452 3000; Mon-Sat daily; Nationaltheatre.org.uk/shows/backstage-tours)

The World's Greatest Dressing Up Box

Want to be the centre of attention without the spotlights of the mainstage? Take a bus south of the river, just ten stops away from the National Theatre to a warehouse in Kennington. Here you can dive deep into a theatre lover's dream at the **National Theatre's Costume Hire**. Anyone can visit these three large warehouses of wonders and take their pick from thousands of beautifully crafted costumes and props for hire. Most of these treasures are made in the National Theatre's renowned workshops and have been featured in their past productions. Be sure to look closely at the costume's tags, they reveal who has previously

National Theatre Costume Deparatment

performed in them. The collection is popular with TV and film companies, as well as schools and am-dram groups, or simply those on the lookout for a fantastical fancy dress outfit. Sift through rails of pretty period petticoats, medieval masks, and Shakespearean suits of armour. You might recognise a few things, such as the barber's chair from Sweeney Todd. Walk amongst the dead, through corridors of coffins, stuffed animals and angel wings. Each piece is unique, no two severed heads are the same. The staff are knowledgeable theatre buffs and friendly personal shoppers. Your wildest wish is their command and they're there to help with material fittings as well as ensuring your items are the perfect fit for your vision. To visit this wonderful walk-in wardrobe and find out information about individual hiring rates, simply ring ahead to arrange an appointment. *(Chichester House, 1-3 Brixton Rd, SW9; +44 020 7452 3970; By appointment Mon-Thurs 9.30am-4.30pm, Fri 9.30am-1pm; Nationaltheatre.org.uk/costume-and-props-hire).*

Need props to dress your set? **Stockyard Prop Hire** is a 60,000-square-foot maze of architectural scenery and backdrops. From period sets to post-apocalyptic, this is the largest collection of backdrops in Europe. *(Unit A, Genesis Business Park, Rainsford Road Park Royal, London NW10; +44 020 8963 9944; Prophire-backdrophire.com)*

Psst! Here's the Key to the City

For two weeks every September, the most secretive spaces in the capital and its outskirts have an open-door policy. **Open House** is an annual festival run by Open City, a charity that campaigns year-round to make London's locked-off architectural gems accessible to all. Find out what it really looks like through the keyhole of 10 Downing Street, or further off the beaten path, take a free tour around Freed of London, a strictly off-limits factory handcrafting ballet shoes since 1929. Follow *@opencitylondon* on Instagram for a sneak peek into some of the sites to arouse your curiosity and plan your snooping ahead of time. The most unusual locations and popular talks require reservations. *(open-city.org.uk)*

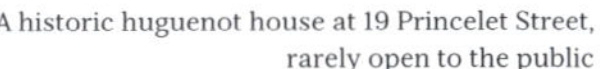

A historic huguenot house at 19 Princelet Street, rarely open to the public

Booklover havens

A Quintessentially Cosy English Bookshop

John Sandoe Books in Chelsea is everything a bookshop should be. Its flourishing window boxes, creaky floorboards and wooden shelving resemble a twee English cottage. It's quiet, cosy and piled high with beautiful old and new books, specialising in the humanities. The booksellers here offer a personal service, promising to track down any book you wish, no matter how rare or recent. You stand a good chance of finding it in store though; the 18th Century premises are home to over 30,000 carefully selected titles, filling every nook and cranny. The building itself is full of stories, and not just those that can be found on the page. This street has seen a whole host of characters over its time. It was once a seedy tobacconist, an antiquities shop and a well-to-do poodle parlour. Proudly independent since 1957 and just a stone's throw from the King's Road, London's counterculture epicentre, John Sandoe Books welcomed the overspill of Chelsea's hippies and punks. Regulars during the Swinging Sixties

John Sandoe Books

included the likes of mod icon Mary Quant and Rolling Stone Keith Richards. It may be a little more mainstream on the King's Road these days, however, the bohemian spirit lives on inside this classic British bookshop. Its fiercely independent essence defies all the trends that have passed outside its windows. As the literary world swings towards digital reading, this place is a powerful reminder that nothing beats the timeless joy of a printed book and the glorious woody aroma of an old bookshop.

(10 Blacklands Terrace, Chelsea, SW3; +44 020 7589 9473; Mon-Sat 9.30am-6.30pm, Sun 11am-5pm; Johnsandoe.com)

Daunt Books

The Unexpected Treasures Hiding in the British Library

There are many reasons to wander into one of the largest libraries in the world, but there is something to be said about actually laying eyes on the documents that were sources for your history books. There is a small corner of the British Library that is filled with wonder. **The Treasures Gallery of the British Library** displays a small fragment of their unparalleled collection of nearly 200 million artefacts. Treasures such as the Magna Carta, Doomsday Book, Gutenberg Bible, and the only surviving original copy of *Beowulf* are displayed alongside the First Folio of Shakespeare. The real treasures though, are the ones written by hand. Gaze in wonder at Lewis Carroll's original copy of *Alice's Adventures Underground*, complete with his own illustrations, which he gave as a Christmas present to Alice Lidell in 1864. You'll find the personal notebooks carried around by Leonardo DaVinci next to Jane Austen's portable writing desk with her handwritten draft of *Pride and Prejudice*. Lennon & McCartney's scribbled lyrics to "I Want to Hold Your Hand" are displayed alongside musical scores hand-annotated by Beethoven and Mozart. What is most striking in the Treasure's Collection is seeing the creative process at work, and the first blank page where some of our most beloved works began. But why not make it an afternoon of library exploration? Head back out onto Euston Road, cross the street and wander into the endlessly fascinating Wellcome Collection, see pg 49.
(96, Euston Road, NW1; +44 01937 546 546; the Sir John Ritblat Treasures Gallery is free, open Mon-Thurs 9.30am-8pm, Sat 9.30am-5pm, Sun 11am-5pm; bl.uk)

Around the World in One Bookshop

Specialising in travel literature, **Daunt Books** in Marylebone is housed in the world's first custom-built bookshop, with Edwardian architecture to show for it. They now have a handful of branches in London, however the original

Daunt Books

Marylebone flagship is the most beautiful of them all, with its Hogwarts-style long oak balconies, William Morris prints and a heavenly stained-glass window arch. The store layout celebrates the joy of the journey; all books are grouped by their relevant country rather than genre, so you'll find phrasebooks next to poetry and regional cookbooks alongside travel guides. True to its spirit, the bookshop itself travels the world in the form of an unlikely fashion item. The iconic bottle-green tote bag is not just a street-style staple for London literary types but has become a coveted symbol of wandering bibliophiles everywhere. If you're looking for a trusty travel companion or simply want to explore the world from your armchair, this is the place. *(84 Marylebone High St, Marylebone, W1U; +44 020 7224 2295; Mon-Sat 9am-7.30pm, Sun 11pm-6pm; Dauntbooks.co.uk)*

London's Literary Lifeboat

Floating gently on Regent's Canal, **Word on the Water** is a 1920s Dutch barge that's home to a sinkable number of second-hand books, from cult classics to contemporary fiction. Snuggle up in the armchair by the woodburning stove below deck and ask for the best story of them all; how the boat full of bric-a-brac and books came to be. Helmsmen Jon and Paddy, with help from their chatty parrot, are happy to tell the tale, which hasn't always been plain sailing. The early days were spent in acute poverty with the pair choosing between coffee or cigarettes as they squatted along the canal with no place to drop anchor. A 6000-signature-strong petition granted them permanent mooring amongst the moorhens by Granary Square, meaning customers could come back without having to track down their location. Choppy waters caused setbacks, such as the time Word on the Water very nearly became Word under Water thanks to a pesky leak. The resilience they've built over the years is much

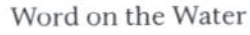

Word on the Water

Word on the Water

needed as towering tech offices, including Google HQ, and modern shopping malls shoot up around them. The luxury landscape of Kings Cross serves as a reminder of why we can never let this ramshackle ark of artists and animals go underwater again. Frequently host to live jazz and poetry readings on the roof deck, it's one of several notable highlights to be discovered on a weekend stroll down the Regent's Canal – see p68. *(Regent's Canal Towpath, Kings Cross, N1C; +4479 7688 6982; Mon-Sun 12-7pm; Wordonthewater.co.uk)*

The V&A has a little-known Victorian library and yes, you're allowed in

If you're looking for a quiet place to surrender to history and creativity, the **National Art Library** is it. Tucked away on the first floor inside the Victoria and Albert Museum, it's got everything you'd want in a historic library; the green reading lamps, the wrought-iron spiral staircase leading up to an elegant mezzanine stacked with precious tomes, mahogany throughout, and the distinct sound of a pin dropping. Surrounded by some of the country's most rare and precious works, including Dickens' manuscripts, Shakespearean folios and Da Vinci's scrapbooks, one might assume that it's the sort of place reserved for high scholars and professionals with special permissions. But three days a week, you're welcome to pick a 19th century wooden desk, which comes with its own numbered key for the duration of your use, a bit like a hotel room, and a view

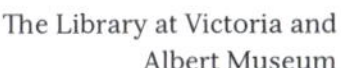

The Library at Victoria and Albert Museum

overlooking the Italianate courtyard. You're welcome to meditate, mull and muse to your heart's content, no appointment necessary, but you might also be inspired to actually mull over some of the incredible material available in the country's leading art and design research library (it's advisable to order items ahead of your visit via the online catalogue). Formed in the late 19th century by artists, designers, and artisans to inspire other creatives, the collection is filled with fine art prints, manuscripts, artist books, graphic novels, decorative arts journals and more; a little-known bonus to the V&A experience (p119). There are a few etiquette rules to bear in mind – no food or drinks, bags must be checked in the cloakroom and only laptops and pencils (not pens) are permitted. To avoid any faux pas, it's a good idea to review the full guidelines beforehand to fully enjoy this historic Victorian library. *(Victoria & Albert Museum, Cromwell Rd, London SW7; +44 20 7942 2000; reading room open to public Tuesday – Thursday, 11am-5pm; Vam.ac.uk/info/national-art-library)*

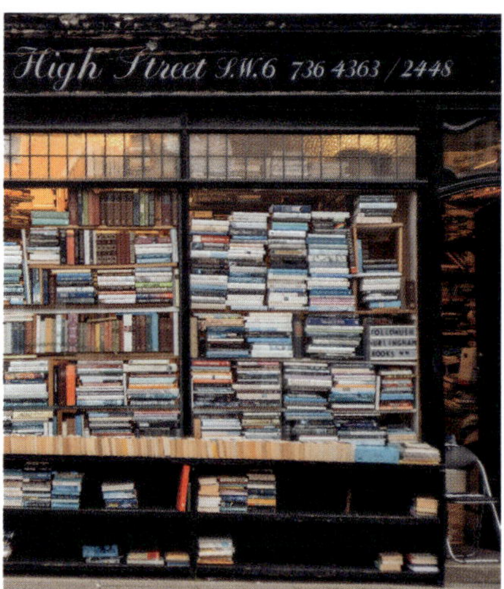

Hurlingham Books

A Book Hoarder's Haven

The old shop front of 91 Fulham High Street is quite the sight. The tall windows are decorated with the spines of a thousand books stacked up to the rafters. But you can never have too many books right? That seems to be the overwhelming theme at **Hurlingham Books**, a bibliophile's treasure trove that's literally bursting at the seams. Steps from the highly exclusive Hurlingham members' club, where William, Kate and the kids play tennis, this bookshop has been open for more than five decades, specialising in second-hand books of all genres (priced at £3-5). Connoisseurs come for the rarer finds, but the friendly owner Ray is on hand for recommendations. For this incurable collector, his career in the book trade was never about the money. Ray has bought so many books

over the years that he has to keep the overflow at a secret warehouse down the road (all one million of them), where a small team is on hand to catalogue his latest buys. His shop isn't always open during regular hours, but if you do find yourself there when it's closed, you'll probably find something to add to your collection on the shelves outside, left with trust for the local community to operate on an honesty system.
(91 Fulham High St, Fulham, SW6, +44 207 736 4363; Mon-Fri 9am-6pm, Sat-Sun 10am-6pm; Hurlinghambooks.com)

From Boston to Brixton, with Books

Are you sitting comfortably? Let's take a moment for a transatlantic tale of one man and his dog. Like many young American college grads, bespectacled beatnik Patrick Kelly visited London in his twenties, fell in love with the city and ended up staying longer than he originally planned. Patrick and his trusty canine companion set up home and shop in Brixton, and together created an unshakeable local literary institution. **Bookmongers** has been a much-loved member of Brixton's community for nearly three decades. Its devoted followers come here to buy, sell and browse affordable second-hand books. There's a cosy emerald couch in an alcove at the back, surrounded by overflowing books divided into subjects with simple scribbled sticky notes. The blues soundtrack and charming serendipitous setting wouldn't be out of place in a Murakami novel. Patrick's beloved pets have come and gone over the years, but live on in the mural painted on the window shutters where they used to be seen dozing. These days he's accompanied by a friendly resident cat, slinking around the shelves, helping you navigate the beautiful chaos within.
(439 Coldharbour Ln, Brixton, SW9; +44 020 7738 4225; Mon-Sat 10.30am-6.30pm, Sun 11am-4pm; Bookmongers.com)

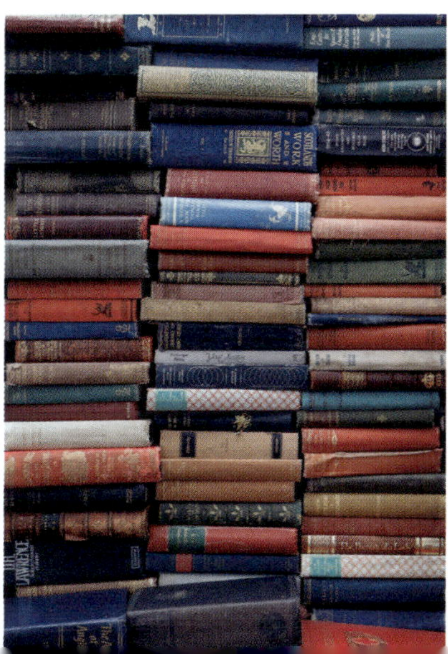

Explorer's Layover in London

The Last Artisanal Globemakers

Ever wondered about the world behind those spinning globes that fascinated us so much as kids? On a quiet Mews just off Stoke Newington Church Street in Hackney, is one of the last companies in the world still making traditionally handcrafted and hand-painted globes; a place that feels every bit like stepping into Jules Verne's brain. Founder Peter Bellerby started **Bellerby & Co Globemakers** when he decided to make one for his father as a birthday present, and the ambitious DIY project snowballed into a company that now employs just under 20 talented artists, craftsmen and cartographers who

Bellerby & Co Globemakers

produce up to 600 bespoke globes a year. Fancy a globe the size of a small comet? They can make it. How about one crawling with mediaeval monsters or detailing the route of the Silk Road? You bet. Film director Martin Scorcese has commissioned four of his own. The largest model is called the Churchill, named after the 50-inch globe once owned by the British Prime Minister, and will set you back a cool £57k. If your global ambitions don't match that budget, you could still conquer the world with a bespoke flat map from £625. If you're in the market for a Bellersby creation and would like to witness what goes on inside this magical workshop, call and make an appointment ahead of time.
(7 Bouverie Mews, Bouverie Road, N16; call +44 20 8800 7235 or email jade@bellerbyglobemakers.com to commission a globe in person; Monday-Friday 11am-6pm; Bbellerbyandco.com)

Bellerby & Co Globemakers

A Cornucopia of Cartography

Whilst GPS and smartphone maps have changed the way we navigate the world, you can't always trust them to inspire the same travel itch like cracking open a beautifully illustrated atlas. Since 1853, intrepid explorers and adventurers have been heading to Covent Garden, and the world's biggest map shop, **Stanfords**. Stocking an unparalleled supply of every map imaginable; from city guides, hiking trails and Admiralty nautical charts to colourful children's maps inspiring the next generation of explorers, Stanfords has it all. When Edward Stanford opened his map shop in 1853, he also had a print works and in-house cartographer, producing what the Royal Geographical Society described as, "the most perfect map of London that has ever been issued." Stanfords flourished with a new breed of explorers leaving London to discover the ever increasing British Empire. Recently leaving their historic HQ on Long Acre for new premises around the corner on Mercer Street, Stanfords also stocks travel books, compasses, survival equipment and the like. Whether you're headed from A to B, or plotting your next adventure, your journey will be all the more rewarding for carrying a map from Stanfords.
(7, Mercer Walk, Covent Garden, WC2H; +44 20 7836 1321; Mon-Sat 8am-8pm, Sun 12pm-6pm; Stanfords.co.uk)

Museums for the Humble Archaeologist

While the crowds flock to the Natural History Museum or the British Museum and partake in the not-so-great British sport of queuing, casually stroll into the quieter but equally captivating museums of the University College of London. Start with the **Grant Museum of Zoology**, housed in an Edwardian library amidst the buildings of the historic Bloomsbury campus in the heart of the city. Founded by an old professor of none other than Charles Darwin, this overlooked museum of animal oddities is certainly educational, but not for the squeamish. In addition to the expected fossils and taxidermy, limits are tested with cabinets filled with jars of pickled bisected brains, a dolphin foetus and tightly packed preserved moles with their pink snouts and fingers pushing against the glass. Cute, and gruesome. As specialists in the unique and unusual, dodo bones are on display along with the rarest skeleton in the world, the quagga, a South African zebra which disappeared in 1883. For a creative night at the museum experience, sign up to one of their 'Dead Life Drawing' evening sessions. Tickets cost £8 and the models stay remarkably still. Finally, don't forget about the little guys often lost amongst the mammoth mammals of the animal kingdom who deserve their own moment in the spotlight. Like nothing you've ever seen before, the Micrarium (meaning, a place for small things) is a tiny museum within the museum, dedicated to the miniscule. A back-lit cave is covered wall-to-wall with 2,300 microscope slides of tiny specimens. It's a thing of visual beauty, all 2.5 square metres of it. Both the Micrarium and the main

Right: The Micrarium at the Grant Museum of Zoology

museum are free to visit. The staff are friendly and happy to assist researchers with closer looks at all their creatures great and small and pickled for your pleasure. *(21 University St, Bloomsbury, WC1E; +44 020 3108 9000; Tues-Fri 1-5pm & Sat 11am-5pm; Ucl.ac.uk/culture/grant-museum-zoology)*

Grant Museum of Zoology

After mammals and Micrariums, it's time to turn your attention to mummies. A two minute's stroll around the corner into a small side street is the **Petrie Museum of Egyptian Archaeology**, housing one of the greatest collections of Egyptian and Sudanese archaeology in the world –around 80,000 objects –in

Petrie Museum of Egyptian Archaeology

what feels like Indiana Jones's storage unit. What it lacks in grandeur, this museum more than makes up for in authenticity; the kind of under-the-radar collection where people who actually call themselves archaeologists would frequent for their own research ... like Indy. Housed above a former stable, the museum is the life's work of 19th-century archaeologist William Petrie and his mentor Amelia Edwards, aka the "Godmother of Egyptology". Before Egyptomania, Howard Carter and his discovery of Tutenkhamun, Petrie and Edwards were collecting thousands of humble and intimate objects to do with everyday life in Ancient Egypt. Displayed in original Victorian-style cabinets, you'll find the oldest woven garment in the world, complete with ancient sweat stains under the arms, as well as shoes, toys, and Roman-period mummy portraits. Like the Grant museum, it's completely free to visit, and the friendly staff couldn't be more enthusiastic to share anecdotes about their own favourite objects in the collection. *(Malet Place, London, WC1E, Bloomsbury; +44 20 3108 9000; Tues-Fri 1-5pm, Sat 11am-5pm; Ucl.ac.uk/culture/petrie-museum)*

Petrie Museum of Egyptian Archaeology

51

04

Lonely Hearts Club, London

Solo travellers, wanderers and Londoners: this is your chance to enjoy life's little pleasures (because there's no one to stop you). People-watch to your heart's content, imagining the stories of passersby; who they've loved or who they've lost. Strike up conversations with the regulars. Eat all the fish & chips you want. Have a good cry at the movies. Join the circus. Be in a world of your own.

"To walk alone in London is the greatest rest." – Virginia Woolf

Feeding a Broken Heart (or a Hangover)

From street food to British comfort food, we can't guarantee this list will cure a broken heart, but there's strong evidence it could help cure a hangover...

Must-Eat Market Treats

On the edge of **Borough Market** is a perfectly nice pub called **The Globe**, but more importantly, the flat upstairs was once the bachelorette pad of the all-too-relatable fictional heroine, Bridget Jones. This is the place where Bridget spent weekends in bed with Daniel Cleaver, made blue soup with Mark Darcy, and had the pair fight over her in the street outside her window. After a weekend full of chardonnay, cigarettes, and bad decisions, you'd usually find Bridget wrapped in her duvet on the sofa, with the only two men in her life who were always there for her: Ben & Jerry. London's foodie revolution hadn't quite kicked off yet in the early noughties, but now, on Bridget's doorstep, she would have all the comfort food thinkable to mend her broken heart, or at least cure her god-awful hangovers.

Borough Market

Borough Market

Borough Market is a farmers' market on steroids. Dating back to the 12th century, the site remains one of the largest and oldest artisanal food markets in London. Traditionally a wholesale market, selling fresh produce to greengrocers, it's now street food central. The sights, the smells, the sounds, oh my! Food porn at its finest. The only trouble is that there's too much to choose from. The market is a maze of passageways and open spaces, an ideal layout for the culinary curious to follow their noses. You can smell **Borough Cheese Company** from a mile away. They specialise in spectacular wheels of comté and gigantic wedges of glorious gouda. If you prefer to go dairy-free, check out **Palace Culture** for their mind-blowing and mouth-watering range of handcrafted vegan cheese. Most vendors are keen to persuade you with

Borough Market

samples, which, if you play your cards right, could be a meal in itself. **Brindisa** is a long-standing Spanish tenant which serves up world-renowned chorizo rolls, the size of the queue proves its popularity. The lively market is a microcosm of London life, with flavours and folks from all over the world. **Joli** is a family-owned stall specialising in traditional Malaysian clay pot cooking. Their name means 'joy' in Chef Salina's regional Baba Malay dialect, and boy, does their Singapore laksa fill you with just that. Things heat up even more at **Pimento Hill**, a stall selling Jamaican sauces that are sure to blow away last night's cobwebs, one of these paired with a sausage roll from **The Ginger Pig** makes for the perfect cross-continental combo. Got a sweet tooth? It's hard to resist

Comptoir Gourmand's French patisserie paradise and its unbeatable chocolate éclairs. The market traders are extremely passionate and knowledgeable about their goods, everything is grown, sourced, cooked and baked personally by the seller. **The Tomato Shop** sells solely its namesake so you know it must be good, each tomato is carefully selected from a valley in the Isle of Wight and boasted about by professional chefs. Whatever you go for is guaranteed to be delicious, and ethically sourced, as all traders must pass the infamous taste test by a panel of impartial judges. If the hangover is still lingering and you need something to wash down the carbs, opt for the hair of the dog approach at **The Cider House** and have a pint of medicinal 'apple juice'. It's best to avoid the lunchtime rush, so if an early morning is out of the question, an extra-long lie-in will come in useful this time.
(8 Southwark St, SE1; +44 020 7407 1002; Mon-Thurs 10am-5pm, Fri 10am-6pm & Sat 8am-5pm; Boroughmarket.org.uk)

Borough Market

The Time-Travelling Fish & Chips Experience

Before you go googling "the best fish & chips in London", consider that a good fish & chips is probably the best it's going to get. This is not fine gastronomy, and you don't need any food critic to tell you where to find a decent greasy fry-up. Instead, ask your London cabby or some hungover club kids, as it's the people's lunch of choice; an honest British staple best left alone. **The Fryer's Delight**, an old-school chippy diner down the road from the British Museum has been going strong since 1962. This cosy little timewarp belongs on the screen, where a Bridget Jones-type hero finds themselves post-breakup, sitting alone in a booth, slumped over the Formica-topped table, and Ozzie, the friendly owner, comes over to refill an empty coffee cup with a sympathetic smile. All for around 10

quid, you can eat your feelings with a hearty meal of battered cod, thick-cut chips doused in vinegar, mushy peas, pickled onions and a canned drink. The massive serving of nostalgia on the side is priceless, of course. *(19 Theobalds Rd, London WC1X; +442074054114; Mon-Sat 11.15am-9pm)*

The Fryer's Delight

A Country Kitchen in Shoreditch

While discovering a hidden green corner in the heart of Shoreditch, stop for a nurturing solo lunch at **Leila's Shop**, a local treasure. Pretty pink radicchio, Scottish Girolles, gooseberries, Trombetta Courgettes and carrots of every colour! Part greengrocer and part country kitchen café, working only with what's in season, Leila's is the place to abide by the agricultural calendar. It's also the place to discover the rarest and most beautiful fruits and vegetables that we rarely get to see outside of chic farm-to-table restaurants. The menu is written on a blackboard and the food is beautifully simple, made with the most delicious ingredients, which you'll be inspired to buy next door from the shop as soon as you're finished. Be prepared to share a table with locals. *(15-17 Calvert Ave, Bethnal Green, London E2; +44 20 7729 9789; Tues-Friday 12pm-4pm; Sat 10am-4pm; Leilasshop.co.uk)*

A Stinking, Stonking Hangover

If you live your life to no set recipe and by the mantra 'there is never too much garlic', then consider this next one your spiritual home. Stinking out Soho since 1992, **Garlic & Shots** does exactly what it says on the tin. All meals in this little London dive bar come liberally laced with garlic. To wash down the food, pick your poison from a menu of 101 flavoured vodkas, many of which also feature garlic. Just remind yourself of the herb's health benefits as it burns down your throat, marinating you from the inside out. There is no chance of encountering any vampires in here, but there sure is an eerie vibe in the gothic crypt downstairs. Chairs and tables spill into the street making it a popular and welcoming spot for all sorts of daytime drinkers; however, the true rock n' roll fiends are those who know to walk straight through the bar to the hidden musical terrace out the back. So, how do you get here? No directions are needed, you'll smell this place a mile off. *(14 Frith St, Soho, W1D; +44 020 7734 9505; Sat 3pm-10pm, Sun-Fri 5pm-10pm; Garlicandshots.com)*

Get your pies before they're gone at London's original fast-food shops

Pie and mash shops were once a staple of London life that could be found on most high streets, particularly in the working-class parts of East London. With their late Victorian decor typically unchanged, they're the sort of establishments where you'll find customers well into their seventies and eighties who can still remember their parents bringing them there as small children **for** cheap and hearty suppers. We're talking about the classic British puff pastry meat pie, mashed potatoes with the famous green parsley sauce known as liquor, and an *optional* side of hot or jellied eel. Legend has it that eels found their way onto the menu as they were the only fish that could survive the polluted Thames. **M.Manze** eel & pie houses were once an empire of fourteen pie shops, though today there remain only three. World War II bombs, the closing of the London docks, and the inflation of real estate costs have taken a toll on the rest. The pick is in Bermondsey, which has survived as an Edwardian time capsule from 1902, all green and white tiles, cosy wooden booths and marble countertops. *(Four locations: Tower Bridge Road, SE1 / 105, Peckham High Street, SE15 / 226, High Street, Sutton, SM1; 204 Deptford High St, London SE8; manze.co.uk)*

M.Manze Pie Shop

Over in Camden Town, **Castle's Pie and Mash** has been open since 1935. More of a 1960s Formica time capsule, Castle's menu is as pleasingly short as Manze's and their liquor recipe is a closely guarded secret; a mixture of flour, water and parsley, all of which you can enjoy for around £5. *(229, Royal College Street, NW1; +44 020 7485 2196).*

Traditional Pie and Mash

The oldest of the bunch is said to be **F. Cooke**, London's longest-running pie shop, where history has been preserved since 1862, from the honest food to the sawdust on the floor. And it's still operated by convivial and proper Cockney proprietors: the grandchildren of F. Cooke himself. You're not coming here for a Michelin-star meal but rather to sample what food was like in London many generations ago. These holdouts are as much thriving community hubs as they are preserved slices of British history, which have survived by doing one thing brilliantly for a hundred years or so – and long may they live. London will miss them when they're gone. *(150 Hoxton St, London N1; +44 20 7729 7718)*

Cream Cakes from the Paris Commune

For more than 150 years, Francophiles have flocked to Soho's blue-and-white striped tearoom for their fill of Parisian pastries. A beacon of butter in the centre of Soho sandwiched in between a bright red pub and a wizard's supply shop, it's not just the glazed fruit tarts, delectable Dijon slices and dreamy creamy eclairs that keep customers coming to **Maison Bertaux**. Upstairs in the oven that's constantly churning out artisanal treats, there's an inextinguishable revolutionary fire that has kept this little café burning bright all these years. It was first ignited in 1871 by Monsieur Bertaux, a Communard fleeing Paris with an armful of recipes and a desire to feed those who needed comfort. Today the boho spirit continues to be honed by Michele, the shop's one-time Saturday girl who never left and now runs the joint 7 days a week. The repertoire has extended slightly beyond its French beginnings to include cream teas, to acknowledge the warm embrace England gave the Bertaux family. *(28 Greek St, Soho, W1D; +44 020 7437 6007; Mon-Sun 9.30am-6pm; Maisonbertaux.com)*

Just Like Nonna Used To Make It

Ultra-urban Peckham is not the place you would expect to find Italian cottagecore, especially just a stone's throw from the tube station, but **Il Giardino** is a slither of Sardinia in the centre of South London's hustle and bustle. A mirage of mustard with green shutters and terracotta tiles; escape to little Italy when you're in need of some TLC from Nonna. Inside it's cosy, comforting, rustic and romantic. You can't go far wrong with pasta & pizza by candlelight and a winding wooden staircase, surrounded by trinkets from family travels. On

Il Giardino

a road of edgy new eateries, this longstanding tiny trattoria delightfully defies trends; no twists on tiramisu, or reimagined ravioli, just tried and tested family recipes that hit the spot every time.
(7 Blenheim Grove, Peckham, SE15; +44 020 7358 9962; Mon-Sat 5pm-11pm & Sun 1pm-10pm)

An All-Day Builder's English Breakfast

Kozzy Café is the kind of place you wish you lived upstairs from. No matter what time you rise & shine, a hearty English breakfast awaits with all the traditional trimmings (bacon, sausage, hash browns, baked beans, black pudding, mushrooms, grilled tomatoes) for an honest £8.75, but they also do great paninis, wraps, smoothies and will put anything you ask for on toast. This charming green corner café in Holborn is what we like to call a builder's café – it's not on anyone's radar except for the local builders and savvy taxi drivers who know where to go for a warm welcome and a delicious, quick and cheap all-day British feast. *(53 Red Lion St, London WC1R; +44 20 7242 8207; open everyday from 6.30am to 4pm; Facebook.com/fastbreakholborn)*

The traditional English breakfast

Kozzy Café

The Underdog Street Food Market

When you've tried all the famous markets, or you're just in search of something a little less overwhelming, in an often overlooked corner of East London, **Exmouth Market** is a charming street decorated with string lights and lined with independent shops, local bars and restaurants, as well as a diverse collective of street food gems serving lunch during the week. An unsung foodie haven, try the delicious rare mushroom medley sandwiches from **Sporeboys** or the jollof rice tubs and Ghanaian stew from **Spinach & Agushi** – wait, maybe also the Turkish tortillas from **Moro**! Once you've got your lunch(es), look out for the archway next to the church marked "Spa Fields Lane", which leads you down an alleyway and into a very pleasant park hiding behind the market where tables and chairs await. *(Exmouth Market, EC1; Monday- Friday 12pm-3pm)*. If the weather isn't playing fair, head inside for cocktails in a bohemian greenhouse at the Bourne & Hollingsworth Buildings (see pg XX).

Where to Start a Conversation (or best overhear them)

A Gentlemen's Club With a (Waxy) Twist

Whether you sport a sleek and skinny dali-esque tash or have the whiskers of a walrus, get ready to meet your tribe of fellow face furniture enthusiasts. Showing hipsters how it's done since 1947, membership to **The Handlebar Club** is open to men with 'graspable extremities of the upper lip'. Beards are strictly forbidden, and any sign of sideburns merging into your moustache is a big no-no, breaking the constitution and punishable by fine. Sounds pretty strict, but these guys sure do know how to grab life by the handlebars. The world's oldest

Handlebar Moustache club plaque at The Heron Bar

whisker club was founded in a London pub in 1947, by ten chaps with one thing in common. Together they fought the facial hair fight against "the bland, the boring and the generic" while enjoying a convivial drink and a game of darts. The group has since grown in strength and length to over 100 members around the world. Those who can, still meet down at the pub on the first Friday of every month, always impressively turned out in their tweeds and ties. Their corner of the Heron Bar is jam-packed with moustache memorabilia from the club's hairy history, including the minutes from the first meeting. Want to get in on the fun but lack the facial fluff? Fear not. Friends of the Handlebar Club is the place for supporters who do not have the necessary qualifications for full membership. *(The Heron Bar, Norfolk Cres, Tyburnia, W2, +44 020 7724 8463; Meetings are held at 8pm on the first Friday of every month; Theheronpaddington.com)*

Eavesdropping at the House of Parliament

It may be one of the most iconic buildings on the London skyline, recognisable the world over, but most people pass by the **Houses of Parliament** knowing little of what really goes on inside. Yet, quite incredibly, members of the public are in fact allowed to drop by the cradle of modern democracy for free. Simply arrive early, and if there's space, you can sit in what's known as the 'Strangers Gallery' and watch the government shape British history. It is a remarkable

and little-known privilege, for not even the King is allowed into the House of Commons. The last monarch to enter the hallowed chambers when Parliament was in session was King Charles I back in 1642 when he stormed in to track down five MPs (members of parliament) suspected of treason.
The Palace of Westminster, to give it the official name, dates back to before the Norman Conquest, although the distinctive Gothic Revival building we know today, described by Tsar Nicholas I as "a dream in stone" was designed by Sir

House of Commons, UK Parliament

Charles Barry in the 1840s after he won a competition to do so. Sequestered inside is a maze of a thousand rooms, joined by three miles of passageways and a hundred staircases, all furnished in British history. But for every statue of Sir Winston Churchill or David Lloyd George, there are quaint, often archaic details and customs. From the Stranger's Gallery, note the two red lines on each side of the House of Commons' floor: they're two sword lengths apart, supposedly designed to stop fevered debates from descending into duels. There may be a total of 650 MPs, but with only seating for 427, on busy days, members have to stand. Enterprising MPs may arrive at 8am however, and leave a prayer card indicating where they wish to sit, with the caveat that they do, in fact, arrive early to say their prayers. If you wish to nab a seat in the public gallery, you can just turn up at the Cromwell Green entrance on St Margaret Street and wait for entry. Tickets are not required for general debates but are required for the Prime Minister's questions. *(Westminster, SW1; +44 020 7219 3000; Galleries are open Mon-Thurs, with the occasional Friday; info & tickets: Parliament.uk/site-information/glossary/public-galleries)*

Voicing Your Existential Shower Thoughts to Strangers

If you often ask yourself questions that you don't have answers to, the weekly **Café Philo at the French Institute** might be up your alley. *The weekly café what,* you ask? Well it's a thing, or at least, amongst Francophiles it is; a grassroots concept born in Paris that regularly brings people together in cafés to discuss and listen to ideas (philosophical or not) while relaxing with a cup of coffee or a glass of wine. Led by the warm and welcoming Christian Michel, the weeks alternate between French and English, and everyone is welcome. Any and all topics brought to the table will be considered, to be discussed in the spirit of tolerance and openness. You don't have to know anything about philosophy to join, just come and meet local musers, rattle your brain, brush up on your French, or just sit back and listen. *(17 Queensberry Pl, Kensington, SW7; +44 207 871 3515; Every Sat morning till 12pm, arrive at 10.15am for a 10.30am start; £2 entry; Institut-francais.org.uk)*

The Conversationalists Pub

Before you walk through the doors of **The French House**, know the house rules: no music, no machines, no television and no mobile phones. And for very good reason – for this is precisely what makes it a haven for conversationalists; a place where friends and strangers alike can talk to each other, you know, like they did in the old days. But what's the "French" connection, you ask? Sometime around the Second World War, this Soho pub, formerly known as the *York Minister*, became a hangout for exiled members of the Free French movement regrouping in London. Even General Charles de Gaulle is rumoured to have written one of his famous speeches here and Edith Piaf is said to have stopped by for a drink in the 40s. Locals started calling it "the French house" and eventually, the name became official. Notable bohemians with a Paris connection began congregating around the bar in the post-war years; painters Lucian Freud, Salvador Dali and Francis Bacon and writers Sylvia Plath and Dylan Thomas became regulars. The legendary London pub is still a magnet for Soho's most interesting characters, from resting actors to fading pop stars, who have stories and memories to share, many of which are captured in the black and white photographs that cover the walls. Upstairs, the dining room is a cosy little oasis of calm to congregate over oysters and impeccable *steak frites*. This is a pub from another time when Soho still embodied *La Vie Bohème*. Vive la French! *(49 Dean St, London W1D; +442074372477; open Mon-Sat 12pm-11pm & to 10.30pm Sundays; Frenchhousesoho.com)*

From Derelict Dock to Creative Quarter

This is the part of the Thames they don't tell you about. Wander off-piste and take a turn down the River Lea, a treasure trove of a tributary. From a thriving Victorian gasworks to an industrial wasteland, **Cody Dock** is now back in business as a creative community space. This forgotten corner of East London remains one of the capital's best-kept secrets. It was brought back to life by residents, artists and volunteers who transformed the space into a social

enterprise with an environmental ethos. The riverbanks of the Lea are now bursting with wildflowers, urban beehives, and an equally buzzing little café. Along with this, you'll find exhibition spaces made from shipping containers and a floating classroom aboard the restored community boat, all available to hire. Talk about regeneration done right! Join the locals for a cosy folk gig, partake in a craftivism workshop or grab a high-vis jacket and a paintbrush and get involved in the process. Cody Dock is still a work in progress and a labour of love – it always will be. That's the beauty of community projects like this, it keeps bringing people together to tend to the plants and watch the birds. What a different world it must be, across the water in the skyscrapers of Canary Wharf. Pick your playground...
(11c South Cres, Canning Town, E16, +44 020 7473 0429; Mon-Sun 9am-5pm; Codydock.org.uk)

How to Lose the London Blues

"When a man is tired of London, he is tired of life."

– *Samuel Johnson*

Afternoon Tea on a Double Decker London Bus

For an exercise in not taking oneself too seriously, experience English tea time while cruising around town from the top deck of an iconic vintage red London bus. Whether you're planning a birthday, bachelorette, or you're simply looking for an out-of-the-box mood lifter, **Brigit's Bakery Afternoon Tea Bus** is probably one of the kitschiest ways to see the city. You can book a table for 2 or 4 people or more, or just rent the whole bus. Along with delicious finger sandwiches, muffins, scones and all the afternoon tea trimmings, champagne, mulled wine and gin cocktails are also available to lift your spirits. *(Bookings at b-bakery.com)*

A Bona Fide Bingo Night

Once home to Britain's favourite Friday night out, purpose-built bingo halls are now few and far between on the London landscape. In the 1960s, bingo became a popular pursuit of post-war housewives, getting them out of the house, into their glad rags and away from their husbands. The buzzing bright lights of Blackpool swept the nation and huge concrete neon halls popped up on high streets all around the country. As tax on winnings rose and indoor smoking was banned, the phenomenon gradually moved online; the only full house you'd find today is on the scorecard – if you were lucky that is. The vast majority of yesteryear's brilliant bingo halls are sadly now crumbling temples of gambling grannies, with hundreds closing their doors for good.

In recent years, bingo has experienced somewhat of a renaissance in the capital, with bottomless brunch spots and nightclubs breathing new life into the old game. However, if you want a taste of the golden age of bingo-going with regulars from that original generation, there's only one place for it. Take a trip back in time to Tooting's defiant **Buzz Bingo**, the world's most jaw-droppingly beautiful bingo hall, disguised as a Russian orthodox church. It's what's on the inside that counts here, a sumptuous gothic gem so unsuspecting that it's easy to pass by. Opened in 1931 as an art deco cinema complete with a Wurlitzer theatre organ, the ornate building became a concert hall ten years later, hosting the likes of Frank Sinatra and The Beatles. By 1976, it became a cathedral to the sometimes competitive sport that is bingo, and not much has changed since. Of course ogle at the awe-inspiring architecture and take a sneaky selfie in the magnificent hall of mirrors, but remember the locals have their head in the game and when they say eyes down, they mean it. Our tip: get familiar with bingo lingo, it's a bit like cockney rhyming slang so many phrases are easy to guess if you use your imagination, like legs eleven (11) or two little ducks (22). Got it? Dabbers at the ready, grab a pew and come join the revolution. *(50 Mitcham Rd, Tooting, SW17; +44 020 8672 5717; Open daily 10am-4am; Buzzbingo. com/club/tooting.html)*

Buzz Bingo Tooting

New Hair, New You

Finally, a hairdresser that gets it. Nick Latham & Sean Paul Nother are the founders of **The Hair Bros**, a refreshing collective of new wave stylists that already know all those vintage references and edgy Parisian It-girl cuts you've been saving on Instagram. Their mood boards dive deep. The modern Brigitte Bardot cut, an Italian 60's bob, a new wave fringe or a more subtle and soft 70s shag? They can recreate all of them in a way that suits you, but equally important to them is that your cut has life beyond the blow dry when you walk out of their salon. Without any pretentiousness, the Hair Bros approach haircuts like paintings, and your face is the canvas. So you'll be asked to arrive with pre-washed, air-dried hair on the morning of your appointment. "Seeing your hair how you would most mornings, is the key to a beautiful haircut in our opinion." A cut (gender neutral) with one of the founders costs £190.00 or from £130.00 with another Hair Bros stylist in residence at the Sydney Street salon in Chelsea. If you need more convincing, head over to their Instagram account @ thehairbros to become totally obsessed. Book well ahead, appointments open up daily, 3 months in advance. *(123 Sydney St ,Chelsea, SW3; Thehairbros.com)*

Cinema Karaoke

Tucked away behind Leicester Square in the heart of Chinatown, **The Prince Charles Cinema** is the only independent cinema in the West End. Since its opening in the early 1960s, the now-vintage holdout has earned cult status, particularly amongst musical lovers, thanks to a popular program of interactive sing-along shows. Screening classics (with lyrics on screen) like *The Sound of Music, Grease, Rocky Horror Picture Show, Dirty Dancing, Moulin Rouge* & *The Greatest Showman,* this is the one place no one will shush you for singing your heart out to your favourite show tunes. *(7 Leicester Pl, London WC2H; +44 20 7494 3654; check the website for its program of "Interactive events: Princecharlescinema.com)*

Basil & Sybil Fawlty await their guests...

Sometimes, dining out just lacks a bit of drama. Sometimes, you just want to see an almighty showdown spill out from the kitchen (but hopefully not land in your lap) and add a bit of spice, laughter and nostalgia to your meal.If you were born after the 80s, you probably won't be familiar with *Fawlty Towers,* the late 70s cult British comedy brought to us by Monty Python member, John Cleese. But for those of us who thought the series was lost to us forever on those old VHS tapes we threw out, rest assured that this spectacle is still very much alive and kicking in the form of **Faulty Towers: The Dining Experience**. To refresh your memory, the plots centre around the hilariously rude owner Basil Fawlty (John Cleese), his fed-up wife Sybil, and a hapless Spanish waiter Manuel as they attempt to cater to an array of eccentric hotel guests on the "English Riviera". This is your chance to be one of those guests. Book tickets to the dinner show at the London hotel where the Beatles once stayed, and where today, a talented cast of *Fawlty Towers* lookalikes perform six times a week. It's a 2-hour show with a set menu, always featuring a soup, a main (usually chicken) and a dessert, but the entertainment is what you're there for and you can be sure to find that devilish John Cleese humour. Could make a great gift for the parents too. *(President Hotel, 56-60 Guilford St, Russell Sq, London WC1N; Bookings & more info: Interactivetheatre.com.au/our-productions/faulty-towers-the-dining-experience)*

London's Secret Portal to a Blockbuster Hollywood Film Set

When you love cinema so much, sometimes it's not enough just to sit in the audience. What if it was possible to travel back to the future with Marty McFly, test your survival skills in a zombie apocalypse or check into the Grand Budapest Hotel? What started out in 2007 as a small events company organising intimate clandestine film screenings has since grown to the phenomenon that is **Secret Cinema**; unforgettable theatrical and immersive film experiences inspired by some of the greatest films of all time. Within a few years of starting up, the young company endeavoured large-scale productions with its *Back to the Future* screenings, set in an elaborate life-size recreation of the 1950s Hill Valley town. Each event that followed outdid the previous one with bedazzling bespoke sets and immersive theatre, allowing film lovers to engage with their favourite characters and become part of the story. If you want to blow someone's socks off for movie night, buy them tickets to the next Secret Cinema production. Once purchased, you'll receive an enticing narrative related to the event, your character, mission and dress code for the evening. More clues are revealed as the date approaches, including the secret location. Once you arrive, your phones will be sealed away, and you'll enter an alternate reality for one seriously thrilling, roller coaster ride of an evening among kindred spirits. *(For more information and upcoming events, see secretcinema.org)*

Can You Hear Laughing Down There?

Small underground comedy clubs are often the breeding ground of up-and-coming talent, while the household names stick to the stadiums. But if a well-known comedian has a tour coming up, or a big gig like the Royal Variety Performance, they might need a chance to discreetly test out their more risqué material on a smaller live audience of guinea pigs first. In the dark, bricked basement of a bar in Greenwich, some of the biggest names in comedy are slipping in via the back door unannounced. **Up the Creek** is a legendary comedy club popular with the locals. It's intimate, cheap, and credited for launching the careers of top-dog comedians who keep coming back. As well as these secret sets, you can boast about seeing the "next big thing" before they were famous, and party with them afterwards at the post-show disco. With a micro-brewery

on site, things can get a little lively, to say the least. Top tip: sign up for the newsletter for the exclusive info, as often the arena-filling names don't get put on the public event listings. Finally, don't forget the golden rule of comedy gigs: avoid the front row, unless you're feeling brave. Going up against the razor-sharp wit of a comedian who decides to single you out as the closest, and easiest target, is like being up the creek without a paddle.
(302 Creek Rd, Greenwich, SE10; +44 020 8858 4581; Thurs 7.30pm-late, Fri 8pm-late, Sat 7pm-late & Sun 7.30pm-late; Up-the-creek.com)

Sky High Cinema

When the sun is shining and the evenings are getting longer, the only way is up, quite literally. London's unofficial summer mantra is, "head up high to the pop-ups in the sky". From May to September, three rooftops in London are transformed into open-air makeshift movie theatres, all kitted out with bars, street food stalls and directors' deckchairs. Five nights a week, **Rooftop Film Club** brings the big screen to a city skyline near you, in Shoreditch, Stratford and Peckham. All films on show are handpicked tried-and-tested classics, think *Dirty Dancing*, *Pulp Fiction*, *Notting Hill* and *Grease* singalongs. There are also popular themed double bills, and cosy blankets if it gets a bit chilly, or if you need something to hide under on fright night. At all of these venues, you're in for a panoramic treat, so wandering eyes are encouraged, and hard to resist. Screenings start at sunset but get there early to take some snaps at golden hour before it's time to get your popcorn and take your seats for a starlit night at the flicks.
(Peckham: Bussey Building, 133 Rye Ln, SE15, 020 7635 6655 / Stratford: 7 & 8 Stratford Multi Storey Car Park, Great Eastern Rd, E15 / Shoreditch: Queen of Hoxton, 1 Curtain Rd, Shoreditch, EC2A, +44 020 7635 6655; Screenings start at sunset; Rooftopfilmclub.com)

Rooftop Film Club

Good places to cry

Cheaper than therapy...

Victorian Writing Prompts in the Park

If you're looking for ideas for your next Victorian melodrama, head to Postman's Park just north of St. Paul's, and the wonderfully touching **Memorial to Heroic Self-Sacrifice**. Dreamt up by artist George Frederic Watts and unveiled in 1900, it is a display of beautifully designed, small tiled plaques, each telling the story of everyday heroes who heroically lost their lives trying to save another. Part of what makes each plaque so moving is the evocative

The Memorial to Heroic Self-Sacrifice in Postman's Park

language used, and the vivid descriptions of the perils and pitfalls of Victorian life. Sarah Smith for example, was a pantomime artist at the Prince's Theatre, who on January 24th, 1863, "died of terrible injuries received when attempting in her flammable dress to extinguish the flames which had enveloped her companion". Others victims were heartbreakingly young, such as David Selves, of Woolwich, who was just 12 years old when he "supported his drowning playfellow and sank with him clasped in his arms, September 12th, 1886." The plaques themselves were mostly designed by William de Morgan, artist at the William Morris & Co, and have detailed floral embellishments. Originally, Watts planned to have 120 plaques in the memorial, but just over fifty were produced, which you can find under a pantile roof built against a red brick wall that lines one side of Postman's Park, one of the largest green spaces in the original City of London. They bring to life a hazardous city, where people seemed to be routinely scalded and scorched, perished in flames, poisoned by gas, falling

in canals, or being struck down by trains or runaway horses and entangled in dangerous weeds. Each tile is a small tale of touching bravery that otherwise might have been forever forgotten.
(King Edward Street, EC1A; open all year round from 8am-7pm or dusk, whichever is earlier)

Spin City

Although a weekly chore, late nights at the laundrette have an air of romance and nostalgia to them. Things can get deep whilst staring at your reflection in the shiny spinning dryer when all you have to do is wait for your wash to finish. Laundrettes are the real bright lights of the big city, but sadly these places that time forgot are becoming a dying breed in London. Dig out your coins and take a trip back to the 1970s at the **Barbican Laundrette**. Dive in for a moment's peace away from the crowds at the Barbican Arts Centre (see p.XX). This glass-fronted local laundrette is a pop of colour and a gentle reminder that people do live and do their laundry, in this iconic brutalist block. The duck egg blue machines and satsuma walls would be sure to catch the eye and imagination of Wes Anderson, or perhaps be the perfect writer's setting for your plot to unfold. The retro fittings and geometric fixtures have captured the lenses of photographers and directors over the years who hire the place out for shoots, so you never know who might be handing back your dropped sock.
(2 Fann St, Barbican, EC2Y, +44 0788 8708 004; Mon-Sun 7.30am-9.30pm; Barbicanlaundretteinfo@gmail.com)

DIY before you Die with Coffee, Cake, Crafts and Coffins

Death doesn't have to be dark, it can be covered in confetti and cat stickers if you want it to be. Funeral chat is a daunting taboo topic that many of us wish to avoid, and ultimately leave until it's too late to share our wishes. **Coffin Club** may sound like a gothic cult, but it's a peaceful club creating a meaningful space to discuss the Big D, freely and honestly. Over tea, cake and surprisingly light chitter chatter, members plan their send-offs and build and decorate their caskets exactly to their taste. Expect impressive designs which celebrate life and the personalities of the crafters within, and spark just as colourful stories. The funeral revolution was born in New Zealand to help people of any age, background, and faith, navigate what can seem like very daunting terrain while raising awareness of funeral poverty. It's also a great way to socialise with fellow mere mortals, and open up conversations about mental health, or just chat about how cool those racing stripes are going to look on your coffin. For anyone who will one day kick the bucket, why not decorate it first? Although hosted in

St Dunstan-in-the-East

a church, Coffin Club is a non-religious community group, open to all of any or no faith. Sessions cost £5, with 'try-before-you-buy" flat-pack coffins provided at a discount. It's my funeral and I'll craft if I want to.
(St Philip the Apostle, Philip Ln, Tottenham, N15, +44 020 3844 8724; See website for next meeting; Coffinclub.co.uk)

The City's Sacred Secret Garden

A short walk from Monument Tube station, tucked away on a small side street in the heart of the city, lies the ruins of an old church overtaken by nature. You can't help but feel like you've stumbled upon a portal to a lost world when you find **St Dunstan-in-the-East.** Dating back to 1100, with a tower & steeple by Christopher Wren, it was damaged beyond repair during the London Blitz and lay as a wreck until the 1960s, when the local council decided to transform the ruins into a public garden. A symbol of the city's struggle and resilience, surrounded by a city of glass skyscrapers, the unexpected site remains largely unknown to tourists. It's as much a fairytale setting for in-the-know event designers as it is for office workers looking for a peaceful escape on their lunch break. But on a weekend, when the bankers have clocked out, this secret oasis is all yours. *(St-Dunstan-in-the-East; St Dunstan's Hill, London EC3R; open everyday from 7am to dusk).*

St Dunstan-in-the-East

Memories are Made (and Triggered) Here

You'd be amazed at how an old cereal box can transport you back to your childhood breakfast table. Celebrating the things that everyday folks leave behind, the "time tunnel" layout of the **Museum of Brands** is an unexpected emotional rollercoaster, as well as a history lesson in British consumer culture. Display cabinets are stuffed to the brim with over 12,000 items that come from the personal collection of eccentric founder and ultimate label lover, Robert Opie. You might not think much of the packaging you're throwing away, but float through the decades in this tunnel of treasures and memories of yesteryear will come flooding back. Recognising the special connection that this unique archive holds for many of its visitors, the museum even became part of an initiative to help spark memories for people suffering from dementia through

Museum of Brands

its forgotten products and packaging of the past. From Victorian times to the present day, you can track how British brands have evolved and how we have evolved with them. Don't resist the urge to buy a bar of Cadbury's chocolate from the café; there's a secluded subtropical garden at the back where you can eat it in peace and pocket the wrapper for the start of your own collection. *(111-117 Lancaster Rd, Notting Hill, W11; +44 020 7243 9611; Mon-Sat 10am-6pm, Sun 11am-5pm; Museumofbrands.com)*

Nature's Nook, Nestled in the West End

On a sunny day at **The Phoenix Garden**, you'll often see artists sketching frogs splashing in the pond and bees on the brambles. The bustle of the West End is not where you would expect to find a leafy oasis of calm, but there it waits, behind the theatres of Shaftesbury Avenue, with a history as varied as its ecology. This serene community garden was once a WW2 bombsite, a pub and lastly a car park in the 1980s. Hidden in the seemingly compact park, there's also a community centre which can be hired out for weddings and events, as a way of supporting the garden and its volunteers. To slightly twist the words of Joni Mitchell, *they put up a paradise and took down a parking lot.* We think she'd like it here. *(21 Stacey St, West End, WC2H; Dawn-dusk daily; Thephoenixgarden.org)*

Party of One

The Kitschiest Dinner Show in Town

Imagine you've fallen into a twisting-and-turning, neon-lit Baz Luhrmann film and you'll almost be able to picture the wild interior of **Sarastro**. Tucked away down a back alley in London's theatre district in the shadow of the Royal Opera House, this place deserves a ranking among the world's most eccentric restaurants. Quite possibly furnished from top to bottom with set dressing and retired props procured from surrounding theatres (some of the staircase bannisters actually did come from the Royal Opera House), book yourself a table in one of the opera boxes and get ready for a show. Thursday nights are Swing & Motown, Friday is Latin music, Saturdays 70s & 80s and Sundays you get opera. The pre-show menu is a tasty range of Mediterranean favourites with an emphasis on Turkish fare. The late founder and creator of this eccentric London gem was Richard Niazi, an opera fan and local character originally from Northern Cyprus who became known as the 'King of Covent Garden' in the 90s. Sarastro maintains his legacy and is still a family business, now run by his daughter and brother. Don't mind the dancing waiters, by the end of dinner, you'll soon be right up there with them. *(126 Drury Ln, London WC2B; +44 20 7836 0101; open daily from midday till late; Sarastro-restaurant.com)*

Sarastro Restaurant

People Watching in the Heart of Fashionable Chelsea

Where best to people-watch but the crossroads of one of London's swankiest neighbourhoods? On the corner of Sloane Square at the intersection of Chelsea, Belgravia and Knightsbridge, you'll find a classic Gallic bistro where the streets are lined with gold, and French rattan table sets. Along with serving up mighty fine croque monsieurs and franco-british fusion breakfasts, **Colbert** is a prime viewing spot for observing "Sloane Rangers" (as the well-dressed Chelsea set are known) go about their daily lives. Take a seat *en terrasse* and enjoy the show. If it's a little chilly for al fresco dining, positioning yourself *au comptoir* is equally appealing. Inside, it's a sophisticated mix of Art Nouveau and dark Victorian features, crimson leather seats and crisp white tablecloths. Framed pictures of French film noir stars adorn the walls, keeping an eye on you as you eat. *(50-52 Sloane Square, Chelsea, SW1W; +44 020 7730 2804; Tues-Sat 8am-10.30pm & Sun-Mon 8am-10pm; Colbertchelsea.com)*

Rekindling the Romance of Botany

While today's scientific world might have lost sight of the romance of botany, once upon a time, the study of plants was the most provocative and desirable virtue of the Enlightenment era. In the 18th century, gardens and greenhouses became a secret haven of discovery, expression and temptation. **Chelsea Physic Garden** was the most important centre for plant exchange in the entire world when the first wave of botanists was sexing up the study of plants, going as far as to juxtapose human reproductive systems with plant anatomy, comparing the *stamen* to a man's phallus, the *style* to a woman's intimates, even the plant petals to a bed and the leaves to the bedroom curtains. Carl Linnaeus, the great Swedish botanist, who made several visits to the Chelsea Physic Garden, identified pollen as the impregnating male sperm that could be carried "promiscuously" in the wind. He described female plants as either virginal or promiscuous flowers that exude a seductive scent when they're ready to mate, triggering the birds, bees and butterflies to join in on celebrating her nuptial rites. Inspired by Linnaean's controversial teachings, Charles Darwin's grandfather, Erasmus, wrote *The Loves of the Plants*, a poem which brought botany to the masses, making it interesting and relatable. This poem served as a young lady's guide to discovering her own sexuality.

Chelsea Physic Garden

In a digital age where many of us feel divorced from the natural world, Chelsea Physic Garden keeps the secret pleasures of botany alive and well, waiting to be rediscovered. As close as you'll get to Eden in London, it's home to 5,000 species of "edible, useful and medicinal" plants from the Atlantic and the largest olive tree in the UK, thanks to the warm microclimate created by proximity to the Thames. Budding botanists can volunteer in the garden, tag along for a bee safari, take a private tour of the Victorian glasshouses or sign up for a composting workshop. Stay for a pastoral lunch or afternoon tea at the Physic Garden Café and keep an eye out on the website for Supper Club events throughout the year. *(66 Royal Hospital Rd, Chelsea, SW3; +44 207 352 5646; Mon-Sat, 11am-5.30pm; Chelseaphysicgarden.co.uk)*

Chelsea Physic Garden

Detox Day

Steamy Encounters in a 1920s Turkish Bathhouse

The 1920s **Porchester Spa** is not just a day spa, it's a survivor from an age when public amenities, much like libraries, were built with integrity. Despite a recent restoration, walking into London's oldest bathhouse still feels like stepping back about a hundred years. The Art Deco marble atrium, that sweeping staircase, the marble columns, green chessboard tiles, original lamps, mirrors and hooks all add to the feeling that you could be spending the day on a period film set. And this is indeed a place to marinate for the entire day if you have one to spare. Take your time wandering from the swimming pool to the Turkish baths to the steam room to the sauna to the beautiful cold plunge pool for that hot and cold therapy, and take a pause with a toastie sandwich delivered from the café, all the while escaping the hustle and bustle of the outside world. Go in with the expectation that this isn't the Ritz, but a public spa from another time. Reintroduced to Britain by the Victorians, Turkish baths admittedly require a little experience to really feel like you know how best to make use of the facilities. As a first-timer, book a treatment (available for the ladies only) to get the lay of the land. The excellent massages which range from the classic Swedish to hot stone, CBD-infused or prenatal, are offered at some of the most reasonable prices in the city starting at £35. A Moroccan body scrub will set you back just £24. Entry to the spa alone for non-residents is £27.50 and includes access to the swimming

Porchester Spa

pool and gym. Mondays, Wednesdays and Saturdays are men's days, Tuesdays, Thursdays and Fridays are for women and Sunday is a mixed session (booking your visit for the day is required ahead). Bring 20 pence for the lockers which are conveniently located right next to the vintage lounge chairs, so you can bring a book or a Kindle for the day without worrying about it getting wet. There's also a bring-your-own towel policy, clothing (swimwear) is optional but body positivity is the overall vibe at this old-world community spa. *(Porchester Spa, Queensway, Bayswater, London W2; +44 20 7313 3858; to book spa facilities only: Everyonespa.com/our-venues/porchester-spa-westminster, to book treatments: porchesterspatreatments.co.uk or call +44 7958 287297/ +44 7506 529644)*

Let's Get Physical

The best way to regain confidence after a break-up? Remind yourself what they're missing and get in tune with your body again. Create your own 80s movie montage sweating it out with some diva 'Flashdance' moves, sexy RnB routines, or really make em' weep with the art of burlesque. When Debbie Moore had her heart broken in her twenties, she turned to her leg-warmers and shook it off in a dance studio. But when her local studio closed down, instead of letting herself off the hook, she decided she could do with having her own place to keep dancing the blues away. After visiting a disused pineapple warehouse in the backstreets of Covent Garden, then a neighbourhood you had to have vision and verve to open anything in, she knew this was the spot. And in 1979, Debbie became the owner and leading lady of **Pineapple Dance Studios**. Moore not only high-kicked her way to owning her own business, but she went all the way to the stock exchange and became the first woman in the country to take her company public. Today, this go-to rehearsal space is quite literally the place to dance with the stars (Madonna filmed a music video here and Beyoncé held auditions here). Open to both members and drop-ins, the studios in the heart of London's West End host over 200 scheduled dance classes each week, from ballet to Voguing, as well as classic 80's aerobics workouts and workshops dedicated to finding body confidence. You can also book private dance classes for a special event, or if you're feeling lucky after a few lessons, maybe even crash an audition. *(7 Langley St, Covent Garden, WC2H; +44 207 836 4004; check the website for schedule; pineapple.uk.com)*

Bathing in Red Wine

Housed in an 18th-century building that was once the home of Peter Pan writer, J.M. Barrie – possibly the only place in London where you can unwind in a 17th-century Venetian well filled with red wine – soothe your soul in the Greco-Roman atmosphere of the **Aire Ancient Baths**. Dip in and out of candle-lit thermal baths with intense massaging jets and finish up in the eucalyptus-infused steam room, all the while being treated like royalty in a peaceful, über luxurious setting of exposed brick and serious mood lighting. The red wine bath is for very special occasions (and would make a pretty special gift at £450 for a 180-minute treatment), but the thermal bathing experiences start at £98. *(2-3 Robert St, London WC2N; +44 20 3830 4610; open everyday; Beaire.com)*

Run away and Join the Circus for a Day

Can't face the treadmill anymore? Here's something different: contemporary circus arts. Located in a stunning converted Victorian power station in Hoxton, East London, **The National Centre for Circus Arts** was founded in 1989 by two pioneering circus performers, Grainne and Paddy Corcoran, offering a range of courses for students of all levels and ages. You can start with a one-off 'Experience Day' on Saturday afternoon and test your climbing skills up silk ropes, jump on trampolines, balance on a high-wire or just juggle a few balls with someone who can teach you a few good party tricks. If you like what you see, you can sign up for an entire term learning how to perfect a handstand, live out your cheerleading fantasies with a beginner's course in tumbling, or go full circus mode and try your hand at trapeze. Acrobatics is a fantastic way to challenge yourself physically and mentally, but it's also incredibly rewarding. Stop clowning around on the elliptical machine and step out of your comfort zone. *(Coronet St, London N1; +442076134141; Experience days on Saturdays, 3.15 – 5.45pm, £49pp; Nationalcircus.org.uk)*

A Vegan Lunch at the Glastonbury Festival Café

It's always sunny in Brockley. Once you find your way out of the train station, a beaming and brilliant shade of sunshine yellow rears its head, whatever the weather. Just looking at this colourful shopfront is enough to raise your spirits and vitamin D intake. Glastonbury festival in coffeeshop form, **The Broca** is full of music, local artwork, and home to a fair few vegans. Forever a hippy at heart, the Broca is an ethical community space, for good food, great coffee and organic groceries. The sandwich and smoothie menus are playful and packed full of veggies and puns. Their animal-friendly ethos goes beyond the kitchen too (check out the Instagram account @dogsofbroca to see why). If your diet (and life) have been a bit beige lately, this is the place to inject some colour. Your mind and body will thank you later. *(4 Coulgate St, Brockley, SE4; +44 020 7277 7888; Open daily 8.30am-3.30pm; Thebroca.com)*

A Rooftop Luxury Spa Kinda Day

Hot tip: you don't have to sneak into Sloane Street's most luxurious hotel to spend the whole day squatting at their health club and spa. Take a dip in the rooftop pool and jacuzzi under the skylight, pop back & forth to the sauna and cosy up in an armchair with your robe, your laptop and a smoothie from the bar, overlooking London's skyline while watching your favourite Netflix shows. Full access to the Carlton Tower's **Peak Fitness Club & Spa** requires booking any 90 treatment (massages start at £195) from Monday to Thursday, or a two-hour treatment on weekends. Isn't your birthday coming up? Go on, treat yourself, and make sure to book a morning appointment to spend the rest of the day soaking up the good life. *(9th floor, The Carlton Tower Jumeirah 1, Cadogan Pl, London SW1X; +44 20 7858 7300)*

Cloudy with a Chance of Cinema

Mellow Yellow Movies at the Oldest British Picturehouse

Imagine walking along Regent Street on a chilly February afternoon in 1896. You see something going on in a small theatre, so you pop in for the price of a shilling. The curtain rises, and British cinema is born. **Regent Street Cinema** is the oldest picture house in the UK, and still one of the most beautiful places to see a film today. With murky yellowy-green seats, a working Compton organ and dome-like ceiling, here is a place to travel back in time with a box of popcorn in hand. As well as being one of the few places showing 16mm, 35mm and Super 8 films, the gorgeous auditorium can also be hired for events. If you're on the other side of town, check out **Castle Cinema** (64 – 66 Brooksby's Walk, London E9 6DA, *thecastlecinema.com*) built circa 1913.
(307 Regent St, Marylebone, W1B; +44 020 7911 5050; See website for schedule; Regentstreetcinema.com)

A Cinema at Your Service

At an influential little movie theatre tucked down a side street in the picture-perfect Hampstead Hills, a soggy Sunday can turn cinematic. **Everyman Hampstead** opened on Boxing Day in the early 1930s, the very first of a small-scale network of boutique cinemas still in operation around the UK. Kitted out with squishy red sofas and armchairs, wine coolers by each seat and waiters on hand for cocktail top-ups and burger delivery, Everyman is not your usual sticky-floored Odeon. With two screens showing a wide array of blockbusters, indie releases and satellite screenings of the Met Opera and the National Theatre, it's popular with Hampstead's bougie boho crowd, especially during the film festival calendar. No doubt at home in the luxurious setting, Princess Margaret even took her kids here to see *High Society* in 1956. It was probably a rainy Sunday then too. *(5 Holly Bush Vale, Hampstead, NW3; +44* 0872 436 9060; *10am daily, see website for screen times; Everymancinema.com)*

Cinématique Chic

Pay a visit to London's Parisian picture house for a night at the French flicks. **Cine Lumière** is a hidden Art Deco auditorium in South Kensington, the epicentre of all things Francophile in the city. It might be hard to find initially, it's hidden within *L'Institut Français du Royaume-Uni*, a cultural HQ and home for Francophiles. This lesser-known independent cinema has two screens: a large 230-seater and smaller boutique room with 35 comfy chairs and an adjoining drinks reception area. If you're learning the language with the safety net of subtitles, take your pick from an eclectic mix of new releases and golden oldies *en français*. Given its close connection with the French Cultural Institute, the cinema regularly puts on special events such as international film festival series,

Regent Street Cinema

director Q&As, and live opera broadcasts from Palais Garnier in Paris. Mini cinéphiles are also spoiled for choice with curated programmes for a range of ages and sensory needs. If you're 25 and under, tickets are just £5, which is even more of a steal when you see the marble staircase and Rodin statue in the lobby. *(17 Queensberry Pl, South Kensington, SW7; +44 020 7871 3515; Mon-Tues 5pm-9pm, Wed-Sun 10am-9pm; Institut-francais.org.uk/cine-lumiere)*

Films for Under a Fiver at London's Cheapest Cinema

If our grandparents knew we were paying up to 20 quid to see a movie these days, they'd probably laugh at us. At South London's beloved **Peckhamplex** every ticket is under five pounds. Single-handedly making movie-going affordable, think of this no-frills theatre like a modern-day equivalent of Shakespeare's Globe. The audience is a lively and vocal mix of local families, hipsters from the art studios next door and Peckham's finest "Jack the Lads". The cinema is old school and independent and you either love it or you don't – it's there to serve a local community, not the pockets of say, a conglomerate headquartered on the other side of the world, happily buying up century-old English cinemas for billions of dollars (you can go to an Odeon for that). Watch the latest blockbusters as well as art house films, screenings of plays and concerts, and Q&As with actors and directors. There are special "watch with baby" screenings for parents every Tuesday (biscuits and tea included), screenings with subtitles for the hard of hearing, and autism-friendly films on the last Saturday of each month. Try to reserve in advance and experience movie-going without breaking the bank. *(95a Rye Lane, Peckham, SE15; +44 844 567 2742; Peckhamplex.london)*

Geek Out Underground at the Cinema Dedicated to Documentaries

Documentaries aren't only for watching under the covers at 3am when you can't sleep. On a rainy day in London, slip into the wonderful world of whatever the hell you like, at **Bertha DocHouse**, the UK's first cinema devoted exclusively to documentary films. No matter how niche or naughty your tastes may be, the expertly curated programme is full of fascinating untold tales, indie movie maker Q&As, international film festival faves, and screenings of obscure deep-cuts you won't find on Netflix. There's always something new to learn. The reclining leather seats are super comfy, just try not to doze off on the shoulder of the person sitting next to you, you're not in your bedroom now. This snug 56-seat cinema is buried deep underground in The Brunswick Centre, a Grade II listed residential centre, which resembles a space-age brutalist greenhouse. So, even after the curtain drops and you walk back up to street level, the scenery is sure to keep the inspiration flowing for that autobiographical documentary you've been working on in your head. *(Bertha DocHouse, Curzon Bloomsbury The Brunswick Centre, WC1N, +44 020 7612 9351; See website for screen times; Dochouse.org)*

The Crate Brewery

05

Don’t Call Me a Hipster, but...

London reached peak "hipster" in the early 2010s and the word itself has since drifted in meaning, without leaving a worthy adversary for defining the archetype of what's 'cool' and counterculture. No one ever wanted to be called a hipster, though everyone secretly wanted to know where they hung out or where they shopped. And then they evolved; got rid of the man buns and thick-rimmed glasses, became more understated and moved from Shoreditch to Hackney and Dalston. The elusive hipster of today is still looking for an escape from what's considered mainstream. Creative, media-savvy and keenly in tune with the way things look, taste, sound, feel and smell, they're still pushing the envelope, and still pretty cool to eat, thrift, drink and dance with.

Dining with the Cool Kids

Glamping Under the Stars & Satellites in Soho

Teleport here: **The Tent (at the End of the Universe).** Indeed, this is what most of us might imagine a tent pitched up in outer space to look like – albeit, a very exclusive luxurious Bedouin tent with a cocktail bar and a world-class chef. Having sharpened his skills at Noma and Momofuku in Sydney, Filipino-born John Javier is a bit of a rock star on the food scene, who landed in London with much anticipation to open his first restaurant here in 2022. Anthony Bourdain called his Chinese food "truly, stunningly delicious", but at this Soho outpost, Javier is experimenting in Middle Eastern cuisine with a cosmic twist. Under floating moons suspended from a ceiling blanketed in LED stars, an eclectic crowd of London cool kids gather in this very intimate space around a limited number of tables sampling Javier's juicy lobster-sized wild tiger prawns and mopping up a bright pink beetroot Borani with some delicious pillowy flatbread. At the heart of this deluxe feast in some other universe, a DJ spins vinyl all night to get you sufficiently in the mood for a post-baklava boogie in the basement nightclub. Oh, and on Wednesdays, they do live jazz with dinner. *(17 Little Portland Street, London; W1; +44 20 3848 7430; open Wed-Sat dinner until late; Little-portland.com)*

Tent at the End of the Universe

Little Yellow Door

The Notting Hill House Party with a History

If the likes of Jimi Hendrix, Nina Simone and Bob Marley were here before you, chances are you're onto a good thing. And so thought the flatmates of **The Little Yellow Door**, four friends who set up their own permanent 'house party' in the hallowed grounds of what was once The Mangrove, an historic café established in 1968 on All Saints Road at the centre of Britain's Black Panther movement. Run by civil rights activist Frank Crichlow, serving home-cooked Caribbean food for the growing community arriving from far-flung islands, the humble but joyful eatery became a meeting place for the Black community in the area, as well as their White allies; artists, authors and actors like Vanessa Redgrave. From the 1960s, right through to the late '80s, Notting Hill was scarred by racial tension and The Mangrove was regularly targeted by police raids. While constantly fighting for its right to exist as one of the first Black-owned establishments in London, a small radical newspaper was also published on the premises and the first contract for the Notting Hill Carnival was written up and signed here (learn more about the carnival's origins on pg 416). After three decades, it was finally priced out and shuttered in 1992. A blue plaque to honour Crichlow was unveiled in 2011.

Today, the neighbourhood spot that became a symbol of Black urban resistance recaptures the intimate, bohemian atmosphere of a clandestine clubhouse, without the police raids. Knock at the door and make yourself at home. Laid out

Little Yellow Door

like someone's private household, as with all good house parties, the kitchen is where it's at. Popping Italian olives in your mouth, you'll hover round the kitchen's island where cocktails, Caribbean punch and snacks are served, before wandering over to the living room and perching on a velvet couch to mingle with other guests playing a spirited game of cards by the fireplace. Shareable plates of truffle arancini and crab mac'n'cheese arrive on the coffee table, and you gladly tuck in. As the evening wears on, you head down to the retro den and raid the fancy dress box, throw on an ill-fitting wig and dance the night away until 2am. You'll have forgotten the history of this place by now, but in the morning, nurse a hangover with Oscar-winning director Steve McQueen's 2020 film *Mangrove*, inspired by the true story of the influential Black radical voices that rallied around the Caribbean café during its long struggle against the establishment. The highly-praised drama should help you recall the significance of the place where you enjoyed one too many cocktails named after Hendrix's 'Bohemian Rhapsody'. *(6-8 All Saints Rd, Notting Hill W11; +44 20 4513 2429; Wed 5pm-midnight, Thurs 5pm-1am, Friday 5pm-2am, open Sat brunch 12-5pm & 6pm-2am; rooms and full venue available for private hire; Book at Thelittleyellowdoor.com)*

Get on the Chef's Carousel

In pursuit of the next big thing, **Carousel** acts as a bit of a talent scout for up-and-coming chefs around the world and invites them to take over the kitchen for a week or two. This airy, high-energy Fitzrovia eatery is perfect for a group dinner with friends – preferably ones who might also take an interest in discovering rising stars. It's the kind of place you can come back to again and again and feel like you're part of a tasting club. While the calibre of talent remains extremely high and the sharing-plate format keeps diners in sync, depending on when you visit, the rotating menu of international chefs means the cuisine can be wildly different from one week to the next, keeping your taste buds on their toes. *(19-23 Charlotte St., London W1T; +44 20 7487 5564; Tues-Sat 12-11.30pm, Sun 12-6pm; Carousel-london.com)*

Look out for the neon sex shop sign

As is often the case in historically seedy Soho, happy endings come from questionable beginnings. **La Bodega Negra** looks every bit the kind of establishment you don't want to get caught sneaking into, but once you hurry past the suggestive neon signs and confirm your reservation (while trying not to look too fazed by the mannequin in a PVC gimp suit at reception), you're in for a fabulous evening at London's finest Mexican restaurant. Swapping the simulated sex shop for a sultry subterranean lair lit by candlelight, settle in with a round of fiery jalapeño margaritas and mezcal shots. The grilled octopus is cooked to perfection, the Lamb barbacoa for two is sensational and their tacos are arguably the best in the city. *(9 Old Compton St, Soho, W1D; +44 020 4580 1186; Mon-Tues 5.30pm-12am, Wed-Sat 5.30pm-1am; Make a booking at the downstairs restaurant at Labodeganegra.com)*

Celebrate in Piri Piri Paradise

Round up the gang and let them know they're in for a slice of the Algarve and some proper Piri-Piri in London. With wood-charcoal grilled chicken brushed with secret spices, traditional Portuguese sharing plates and an onsite bakery churning out fresh pastéis de nata for pud, **Casa do Frango** serves up the finger-lickin' goods. Situated around the corner from Borough Market, dinner can be found in a 19th century industrial warehouse with large rustic tables ideal for group feasting, ceiling-to-floor arched windows and greenery draping from the skylights. Start with an order of Piri-Piri margaritas and you'll soon forget you're actually in overcast South East London. PS: there's an intimate secret bar through an unmarked door in the restaurant for your post-feast digestif – this sultry little spot would also be perfect for a more privatised evening amongst friends, sipping on Portuguese cocktails and passing around Iberico croquettes. *(32 Southwark Street, SE1; +44 020 3972 2323; Mon-Sat 12pm-11pm, 12pm-8.30pm on Sunday; Casadofrango.co.uk)*

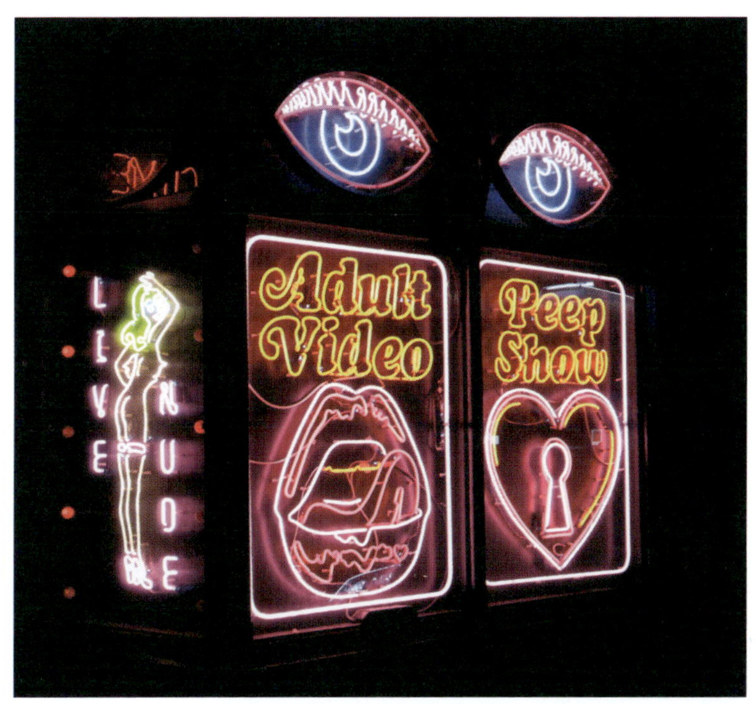

La Bodega Negra

A Maximalist Italian Feast

Looking for London's most Instagrammable restaurants? That label can have some people rushing for a reservation and others running for the hills, but if the maximalist interior design trend fills you with joy, go ahead and indulge yourself. We're talking about the growing family of Italian eateries from the successful hospitality group, Big Mamma. Of the five restaurants in London so far, personal preferences include **Carlotta** (a retro celebration of Italian-American kitsch), **Circolo Poplare** (Sicily on steroids), and **Jacuzzi** (reminiscent of a Venetian villa). True to the Big Mamma name, the portion sizes, like everything else, are gloriously gigantic and extravagantly served on gorgeous signature house crockery. Lemon meringue pie is scandalously sky-high and spaghetti carbonara is swirled straight from a wheel of pecorino cheese in front of your very eyes by flirty Italian waiters. Pure theatre, and the best news is that it all tastes as good as it looks. Book ahead if you're a big group, otherwise, walk-ins are welcome. Arrive early, and hungry. *(Circolo Poplare: 40-41 Rathbone Pl, Fitzrovia, W1T; open everyday; Bigmammagroup.com/circolo-popolare / Carlotta: 77, 78 Marylebone High St, W1U; open everyday; Bigmammagroup.com/en/trattorias/carlotta / Jacuzzi: 94 Kensington High St, W8; open everyday; Bigmammagroup.com/en/trattorias/jacuzzi)*

Soirées at Jacuzzi

Find more enticing and edgy eateries in secret bars & restaurants, pg 269

BOXE
PUGILISTICA LUCCHESE
BALDINI VERNICI
LA ROCCA
SYRACUSA
ITALIA

Carlotta

Dancefloor Diaries

Social Clubs of Bygone Britain

Happily stuck in a time warp, a night at the **Moth Club** is a bit like finding yourself back at a 1970s school prom – in the best possible way. This East London venue is a tarted-up old working men's club with most of its original paraphernalia still on the walls alongside a David Lynch disco hall aesthetic that attracts a hip Hackney crowd like moths to a flame. During the week you can catch an intimate gig with rising British bands. Get on your feet to see them up close & personal or watch comfortably from the sulky, vintage velvet-covered booths. The weekend dance parties on Fridays and Saturdays alternate between cool 80s hits and the latest pop and R&B floor fillers. Reliably cheap drinks and good vibes, this gem sparkles brighter than the glittering gold ceiling. *(Valette St, London E9; +44 20 8985 7963; open everyday, Sun-Thurs from 7pm-12am and Fri & Sat until 3am; Mothclub.co.uk)*

Working Men's Clubs began emerging during the 19th century, particularly in industrialised areas where there was a growing need for spaces where blue-collar workers could socialise, unwind and find camaraderie, but declining membership in recent decades has seen many historic clubs struggle to remain open. However, a few of these local treasures have evolved with the help of an inclusive new generation. On a stage backed by gold tinsel fringe curtains and a giant pink light-up heart, the wonderfully camp DJ sets, drag performances, karaoke nights and sexy poetry jams have proved to be the unlikely lifeline the **Bethnal Green Working Men's Club** needed. Having moved into the traditionally working-class areas of London, such as Shoreditch and Dalston, the queer community has played an important role in reviving many of East London's neglected venues. Still very much reminiscent of its 1950s roots, and still hosting a club co-existing in the basement of the red brick Victorian building, the BGWMC is an encouraging example of how to successfully maintain working-class institutions while embracing the growth and diversity of younger generations. Come for the promise of a kitsch time capsule, stay for the wildly creative entertainment. *(42-46 Pollard Row, London E2; +44 20 7739 7170; open Wed-Sun; check out the line-up at Workersplaytime.net)*

Effra Social is an old Victorian social club for Brixton's Conservative party members, rescued from neglect and gloriously stuck in the sixties. Adorned with its original vintage furniture, old Blighty memorabilia and plenty of pictures of a youthful Queen Liz, it's said that Winston Churchill used to enjoy a tipple here, as did former PM John Major. Despite holding onto its history, the clientele is quite different today and politics are best left at the door. This Georgian townhouse is now an unpretentious weekend hangout with a retro village hall feel, home to

Moth Club

roast dinners, live music, indie discos, bingo and a notoriously tricky Tuesday night pub quiz. *(89 Effra Rd, Brixton, SW2; +44 020 7737 6800; Mon-Wed 11am-11pm, Thurs 11am-12am, Fri-Sat 11am-1am & Sun 11am-11pm; Effrasocial.co.uk)*

For a similar vibe, also check out the Rivoli Ballroom on pg 45

The Great British Gatsby

Pssst! There's a portal in central London that'll take you back in time to the 1920s (or thereabouts). Just look for the single candle outside the door. The top-secret **Candlelight Club** authentically captures the frivolity of jazz-age antics as conjured up by F. Scott Fitzgerald himself. Once a month, a unique London location transforms into a clandestine club complete with a cigar and cocktail bar, live jazz, cabaret, and usually ends in an everyone-on-their-feet conga line. In true speakeasy style, this raucous prohibition-thwarting party stays on the move to avoid being unmasked by the 'authorities'. The address and password will be revealed to guests two days before the event. The New Orleans Mardi Gras and Halloween ball are parties not to be missed and book early for the NYE special which is guaranteed to blow away the cobwebs. England's response to Gatsby has an enviable address book of tarot readers, swing orchestras, burlesque acts, portrait artists and fortune tellers, as well as a directory of vintage costume hires and hair parlours which you can find on the website if you need some help with the strict flappers and dandies dress code. Just go easy on the hairspray as the mystery venue is completely illuminated by hundreds of candles. *(Standard entry costs £25 but there's also a three-course champagne dinner option for those after the full Long Island lifestyle experience. Check Thecandlelightclub.com for dates, details and tickets; +44 077 6862 8788)*

Nineties Indie Night

Performing at the **Shacklewell Arms** is a bit of a rite of passage for cutting-edge, unsigned and underground bands. This friendly, buzzy little corner pub in Hackney is one of the best places in London to see exciting young talent up close and personal, reminiscent of Camden's disappearing indie gig scene that nurtured the likes of Oasis, The Libertines and Amy Winehouse. Always on the wavelength of cool new music, the venue's line-up covers everything from indie, new wave to post punk, goth, and alternative R&B (Solange Knowles, Dev Hynes and Mark Ronson have all been known to turn up here and perform or DJ). The eclectic vintage decor feels a bit like you're inside a Christmas tree; the pub is at the front and at the back, the stage, dance hall and fairy-lit terrace await. If you get peckish, there's a life-saving selection of delicious Lebanese street food on offer. A place for friends to dance and frolic together until the wee hours, the Shacklewell is well worth the trek even if you're coming from South London – the buses run all night and there are reputable cab firms in the area. *(71 Shacklewell Ln, Hackney E8; Mon-Thurs 4pm-12am, Fri 4pm-3am, Sat 12pm-3am, Sun 4-11pm; for upcoming gigs, check the Shacklewellarms.com)*

Dinner & Dancing for the 30+ Club

Part pub, part restaurant and part Victorian playhouse of faded grandeur complete with peeling wallpaper, vintage Chesterfields and massive chandeliers, **Paradise by Way of Kensal Rise** is a beacon of familiarity in an ever-evolving area of London. This local holdout has seen the Gen Xers and millennials of North Kensington through many first dates, numerous relationships, career milestones and post-work benders, but even as time marches on, Paradise remains a reliable night out. Enjoy a romantic roast, meet up with old friends for drinks, or mingle with the down-to-earth crowd at the bar before heading upstairs to dance off dinner with a blend of 70s and 80s pop, hip hop and party classics. For thirty and forty-something Londoners who can't/ won't commit to a real night of clubbing, it's just the right dose of a good time. *(19 Kilburn Ln, London W10; +44 208 969 0098; open Wed-Sun from 12pm and until 2am on weekends; Theparadise.co.uk)*

London Club Kids

Once a nightclub becomes popular, according to the rulebook of cool, it loses its sheen. But there are always some that defy the rules...

- **Koko**: An historic theatre palace in Camden with a wide array of music nights from hip-hop to electronic, as well as a stellar concert line-up of live concerts. Dance the night away under a massive disco ball and explore the labyrinthine venue with cocktails in hand – you might even bump into a member of the royal family having a boogie. *(1a Camden High St, NW1; +44 20 7388 3222; Mon-Sun; Koko.co.uk)*

Koko in Camden

- **The Notting Hill Arts Club:** On a really good night, you might leave wondering whether this is West London's answer to New York's CBGB. It's all about countering the mass music wave at this cosy underground venue, which for three decades, has acted as a springboard for some of the industry's biggest music performers. Amy Winehouse, The Libertines, Lily Allen, Ed Sheeran, Mark Ronson, and Bruno Mars all gigged here before they became household names. Who will be next? *(21 Notting Hill Gate, Kensington, W11; +44 208 460 4459; Mon-Sun; Nottinghillartsclub.com)*

- **The Box Soho:** Worth the wait to get inside for a creative Burlesque show of impressive talent – the secret room downstairs is pretty wild. *(11-12 Walker's Ct, Soho W1F; +44 20 7434 4374 open Wed-Sat; Theboxsoho.com)*

- **Fabric:** Wear comfy dance shoes to explore this legendary playground and immerse yourself in various styles of electronic music with an incredible sound system. *(77A Charterhouse St, Farringdon EC1M; +44 20 7336 8898; Mon-Sun; Fabriclondon.com)*

- **Colour Factory:** This is Hackney Wick's proudly Black-owned nightclub and music venue championing up-and-coming, diverse, female and queer talent. *(8 Queen's Yard, Hackney E9, Mon-Sun; Colourfactory.com)*

- **Village Underground:** Cutting live music acts hosted in a Victorian warehouse depot in Shoreditch with a creative workspace housed in decommissioned tube carriages on the roof. *(54 Holywell Ln, Shoreditch EC2A; see Villageunderground.co.uk for events)*

Notting Hill Arts Club

Crate Brewery

Social Playgrounds in the Sun

The New East London

Hackney Wick's transformation from an industrial wasteland to a vibrant, even charming social scene began in the 1980s, in the wake of Britain's 'Winter of Discontent'. Warehouses were repurposed into creative spaces, fostering a community of artists, musicians, and entrepreneurs. Naturally, the after-work bar scene followed in the form of breweries and canalside hangouts, mirroring the area's artistic and eclectic vibe. With a prime location overlooking the Lea Navigation Canal (once a busy little highway for tugboats during the Industrial Revolution), **Crate Brewery** is a handsomely renovated old print factory and former art squat. On a warm summer's eve, find your spot next to the river under the string lights with a stone-baked pizza and fresh home-brewed beer. Drink in the atmosphere – the Hackney Wick hipsters have a good thing going. Upstairs is **Silo London**, the world's first zero-waste restaurant, with a Michelin *Green* Star to boot (*Silolondon.com*). In fact, the entire neighbourhood is committed to doing their bit for the planet. Once one of 19th century London's worst culprits for industrial pollution, it's now a dynamic community of eco-friendly social hubs and microbreweries, playing a pivotal role in shaping the cultural landscape of Hackney Wick. Watch this space. *(Unit 7 Queen's Yard, London E9; +44 7547 695841; open Sun-Thurs 12pm-11pm, Fri & Sat until 1am; Cratebrewery.com)*

Rooftop Hopping and Hipster Watching

In the summertime, the arty crowd south of the river likes to get high. As the sun sets, there are two main places you will find Peckham's hipsters and it certainly isn't street level. Perched at the top of a car park is **Frank's Café**, a buzzing bucket-list Campari bar with 360° views of London, accessed by a bubblegum pink staircase. Expect ambient tunes, street food snacks and good vibes guaranteed. *(7th – 10th Floors, Multi-Storey Car Park, 95a Rye Lane, Peckham, SE15; +44 075 2860 0924; open in Summer Thurs-Sun 11am-11pm; Closed Winters; Boldtendencies.com)*

The other half of Peckham's cool kids who aren't at Frank's, will more than likely be found atop the **Bussey Building** across the road. The healthy rivalry between these two bars makes for ideal rooftop hopping. Day drink in one and finish the night in the other. Once a former cricket bat factory, then a 1930s department store, the Bussey Building is now a stalwart of Peckham's creative quarter, hosting live theatre, fitness classes, exhibitions, raves and a rooftop film club (p218). If something can be 'popped-up', this is where you will find it first. Like Frank's Café, the tropical rooftop bar in the Bussey Building opens in May with last call at the end of September. Any events outside of summer will be listed on their website. *(Roof B Bussey Building, 133 Rye Ln, Peckham, SE15; +44 020 7635 6655; Mon-Fri 5pm-11pm & Sat-Sun 12pm-11pm; Busseyrooftopbar.com)*

The Boat Bar That Rocks

Drop your anchor, climb aboard, and join the party. With stunning views of the Houses of Parliament and a soundtrack of funk and jazz, **Tamesis Dock** is a boho booze cruise permanently moored smack bang in the city centre. The perfect drinking spot to watch the sunset, grab a pizza and catch some live music. Since the late noughties, this converted 1930s Dutch boat/bar has been one of the city's most loved spots for a nautical night out. The lower deck, with its funky Austin Powers-era decor, makes for an intimate and charming floating auditorium for staging live gigs and open mic nights (musicians searching for a quirky venue, take note). Just beware of your sea legs when disembarking, nothing to do with their never-ending selection of local beers, of course. *(Albert Embankment, Vauxhall, SE1; +44 020 75821066; Mon-Sun 11am-1am; Tdock.co.uk)*

Sunset Pints

One of London's summer pleasures is the bustling beer garden, and tucked down in Wandsworth is perhaps the capital's finest. **The Ship** offers a spacious outdoor garden on the banks of the Thames, with uninterrupted river views. The pub started life as a boatman's tavern in 1786 and flourished during the Industrial Revolution when Wandsworth was teeming with riverside wharfs, and the old Young's brewery down the road still delivered casks of Special and Ram Rod strong ale by horse and cart. Today, the Georgian interior of The Ship has been renovated into a charming gastropub, but the chief draw is still the garden, the perfect place for a lively summer session by the Thames. *(41, Jews Road, SW18; +44 020 8870 9667; theship.co.uk)*

For more al fresco playgrounds, check out the secret beer gardens on pg 279.

Tamesis Dock

The Little Black Book of a Thriftaholic

Play the London Charity Shop Lottery

Wherever you see a charity shop in London, a beloved fixture of the British high street, don't hesitate to go in and have a look around. Sometimes you win Burberry cashmere or a rare Laura Ashley dress, and sometimes you lose. Oxfam, Salvation Army, the British Red Cross; shop with a good conscience and play them all, especially the ones in London's priciest postcodes. With millionaires in residence in the surrounding mansions of the **British Red Cross Shop**, **Chelsea**, you never know what London's wealthiest are discarding from their designer wardrobes. *(69-71 Old Church St, London SW3; +44 20 7376 7300; Mon-Sat 10am-6pm, 12-5pm Sunday; Facebook.com/BRCChelsea)*

Home to London's coolest cats from Harry Styles to Kate Moss, Primrose Hill has a lovely little cluster of clothing, interiors and wellness boutiques, but at the top end of Regent's Park Road, you'll find **Mary's Living & Giving Primrose Hill**, a cosy charity shop full of all sorts of pre-loved gems donated by locals of this North London village. *(109 Regent's Park Rd, London NW1; +44 20 7586 9966; open Mon-Sat 10am-6pm, Sun 12-4pm; Savethechildren.org.uk/shop/marys-living-and-giving-shops/primrose-hill).*

Helping to fund a fairer fashion world, you'll notice **Traid** on trendy high streets across the city, but the South London Brixton store is the mothership. This isn't a musty charity shop of mismatched crockery and jigsaws with missing pieces, it's packed with modern and vintage street-style staples, all in excellent condition, ready for their second outing. They have 5 big bargain clear-outs a year, ending in the queuing-in-any-weather-worthy £1 sale. Keep an eye on their website for mending workshops, designer Q&As and late-night openings. *(2 Acre Lane, Brixton, SW2; +44 020 7326 4330; Mon-Sat 10am-6pm & Sun 11am-5pm; Traid.org.uk)*

West London's Wardrobe Secrets

If you like your vintage with some provenance (and the chance of bumping into a celebrity), you'll want to track down the bona fide collectors. One doesn't just stumble upon **Rellik**, a veritable archive of fashion history tucked away under a 1960s housing estate in North Kensington. With regulars like Kate Moss and Lady Gaga, it feels like a genuine industry secret that should be by appointment only (though there is a doorbell to enter), but luckily, anyone can browse all the expertly curated 1980s Vivienne Westwood or 1970s Halston that the heart desires. eBay has nothing on this place, with the friendliest of staff and very reasonable prices for such a precious inventory. *(8 Golborne Rd, London W10; +44 20 8962 0089; Tues-Sat; 11am-6pm, 12-5pm Sun; Relliklondon.co.uk)*

Making your way down Portobello Road, sandwiched in between a tattoo parlour and a souvenir shop, **One of a Kind Fashion Archive** is a destination for die-hard vintage collectors, curators, stylists and celebrity rock chicks. Raising the bar, you'll need an actual appointment for this shoppable museum of fashion that has an unbeatable catalogue of 90s and early 2000s style. Book your time slot via the website. *(259 Portobello Rd, London W11; Oneofakindarchive.net)*

Picture where Oscar Wilde might have shopped in London and you'll find something pretty close to what could've been his dressing-up box at **Hornets**. "We sell style – not fashion", says *William* Wilde (aka The Guvnor), the fascinating chap behind this men's vintage boutique catering to London's dapper dandies, hidden away down a picturesque leafy passageway behind Kensington High Street. Meeting Bill is enough of a reason to pay a visit. Every inch a true English gent, he emerges from behind the counter, walking cane first, in an immaculate three-piece suit. He's the type of character tourists imagine London must be filled with. It isn't, of course, but that's what makes Mr Wilde and his shop so special. In the 60s, his dapper demeanour and style earned him a reputation while working as a jobbing actor, playing assassins and doctors on British TV shows. Not long after, he moved from one glamorous industry to another and fell head over polished heels into the fashion world. For more than

English Dandies catching rays
outside the Hornets shop on Kensington Church Walk

20 years, 'The Godfather of Style' and his small team of sartorial experts have been dressing distinguished gents (and dames) in vintage Savile row suits, Harris tweed and handmade brogues. The boutique's motto of 'style – not fashion' goes beyond a tagline to a code of living. It's more than just refining your wardrobe, customers will learn the history of their collector's item and pick up lessons in dandy decorum. Famous for avoiding fashion trends in favour of classic cuts, members of the royal family have been known to pop in, proving no one is too posh for a second-hand shop. Bear that in mind when someone quietly slips into the fitting room next to you. *(2 Kensington Church Walk, Kensington, W8; +44 020 7937 1515; Mon-Sun 11am-6pm; Hornetskensington.co.uk)*

The Last Record Shops of Notting Hill

Let's go back for a moment to the swinging sixties in London's Notting Hill: Portobello Road is the main artery of the hippie movement, heaving with bohemian musicians and freethinking "freaks", as they're known to the establishment. Jimi Hendrix hasn't yet taken a fatal overdose in his flat and British counterculture is on the rise. Today, it's no secret that Notting Hill has become the poster child for London gentrification, which makes the last indie record shops standing all the more special.

Hitchhiking across America in the 1970s, **Rough Trade** founder Geoff Travis was struck by the legendary City Lights in San Francisco, where customers were just as encouraged to linger among the stacks as much as buy any books. Travis

planned to do the same with records, and opened Rough Trade in 1976, on what was then, a down-at-heel street off Portobello Road. The record shop swiftly developed a community centre feel, fuelled by the explosion of punk music, where lovers of independent music could spend hours browsing racks of punk and reggae records, and post ads recruiting band members. Travis also set up a network with other indie record shops, called The Cartel, making underground vinyl easier to find. A record label followed, putting out seminal music by the likes of Stiff Little Fingers, Cabaret Voltaire, the Fall and the Smiths. Branches of Rough Trade are today open as far afield as Williamsburg, Brooklyn, but its heart remains at the small shop with the punk vibe in Notting Hill.*(130, Talbot Road, W11; +44 020 7229 8541; Mon-Sat 10am-6.30pm, Sun 11am-5pm; roughtrade.com)*

A whopping 90% of independent record shops in Britain have been lost since their heyday in the 70s and 80s, but **Honest Jon's** is another rare survivor. Since its doors opened in 1974, you've been able to find rare vinyl here at a great price. Sift through a stellar collection of reggae, dub, blues, jazz, dance, funk, soul etc. If you're not sure what you're looking for, the staff are friendly and approachable; tell them what you like and they'll emerge with a pile of records to listen to at the counter. Inside this little timewarp, you can imagine what Portobello Road used to be like. *(278 Portobello Rd, London W10; +44 20 8969 9822; Mon-Sat 10am-6pm, Sun 11am-5pm; Honestjons.com)*

Music & Video Exchange is the unapologetically grungy holdout at Notting Hill Gate that's been buying & selling since 1967. Take your old media here for some quick cash or restock, choosing from a mountain of reasonably well-arranged second-hand vinyl, CDs and cassette tapes. They have a particularly good selection of old country and 50s rock. The staff can admittedly be a little grumpy (fitting for the enduring anarchist vibe) but a necessary stop for collectors who are happy to thumb through records without assistance. *(38 Notting Hill Gate, London W11; +44 20 3404 5200; open everyday 10am-8pm; Mmfeshops.com)*

People's Sound Records was founded in the 1980s by the late Daddy Vego, a local legend and wise old Rastafarian who mentored troubled youngsters, encouraged new talent and introduced the foundations of Jamaican sound system culture and reggae music to the UK. His younger *bredren* continue his legacy at the store today and there isn't a reggae tune that this place doesn't

People's Sound Records

have. During Notting Hill Carnival, this is where you'll witness an entire street doing the electric slide, dancing to the tunes pumping out of their famous sound system jacked into the heavy-duty socket above the door. This little reggae specialist shop, unchanged and authentic as ever, defies the gentrification that's been engulfing a road which was once a major hub for civil rights activism. People's Sound Records is not just a music store but a cornerstone of British-Caribbean history and culture that has almost vanished in Notting Hill, where people like Daddy Vego laid the foundation for modern multicultural London. *(11 All Saints Rd, London W11; +44 20 7792 9321; Mon-Sat 10am-7pm)*

An Eastenders Market Day

Perhaps you've heard of Britain's popular soap opera *Eastenders*, the long-running BBC series that centres around a neighbourhood of working class Londoners who live on their famous but fictitious Albert Square in East London. Aside from the never-ending drama, it paints the picture of a London village where everyone knows each other; you get the gossip from the market peddlers, the barman at the pub is always there to lend an ear and you can probably count on running into your ex at the laundrette. Does such a London even exist anymore? The decline of the British high street isn't exactly a new phenomenon, and the same goes for the weekend markets, which have been the pride of East London for centuries. They aren't all gone luckily, and there are a few special ones with a community feel that loosely fit the description of an Albert Square.

Start off in Hackney with an early morning visit to **Columbia Road Flower Market**. Originally used as a pathway that led sheep to slaughter in the early 1800s, it became a flower market in the Victorian era and remains an epicentre of a thriving community, even through the neighbourhood's 21st century changes. As long as Columbia Road's chic boutiques and cafés that now occupy the 18th century terraced houses keep attracting the hipsters and well-heeled Londoners, the flower market will continue to bloom. The vendors, whose booming voices can be heard over the market hum, start setting up their stalls at four in the morning. Their families have been speaking the secret language of flowers for generations. Do arrive early-ish because they don't call it the 'Highway of Hackney' for nothing, but stick around long enough to witness the fashion peacocking. *(Columbia Rd, E2; Sundays 8am-3ish; Columbiaroad.info)*

Columbia Road Flower Market

Vintage Heaven on Columbia Road

Broadway Market

With a bouquet in hand, take a 15-minute stroll north over the Regent's Canal to **Broadway Market**, a working Victorian market which is said to have inspired BBC's *Eastenders*. Go with an empty stomach and drift through a kaleidoscope of tastes and cultures: street food stalls, bookshops, pubs, restaurants and cafés. Look out for the novelty Yorkshire Pudding Wrap from Yorkshire Burrito or the lobster mac & cheese from Fin and Flounders and wash it all down with some fresh oysters from Oyster Boy. *(Broadway Market; London Fields E8; Sat 9-5pm & Sun 10-4pm; Broadwaymarket.co.uk)*

Licking your fingers through London Fields, one of Hackney's most popular parks, make a detour to **Fassett Square** (E8), which any self-respecting *Eastenders* fans will no doubt recognise as a doppelganger of the BBC's iconic Albert Square, complete with late Victorian houses, a pub on the corner and a communal garden surrounded by a wrought iron fence. This is no coincidence; the first pilot episode for the programme was filmed here in 1985 before shooting moved to a studio.

Our final eastenders market is **Chatsworth Road Market**, a carnival of colour, conversation and independent traders. One of East London's biggest markets, the faithful traders have been gathering weekly since the 1930s. Despite fizzling out in the 90s, the market rose again from the ashes in 2010 thanks to efforts from community groups and has continued to be a stalwart smash hit from then on. Proactive and protective E5 locals take city planning into their own hands to ensure the street retains its unique character and residents don't get priced out. Traders who live nearby get first dibs on market spots and must meet community needs and values. There's also an entrepreneurial scheme for residents who wish to test-run business ideas through subsidised pitch rents. Even when the Sunday stalls have packed up, chain stores are few and far between on this street. Like the community that lives here, Chatsworth Road, known as 'Chats' by locals, is a diverse and vibrant village of shops and surprises on all days of the week. An old-school hair salon neighbours an eco-friendly toyshop and Jamaican takeaways live side-by-side with a jam boutique. For everyday essentials or unusual artisan gifts, Chats has got you covered, with plenty of coffee pit stops along the way. *(46-51 Chatsworth Rd, Lower Clapton, E5; +44 020 8356 5300; Sun 11am-4pm; Chatsworthroade5.co.uk)*

Discover more of London's street markets. South: Borough Market on pg 201, Maltby St Market on pg 41 and Brixton Market on pg 413. West: Golborne Road Market on pg 298. North: Exmouth Market on pg 210.

CHEESE & WINE

06

I Know This Great Little Place

Here's the thing about secrets: they don't help people stay in business and they don't save precious places from being turned into supermarkets. Our philosophy: if you find someplace special, tell a friend. Let's lift the curtain and put a spotlight on the makers, the artisans, the shopkeepers, urban farmers and family-run restaurants preserving the character of the city's past. When the world has gone mad, the hope is you'll still have that great little place you can go back to where everything is just the same as it always was.

Time Travelling Shops

The Magical World of London's Oldest Art Shop

The sign outside the door reads *artists' colourmen*, which was the term in use when Louis Cornelissen set up shop in the 19th century. **L. Cornelissen & Son** has been catering for the capital's most colourful minds since 1855. Handmade watercolour paints, luxurious gold leaf, ornate calligraphy nibs and ink made from the fermented galls of oak trees – this is where artists get themselves a couple of grams of the good stuff. We're talking specialised, hard-to-find, high-end gear. Firmly rooted in tradition still, the staff here today are artists themselves with extensive product knowledge, on hand to help you find the truest blue, or most curious shade of crimson. The shop is a masterpiece

L. Cornelissen & Son

in itself; think Hobbycraft meets Hogwarts; mysterious dark drawers and spellbinding shelves lined with antique jars of powders and pastels, each with a handwritten label for their magical shade names. Everything looks too precious to use, but go get messy. We insist. *(105 Great Russell St, Bloomsbury, WC1B; +44 020 7636 1045; Mon-Sat 9.30am-6pm; Cornelissen.com)*

L. Cornelissen & Son

A Quieter Alternative to Portobello Market

Not to be confused with Camden Market, **Camden Passage** is a charming sliver of old Islington tucked behind the main thoroughfare. Free of cars and crowds, antiques traders have been setting up their stalls here on Wednesday and Saturdays since the 1960s and the small shops behind them deal in niche collectibles and vintage clothing throughout the week. Where Portobello Market has fallen short in recent years thanks to an influx of overtourism, authentic dealers can still be found here in the calm of their own little colourful and cobblestoned North London village. *(Nearest tube station is Angel).*

Camden Passage

When your coffee craving kicks in, pop into **Redemption Roasters** at the end of the passage, an unusual coffee shop and bakery that works alongside ex-offenders to offer them training and work as baristas. This used to be the site of an old vintage shop and hidden in the basement, you'll discover a wondrous and unexpected grotto and garden now used as a seating area to sit and sip in the surreal surroundings. *(96 – 98 Islington High Street, N1; open everyday; redemptionroasters.com/locations/islington-high-street)*

Stay in Islington for lunch at the Albion (pg 280) or catch a show at one of the area's historic pub theatres (see pg 177).

The World's Oldest Hat Shop (with a secret unofficial museum at the back)

Why did men stop wearing hats? Where have all the elegant fedoras, bowlers, and top hats gone? There are theories that come together to explain their gradual disappearance from everyday society, but the simplest explanation lies with the rise and evolution of the automobile. The advent of the four-wheeled engineering marvel brought forth the beginning of the end for the gentleman's hat when it alleviated the need to protect one's head from the elements. But if cars are slowly being driven out of major cities in a bid to curb climate change, surely rainy London town is due for a hat comeback. Nothing is quite as sartorially iconic as a London gent in a bowler hat and in fact, the very shop that created the bowler is still around today. Founded all the way back in 1676, **Lock & Co. Hatters** is officially the world's oldest hat shop. Lord Nelson wore a Lock & Co hat to the Battle of Trafalgar, and Sir Winston Churchill completed his trademark look with one. Many of the hats are still made on the premises which include a wide range of elegant women's hats as well (the Duchess of

Lock & Co. Hatters

Cambridge shops here). Whether you're looking for a felt trilby, a distinguished homburg, or an elegant straw panama, the milliner's credentials are without parallel. The appearance of the shop has changed very little over the centuries and every customer is measured using a 150-year-old custom-fitting device known as the *conformateur*. This steampunk-looking contraption is still used at the shop every day to outline an exact head shape, and within the business' archives, the conformateur patterns of everyone from Oscar Wilde to Princess Diana are kept on record. Should you choose to purchase a Lock & Co hat, arguably the quintessential English souvenir, don't leave without asking to see their secret hat museum at the back of the shop. Highlights include a thank-you note from Charlie Chaplin and Jackie Kennedy's signed conformateur pattern, among other rare keepsakes of famous clients who have passed through the shop's doors in its 340-year history. *(6, St. James's Street, London, SW1; +44 020 7930 8874; Mon-Fri 9am-5.30pm, Sat 9.30am-5pm, closed Sun and Bank Holidays; lockhatters.co.uk)*

On the Beat with London's Most Elegant Police

In Mayfair's elegant **Burlington Arcade**, a 19th-century shopping mall, the highly exclusive glass-covered walkway is still patrolled by the Burlington Arcade Beadles, the oldest and smallest private police force in Britain. Lord George Cavendish established the prestigious shopping arcade in 1819, about a decade before the birth of the Metropolitan Police, and needed some way to protect the "sale of jewellery and fancy articles of fashionable demand". The first Beadles couldn't have been more imposing: veterans of the Battle of Waterloo, drawn from Cavendish's former regiment, the Royal Hussars. Still today, the Beadles dress in Regency finery that wouldn't look out of place on the parade ground – top hats, frock coats and pristine uniforms designed by Henry Poole of Savile Row. They continue to maintain the peace in the glittering arcade,

Burlington Arcade

protecting such prestigious shops as Hancock's, the jewellers who make the Victoria Cross, and enforcing the sometimes quaint rules, such as no running, singing, or whistling – the latter dates back to time when it was still the secret code of youthful pickpockets. Take the little-known tour of the arcade with the head Beadle and learn about all the secret details of London's original department stores – secret underground passageways included. *(51 Piccadilly, Mayfair, W1J; +44 20 7493 1764; Mon-Sat 8am-8pm, Sun 11am-6pm; enquire about tours with the Beadles via Burlingtonarcade.com)*

Books for Cooks

Secret Bars & Restaurants

This must be the place...

Lunch From the Back of a Bookshop

A handful of tables are squeezed in between bookshelves of **Books for Cooks**, where as it happens, they actually cook from the books. From Monday to Friday, a recipe *du jour* is plucked from the pages of a cookbook amongst the shelves; perhaps a classic risotto from a rare out-of-print edition that you can't find elsewhere, or a fresh and zingy dish from a new best-seller; and served up for lunch. Eric Treuillé, a dry-witted Frenchman runs the show from his test kitchen at the back, whipping up what often ends up as an outrageously underpriced three course meal for around £7. He doesn't take reservations but you'll want to arrive before lunch is served at midday (11.30 am to guarantee a table). Think of it like eating in your grandmother's kitchen – she wouldn't have you asking for your sauce on the side or gluten-free bread, and neither will Eric (although Tuesdays are vegetarian and Fridays are pescetarian). The ingredients are bought fresh each morning, usually from Portobello Market around the corner, and service ends when the food runs out. Don't miss a chance to eat at the world's best smelling bookshop. *(4 Blenheim Crescent, W11; bookshop open Mon-Sat 11am-5pm, no lunch on Saturdays, afternoon cooking workshops available upstairs; see Booksforcooks.com for more info).*

Books for Cooks

Supper Clubs and Secret Pleasure Gardens in Vauxhall

We'd wager most Londoners don't know there's a lavender field in the middle of Vauxhall harvested every summer and sold locally. Largely dismissed as a forsaken industrial area south of the river, this should make it even more satisfying when you decide to give it a chance and venture off the beaten path to discover Vauxhall's delightful and overlooked little village. A very good place to start is Bonnington Square, one of London's lesser-known radical pockets of recent past. The quiet leafy lanes surrounding a wild community garden are kept pretty hush-hush, not to mention its secret history as one of Europe's

Bonnington Square

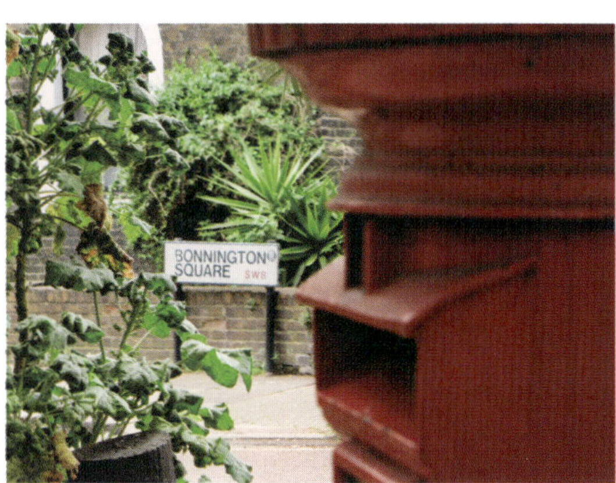

longest surviving experiments in urban living. In the late 1970s, the rows of Victorian houses in these secluded streets were abruptly cleared of their occupants and destined for the wrecking ball until a local shopkeeper used legal action against the council to successfully halt its demolition. In the years that followed, the abandoned homes were almost completely occupied by squatters who formed a housing cooperative and ultimately won the right to legally lease the buildings. A fully-fledged artistic community blossomed, complete with a volunteer-run café, vegetable garden, wholefoods shop and even a disco. A mini Freetown Christiania if you like (sans tourists), this story goes down in squatting history as an example of utopian living done right, and many of the enterprising hippies that wound up here all those years ago are still homeowners in the square today. While aspects of the commune's lifestyle have inevitably disappeared over time, Bonnington's Square's small garden remains at the heart of Vauxhall's hidden anarchist history. The Pleasure Garden, cultivated on a former WWII bomb site, is still maintained collectively by the residents and open to visit; home to an oasis of tropical and native plants, sculptures, and an old industrial wheel salvaged from an abandoned marble factory nearby. Across the road is the old corner shop that belonged to the Turkish shopkeeper who

Italo Delicatessen

Model village in Vauxhall Park

originally led the fight to save the square from demolition. Today it's a friendly Italian deli where the palpable community spirit continues to thrive. **Italo** looks like a Vespa in café form, with its bold blue shopfront, retro red diner chairs and vintage posters. The homemade rosemary focaccia sandwiches (or "superstar sarnies" as they like to call them) pair very nicely with a Campari spritz, and you'll be hard-pressed to find a prettier patio for lunch in all of South London. But if you're really in the know, you'll find yourself a seat at one of their supper clubs, where up-and-coming local chefs take over the deli's kitchen and host a small group on a long table set up on the cobbled street (supper club dates and booking links are shared on the Instagram account @italo_vauxhall_). Inside, amidst the tins of giant olives and inviting Italian produce, look out for a copy of the local newspaper booklet they publish. Stock up on local lavender harvested by the community from nearby Vauxhall Park where the maze of indigo blooms is tucked away behind a miniature model village – very much worth a visit. *(13 Bonnington Square, Vauxhall, SW8; +44 020 7450 3773; Bonningtoncentre.org)*

A few steps away, **Bonnington Café** is the old squat's canteen. Run successfully by a collective of rotating chefs for 20 years, it still plays an important role in the community despite a prolonged closure during the pandemic when management and landlord disagreements bubbled to the surface. Opening hours can be sporadic and will probably always remain dependent on members of the community, so if you're not a local who has the good fortune of happily stumbling upon an open door, it's best to check in on the association's Instagram account (*@bonnington_centre*), which shares all the information on upcoming local happenings, including supper clubs, art shows, workshops and even small festivals on the square. *(11 Vauxhall Grove, Vauxhall, SW8; Bonningtoncafe.co.uk)*

Head back into Bonnington Square to find the community's best-kept secret: another, even larger garden nestled behind a passageway between two Victorian brick houses in the northeast corner. Created by the residents in the 1980s on an abandoned lot given up by the council, **Harleyford Road Gardens** is an enchanting and untamed tapestry of meandering trails dotted with mosaic tiles, serene water features and inviting reading nooks. Where the Bonnington squatters once grew their vegetables, enjoy a moment of solitude hidden away from the chaos of the outside world, surrounded by the whispering leaves and the occasional glimpse of wildlife darting through the underbrush. *(Find the entrance between 31-41 Bonnginton Square).*

Finally, take your exit from the gardens on the Harleyford roadside and trot down the street to convene with a herd of alpacas that live at the **Vauxhall City Farm** (*Vauxhallcityfarm.org*) on the edge of a local park. This also happens to be the site of the infamous **Vauxhall Pleasure Gardens**, a name you might recognise from the classic 19th-century English novel, *Vanity Fair* (or more recently, it was reimagined in Netflix's *Bridgerton*). While it still goes by the same name, this seven-acre park isn't quite the legendary attraction it once was, so you'll need to tap into your imagination for this.

Vauxhall Pleasure Gardens in about 1779, by Thomas Rowlandson

At the heart of Georgian London's entertainment and social scene, the original enclosed gardens were at one time home to opulent Italianate piazzas, Rococo "Turkish" tents, Chinese-influenced pavilions and faux classical ruins, as well as plenty of society intrigue, scandal and excess during the summer. The gardens became so well-known and widely synonymous with the idea of entertainment that for well over a century, the mere mention of the word 'Vauxhall' to anyone in Western society would have been akin to a casual reference to Broadway today.

Alas, the once iconic destination fell out of favour by the mid-19th century and spent the next hundred years disappearing from our collective memory as the capital expanded. This overlooked pocket of London may be surrounded by high-rise apartments and office blocks today, but if you care to take a closer look, Vauxhall is hiding plenty of charming little secrets. Find yet a few more, over on pg 140 and 177.

A Cocktail Theatre, by Appointment

Let's be honest, speakeasies have largely lost their thrill. But the fact that **Lounge Bohemia** is hidden down a staircase behind an unmarked door next to a kebab shop is probably the least interesting thing about it. There are some special meals that stay etched in your memory forever, but the same can rarely be said about a round of cocktails. Paul Tvaroh's appointment-only cocktail experience, however, is very likely to be an unforgettable one. In fact, to call his concoctions "cocktails" feels like a disservice. These molecular creations are little works of art that take you on a sensory discovery of alcohol in all its forms and textures. Expect to eat, drink and breathe his offerings from various sculptural vessels; a rare seashell, a miniature diorama or a delicate hand-blown sculpture – but never just a glass. Expect to be introduced to ingredients you've never heard of, like chocolate caviar or vaporised salt. Recommended as part of a six-course tasting menu, each course comes with its own story and splash of theatre. The den-like lounge is a subtle ode to 1960s Soviet design and Paul Tvaroh's Czech roots, furnished with several pieces that may very well have come from his own grandmother's living room.

Something to keep in mind if you read through some of the disgruntled online reviews regarding their customer service: there's a certain level of decorum expected here from clientele that's somewhere on par with how you might behave when you're in the presence of a well-respected sushi master. Go with that mindset and the evening will be spectacular. The level of talent here certainly deserves a measure of awe and respect, and quite frankly, being slightly scared of the cocktail master only adds to the mystique of it all. *(1e Great Eastern St, London EC2A; by appointment only: +44 7720 707000; open Mon-Sat 6pm-12am & until 11pm Sunday; Loungebohemia.com)*

Floating to Old Hong Kong

Take a tip from a Beatle (and vegetarian since 1975), Sir Paul McCartney himself. **The Feng Shang Princess** is a totally unexpected but idyllic floating Chinese restaurant tucked away down at the end of Regent's Canal, assumed to be the former Beatles' favourite restaurant because he was spotted there a few times (but we'll go with it). The impressive, bright red three-tiered pagoda, hand-crafted in the 1980s, was actually London's first floating restaurant of its kind. As soon as you step on board, you can just smell that you're going to eat well. They do a Hong Kong-quality wonton soup, the crispy beef is to fight for and tofu/vegetarian options are plentiful (consider the very special "veggie duck" with pancakes). A little pricey but as good a choice for a solo feast with a book as it is for a special occasion date at sunset when the lights reflect on the canal. *(Southern Star Cumberland Basin, Prince Albert Rd, Regent's Park NW1; +44 20 7485 8137; open Mon-Fri 6-11pm, Sat & Sun 12pm-11pm; Fengshang.co.uk)*

The Feng Shang Princess

A Slice of Sicily Under A Brutalist Tower Block

Tucked away beneath the colossal concrete conversation starter that is Trellick Tower, sits a secret Sicilian restaurant. **Panella** is a real-life Italian living room full of chit-chat, kitchen clatter and massive portions of pasta. Through the hatch is married couple Giuseppe and Caterina who run the ship and spread their love of seasonal Sicilian cuisine. The casual menu changes daily so grab a plate and get sucked into the super fresh salad bar for a bit of everything. Don't skip the arancini and the gnocchi sprinkled with pick-your-own parsley from the pots on the table. With authentic cannoli on offer too and the encouragement of your adopted Italian parents for the day, it's unlikely you'll leave empty handed. The ideal pitstop for when you get peckish on your search for the Portobello Road of yesteryear, see pg 296. *(15 Golborne Road, Kensal Green, W10; +44 074 6749 6655; Mon-Sat 9am-5pm; Panellalondon.co.uk)*

A Birds Eye View of Portobello Market

For as long as locals can remember, although it's changed hands over the years, there's always been a rooftop restaurant with a discrete people-watching terrace (heated and covered) overlooking the Portobello Road where it crosses with Lancaster Road. Hidden above a cornershop, accessed via a stairwell from the market road, today it's a family-run Lebanese restaurant called **Akoya**. But in all honesty, it's not the food (although the mezze is very good), nor the decor (cosy but slightly overdone with the faux flowers), nor the friendly service that will continue to lure us here. It's quite simply that location; a secret-ish place to watch the iconic Portobello Road market with a birds-eye view above the madding crowd. And if there isn't a seat on the terrace available, we'll come back another time to perch in our little nest, but keep it in your backpocket when traipsing down this world-famous thoroughfare of trade. *(253A Portobello Rd, London W11; +44 7979 797961; open everyday 12pm-11pm; Akoyaldn.uk)*

The Notting Hill Pub With a Spicy Secret in the Back

If you're looking for a traditional English pub with a little extra twist, **The Churchill Arms** is it. The fact that it's been called London's most colourful pub isn't even what makes it most special (but rumour has it they do spend upwards of £25,000 annually on the facade's extravagant floral displays). Inside, you've got all the traditional cherry wood furnishings of a classic pub, enhanced by

The Churchill Arms Thai restaurant

a rip-roaring display of British kitsch hanging from every inch of the ceiling. Veer to the right of the main bar to the back, past the fireplace and discover the pub's unexpected spicy little secret – a tropical Thai restaurant. Surrounded by ferns and fairy lights in a charming greenhouse-inspired setting, you'll find authentic family recipes on the menu from the Thai chefs that moved into the pub's backyard some 20 years ago. Try the *Pad Siew* noodles and spicy *Kaeng Par* curry that wash down perfectly with a nice cold pint of British beer. *(119 Kensington Church Street, London, W8; +44 20 7727 4242; open everyday from midday; churchillarmskensington.co.uk)*

Churchill Arms Thai restaurant decor

A Turkish Delight Nestled Amongst the Skyscrapers

Like a time travelling spite house, seemingly there just to irritate the less fortunate-looking neighbouring tower blocks of Bishopsgate, the **Victorian Bathhouse** is an architectural oddity, to state the obvious. Turkish bathhouses were very popular with the Victorians when most Londoners didn't have everyday access to bathing facilities. This one was built in 1817, survived the Blitz, and held its ground when they modernised the financial heart of London. Post-war fuel costs put the bathhouse out of business in 1954, though its lights flickered on and off as a restaurant and then a nightclub for many years. By the time events company Camm & Hooper got the keys, this Victorian gem had seen much better days, requiring careful restoration work to uncover the original finishes, Arabic mosaics and rich tilework. Resembling a veritable miniature mosque above ground, don't be deceived by its size – down a spiral staircase

Victorian Bathhouse Bishopsgate

awaits a cavernous space for up to 150 party guests. Where the cold pools and marble-lined hot rooms once preened city gents to perfection, Londoners can now celebrate with a cocktail in the secret alcoves of the subterranean jewel for seasonal ticketed events or private parties. The by-appointment space can play host to events of all shapes and sizes from themed birthdays (from 20 people at £30 a head) to intimate weddings and professional occasions. Of course, it wouldn't be a bathhouse without a bath, which has been repurposed as a champagne cooler. *(7-8 Bishopsgate, Churchyard, EC2M; +44 203 617 9944; Follow the IG account for upcoming events @Victorianbathhouse or visit Victorianbathhouse.co.uk for more details)*

Criminally Good Cocktails

Come prepared to your appointment at **Evans and Peel Detective Agency** with your story straight and supplementary evidence up your sleeve in the event of probing. Most importantly, don't linger too loudly or too long outside the nondescript noir door – this is top secret business. Once you've been buzzed in, head downstairs to the detective's vintage bureau and state your case. A mysterious figure, with a surprising American accent, will grill you to verify their investigations before divulging their findings through, yes *through*, a dusty bookcase. A prohibition safehouse serving up clandestine cocktails, shaken not stirred, it's a secretive setting for interrogation and intoxication, with dim lighting and sultry live jazz from Thursdays to Saturdays. Like the unsuspecting entrance, faux bookcase and dodgy New York accent, not all is as it seems. Look out for the cast iron radiator on the wall by the bar, it doubles as a beer tap serving 'radiator moonshine'. You can also negate the coded newspaper menu and order, under your breath, the private and confidential Old Fashioned, concocted by candlelight from paper-bagged bottles in front of your eyes only. The perfect drink to kick back with and swirl around the tumbler as you close the case and end the night. *(310C Earls Court Rd, SW5; +44 020 7373 3573; Tues-Sat 5pm-1am; Evansandpeel.com)*

Find more hidden bars for date night on pg 57 and in-the-know spots in Dining with the Cool Kids pg 237

Secret Beer Gardens

Scotch Eggs in the Backyard of the other Windsor Castle

The **Windsor Castle Pub** is nowhere near the actual royal castle in Berkshire county, but once upon a time, patrons supposedly had a clear view of its royal namesake from this two storey cottage on a hill – Notting Hill, that is. This should give you an idea of how long the Grade II listed watering hole has been around for. The interior was refitted in 1933 and hasn't been touched since, maintaining the charm of an inter-war rural English pub, with itty-bitty old doorways leading to the "Sherry Room", once reserved for ladies, with a fireplace and Great Oak panelling. It makes for a wonderfully cosy and atmospheric nook in colder weather, whilst the secluded walled garden at the back is an ideal summer hideout. On a sunny day, it's well attended by locals who come for the excellent Scotch Egg or the sticky toffee pudding with bourbon vanilla ice cream after a game of tennis in neighbouring Holland Park. *(114, Campden Hill Road, Kensington, W8; +44 020 7243 8797; Mon-Sat noon-11pm, Sun noon-10.30pm; thewindsorcastlekensington.co.uk)*

The After-Party Pub

Walking into **The Magic Garden** is like turning up to *that* after-party of a friend of a friend's friend. You don't know where you are or what's going on, but it's exactly what you need right now. In the garden at the back there's a spray painted old black cab lit up with fairy lights. A bunch of barefoot pixies – oh wait, *people* – lounge on a mishmash of sofas covered in colourful cushions and blankets. Back inside this bohemian Narnia, there's Mr Tumnus in a bucket hat (that's the DJ) behind the decks. That feeling of dread dawns on you that the night's nearly over and you must find your way home from this foreign land. Fear not! You're only in a pub just a stone's throw from Battersea Park and the party continues tomorrow. *(231 Battersea Park Rd, Battersea, SW11; +44 020 7622 4844; Sun-Thurs 10.30am-12am & Fri-Sat 10.30am-2am; Magicgardenpub.com)*

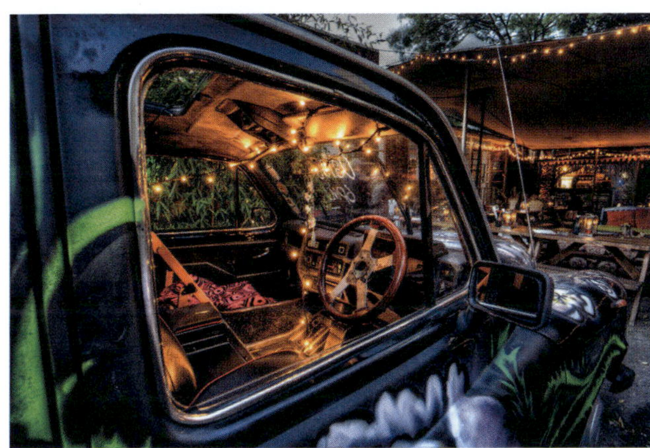

Magic Garden

A Fish & Chips Wedding Under the Wisteria

A pub isn't usually the first place that comes to mind for a wedding venue, but many of London's historic boozers are just as well suited for an intimate and romantic celebration as they are for a first date. Many of the pubs you'll find in this book would do nicely for a low-key city wedding, but **The Albion** is perhaps the one that takes the cake. On a leafy residential corner of Islington, this seriously handsome Georgian gem was once a tea house. Elegant fireplaces, cosy wood panelled rooms and carefully restored period furnishings embrace the area's pastoral past (one street over on Liverpool Road, you can still see the raised pavement that separated pedestrians from the cattle path). Around the back of the Albion's bar, the dining rooms look out on the enchanting walled garden through a set of French doors, where smart teak tables and benches sit under a glorious lilac canopy of wisteria in the warmer months. It doesn't take much more than some cheerful bunting and a few string lights to make this garden into a bride's fairytale wedding, or any occasion for that matter – It girl Alexa Chung and Burberry celebrated their own fashion union here one balmy summer eve. Wedding talk aside, if you're spending some time in Islington, perhaps after a spot of antiques shopping down Camden Passage (see pg 265) this is your pub. Happiness is sitting under their attractive green striped parasols with a plate of crispy haddock and thick chips, a glass of Pimms in hand and rogue vines of wisteria dangling close enough to tickle your ear. *(10 Thornhill Rd, Islington, N1; +44 207 607 7450; open everyday from midday to 11pm; the-albion.co.uk)*

Riverwatching with a Roast

One of London's most pleasant walks is the stretch of the Thames Path that passes through Fulham. Stroll along the river past leafy narrow streets, still lined with Victorian two-up and two-down houses, through lush Bishop's Park, and give a nod to London's oldest football club, Fulham FC, which has kept its original 19th century brickwork exterior, and a village cottage on the corner. An ideal pitstop is **The Crabtree**, a welcoming riverside Victorian public house whose main draw is the enormous outdoor garden shaded by an old willow tree (which replaced the namesake crabtree). The pub boasts mesmerising views over the Thames, especially during the summer when the sunsets cast a cinematic glow over the waters. Positioned on a natural inlet, it's the last of the many riverside taverns that once existed along this stretch of the Thames as early as the 1760s. Often quiet, though busy with home fans on match days (with which the superb staff copes impressively well), the pub is renowned for its Sunday roasts and summer BBQs. Also, the Monday night mussels are a treat to devour by the water's edge. *(Rainville Road, W6; +44 020 7385 3929; open everyday from midday to 11pm; thecrabtreew6.co.uk)*

Family Recipes from the Continent

Comfort and Cannellini at Mom & Pop's Italian Corner Shop

Sitting pretty in its old Grade II Victorian corner shop, **Ida** is the type of place you wish you could call your local. The lucky residents of Queen's Park get to transport themselves to old world Italy almost every night of the week via the authentic cuisine and warm hospitality of husband and wife team, Avi and Simonetta. This is the simple story of an Italian family that became passionate restaurateurs in London town. The couple run the place with their children who will take the helm one day. "Ida" was Avi's mother, who lived in a medieval hilltop town called Cupramontana and passed on her love of cooking, including her homemade, hand-rolled pasta recipes and a slow-cooked cannellini stew that feels like a warm hug. Tables have crisp white tablecloths and you can follow the family history in the mishmash of handpicked artwork and photographs on the walls. The old-fashioned starched linen curtains that hang halfway in the windows would have reminded *Nonna* of home. In short, it's got all the right ingredients for one of the most authentic Italian meals in the city. PS: a local's secret: don't miss out on the monthly Italian cinema Sunday supper clubs. Watch 'Dolce Vita' classics over a three course meal inspired by the sights and sounds of the evening's chosen film. *(167 Fifth Ave, Queen's Park, W10; +44 208 969 9853; See the website for cinema supper clubs: idarestaurant.co.uk)*

Ida

The One the Foodies Don't Want You to Know About

For most central Londoners, Peckham is a few Tube stops too far to travel on the premise that a little-known Balkan restaurant is going to rock their world. And that's just how in-the-know foodies and locals would like to keep it. **The Peckham Bazaar** has been an under-the-radar neighbourhood gem for a few years now since it took over a local corner pub with an old red telephone booth hugging its terrace. Romantic, rustic and passionate about grilling things over charcoal, the restaurant's currency is flavours that are smoky and sing of the simple pleasures of summer in the Eastern Med. Owner and Albanian native, John Gionleka, describes his menu as steeped in all the scenic romance of "former Ottoman lands, from the Dinaric Alps to the beaches of Anatolia." Share the salt cod croquettes, the marinated octopus & white tarama, and some lip-smacking-good juicy lamb cutlets with vanilla baked beans (yes you read that right), all washed down with sparkling Greek wine. Save room for that heavenly date molasses ice cream and chocolate tart. In winter, it's a cosy, moodily-lit old world space with oil lamps flickering to the sound of Balkan folk music, and come summer, the fairy-lit terrace is a dream. The truth is, this pocket of Peckham is blessed with good restaurants that will keep you coming back to explore. Get talking with the Bazaar's charming team for a few local tips. *(119 Consort Rd, Peckham, London SE15; +44 208 732 2525; Peckhambazaar.com)*

A Tuscan Family Lunch

Put on your Sunday best and head to lunch with **La Famiglia**, your adopted Italian *famiglia* in Chelsea that is, where they greet you like cousins, treat your children as their own and serve you like a *nonna* fattening up her grandkids. This upmarket Italian restaurant has been tucked away behind the King's road for decades, transporting faithful clientele back to summers in Tuscany with their signature blue and white tiles and secret garden at the back. A special mention for their Mozzarella in Carrozza (deep fried mozzarella with a secret tomato sauce recipe): pure joy and comfort on a plate. *(7 Langton St, London SW10; +44 20 7351 0761; open Tues-Sun for lunch & dinner, Lafamiglia.co.uk)*

The Village Taverna

Hillgate Village is a quiet candy-coloured village tourists don't know about on the south side of Notting Hill. Picture perfect pastel painted brick cottages, once home to the bakers, blacksmiths, bootmakers and bricklayers of North Kensington when it was still considered a slum, are now worth millions of pounds each. The lucky residents have two cosy pubs within a stone's throw, but the local haunt you should come for is a chic Greek taverna with a hidden back garden for summertime lunches. In 2012, **Mazi** took over from the previous and well-loved Greek taverna that had been operating here since 1957, but the more recent family-owned replacement turned out to be a very welcome and

Peckham Bazar

lasting addition to the village. Take yourself back to the Cyclades with tapas starters served up in little mason jars to share. You might find yourself ordering a second round of the feta tempura prawns, but leave some room because nothing on the menu disappoints. Mazi means 'together', which is just what this restaurant is for; catching up with friends in the taverna's white-washed garden and planning your next holiday to the Greek islands. Book an early seating to ensure an al fresco table. *(12-14 Hillgate St, W8; +44 20 7229 3794; open everyday for lunch & dinner; Mazi.co.uk)*

Mazi

Dive Bar Jukebox

The Red Glow Under the Bridge

When is it ever a bad idea to follow the glow of a red neon sign? From experience, very rarely. **The Bridge** in Shoreditch glows like a fireplace with red lights. Take refuge from the cold in this Dickensian-style joint, which from the outside looks like an old Victorian sweet shop. Open the maroon coloured door to a sweet shop of its own kind; a shaken-up chocolate box of gaudy lamps, old framed photographs and tiny trinkets from bygone eras. Check out the antique cash register behind the bar while you wait for the best espresso martini in town. Head upstairs to the parlour where the crimson theme runs through the drapes and plush sofas. Settle into the big baroque armchairs, with just the rumble of the trains overhead to remind you of the outside world.
(15 Kingsland Rd, Hackney, E2; +44 020 3489 2216; Sun-Wed 2pm-2.30am, Thurs-Sat 2pm-3am; Facebook.com/thebridge15)

Through the Keyhole of Old School Soho

Soho in the '60s glowed fluorescent red. Dotted all over the district were open doorways with subtle makeshift signs advertising 'sexy models upstairs'. There are still plenty of these seedy stairways, known as 'Soho walk-ups' to climb today, but consider that the way to a good time and a slice of sexy sixties Soho isn't always *up*. Head through the unmarked entrance and down the scruffy staircase of 57 Greek Street (an address just a couple of doors down from an actual Soho walk-up at No. 52). No handwritten signs or red lights indicate what's through the broom cupboard door in the basement, it's a word-of-mouth subterranean secret. Slip into the last of London's real deal speakeasies, a portal to Soho's hedonistic golden days. Formally the New Evaristo and sometimes called The Hide Out, this legendary time warp dive bar is known to locals as **Trisha's**, after proprietor Trisha Bergonzi. Once an Italian drinking and gambling den, remnants of its former life adorn the windowless walls today in the form of black-and-white pictures of Sinatra, Bogart and the Pope. It's easy to imagine the Sopranos laying down their cards on the green chequered tablecloths, under low lights and a cloud of smoke. Most nights nowadays, you'll find some old crooners propped up at the bar and an Edith Piaf doppelganger in the corner, warming up for her after hours jazz number. Technically it's a members' club, but details are vague, a bit like a house party with an open-*ish* door policy. It's a humble and casual set up so you may just have to sign in or pay £20 entry for lifetime membership to Trisha's front room. Although tempting to keep this one under wraps, for the last 80 years Trisha's

has survived paycheck to paycheck. Rising rents means it has sometimes come dangerously close to going under and forced to call on support from devoted patrons. Secrets don't save precious spaces like this one, so help an old girl out and tell a friend.
(57 Greek St, Soho, W1D; +44 020 7437 9536; Mon-Sat 5.30pm-1.30am & Sun 5.30pm-1am; facebook.com/TrishasSoho)

Escaping the Oxford Circus

Tucked away down a snug alleyway off Oxford Street might be just the refuge you need away from the crowds of shoppers. **Bradley's Spanish Bar** is a harmonious hodgepodge of Spanish and English influences. Quench your thirst with their huge range of draught Spanish beers and house sangria. If you're looking for some patatas bravas to soak up the alcohol, you're in the wrong place. The only food served here is strictly English tapas, in the form of crisps, nuts and pork scratchings, just as the regulars like it. This tiny two-level hideout is known for its 1970s vinyl jukebox, which is as old as the pub itself. It seems the same can be said for the flea market furniture and cross-continental trinkets on display. The ever evolving and modernising city is closing in on historic Hanway Street, and Bradley's is an example of an old school watering hole where time stands still. So make yourself at home in this quirky Anglo-Spanish living room open to all.
(42-44 Hanway St, Fitzrovia, W1T; +44 020 7636 0359; Mon-Thurs 12-11.30pm, Fri-Sat 12pm-12am & Sun 12.30-10.30pm; Bradleysspanishbar.com)

The Bridge

The garden at Number Sixteen, SW7

07
The Anxious Host

Whether you live in London or you've been nominated to lead the way on a friends or family trip to the city, as much as we love them, when your people come to town, anxiety levels go up. But hang on, what if you don't take it upon yourself to make exhaustive itineraries and plan every minute of the day? People-pleasing is a thankless job. And you know what people appreciate more? Someone with good suggestions. Share your ideas with friends and family – create your adventure together. You might even leave this book on their night stand and ask them to pick out a few things they like the sound of. Life is unpredictable, so take the pressure off and put yourself on a more level playing field for turning the situation around if things go awry. In this chapter, we'll zone in on some first-time visitor requests and how to put your own spin on them. If the kids are coming too, get ready to revisit your childhood and possibly, enjoy it more than they do. And finally, if there's a special occasion on the cards, consider the shortlist of locations locked down. Now, go and enjoy London with your guests.

Afternoon Tea Done Right

Locals and tourists alike all love a cream tea every once in a while. It's a necessary indulgence for even the most jaded of Londoners. For your convenience, below you'll find a selection of some genuinely good Earl Grey-infused experiences, particularly handy for when your extended family comes into town, appointing you as the master of afternoon tea ceremonies. All that's left to do is tuck in and settle the long-standing debates of how to pronounce 'scone', and whether it's jam or cream first.

A Secret Chelsea Garden

The mid-Victorian white stucco terrace at **Number Sixteen** is a boutique hotel that feels less like a hotel and more like the London pied-à-terre of your wealthy, bohemian fairy godmother. Float through a series of deliciously *Alice in Wonderland*-esque salons to **The Orangery**, the in-house restaurant which begins in a bright conservatory and leads out onto a private, leafy garden where all of a sudden, it becomes hard to believe you're still in the heart of London. Just about the only noise disturbance here is the oversized goldfish, belly-flopping in their shallow pond that runs down the centre of the garden, stopping before a wooden gazebo with cushioned seating and a table set for afternoon tea. The service includes a selection of sandwiches and an array of delicious cakes for £45 per head, with the option to add a glass of champagne. Book in advance and ask for the table in the gazebo or under the oak tree. *(16 Sumner Pl, Kensington, SW7; +44 20 7589 5232; open everyday; Firmdalehotels.com/hotels/london/number-sixteen).*

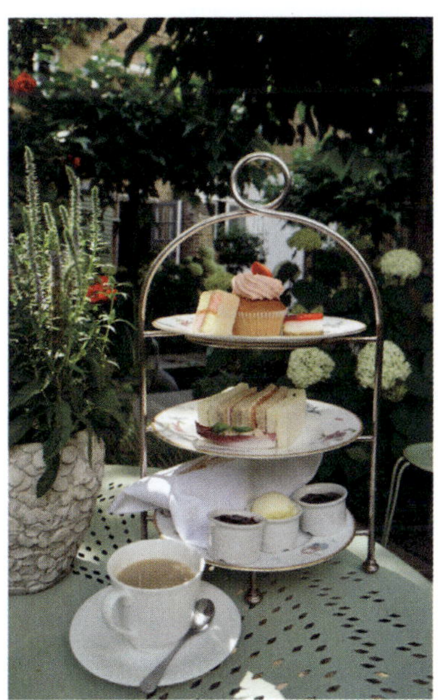

Afternoon tea in the garden of Number Sixteen

Cosy as Tea Cosy

Despite being just down the road from Buckingham Palace, **The English Rose Café and Tea Shop** is the real deal, with all the charm you'd hope for when imagining a quaint British tea room. This family-run independent does the British tradition of afternoon tea properly, and inexpensively, with dainty teacups, your Grandma's floral wallpaper and the top-notch cucumber sandwiches and homemade Victoria sponge cake to match. *(4 Lower Grosvenor Pl, Victoria, SW1W; +44 020 7976 6280; Fri-Sun 10am-4pm; Theenglishrosecafe.co.uk)*

A Dollop of Georgian Drama

The **Zetter Townhouse Marylebone** is an historic townhouse turned boutique hotel that feels like stepping into the home of the famous eccentric Lord Byron. The scarlet red maximalist parlour, adorned with antique treasures is the cosiest of winter retreats sequestered behind busy Oxford Street. The fire is going, the servings are generous and cocktails are optional but highly recommended. High tea from £45. *(28-30 Seymour St, Marylebone W1H; +44 20 7324 4544; afternoon tea served Wednesday to Sunday, 12pm-4.30pm; Thezetter.com/marylebone)*

A rumoured Kensington hideaway of the late Princess Diana

Serving simple but delicious little finger sandwiches and crumpets with tea and cream since 1963, the **Muffin Man Tea Room** looks very much like a humble English granny's cosy conservatory. Seemingly stuck in a timewarp when Laura Ashley was all the rage and Diana was still living nearby at Kensington Palace (and said to occasionally frequent the comfortingly under-the-radar tea room), if you're looking for a truly authentic local spot without the tourist price tag, this would be it. We're not sure how Diana took her tea, but you'll get the full afternoon tea experience for under £9. An old-fashioned tea room, just like they used to make 'em, before they became a British tourism commodity – thank goodness this place is still around, for now. *(12 Wrights Ln, Kensington, London W8 6TA, UK; open everyday from 8am-8pm)*

A Victorian Winter Garden

As an enchanting alternative to the more obvious choices for a glitzy afternoon tea at Claridges or The Ritz, opt for one of London's most overlooked palatial hotels, **The Landmark**, which first opened in 1899 as the grandest of railway hotels. Take your tea under the soaring palm trees of an awesome eight-storey Victorian glass atrium with a live harp serenading you throughout. Splurge on a decadent and delicious tea service for £70 a head, but when you can peel yourself away from the heavenly winter garden, take a sneaky wander around this labyrinthine grande dame. *(222 Marylebone Rd, NW1; +44 20 7631 8000; Mon-Friday 3-5pm, Sat & Sun 1-5pm; Landmarklondon.co.uk)*

All Aboard London's Travelling Tea Bus

For an exercise in not taking oneself too seriously, experience English tea time while cruising around town from the top deck of an iconic vintage red London bus. Whether you're planning a birthday, bachelorette, or you're simply looking for an out-of-the-box mood lifter, **Brigit's Bakery Afternoon Tea Bus** is probably one of the kitschiest ways to see the city. You can book a table for 2 or 4 people or more, or just rent the whole bus. Along with delicious finger sandwiches, muffins, scones and all the afternoon tea trimmings, champagne, mulled wine and gin cocktails are also available with your bus ticket. Peppa Pig-themed tours are also on offer for the kids. *(Bookings at B-bakery.com)*

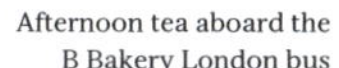

Afternoon tea aboard the B Bakery London bus

Tea house by day and theatre by night

The Tea House Theatre is an old Victorian corner pub that was built the same year as London Bridge in 1886, but today the pint glasses have been replaced with dainty china teacups. Set yourself up by the fireplace, surrounded by cosy leather armchairs, mismatched rustic furniture and stacks of board games. They have a surprising selection of homemade loose tea blends to choose from for afternoon tea, which at £24.50 a head, comes with a cake stand filled with all the finger sandwiches, freshly baked scones and brownies you can eat. Stick around until dark when, several evenings a week, the space turns into a makeshift theatre, host to small-scale adaptations of Victorian thrillers, jazz and poetry nights, acting workshops, a regular debate club, as well as an eclectic variety of unusual events such as lock-picking classes. After tea, continue your discovery of Vauxhall's little hideaways and some of London's best-kept secrets on p270. *(139 Vauxhall Walk, Vauxhall, SE11, +44 207 207 4585; Mon-Fri 9.30am-10pm, Sat 9am-10pm, Sun 9.30am-8pm; teahousetheatre.co.uk)*

Kill two birds with one scone

Treat yourself twice and combine your afternoon tea with some world-class art & culture at **The Wallace Collection**. The West London is mansion packed with Rococo treasures (Fragonard's, *The Swing* is in the house) and priceless antiques, many from Versailles (flip to pg 117 to learn more about its treasures). The museum's pretty pink-hued restaurant is set in an elegant glass-roofed courtyard and sculpture garden, which serves a perfectly good afternoon tea with a glass of champagne for £45. The museum is free. *(Hertford House, Manchester Square, Marylebone, W1U; +44 207 563 9500; afternoon tea served everyday between 12-12.30pm and 2.30-5pm; Wallacecollection.org)*

A Sip of History at London's Oldest Tea Shop

Looking for some historical context on the star ingredient? **Twinings** has been selling tea for over three hundred years, so they know a thing or two about pouring us a cuppa. The flagship store, which looks like a Georgian-era toy shop on the Strand, is London's oldest tea shop. And it's not only home to a mini museum of tea chests, caddies, pots and old advertisements, but a tea "bar" too, which hosts a range of excellent masterclasses, including one dedicated to the ceremonial culture of it all. If you have some burning questions about tea etiquette, this is the place to ask. A 2.5 hour masterclass costs £60 per person. *(216, Strand, WC2R; +44 020 7353 3511; Mon-Fri 9.30am-7pm, Sat-Sun 11am-6pm; Twinings.co.uk/pages/tea-masterclass-tasting-experience)*

Prêt-à-Portea

For a more playful take on a British tradition that's sure to be a hit with young and young-at-heart fashionistas, bite into a tiny Vivienne Westwood jacket or a buttery Prada handbag among other delicious bespoke biscuits and couture cakes served with your "Prêt-à-Portea" at **The Berkeley** hotel. £80 a head. *(Wilton Place, Knightsbridge, SW1X; +44 20 7107 8866; Mon to Sun 1 pm – 5.30pm; The-berkeley.co.uk/restaurants-bars/afternoon-tea)*

The Classics, Revisited

A few of London's greatest hits, from a different perspective

Be the Harrods Tour Guide with the Good Trivia

With guests in town, a trip to London's most luxurious and famous department store is always on the bucket list. And a place as iconic as **Harrods** is best visited with a sense of its history, along with some of its more peculiar secrets. Charles Henry Harrod may have started it all with a one room grocer's, but his shop would swiftly grow into the landmark store it is today, with over 330 departments spread over a million square feet of opulence and luxury, covered in 11,000-12,000 light bulbs. It's rumoured some 300 bulbs need to be replaced everyday. Wealth and elegance of course go hand-in-hand at Harrods, where a dress code is still in place. And for those with riches left over after an extravagant shopping spree, the store still offers its original Victorian safety deposit boxes and strong rooms, well worth a visit.

Harrods was the first department store in Britain to install an escalator; shoppers who braved the contraption had their nerves steadied with a snifter of brandy when they reached the top. In keeping with the store's motto of *Omnia Omnibus Ubique* (all things for all people, everywhere), up until the year 1916, the department store offered packages of morphine and cocaine complete with syringe and spare needles, which was recommended as "a useful present for friends at the front". Harrods also had its own shoppable zoo, controversially selling crocodiles and baby lion cubs. Christian the Lion was purchased from the pet shop in 1969 and became the local mascot on nearby King's road before he was justly reintroduced to the African wild.

Visit the toy department, where the most famous bear in the world was once sold; a 1921 Christmas present for a young boy by the name of Christopher Robin Milne, who he named Winnie-the-Pooh. From the fantasy Egyptian Room to the churchlike extravagance of the historic Food Hall (circa 1903), brave the crowds of green bag carrying shoppers and look out for your own secrets hiding in plain sight at the grandest shop of them all. *(87-135, Brompton Road, SW1X; +44 020 7730 1234; Mon-Sat 10am-9pm, Sun 12pm-6pm; harrods.com)*

Poking around the Natural History Museum's Basement Storage

Why are so many things kept behind-the-scenes at museums? London's **Natural History Museum** opened up an entirely new wing, in part, to fix that problem. The iconic 19th century treasure trove of natural wonders is an evolving mixture of old and new, one of its most significant new additions being the Darwin Centre, a glass box located to the side of the original cathedral-like building, containing 27 kilometres of shelves that hold some 22 million animal specimens. The Natural History Museum is free and a must-see for any London visitor, but the 45-minute behind-the-scenes visit of the Darwin Centre's **Spirit Collection** is the most fascinating way to spend an extra £25. Get into the basement vaults and labs with an archivist for a close look at the museum's rarest specimens stored in alcohol (hence the name, the Spirit Collection), some preserved for hundreds of years, too special and fragile to exhibit publicly. Meet Archie, a 8.62-metre-long giant squid, as well as some 250-year-old fish collected on the Captain Cook expedition and specimens collected by Charles Darwin that still have his little handwritten labels on their tails. This is where the real scientists hang out in their lab coats with one of the biggest and best collections in the world. *(Cromwell Road, South Kensington, SW7; Spirit Collection daily tours meet by the Turbinaria coral bay in Hintze Hall; Book tickets ahead at Nhm.ac.uk/events/behind-the-scenes-tour-the-spirit-collection.html)*

Natural History Museum

Searching for the Portobello Road of Yesteryear

Depending on how frequently one visits flea markets and street markets, Portobello Market may or may not feel like a place that's lost its authenticity, but to the average Londoner or owner of this book, chances are it'll feel like a Disney-fied version of what it once was. There are worse 'tourist traps' to wander into, mind you; for a first time visitor, it's a colourful rite of passage to ride the wave of tourists that flock here every weekend. And as luck would have it, there is a pot of unpolished gold at the end of the riotous rainbow.

If you want to get a glimpse of the Portobello Road of yesteryear, make your way to the end of it, all the way at the top, where the Westway bridge looms above. Historically an antiques market since the 1940s, Portobello Road isn't quite the same old peddler's street they sang about in the musical, *Bedknobs and Broomsticks*, but if we're looking for the last of the traders who still remember what it used to be like, this is where they'll be. Look out for the arcades of Portobello too; hidden indoor alleys behind the buzz of the street food stalls. They tend to go overlooked by tourists, but remain home to seasoned antiques dealers. Duck into **Portobello Green Market** by the Westway where genuine vintage clothing sellers cluster together under white tents. On the next block, you'll find the faded red cornershop of **L H Cook Furnishers** at number 298, **a** family-run, independent business going strong since 1962, selling reasonably priced second-hand furniture. Just across the street, **Honest Jon's** is a reggae record shop that opened its doors in 1974 (find more like this in 'the Last Record Shops of Notting Hill' on pg 254). Continue two minutes up the road to reach our final destination: **Golborne Road**, a hidden corner of Notting Hill where remnants of the old Portobello linger amidst a small community of diverse cultures.

Portobello Road

While most tourists stick to the main drag, Golborne Road remains somewhat a local's secret. The infusion of Portuguese, Moroccan, Spanish, Caribbean and English influence carved into this North Kensington village make it feel like a little United Nations. Omar, the owner of **Fez**, a mini North African bazaar, left Morocco with only a rucksack and travelled around until he eventually settled at 71 Golborne Road. His shop, carrying Moroccan ceramics, glassware, lanterns, slippers, djellabas and hand-embroidered bags, has been in business for a quarter of a century now. Across the road is **Le Marrakech**, the trusted village butcher, and **L'Etoile de Sous** on the next corner, sells fresh Moroccan pastries.

Alice's antiques shop on Portobello Road

Portobello Road

The presence of the Moroccan community here, along with the Portuguese, began with the migrations of the late 1960s and early 1970s, in response to the flood of recruitment in the hospitality industry. **Café O'Porto** competes with another Portuguese institution, **Lisboa Patisserie**. The two old-school eateries pledge fierce allegiance to their hometowns and play out their rivalry on Golborne Road. Interlaced with the international flavours are the kinds of antiques and interiors shops that should've maintained centre stage on Portobello Road; **88 Antiques** is the longest running business on Golborne Road, **Universal Antiques** next door is an eclectic cabinet of curiosities and **Les Couilles du Chien** across the street is a jumble of eccentric pieces, straight out of a Brighton beach arcade.

Now, we can't ignore the elephant in the room that is **Trellick Tower**, North Kensington's dominant landmark. Yawning upwards at the end of Golborne Road is Ernö Goldfinger's 31-storey megalith of concrete brutalism, reminiscent of Stalin's Russia. Love it or loathe it, the tower is looked up to today as an icon of postmodernism. Architecture students flood in every other week to study the tower as a classic example of post-war public housing. Before it became one of the most desired addresses for postmodern design lovers, Trellick Tower did indeed have a truly appalling reputation. In the 1970s, newspapers regularly ran headlines like, "Pensioner Dies in Prison Flats". Though it is a brute, Trellick certainly has a whiff of the distinctive. If you curl around the end of Portobello Road, there towers that unique profile; Trellick is still standing. Trellick is a listed building. Get closer. Enter the lobby and you are met with marble floors, bright new lifts and a concierge. Young families, professionals and pensioners breeze in and out. Though most flats in Trellick are still council-owned, there are many private owners too. If they do ever come on the market, they change hands for upwards of £600,000. Stop in for a snack at the base of the tower at **Panella**, a well-hidden Sicilian canteen loved by locals (from our secret restaurants on pg 274). Around the corner, dive into Kate Moss' favourite vintage closet at **Rellik**, (see pg 252) one of London's best kept fashion secrets, hiding at the end of our rainbow.

Kew Gardens: A Rainforest in an Upturned Ship

Close your eyes and think of England, what do you see? Perhaps a summertime romp around a gorgeously grand English garden plucked straight from a period romance novel. At **Kew Gardens** in leafy West London, your *Pride and Prejudice* fanfic comes to life, although you'll have to find your own Mr Darcy. Founded in 1840, and beautifully maintained ever since, Kew is home to a beast of a botanical garden, the largest and most diverse in the world, with more than 30,000 different kinds of plants. The *pièce de resistance* is the Palm House, a magnificent glass jungle resembling a washed-up submarine. In fact, architects borrowed cutting edge techniques from the shipbuilding industry when designing the giant Victorian greenhouse as it was the world's first to be built on this scale. As well as being lovely to look at, the ornate plant palace is a laboratory of research for the site's resident scientists; much of its insides are

Kew Gardens

medically magic, endangered, or extinct in the wild. While you're in there, say hello to Techno the Chinese water dragon, you can usually find her chilling by the papaya tree.

The tropical Palm House is a favourite with visitors, however there are quieter parts of the 300-acre grounds which are often overlooked, especially during busy times. Take a trip up to the treetops on an 18-metres-high walkway offering a spectacular view of the forest under foot. Pause for a moment's peace and a picnic lunch in the manicured Japanese Garden. Lastly, hidden down a side path from the Temperate House, there's a gallery of over 800 historical botanical artworks. It's the only permanent exhibition by a female artist in Britain. The lesser-known **Marianne North Gallery** (included in the main ticket price) is the result of a radical Victorian woman defying all social conventions of her time and travelling the world with just an easel as her companion. Marianne traversed treacherous terrain to paint exotic and flowers on the brink of extinction in their natural habitats, all of which are exhibited in geographical order so you can follow in her footsteps.

If you're visiting Kew in the winter months, you will be happy to hear that the tropical glasshouses are constantly in bloom and toasty-warm no matter the season. In fact, Christmas is a particularly magical time as they light up and sparkle after dark as part of a festive light trail. It's a big hit with kids, and enough to get even the grumpiest of scrooges in the holiday spirit.
(Kew, Richmond, TW9; +44 20 8332 5655; Open daily from 10am, closing time differs with seasons; Kew.org)

Kew Gardens

Kew Gardens

The Modern Mary Poppins Playbook

London with kids ... (or just the big kid inside).

If Aladdin's Cave was Full of Toys

Victorian children would spend hours assembling and staging their own miniature productions of *Cinderella, Hansel & Gretel* and *Punch & Judy*. In the 1850s, Benjamin Pollock began designing, colouring and printing little theatres on paper and card, that came complete with painted backdrops, stage curtains and costumed characters. Find some time to visit **Benjamin Pollock's Toyshop** in Covent Garden, the toyshop where you can still buy hand puppets, vintage board games, toy theatres, shadow boxes and everything else you need to drag children away from the screens and back into a world of old fashioned storytelling, imagination and magic. (*44, The Market, Covent Garden, WC2E; +44 20 7379 7866; Mon-Wed 10.30am-6pm, Thur-Sat 10.30am-6.30pm, Sun 11am-6pm; pollocks-coventgarden.co.uk)*

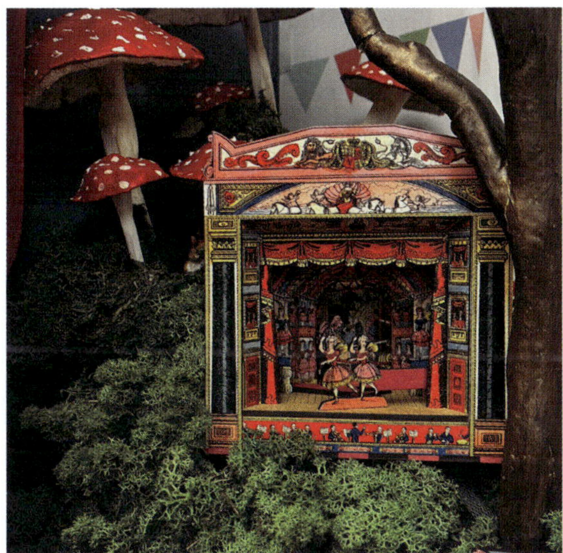

Sleeping Beauty Reverie Miniature Theatre

Tinkerbell Lives in Clapham

Who doesn't want to meet a fairy and explore their house? Yes, of course – it's for the kids, right you are! **Fairytale House Clapham** is an enchanting hideaway conjuring up immersive 'Fairy Training Adventures' hosted by a real-life fairy in her magical house of twinkling lights, hidden treasures, potions and spells. The resident fairy goes all out with planning birthdays too. Before your visit, you receive a package in the post with handmade invitations to send out to friends along with a key to the fairy house. Everyone gets to take home their own wings, wands, cookies and gift bags. *(Book in advance, available for birthdays and private visits, from £139 for age 2 and up for groups up to six; Fairytalefriends.co.uk/birthdayvisits)*

A Joy Ride through Time on London's Forgotten Mail Train

Ask a Londoner about the subterranean Royal Mail train and chances are, they won't have a clue what you're talking about. For seventy five years, the British postal system ran a narrow gauge railway beneath the city's gridlocked streets, secretly whizzing the public's post (and sometimes postal workers) along the tracks to different stations and sorting offices. Stretching 10km from Paddington to Whitechapel, by 2002, it had become an uneconomical service, losing an estimated £1.2M a day, and quietly shut down. For almost a decade, the abandoned stations and tracks stood in silence; the toy-like trains frozen in time, occasionally being visited by underground explorers for a rare photo opportunity.

The Mail Rail at the London Postal Museum

Recognising the appeal of this forgotten little railway, in 2017, **The Postal Museum** announced its intention to officially open part of the network to the public. You can now journey back in time on a toy train (not all that dissimilar to the original ones used by postal workers) through the old tunnels and decommissioned station platforms. If you aren't claustrophobic, the highly impressive 15-minute Mail Rail experience is undeniably the highlight of the Postal Museum, which is situated on what was the largest postal sorting office in the country. The museum is great for kids, who can busy themselves decoding Morse messages, send letters with a vacuum pipe, try on replica vintage postman uniforms – or design one for the future. As technology continues to fast-track the art of letter writing from daily life to our history

books, this wholesome museum feels like a comforting blanket of nostalgia that wraps around you at every corner. Look out for England's retired post bus, the delightful red minivans that both delivered mail and served as the only public transport in some of the UK's most remote areas. Scrapped around the same time as the Mail Rail in the 2000s, one could journey across the English countryside on a trusty red post bus, bouncing around in the back with sacks of people's mail, and pay for the bus' fare with stamps!
(15-20 Phoenix Pl, London WC1X; +44 300 030 0700; Wednesday to Sunday 10am – 5pm; Postalmuseum.org)

Really, really Old School

Kids these days – do they know how good they have it? A visit to the **Ragged School Museum** might just see to it that they do. Named after the state of the clothes worn by destitute children at a time when London's East End was plagued by disease and poverty, "ragged schools" emerged as vital charitable organisations providing free education in Victorian Britain. Telling an important and sadly still-relevant story, the museum is housed in the same building where the largest-ever ragged school was opened by Irish philanthropist Dr Thomas Bernardo in 1877. Today you can visit Victorian classrooms equipped with original blackboards, antique school desks, authentic slate writing boards and even the dreaded dunce hats – all to leave today's iPad-learning generation open-mouthed. There's plenty to learn and look at for grown-ups too and the information panels are packed with curious and jarring facts (if you can stop your kids from dragging you away to the next exhibit). On the second floor there's also a recreated kitchen from the 1900s which shows what life was like for families who lived in a single room with no electricity or water. The kids can dress up (mop hats included) and re-enactments of Victorian lessons take place the first Sunday of every month. Miss Perkins is most probably the strictest teacher in the whole of London, so best be warned not to put a finger out of place in one of her classes. And if they're good, you can treat them to tea and cakes at the onsite café after class. *(46-50 Copperfield Rd, Tower Hamlets, E3; open to the public Wed-Thurs and the first Sun of each month 2pm-5pm, the Victorian lessons run the first Sun of each month 2.15pm-3.30pm; +44 208 980 6405; Raggedschoolmuseum.org.uk)*

Camden's Unofficial School of Creativity

On a chilly October evening in 1966, crowds of people were queuing down the road to attend the opening night of the **Camden Roundhouse**, where Pink Floyd performed their first big gig. The legendary venue went on to stage concerts by Dylan, Hendrix and Bowie, and it hosted the "Dialectics of Liberation" conference attended by Allen Ginsberg. In the 70s, it was riddled with thrashing punks who came to see the Ramones, and in the 90s it was booming with neon ravers. Today, the arts centre runs a Young Creatives programme put in place to help the next generation of cultural revolutionaries find their feet. From drop-in drama clubs and playwriting workshops to after-school sessions with the circus, everyone can take part in the youth program's creative projects (from 11 to 30 years old) and get access to top-notch media suites, equipment and rehearsal rooms from one pound an hour. *(Chalk Farm Rd, Camden Town, NW1; +44 300 678 9222; Roundhouse.org.uk/young-creatives-11-30)*

Punch and Judy have still got it

Little Londoners are in on a big secret. Far from the West End, on the edge of a leafy garden in Islington, lies their very own mini theatreland. Since opening its doors in 1961, **Little Angel Theatre** has been handcrafting magical and moving puppet shows guaranteed to tug at your heartstrings and get everyone shouting, *he's behind you*! Stories are tailored to age groups, from toddlers to 12 year-olds, and enjoyable for grown-ups too. The Blue Peter badge-worthy puppets, along with the hand-crafted set, pews and props are brought to life in the adjoining atelier. For those who struggle to sit still, there's a programme of craft workshops to inspire the next generation of marionette masters. *(14 Dagmar Passage, Islington, N1; +44 020 7226 1787; See website for performance schedule, the box office is open Mon-Fri 10am-1pm; Littleangeltheatre.com)*

Across town, floating on the canals of Little Venice is the **Puppet Theatre Barge**, a warm and gentle space for little folks' big imaginations where ducks float past the portholes. A family business for three generations running, this 72 ft-long Thames lighter was charmingly converted into a teeny-tiny puppet playhouse in 1982, comfortably seating an audience of up to 50 people; children and their grown-ups. For adults, it's a chance to see inside one of the quaint little houseboats on the Regent's Canal, and as for the kids? Transfixed – you'll never see a boatload of children sitting so quietly and attentively. Everything from

Barge exterior

the stage lighting to the voice acting and the surreal movements of the string marionettes is entirely enchanting; entertainment from another time that you can't really put a price on. *(Rembrandt Gardens Little Venice, opposite 35 Blomfield Rd, London W9, +44 20 7249 6876; the earlier you book the closer you'll be seated to the stage; see the website for show times: Puppetbarge.com)*

All Aboard the Nostalgia Express

Museums generally only display a fraction of their inventory, the rest held in storage, but when your museum is Covent Garden's popular London Transport Museum and your items are literally the size of a bus, the overflow is enormous. Step forward the astounding **London Transport Museum Depot** in Acton Town, a cavernous warehouse that looks a lot like an actual train depot with an enormous collection of over 320,000 artefacts charting the evolution of London's urban transit history. Horse drawn buses rest alongside the iconic red Routemasters, next to the motorised buses requisitioned to transport soldiers to the Western Front trenches; all waiting their turn to be displayed at the bustling main museum in the West End. The depot holds Edward Johnson's original wooden printing blocks that gave London Underground its distinctive font, whilst you can see how the Tube map evolved from the first, slightly more geographically accurate maps, to Henry C. Beck's iconic rendition we know

London Transport Museum Depot

today. Take a seat in the retired Underground trains, trolleys and buses, reading the old Tube maps, enjoying the period ads, and picturing the untold number of commuters who once sat in your seat.
(118-120 Gunnersbury Lane, Acton Town, W3; +44 0343 222 5000; only open to the public on Open Weekends or by a pre-booked guided tour, held on some Fridays and Saturdays. See the website to book: ltmuseum.co.uk/visit/museum-depot)

Ghoulish Gifts for the Monster in Your Life

From the outside, this navy-blue shopfront with windows full of jams and chutneys resembles a trendy urban farm shop. A typical East London concept store, you might think. Well, think again. At the stroke of midnight, werewolves, zombies and gremlins queue up outside **Hoxton Street Monster Supplies** to get their claws on their weekly provisions. Luckily for us humans, we're permitted entry during the day, at our own risk, to stock up on monstrous delicacies such as cubed earwax, fang floss and salt made from the tears of anger. A jar of the thickest human snot, which tastes suspiciously and deliciously like lemon curd, is not only a curious unconventional gift for your little (and big) monsters, but

Hoxton Street Monster Supplies

all proceeds go to the Ministry of Stories, accessible via a secret door in the shop. This initiative, founded by author Nick Hornby, sees professional writers mentor young kids in the art of story writing, encouraging them to concoct their own magical and monstrous creations. They also run a post-mortem postal service, connecting curious humans with lonely monsters. Letters cost £5 and original responses from your petrifying pen pal can be collected in-store or posted via broom delivery for an extra £1. Mind out for Wells the invisible cat on your way out, he can be a little frosty towards humans.
(159 Hoxton St, Hoxton, N1; +44 020 7729 4159; Thurs-Fri 1pm-5pm & Sat 11am-5pm, Closed Sun-Wed; Monstersupplies.org)

Don Draper's Weekend to take the kids

This one is for the parent who gets nominated to organise a pre-teen birthday party. **Bloomsbury Bowling Lanes** is a time-warp within a time-warp; a 1950s-themed venue that was opened in the early 2000s and, comfortingly for some, hasn't changed much since. Accommodating parties of up to 25 guests, everyone can bowl, game, eat, sing and dance, all in one sprawling subterranean space, while you sit back with a cocktail, a giant pizza and some decent diner food in a red leather booth. Karaoke rooms are available to book and if you've still got the energy, send the kids home and throw down some moves to some cheesy golden age classics on the dancefloor, open until 3 am on weekends.
(Tavistock Hotel, Bedford Way, London WC1H; +44 207 183 1979; bloomsburybowling.com)

Where to Really Stretch their Legs (besides Hyde Park)

Wimbledon and Putney Commons should be more celebrated as one of London's best natural assets, particularly for parents. At the end of the District line, a five-minute bus ride from the station, you'll be greeted by acres of open fields, trees to climb, lush forests of ferns and streams, and at the centre of it all, a two-hundred-year-old windmill, one of four in the London area. The **Wimbledon Windmill Museum** would look more at home in Holland, but it was built here as a working corn mill in 1817 to provide flour for locals. In the 1970s, the whimsical relic was turned into a free museum, where you can now discover the history and science of windmilling, have a go at grinding flour, and on the upper floor, step inside the preserved Victorian living quarters where Robert Baden-Powell stayed in 1902 to write *Scouting for Boys*. Factor in lunch at the neighbouring tea rooms or the Fox & Grapes pub on the edge of the commons, and it all makes for a cracking family day out.
(Wimbledon Common, SW19; the museum is open from March – October, Sat 2pm-5pm, Sun 11am-5pm, and Bank Holidays 11am-5pm; Wimbledonwindmill.org).

Pirates and Police

Tucked inside what was once a carpenter's workshop at Wapping police station, the **Thames River Police Museum** brims with a jumble of artefacts like in an old sailor's cabin. This small and offbeat museum visited by appointment-only is dedicated to the early days of the special police force that was tasked with guarding the once crime-ridden docks of the Thames. Tackle theft and ship lootings were common in 1800s London. Hundreds of ships would be moored on the river, transporting cargo from near and faraway lands, tempting thieves from all over town to get their hands on these wares. After being welcomed by a retired officer, browse Victorian diving uniforms, antique handcuffs and sabres. In the extensive collection of photographs, drawings and newspaper cuttings spanning the centuries, you'll be able to see how London's lifeline went from underdeveloped dock to a huge international trade powerhouse, to the more leisurely pace of the present day. *(98 Wapping High St, Wapping, London E1W; thamespolicemuseum.org.uk)*

After your visit, follow the cobblestones a few doors down and stop for lunch at the **Captain Kidd**, an atmospheric pub hidden away inside an old coffee warehouse, serving cheap pints and views over the river. Designed like a ship's hull, it was named after the 17th-century pirate, William Kidd, who was executed nearby at, you guessed it, **Execution Dock**. Continue your swashbuckling Thames crawl to the macabre historical landmark, just a ten minute's walk upriver, where you can see the old gallows on the shore line, accessible at low tide via the back of another historic riverside pub, **The Prospect of Whitby**. And just in case you're wondering, children, supervised by an adult of course, are welcome patrons of most London pubs. (*Captain Kidd: 108 Wapping High Street, E1W; +44 20 7480 5759; open everyday; Thecaptainkidd.co.uk / Execution Dock & The Prospect of Whitby: 57 Wapping Wall, London E1W; +44 20 7481 1095; open everyday; Greeneking.co.uk/pubs/greater-london/prospect-of-whitby)*

Wizards in Soho

Still awaiting a Hogwarts acceptance letter? Find a fast-track portal to Diagon Alley hiding in London's Soho. **House of MinaLima** is a design wizard's destination created by the studio behind the graphic universe of the Harry Potter and Fantastic Beasts films. Design duo Miraphora Mina and Eduardo Lima brought their whimsical world to a townhouse on Wardour Street where you can wander through the creaking rooms, immersing yourself in the imaginative artwork and set design of Harry Potter's world. An unofficial free museum of sorts for Hogwarts fans (or just fans of whimsical graphics and prop design), MinaLima is also a purveyor of memorabilia and replicas of props from the movies, as well as signed books, prints and other quirky little gifts. Keep the fantasy going around the corner on Greek Street at **The Wands & Wizard Exploratorium** (*Wizardexploratorium.io*) an immersive experience for young wizards and mad scientists.
(157 Wardour St, London W1F; +44 20 3214 0000; open everyday 11am-6pm; minalima.com)

A Little Engineer's Big Day Out

For kids with a fascination for great big hulking machines and parents who hope it means they've got big ideas as future engineers, it's highly recommended to plan a big day out to the **Kempton Steam Museum**. Home to the world's largest working triple-expansion steam engine (think four double-decker London buses high), the volunteer-run museum is situated on the site of the former Kempton Park Waterworks, which once powered London's water supply

House of MinaLima

system. To witness these century-old engines in action, a colossal symphony of heaving and grunting Victorian machinery recalls what it must have felt like to stand inside the belly of the RMS Titanic's engine room. In fact, they are so similar in design and size, Kempton's engines have made cameos in a number of notable films and documentaries about the ill-fated vessel. Open to the public at weekends, a talented team of volunteers brings the Industrial Revolution back to life, puppeteering engines and turbines of titanic proportions in a remarkable homage to the marvels of Victorian engineering that transformed the world. If you or your future engineer fancy a go at operating one of the world's largest stationary steam engines, the museum offers 'drivers experiences' – a training day spent in the engine house learning how to control them first-hand. The experience costs £110 for adults or £40 for under-16s (minors must be over 1.4m tall). Come in overalls and leave with a signed certificate and your mind very much blown. Don't miss a ride on the little steam train outside the museum before you go.
(Kempton Park Waterworks, Snakey Lane, Hanworth, Middlesex, TW13; +44 1932 765328; see website for open weekends, admission free for under 18 and £10 for adults; Kemptonsteam.org)

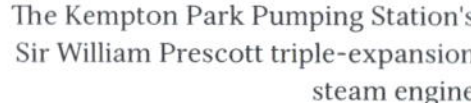

The Kempton Park Pumping Station's Sir William Prescott triple-expansion steam engine

Cookie Monsters

Behind a whimsical illustrated shopfront and smart monochrome awning, London's most charming biscuit shop doubles as a **Little School of Biscuiteers**. Gather your budding bakers (age 7 and up) for an hour of delicious creativity spent icing their own tin of biscuits, guided by the house baker. Each student takes home their own apron and certificate of 'Biscuiteers Icing Brilliance'. For private birthday parties, children can choose their own icing theme and the day wouldn't be complete without their own bespoke cake.
(Locations in Notting Hill and Belgravia; classes from £49; find information for bookings at Biscuiteers.com/boutique-icing-cafe/childrens-icing-parties)

Enjoy the Big Screen with your Little One

On Monday mornings, the iconic **Electric Cinema** in Notting Hill has a BYOB policy. You may be thinking, "that's a little early for boozing?" but hitting the bottle in the AM is perfectly acceptable when it's full of milk. Bring-Your-Own-Baby to see that film you've been meaning to catch but haven't been able to find yourself child-free. It may sound like a horror fest, but **Electric Scream!** is a safe space for babies (and parents) to scream, cry and whimper without judgement. Park your pram at the back of the auditorium and have drinks and snacks brought to your plush red seat. The lights and volume are lowered to protect little eyes and ears, but films are subtitled so you can stay on track even if it isn't naptime for everyone. Babies under one are welcome rather than roaming toddlers, so you don't have to worry about PG age ratings and getting trapped in a Disney film. There's plenty of time for that in a few years. To reserve a ticket, give them a call.
(191 Portobello Rd, Notting Hill, W11; +44 020 7908 9696; Monday mornings, see website for film times; Electriccinema.co.uk)

Child-Friendly Brunching on the Beatles Barge

Floating restaurants are usually crowd pleasers when it comes to family meals out, but one that is plastered in playful pop art is a guaranteed hit. Not just any old paint job, the exteriors of **Darcie & May Green**, conjoined twin canal boats moored in Paddington, are designed by Sir Peter Blake, the godfather of British pop art and co-creator of the iconic album artwork for the Beatles' *Sgt Pepper's Lonely Hearts Club Band*. Climb aboard the funky floating piece of art for posh bacon butties, squidgy banana bread, perfect flat whites and brilliant babycinos, brought to you by Melbourne's café culture maestros. There's something to float everyone's boat. Got a babysitter for the evening? This double decker Aussie eatery burns the candle at both ends and so should you too, come back for rooftop cocktails after bedtime.
(Sheldon Square, Paddington, W2; +44 020 3935 9045; Mon-Fri 9am-10pm & Sat-Sun 10am-10pm; Daisygreenfood.com)

The Museum of Play

The best "nanny" in London is free. The **Young V&A** is an absolute godsend for parents of young children (we're talking all the way up to the age of about 14). A branch of the hugely popular V&A museum (pg 119) housed in a beautiful Victorian building in East London, the curators of this museum clearly know what it takes to nurture small humans (and what it takes out of the adults). Divided into three parts – play, imagine and design – the exhibits are thoughtful and inclusive, offering not just things to look at, but *activities* for children of all abilities and interests; things they can actually touch and play with. There is a miniature village of toy houses, a theatre for the kids to do some play acting and dress up, story time several times a day and creative workshops to join, or not. It can also just be a beautiful giant indoor playground for them to run around in without hurting themselves. Babies have their own calmer area to play and parents are entertained too with audio guides delving into the design, history and evolution of toys from their own childhoods. Just like the perfect Mary Poppins, everything has been thought of at the Young V&A, so parents can relax and focus on enjoying time with their children. *(Cambridge Heath Rd, Bethnal Green E2; +44 20 8983 5200; open everyday from 10am-5.45pm; Vam.ac.uk/young)*

The Young V&A

Jazz Obsessed Dad is Coming to Town

Somewhere to tap your feet

A low-key time capsule of music history

The spirit of 1950s & 60s counter culture lives on in Earls Court's legendary **Troubadour.** Going strong since 1954, this coffee house and music venue is a charming mix of the Parisian Latin Quarter, with its outdoor bistro tables, and the old folk music clubs of Manhattan's Greenwich Village; it's no wonder that this was where Bob Dylan held his first performance in London. With its weathered exterior, the much loved Troubadour was the bustling centre of London's underground artistic scene: Jimi Hendrix, the Rolling Stones' Charlie Watts (who was discovered here), Ronnie Wood, Joni Mitchell, Led Zeppelin and jazz great Lionel Grigson, all played in the cosy café where the 'Ban the Bomb' movement was formed, *Private Eye* magazine was published, and the Black Panthers met after the 1968 Paris riots. Whether you're enjoying the free folk, jazz and blues music jams still held downstairs, or a drink in the secluded back garden, or a late night supper on the outdoor tables lining Old Brompton Road, the Troubadour makes for a swinging soirée from a bygone era. *(265 Old Brompton Road, SW5; +44 20 7341 6333; the café is open Sun-Wed 9am-12.30am, Thurs-Sat 9am-2am; the music club is open Sun-Wed 7.30pm-12.30am, Thurs-Sat 7.30pm-2am. Reservations are recommended; Troubadourlondon.com for details about upcoming music events)*

London's Jazz Mecca & Supper Club

A long standing staple of late night London, **Ronnie Scott's** isn't just an institution, but the definitive home of British jazz. Working as a tenor saxophonist aboard the touring Queen Mary in the late 1940s, Ronnie Scott was inspired by New York's bebop clubs to recreate something similar back home. First existing in a small basement space on Gerrard Street in 1959, and since 1965, on nearby Frith Street, Ronnie Scott's swiftly became to Soho what Birdland was to 52nd Street in Manhattan. Co-founded with fellow musician Pete King, the supper club with a smoky atmosphere, where sharply dressed clientele drank smooth tipples long into the night, soon attracted the greatest names in jazz: Ella Fitzgerald, Stan Getz, Chet Baker, Count Basie and countless others. Ronnie Scott would often act as host, quipping that his club "was just like home. Filthy and full of strangers." Given a revamp in 2006, the club retains its 1950s charm, with the tables crammed right against the performers, and still welcomes the finest musicians to its hallowed stage. *(47 Frith Street, Soho, W1D; +44 20 7439 9747; show times are in two sittings, 6pm-10pm and 10:30pm-3am, advance bookings are recommended; Ronniescotts.co.uk)*

Jazz Amongst the Tombstones

At the northeast corner of London's most famous squares, look for the lone glass elevator shaft in the shadow of the church steeple with the blue clock face. Press the button to the only place this glass box will take you: the crypt. Escape the crowds of Trafalgar Square, and descend into the **Café in the Crypt** lying underneath historic St Martin-in-the-Fields, where every Wednesday night you can enjoy live jazz surrounded by ancient tombstones. St Martins is one of London's most famous churches, with worship here dating back to the medieval times. Despite the prominent tourist location, St Martins is still a thriving church, known particularly for its sterling work with London's homeless, funded partly by programmes like the jazz nights held in the Café in the Crypt. The low, brick vaulted ceilings, and old gravestones set into the floor create an atmospheric backdrop for some of London's finest jazz musicians, with food and drinks available from the bar. The repertoire strays from jazz on other nights to classical, country, motown and the best of West End musicals, and the café is open for business everyday. See the website for details. *(St Martin-in-the-Fields, Trafalgar Square, WC2N; +44 20 7766 1158; Jazz Nights at the Café in the Crypt are every Wednesday 8pm-10pm, café open Mon, Tues 10am-7.30pm, Wed 10am-6pm, Thurs-Sat 10am-7.30pm, Sun 11am-7pm; Tickets from £9 via Stmartin-in-the-fields.org/crypt-lates)*

For punks who love a bit of jazz

Sandwiched in between a souvenir shop and a lingerie shop on London's busy Oxford Street, a stairwell leads down to one of the most storied music venues in the city. **The 100 Club** was opened in 1942, originally as a jazz and swing venue, reassuringly located underground in case of an air raid. Part nightclub, part bomb shelter, it became popular with American GI's and Louise Armstrong was among the first of many legends to perform there, followed by Billie Holiday and Muddy Waters. As Britain's Punk movement emerged in the late 70s, the club's direction shifted gears and became a hub for the growing subculture. The Sex Pistols, The Clash, Buzzcocks, The Stranglers and later, Britpop bands like Oasis, all played at the intimate venue, but one night was still always reserved for trad jazz. Today, the line-up mostly alternates between punk, indie rock, jazz and something in between called Northern Soul, a genre born out of the British mod scene, based on American soul music with a faster tempo. Tuesday nights are always blues nights, and there's a recurring spot for swing bands, with the occasional household rock legend passing through for a secret gig. The scruffy decor hasn't changed since the 70s, the drinks are still cheap enough and the talent is close enough to see them sweat. Exactly as it should be. *(Century House, 100 Oxford St, London W1D; open everyday from 7.30-11pm; for gig listings see The100club.co.uk/events-calendar)*

Literary London's Cocktail Club

We've all heard of Hemingway and his band of literatis and artists that shook up Parisian society throughout the 1920s, whom we nostalgically call the "Lost Generation". London had the "Bloomsbury Group", a collective of English eccentrics across the channel known for their rebellious lifestyles and liberal attitudes that often overshadowed their talent as writers and artists. Virginia Woolf was among them. Entwine yourselves in the love triangles of the decadent and debaucherous British bohemians in their old stomping ground at **The Bloomsbury Club**. You're in for 1920s live jazz several nights a week, a cocktail menu inspired by tarot cards and a decor of wood-panelled walls lined with antique books. *(16-22 Great Russell St, WC1B; +44 020 7347 1222; Tues-Sat 5pm-1am, Sun-Mon Closed; Thebloomsburyclub.com)*

Don't miss an unforgettable evening with cocktails and swing music in an abandoned wartime Tube station at Cahoots on pg 43. Also, check out Oliver's Jazz club on pg 114, the Hampstead Jazz Club on pg 33 in Chapter 1 and the Nightjar in Chapter 2 on pg 64.

Ronnie Scott's

So you're celebrating something special...

Keeping it Intimate

- **Midnight Apothecary**: At the whimsical rooftop cocktail garden above a forgotten entrance to Thames foot tunnels, roast marshmallows over personal fire-pits with botanical cocktails, foraged ingredients from the surrounding rooftop herb garden. Beneath lies a historic entryway to the subterranean Thames tunnel, doubling as a secret theatre for clandestine concerts. Entertain up to 30 guests with a starting budget of £1400. *(Thebrunelmuseum.com/venue-hire/midnight-apothecary-rooftop-bar-exclusive-hire)*

Roof Garden at night

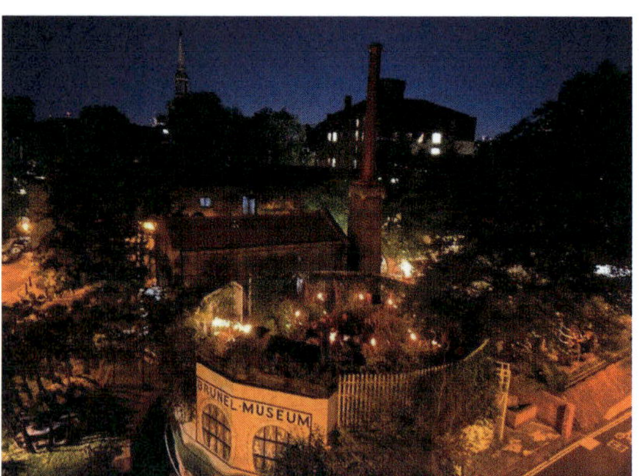

- **Maggie Jones's Restaurant**: Theatrically decorated with floor to ceiling bric-a-brac, run by warm and welcoming staff, Maggie Jones still remains a firm favourite with the royal residents of Kensington Palace (see pg 75). Join friends around one of their large tables that seat up to 20 people. (*Maggie-jones.co.uk/bookings.htm*)
- **The Pig and Butcher**: Host a feast in a farmhouse kitchen complete with a wood burning stove in North London, comfortable seating 16-24 guests. Perfect for a big family reunion or birthday lunch. (*Thepigandbutcher.co.uk/private-dining*)
- **The Last Tuesday Society & Absinthe Parlour**: For a truly out of the box event, book a banquet in the basement museum of 'one of the great latter-day collectors', Mr. Victor Wynd. Treat your guests to an absinthe tasting, a tarot reading or a taxidermy class, seated around a Sarcophagus, surrounded by skeletons and sea monsters. Accommodating parties from 6 to 75 people with a private hire fee starting at £100. Jump to pg 340 to learn more about the unusual society and museum. *(Thelasttuesdaysociety.org/private-hire)*

Bourne & Hollingsworth Buildings

- **Bourne & Hollingsworth Buildings**: Ready to host groups of 12 or up to 250 guests, there are many layers to this black brick clubhouse in Clerkenwell, including a greenhouse and a secret underground den decked out in bohemian kilims. You can rent out the entire building or just one of the spaces, ideal for smaller parties, creative meetings or perhaps your own product launch. (*Bandhbuildings.com/weddings-at-bh-buildings*)
- **The Union Club**: On the roof of a 280-year-old Georgian town house in Soho, decorated with French street lights and eclectic art and antiques, there's a hidden gem of an al fresco terrace that would be magical for an engagement party. It has a capacity for 40 standing or 25 sitting down. *(Unionclub.co.uk/hire)*
- **Brigit's Bakery Afternoon Tea Bus**: Whether you're planning a birthday, a bachelorette, or you're simply looking for a whirlwind mood lifter, taking your Afternoon Tea on an iconic London bus is probably one of the kitschiest ways to see the city (see pg 214). You can book a table for a few friends or rent the whole bus. Along with finger sandwiches, muffins, scones and all the afternoon tea trimmings, champagne, mulled wine and gin cocktails are also available to lift your spirits. *(B-bakery.com)*
- **The Bedouin Tent**: An unexpected venue set in a beautiful courtyard garden, this tent woven from goats hair, is perfect for talks, workshops, conversations and intimate music concerts. (*Stethelburgas.org/venue-hire*)
- **Go Boat**: Explore the royal waterway on your own self-driving electric boat. From £85, you can play pirates down the canals at a speed of about 3 knots – no licence required – and they even have boats with heated seats. Ideal for a small children's birthday party or a low key celebration with up to 8 friends. *(Goboat.co.uk)*

- **Villa di Gennario**: How about an Italian dinner party? Take your friends to a Tuscan villa in Chiswick (see pg 147) with a choice of private dining rooms for up to 22 guests. (*Villadigeggiano.co.uk*)
- **Tap & Bottle**: The "snug room" of this historic Georgian townhouse (see pg 56) would make for an excellent office party or professional event for up to 30 people with in-house catering available. *(Tapandbottlelondon.co.uk/private-hire)*
- **Number Sixteen, The Orangery**: A secret garden in Chelsea awaits behind this mid-Victorian white stucco terrace house turned boutique hotel. The bright conservatory leads out onto a private, leafy garden where over-sized goldfish swim in a shallow pond that runs down the centre of the garden leading to a wooden gazebo. This would be very chic for an intimate ceremony and cocktail reception. *(Firmdalehotels.com/hotels/london/number-sixteen/weddings/ceremony)*

The Big Bash

- **Little Nan's Bar**: This kitsch-tastic venue under Deptford's disused railway arches is adorned with fairy lights, union jack bunting, plastic pink flamingos, vintage royal family memorabilia and British tchotchkes. For birthday celebrations they'll design and name one of their signature teapot cocktails in your honour and for something with a larger guest list, their event space "Grandad's Shed" is available to book for soirées of 65 –110. *(Littlenans.co.uk)*

Little Nan's Bar

- **The Victorian Bathhouse**: An Arabian Nights costume theme is practically mandatory at the historic Turkish baths (see pg 276) tucked away in the City of London with a capacity of 150 guests. (*Cammhooper.com/venues/victorian-bath-house-london*)
- **The Albion**: Get married at one of London's most beautiful pubs with a garden covered in wisteria (see pg 280). Its garden caters for up to 120 guests and will offer all-day barbecues and spit-roasts in the summer. *(The-albion.co.uk/events-weddings)*

- **Two Temple Place:** Party like an Astor in one of London's hidden architectural gems, a neo-Gothic mansion on the embankment once owned by William Waldorf Astoria (see pg 166). Visit the mansion for one of its cultural exhibitions and fall in love with this one-of-a-kind venue that hosts up to 300 guests. (*Twotempleplace.org/venue-hire*)
- **The Phoenix Garden:** Get hitched in a secret garden in the city surrounded by flowers and birdsong (see pg 223) The award-winning community retreat has an indoor pavilion with a capacity of 150 guests. (*Thephoenixgarden.org/hire-us*)
- **The Prince Regent:** Serve up to 80 guests fresh oysters and champagne as you cruise down London's Regent's canal on a historic tug boat. (*Londonshellco.com/the-prince-regent*)
- **Brunswick House:** This lone Georgian mansion in Vauxhall is home to one of England's most important architectural salvage companies; part showroom, part restaurant, café and events venue (see pg 140). The ambiance caters to a hip and informal new generation of antique lovers and the food and wine selection is just as thrilling as the decor. The choice of spaces is quite decadent – you can feast in the library, party in the smoking room, recover in the saloon and finish in the crypt. Capacity ranges from 12 – 110 seated or 50 – 250 standing. *(Brunswickhouse.london/venue-hire)*
- **Sessions Arts Club:** Behind a very smart red door of a very smart Palladian-style building in Clerkenwell, awaits one of London's most surprising restaurants in Sessions House (see pg 66) a Grade II listed landmark that's had several lives. Available to hire with a capacity of 100 guests whose jaws will most certainly drop as they enter the Dickensian vaulted space that used to be an old judges dining room. Throw a time travelling secret dinner party in this candlelit mansion with beautifully distressed walls, lunette windows and bohemian decor that lure you into another place and time. *(Sessionsartsclub.com)*
- **Leighton House:** Queen Victoria partied here so why not you too? The Kensington bohemian mansion of Frederic Leighton, a well-travelled 19th century painter, is now a spectacular house museum (see pg 129) and also makes for an unforgettable setting to host a cultural event or even a wedding for up to 150 guests. *(Rbkc.gov.uk/museums/venue-hire)*
- **Rivoli Ballroom:** Throw a 50s-themed dance off at one the last of London's lost ballrooms (see pg 45) which remains intact and unchanged, with its original vintage décor; a Grade II listed vision of crimson, with Chinese lanterns, French chandeliers and kitsch glitterballs hanging from the ceiling. *(Rivoliballroom.com/hire)*

For children's party venues, see pg 303 and for special anniversary dinners, see pg 66.

08

Down the Rabbit Hole

We all have it; that itch to explore and discover what lies behind the closed doors of our cities, unseen beneath our feet or up on the rooftops. Or is something we're not seeing simply hiding in plain sight? Urban environments are full of strange little secrets and if we're curious and observant enough, we might just find that trapdoor to a hidden level in the game of life. Let's take a tumble...

Abandoned & Underground

"Please, mind the gap."

Ghost Stations and Entombed Museums

Little do London commuters know, as they travel through the maze of the Underground, what may lie just on the other side of a wall. The Tube network has somewhere in the region of 40 "ghost stations", abandoned stops on the transit system that once thronged with commuters, but are today sealed up and forgotten deep underground. Their tiles are cracked and faded, the unused platforms covered in dust and in some rare cases, advertising from another era is frozen in time on the walls. At Notting Hill Gate station in 2010, some routine works were underway when a series of decommissioned public passageways were re-discovered after 50 years, revealing a veritable mini museum of vibrant vintage advertising from the late 1950s. Presumably still entombed in the darkness, it was decided that the collection of posters should be left in situ as a time capsule and the passageways were once again sealed up.

Stepney Green Station

Rush hour might not seem so dull when you know places like that exist, and there are plenty of opportunities to catch intriguing glances of this forgotten London from the comfort of your own Tube seat. Take the Piccadilly Line between Green Park and Hyde Park Corner, and on the right hand side window you'll see the concrete tunnel suddenly change into brickwork. It is a fragment of **Down Street**, a station in Mayfair that was so short-lived, it never made it to Harry Beck's seminal 1933 Tube map. Down Street may have closed a year earlier, but was used extensively during World War II as the bomb-proof headquarters of the Railway Executive Committee, and by Winston Churchill before the Cabinet War Rooms (see pg 329) were ready. Churchill called the abandoned station the 'burrow,' and its location was so secret, its official address was listed as somewhere else in London. You can visit the warren of tunnels and platforms on the London Transport Museum's "Churchill's Secret Station" tour. *(Ltmuseum.co.uk/whats-on/hidden-london/down-street)*

Ghost Tube Stations

Down Street Tube Station

Stay on the Piccadilly Line towards Heathrow, and by Osterley station, you'll pass right through the abandoned platforms of the original Osterley and Spring Grove station. The stop was closed in 1934, when the new Osterley was opened a few hundred yards down the line. The original station is still there though, only today it's home to a charming secondhand bookshop. Glance above the bookshelves of **Osterley Bookshop** and you can still see the bricked up arches that once led down to the platforms. *(168A Thornbury Rd, Osterley, Isleworth TW7; +44 20 8560 6206; open everyday from 9.30am-5.30pm)*

Notting Hill Gate's entombed post-war posters

The Bull & Bush station on the Northern Line was intended to be the deepest station on the Underground, but was never opened to the public. Between Hampstead and Golders Green stations, the eagle-eyed will spot an unfinished platform and staircase. But one of the best-preserved of London's ghost stations is **Aldwych** (once called The Strand), a little-used, one-station spur on the Piccadilly Line. From the distinctive ox blood red exterior to the beautiful original Leslie Green tile work in the ticketing office and preserved platforms, Aldwych has seen a new lease of life as a filming location. There are other ghost stations all over London and a good place to start your research is at the excellently comprehensive *Underground-history.co.uk*. The hidden stations beneath our feet can, on occasion, be legally explored up close (including Aldwych) on one of London Transport Museum's spellbinding "Hidden London tours". (*Details of the London Transport Museum's Hidden London Tours can be found at Ltmuseum.co.uk/whats-on/hidden-london, sign up for the newsletter to be notified first about ghost station visits)*

Find another ghost station where they serve cocktails with live jazz on pg 43

A Gourmet Dinner on the Tube

The average commuting Londoner spends up to 75 minutes a day on the Tube. Convincing one to get back on the Underground for dinner would probably seem counter-intuitive, but we're not talking about a late night bacon butty and a bag of crisps to chomp on the last train home. No, we're talking about a six-course Latin-inspired tasting menu and an entirely unique dining experience served up inside a decommissioned 1967 Victoria Line Tube carriage stationed at the Walthamstow Pumphouse Museum. **The Supperclub Tube** began as a small endeavour in a Brixton flat in 2013, but things really took off when the founders "upgraded" for a more unusual setting. If you've ever ridden the London Underground before, it may take a little getting used to seeing people actually talking to each other on the Tube, let alone drinking glasses of wine or enjoying Cuban shredded brisket. But in case you need one, here's a fitting conversation starter: the oddly comforting allure of London's vintage Tube textiles (the very ones you'll be sitting on). It was a woman who designed many of those iconic patterns for the city's public transport, and fun fact – she was a distant cousin of Karl Marx. Her name was Enid Marx, and in 1937 she was selected to design the moquette seat fabrics for London's public transport, using patterns that could hide wear and dirt, but also avoid the "dazzle" problem – the potentially nauseating effects of a pattern in motion. These versatile and often overlooked textiles have long accompanied generations of Londoners around the city on one of the oldest subway systems in the world. They can evoke all sorts of emotion and nostalgia, triggering fond memories of journeys made around London over the years. Chances are, the ones you make while dining aboard a 1960s Tube carriage will likely be among the most memorable. *(Walthamstow Pumphouse Museum, South Access Road, London E17; Thursday-Saturday dinners 7pm-9.30pm; £67 per person, prepaid reservations only for parties of 2 to 12; Supperclub.tube)*

The Supperclub Tube

Stepping into Winston Churchill's Brogues

Buried deep beneath the streets of Westminster is a complex of bunkers, corridors and meeting rooms where the Second World War was waged in secret. As the German air force devastated Britain and the threat of invasion mounted, here Sir Winston Churchill, his Cabinet and Chiefs of Staff desperately plotted to secure Britain's defence, in what has become known as the **Churchill War Rooms**.

Churchill's bedrooms at the Churchill War Rooms

In guide books, the underground nerve centre is listed as a museum, but it is really a place frozen in time; a bonafide World War II time capsule. After the last German V2 rocket landed in London, the government returned to its duties above ground, and the War Rooms were simply sealed up and forgotten for forty years. The hidden bunkers were reopened to the public in 1984, through a small entrance under a statue of Clive of India, where Londoners discovered the War Rooms remarkably preserved. One of the main corridors still has its weather board in place, where a card strip would indicate whether the day would be sunny, rainy or cloudy. During air raids, the indicator was always changed to 'windy' as a joke. Sleeping quarters still have night time reads on the side tables and neatly folded pyjamas on the bedspreads. Wander down narrow, dimly-lit corridors to find the Cabinet room, where, as the Battle of Britain raged overheard, tensions must have been on a knife's edge. The map room was updated with daily intelligence and still plots the final front lines of the war, marked by pins joined together with wool string. One small room, disguised as a bathroom, was of utmost importance: it contained a transatlantic telephone line direct to Washington DC, used by Churchill to talk with Franklin Delano Roosevelt. Peek in here, half expecting to catch the lingering scent of Churchill's cigar. Today the War Rooms are run immaculately by the Imperial War Museum and look just as it did when the lights were finally turned off in 1945; much

more than a museum, the weight of history and the decisions made here deep underground are still palpable today. As Churchill himself put it: "this is the room from which I will direct the war."
(Clive Steps, King Charles Street, Westminster, SW1A; +44 20 7416 5000; open everyday 9.30am-6pm; Iwm.org.uk/visits/churchill-war-rooms)

A People's Shelter from the Blitz

Walk around Clapham and you'll find several unusually large concrete cylinders. With no windows, there's little indication of what these urban anomalies might be. They are in fact remnants of a desperate chapter in London's history; entrances to the deep-level shelters of World War II. During the terrifying height of the Blitz, many Londoners sought safety in the Underground, but the Tube stations didn't always offer enough protection. Down the road from Clapham, plaques at Balham station tell the story of how a direct hit in October of 1940, killed over sixty people sheltering on the platforms. Something deeper underground was needed and the answer came in the form of the Northern Line.

In the 1930s, work had begun on an express line, with tunnels being dug below the existing Tube line. During the war, these were swiftly repurposed into Deep-Level shelters, eight in all, and each capable of sheltering 8,000 people with vital ventilation, medical and canteen facilities. After the war, they were closed to the general public, but at **Clapham South Deep Level Shelter**, it is possible to relive this dark chapter of London history by booking a spot on the London Transport Museum's sterling 'Hidden London' tour. Step inside the curious concrete portals at street level, and descend 180 stairs into a subterranean labyrinth. The Clapham South Deep-Level shelter ran for over a mile, and the tunnels are still eerily filled with empty bunk beds. The original 1940s signs are still there, pointing the way to each shelter, named after Royal Navy admirals. By the time the Deep-Level shelters were finished, London continued to be devastated by the ferocious V1 & V2 rocket attacks, and these tunnels offered vital protection. They worked so well that General Eisenhower commandeered one at Goodge Street as his personal headquarters while Clapham South saw further use after the war as temporary accommodation for West Indian immigrants arriving on the *Empire Windrush* in 1948. Venture through this forgotten subterranean world, buried deep beneath the streets of London, for a visceral reminder of what war feels like for innocent civilians. *(Clapham South Deep-Level Shelter can be found on the south side of Clapham Common, SW12; +44 0343 222 5000; tours are run regularly and can be booked at Ltmuseum.co.uk/whats-on/hidden-london/clapham-south; a second, sealed up entrance to the shelter can be seen down the road, at 4 Balham Hill Road, SW12)*

Tipple in the Toilet

Isn't there something hugely satisfying about abandoned public infrastructure that finds new purpose? Especially when it involves something sensible, like bringing in booze. There's an unassuming traffic island in Bloomsbury not far from the British Museum, and for a long time, below it, a rather beautiful example of a Victorian water closet (or WC, as they once said) sat abandoned in the darkness. The 120 year-old subterranean site has since received a thorough scrubbing and in its reincarnation has kept the name **WC (Bloomsbury)**, only this time, it stands for "wine and charcuterie". The speakeasy below the street is far from your bog-standard bar. It's stylishly modern but pays homage to its WC roots, with original Victorian tiling, authentic porcelain pieces, reclaimed mahogany, salvaged leather booths and of course, the toilet cubicles, now functioning as cosy dining nooks. Spend a penny on organic wines paired with tempting cheese and meat boards, perfect for candlelit grazing. Once you're satisfied that evening drinks in a Victorian public toilet is in fact *not* a terrible idea, take a date to discover **WC Clapham**, the first water closets converted by WC Bars back in 2014 at Clapham Common Underground station. Popping to the loo has never been so chic.

(WC Bloomsbury, Guilford Place, Lamb's Conduit Street, WC1N; +44 20 3011 2115; Mon-Wed 5-11pm, Thurs-Sat 5pm-midnight, Sun 5-10pm / WC Clapham: Below Clapham Common South Side, SW4; +44 20 7622 5502; Tues-Thurs 5-11pm & Fri-Sat 5pm-12am; Wcbars.co.uk)

WC Bloomsbury

WC Clapham

A Scavenger Hunt for Buried Burial Grounds and Roman Baths

Somerset House is one of the most famous addresses of central London, a majestic Neoclassical complex on the south side of the Strand, with a grand courtyard that has become home to London Fashion Week, music concerts, art events, and in the winter, an ice rink. But little do thousands of visitors realise that there's a secret world hidden underfoot; a forgotten Tudor graveyard, known chillingly as the **Deadhouse**. In its earlier incarnation as a Tudor palace, Somerset House was the official residence to three different queens of England, including Henrietta Maria of France, wife to King Charles I (the one that got his head chopped off), who had a chapel built on the grounds complete with a burial site. In the 18th century, architect Sir William Chambers called for it all to be demolished, saving only the burial grounds, which were entombed underneath Somerset's main quadrangle, roughly where the water fountains are today. Seek out the only five visible tombstones that remain, by way of the atmospheric 'lightwells'; three sunken passageways on the edges of the quadrangle that have become a favourite shooting location for portraying gothic and Victorian London in period productions. Explore solo, keeping an eye out for signs of a skull and crossbones and Latin inscriptions in the walls. Alternatively, Somerset House hosts a very good Historical Highlights Tours worth the ticket. *(Somerset House, Strand, WC2; +44 020 7845 4600; the quadrangle is generally open to the public everyday apart from Christmas Day, 8am-11pm. Special events are usually ticketed. Tours are on Thurs 1.15pm and 2.45pm, Sat on the quarter past the hour, from 12.15pm to 3.15pm, see Somersethouse.org.uk/whats-on/historical-highlights-tour)*

Some of Somerset's guided tours also take in the peculiar story of the 'not quite ancient' Roman baths next door. Tucked away behind a side street on the Strand, past the Aldwych 'ghost' Tube station (see pg 327), look for the small archway on Surrey Street with a plaque suggesting that if you go 'down steps, turn right,' you'll find a 'Roman Bath'. True enough, at the end of a narrow alleyway, you'll find the **Strand Lane Roman Baths.** Lined with brick, and set into the floor, it's easy enough to imagine the Romans of *Londinium* enjoying the calming spring waters. But despite an official National Trust sign, and an older, worn sign from the 19th century claiming that the baths are 'nearly 2000 years old!', the whole ancient site is a fiction. The baths are in fact an old cistern from the 1600s, used to feed the fountains of Somerset House next door. The cistern might have been completely forgotten about, had an enterprising owner in the 1830s, a Mr. Charles Scott, not hit upon the idea of pretending they were ancient Roman baths to attract customers. His advertising gimmick started to appear in London guide books, inviting gentlemen to cure their aching muscles in one of the oldest structures in London, 'as far back as the reigns of Titus or Vespasian, if not of Julius Cæsar himself!' Even Charles Darwin was taken in, the Strand Roman baths appearing in *David Copperfield*, where he took, "many a cold plunge." The Romans may loom large in London's history, but remnants of old *Londinium* are scarce, and alas, not hiding down Strand Lane (follow the page to find the real deal). The cisterns however, remain a fascinating curiosity, albeit the figment of a 19th-century gentleman's imagination. *(5, Strand Lane, WC2R; The baths are managed by the National Trust, and can be viewed by appointment, at least one week in advance, April-Sept 12pm-4pm, Oct -March 12pm-3pm; email dcreese@westminster.gov.uk or call +44 20 7641 5264 for more information)*

Deadhouse

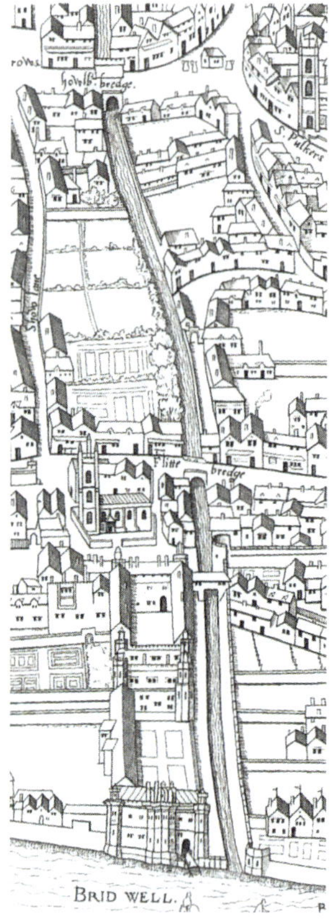

The southern reaches of the Fleet river as shown on the 16th century Copperplate Map

Glimpses of the Hidden River

Stand over an anonymous street grate outside The Coach pub on Ray Street, Clerkenwell, and you'll hear the sound of rushing water. This isn't just any commonplace sewer, but one of the last traces of London's lost river, **The Fleet**. Buried over since Victorian times, the Fleet was once one of the capital's major water thoroughfares. You can still see its source, two ponds on Hampstead Heath that used to be natural springs. From here, the Fleet passed through what is now Camden and Farringdon, before emptying into the Thames at Blackfriars Bridge. For most of its urban existence (so that'll be when the Romans arrived), the Fleet was an eyesore, often used as an open sewer and lined with slums, prisons and filth. After the Great Fire of London in 1666, Sir Christopher Wren attempted to remodel the river with stone embankments, a canal and bridges, but the Fleet remained squalid, moving Jonathan Swift to pen a poem in 1710, noting how it was filled with "Sweepings from Butchers stalls, Dung, Guts and Blood." Conditions weren't much improved in Charles Dickens' time: he set Fagin's den in *Oliver Twist* near the Fleet in Saffron Hill. The turgid canal was eventually bricked over in the Victorian era, but the water still flows from Hampstead, and you can catch other glimpses of the lost river; through a grating in the middle of Charterhouse Street where it crosses Farringdon Road, and underneath Blackfriars Bridge, spy an archway where the Fleet empties into the Thames. The history of the Fleet dates back to Anglo-Saxon times, but it remains hidden and forgotten, deep underneath the streets of London.

The Remains of a Roman Gentleman's Club

The glassy skyscrapers in the City's financial epicentre aren't as transparent as they may look. The Square Mile holds some pretty ancient secrets, you just have to dig a little deeper to find them, which is exactly what excavators did in 1954 during the construction of a towering office block. In amongst the rubble, they made one of the most important and intriguing archeological discoveries of 20th-century Britain. And today, in the bowels of the ultramodern Bloomberg HQ, lies a layer of old Londinium; history's first gentlemen's club of sorts, set in a curiously cavernous Roman temple. The **London Mithraeum** is a subterranean shrine to the cult of Mithras, a deity famous for slaying a primordial bull. Much of the beliefs and practices are shrouded in secrecy, like all the best cults, but it's thought that almost 2,000 years ago worshippers of this male-only Roman religion would meet here to drink, dine and behave badly. Today, people of all genders and beliefs are free to wander around the restored remains and see some of the 14,000 artefacts found at the site, including the earliest ever handwritten document in the form of some squiggles on a wooden tablet from AD 57. With the help of high-tech hazy lighting and audio installations of Latin chanting, the long lost Londoners' secret society comes alive. It's eerily immersive, and gets you thinking, what else is buried away in the basements of those high-rise temples of money back on street level? Read on... *(12 Walbrook, The City, EC4N; +44 020 7330 7500; Tues-Sat 10am-6pm, Sun 12-5pm; Londonmithraeum.com)*

A Medieval House of the Dead

Make sure to look down at the pavement when walking through Spitalfields, to find preserved under a pane of glass, a chilling remnant of a medieval London: the ancient **Charnel House, Spitalfields**. Centuries ago, this underground vault was piled high with human bones collected during the great famine of the 1300s. This eerie ossuary, once attached to the hospital of St Mary's Priory, was unearthed under a building site in 1999, where it had lain undisturbed for hundreds of years. It's getting harder to find traces of the old, working class Spitalfields amidst the sweeping redevelopment of the neighbourhood, let alone a haunting relic of medieval London. Thankfully, the developers incorporated the site into the project preserving the charnel house under glass, and setting a stairwell into the ground to provide a closer look at the underground bone store. *(Bishops Square, Spitalfields, E1)*

Fiesta in the Crypt

Here's where to eat your daily bread and drink water turned to wine 'like a good Christian'. Below the church where ex-prime minister John Major got married in 1970, lies a secret Spanish tapas bar where thou shalt have fun. The bare brick arches of the candlelit crypt makes **Gremio de Brixton** a hallowed haunt for Brixtonians to spend evenings sipping sangria and munching on padron peppers and crispy calamari. Things get slightly unorthodox on the weekend when Latino bands, Flamenco dancers and DJs get the fiesta in full swing. *(Basement of St Matthew's Church, Brixton Hill, SW2; +44 020 7924 0660; Wed-Thurs 5-11pm, Fri 5pm-3am, Sat 2pm-3am & Sun 1-8pm; Gremiodebrixton.com)*

Tunnelling through Time beneath the Thames

London's bridges are famous, but there are other, lesser-known ways to cross the River Thames. Hidden out of sight is a system of foot tunnels buried beneath the river, one of which was once called the Eighth Wonder of the World. **The Thames Tunnel** was the first underwater tunnel in the world, a prodigious

The Thames Tunnel

feat of engineering by Marc Isambard Brunel and his son, Isambard Kingdom Brunel. The 1,300-foot-long tunnel ran between Rotherhithe and Wapping in the East End, and swiftly became one of Victorian London's must see attractions when it opened in 1843. Seventy-five feet below the Thames, the tunnel's archways were lined with market stalls selling trinkets, souvenirs and Victorian fast food, but with time, it also became a popular subterranean lair for thieves and prostitutes. The pedestrian passageway was converted into a railway in 1869, and is still used by the London Overground, which means you can catch glimpses of the forgotten endeavour from the train window. Or visit the Brunel Museum in Rotherhithe and you can step inside the engine house and wondrous Grand Entrance Hall, which has been turned into an imaginative underground theatre, arts space and secret cocktail bar (see pg 59). But if you head eastwards along the Thames, you'll find two tunnels where it's still possible to walk under the river.

The entrance to the **Woolwich Foot Tunnel** isn't exactly easy to find; behind the Waterfront leisure centre, there's a distinctive octagonal shaped building that serves as the southern entrance to a 1,644 foot-long tunnel connecting Old Woolwich to North Woolwich. Built in 1912, the eerily-lit tunnel is still open to pedestrians and cyclists. The **Greenwich Foot Tunnel** is a slightly less ominous-looking route under the Thames, lined with white tiles and sporting grand domed entrances at Greenwich and Millwall. The 1,215 foot-long tunnel lying fifty feet below the Thames opened in 1902, and is still open to pedestrians. Whilst most people cross the Thames by bridge or tube, next time, choose to venture underground in the submerged world of the Thames foot tunnels. *(Brunel Museum, Railway Avenue, Rotherhithe, SE16; +44 020 7231 3840; Mon-Fri 12pm-4pm, Sat-Sun 10am-5pm; Thebrunelmuseum.com; the Friends of Greenwich & Woolwich Foot Tunnels at fogwoft.com is an excellent resource to find out everything you need to know about the tunnels under the Thames).*

The Prison Under the Gin Palace

Gin palaces were by design, much more lavish spaces than your local pub, even though ultimately they all became known as pubs by association. A direct influence on later Victorian pubs during the peak era of pub building, it's thanks to the gin palaces that so many of Britain's neighbourhood establishments are furnished with polished and carved mahogany and embellished with brass, engraved glass and mirrors. Most gin palaces however, had unlikely humble origins as converted chemists. Gin originally had medicinal associations and patrons bought it to take away, or drink it standing at the counter. It was this seemingly virtuous shop counter, over which many dubious medicinal cures were traded, that ultimately led to the concept of a "bar" as we know it today. **The Viaduct Tavern** is the last remaining example of a 19th-century gin palace in the city, resplendent with glittering mirrored murals that reach floor to ceiling, gilt edges everywhere you look, and a sumptuous bar with an ornate ceiling. It also has an original ticket booth at the back, where thirsty patrons once bought tokens to use at the bar so the landlord could keep an eye on the house earnings himself. But lurking underneath the fabulous bar room is something much grittier; a remnant of a place that once filled Londoners with dread; the infamous Newgate Prison. Hidden away in the cellar, amongst the beer barrels and dusty drink crates are the assumed to be original prison cells.

Newgate's reputation as a terrifying prison was well founded; for over 700 years, untold numbers of criminals were locked up in what one witness described as "a massive monolith of windowless brick" until it was demolished in 1904. With the prison teeming with criminals, overcrowding saw more jails being dug underneath Newgate Street, the last surviving of which can be seen in the cellar of the Viaduct Tavern. Ask nicely and a member of the staff will escort you downstairs where you'll find what looks like rows of rusted, ancient prison bars. Whether the local lore is true or not, the Viaduct Tavern remains a glorious place to spend a quiet afternoon, basking in the gilded decor of what was aptly once called a (gin) palace. It's also the perfect pitstop within walking distance of Barts Pathology Museum (pg 345) and the Memorial to Heroic Self-Sacrifice, (pg 219). And just outside (formerly the site of Newgate prison's main execution grounds, where hundreds of prisoners would have been executed) cross the street towards the railings of the Holy Sepulchre Church and find what claims to be London's first drinking fountain. *(126, Newgate Street, EC1A; +44 020 7600 1863; Mon-Fri 12pm-11pm, Sat 12pm-8pm; Viaducttavern.co.uk)*

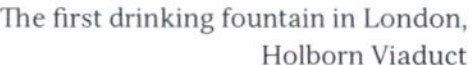

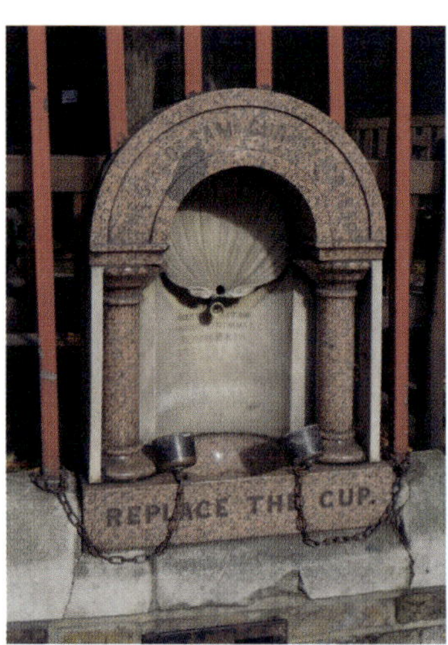

The first drinking fountain in London, Holborn Viaduct

A Theatrical Underworld hiding beneath Waterloo Station

You won't be able to easily explain what you experienced in a disused maze of vaulted tunnels running below Waterloo station known as **The Vaults**. Immersive theatre is their game, but on any given night, you might tumble down the rabbit hole with the maddest of hatters and indulge in a debaucherous cabaret dinner show, or follow a cast of singers through the tunnels in a walk-through opera, or discover an artist-run hidden jazz club. The starting point is the Leake Street graffiti tunnel, which was founded by Banksy in 2008, where you can view the ever-changing work of street artists at any time. Once inside The Vaults, dreamlike experiences are crafted in a labyrinth of tunnels and rooms, where grown-ups remember what it's like to play. When was the last time you were mesmerised? *(Leake St, Bishop's, SE1; +44 207 401 9603; check the website for updated schedule; Thevaults.london)*

Join the Society of Underground Explorers

A trip down the rabbit hole can sometimes be risky business, especially if you're a first timer and that rabbit hole is a nuclear bunker purposefully closed off from curious minds. You'll be in safe hands with **Subterranea Britannica** though, a specialist society for explorers of underground spaces, covering all manner of sites, from Neolithic mines to secret Cold War hideouts. The community of cave-loving men and women that make up Sub Brit don't just scratch the surface, they dig deep. Members have uncovered witches' marks which were long overlooked as idle graffiti, traversed tunnels off the beaten railroad track and discovered one of Churchill's previously inaccessible backup bunkers, hidden under a housing estate in Dollis Hill. Findings from expeditions have built up a comprehensive map of UK and overseas abandoned wonders, at your disposal on their website, where you can study their best discoveries in Greater London (Subbrit.org.uk/locations/greater-london). Membership costs £25 a year and includes invites and information on upcoming explorations, history seminars, meetings and copies of Subterranea, their underground society magazine, full of secrets you are encouraged to keep close. *(Visit subbrit.org.uk)*

Chislehurst Caves, one of the subterranean sites listed in Subterranea Britannica's archives

Cabinets of Curiosity

"I'm so bored of contemporary museums and their desperate attempt to classify and make sense of everything. The world is one big, glorious mess and we should celebrate that."

– Victor Wynd, founder of The Last Tuesday Society

Absinthe and Mermaids in an East London Wunderkabinett

Any 'museum' that pairs weird history with strong cocktails is a museum that has our vote. Viktor Wynd's **The Last Tuesday Society** has actually been around since 2005 as London's longest running literary salon, notorious for surreal and spellbinding parties. It was only natural then, that when Wynd decided to transform the society's East London headquarters into his own idea of a museum / curiosity cabinet, there would be absinthe, eccentric dining (with stuffed long-dead lions at the table, of course) and a whole lot more. The bar, known as the Absinthe Parlour, serves its own brand of East London-distilled absinthe called the Devil's Botany, along with other wickedly strong cocktails, and guests can pair tastings with tarot and palm readings, anthropomorphic taxidermy classes or personally-guided tours of the basement museum by Mr. Wynd himself. A fascinating character and former Parisian, described as "one of the great latter-day collectors", and by John Waters as a "sick orchid", his collection includes mermaids, stuffed squirrels playing cards, dodo bones,

The Last Tuesday Society & Absinthe Parlour

Napoleon's death mask, dandy relics and old master etchings. The upstairs parlour or even the whole curio museum can be yours if you want to rent it out for a very unordinary banquet (see page 318), seated around a sarcophagus, surrounded by skeletons and sea monsters. *(11 Mare Street London E8, Hackney, +44 208 5335297; Tues – Fri 3pm – 11pm, Sat 12pm-11pm, Sun 12pm – 10pm; Thelasttuesdaysociety.org)*

The Last Tuesday Society
& Absinthe Parlour

Sure to delight and disgust everyone who visits

File this museum under "dark tourism". Eye-opening, fascinating and thoroughly educational, but even for the most medically-minded, it's advisable to go to the **Hunterian Museum** on an empty stomach. This peculiar museum, tucked away inside the England College of Surgeons, is packed to the gills with pickled specimens of human and animal remains, most of which were being collected by one guy, over 250 years ago. ("That guy" is John Hunter by the way, also known as the father of scientific surgery). But you don't have to be a doctor to appreciate this museum. For those who don't work in the profession, the recently refurbished museum now boasts some world-class exhibiting that really helps explain what exactly you're looking at and why it's important. The Hunterian is a must-see for anyone interested in science, biology and macabre history, but also highly recommended for anyone who is just generally interested in what it means to be human. Well-paired with a visit to the John

Soane Museum across the square (see pg 141), think of it like a grown up version of the National Science Museum, free of charge. *(The Royal College of Surgeons of England 38, 43 Lincoln's Inn Fields, London WC2A; +44 20 7405 3474; pre-booking a time slot recommended, open Tues to Sat 10am–5pm; Hunterianmuseum.org)*

An Optical Wonder Cabinet in the Basement

They say that in art museums, the eyes of masterpieces seem to follow you around the room, but at the **British Optical Association Museum**, there's no escaping its wunderkammer of glass eyes that are absolutely staring right back at you. Founded in 1901, this quirky repository of 28,000 eye-related artefacts is the world's oldest optical museum in the world. Today, housed in the basement

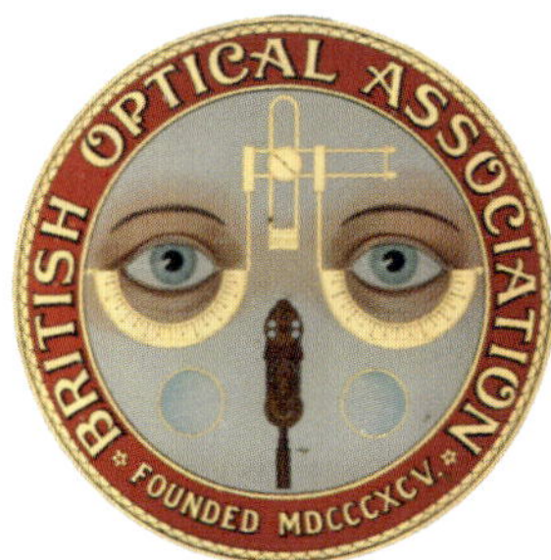

Left: British Optical Museum Association
Opposite: Horniman Museum collections

of the College of Optometrists in Charing Cross, the compact but unparalleled collection of ocular oddities is one of London's little known museum gems. The history of spectacles, from the earliest examples to the late Queen Mother's specs are displayed alongside every pince-nez, monocle, and model of eyewear imaginable – even the ancient artificial eyes placed on Egyptian mummies. The standard tour is 40 minutes and free, but for a small fee, a guide will take you on a full building tour. It's the kind of happy accident that you stumble upon while trying to kill some time in the neighbourhood, but should really be sought out by anyone with an interest in medical ephemera, or secret museums for that matter.

(The College of Optometrists, 42 Craven Street, WC2N; +44 207 839 6000; open most weekdays but only by advanced appointment; College-optometrists.org/the-college/museum.html)

The Little Laboratory that Changed the World

One of the most important rooms in modern world history can be found in a corner of St Mary's Hospital, Paddington. There you'll find a small, slightly untidy laboratory looking much as it did in 1928, when Sir Alexander Fleming discovered penicillin. Preserved today as the **Alexander Fleming Laboratory Museum** it's possible to step inside and see the shelves crammed with petri dishes, journals, microscopes and test tubes where the antibiotic that revolutionised medicine was first discovered, almost by accident. Known for keeping an untidy lab, Fleming had gone on a family holiday leaving a stack of petri dishes to one side. Returning several weeks later, he noticed that a fungus had started to grow on one of the cultures of staphylococci, a bacteria that causes sore throats. Peculiarly, the fungus had created a bacteria-free circle around itself, killing the germ. Fleming deprecatingly called his breakthrough discovery 'mould juice,' before identifying it as a rare strain of *penicillium notatum*. Today Fleming's laboratory, the place where mankind got control over its future, is now a visitable time capsule Monday through Thursday, although making an appointment is recommended. A friendly onsite archivist will give you a fascinating crash course on the accident that would save untold numbers of lives, and leave you wondering, what other marvellous things are still waiting to be discovered? *(St Mary's Hospital, Praed Street, W2; +44 020 3312 6528; the laboratory museum is open Mon-Thurs 10am-1pm; Imperial.nhs.uk/about-us/who-we-are/fleming-museum)*

An Eccentric Explorer's (Free) Museum of Unexpected Treasures

When Victorian gentleman, philanthropist, world traveller and artefact collector Frederick John Horniman began to take over the family home with his collection of curios, his wife gave him an ultimatum: "either the collection goes or we do!" And so the **Horniman Museum & Gardens** was born, a vast and eclectic assortment of anthropological and natural curiosities.

When Horniman inherited his father's tea business, at one point the largest tea trading company in the world, he did the sensible thing and began to travel the globe. Horniman became the archetypal Victorian gentleman collector, journeying to Egypt, Sri Lanka, Burma, China, Japan and North America, scouring the world for specimens that took his fancy. Today, housed in a delightful Arts & Crafts inspired building in Forest Hill, a leafy residential area of South East London, the collection stands at around 350,000 artefacts, complete with a butterfly house, an aquarium and sunken gardens. Wander amidst the cabinets of curiosities, ogling at thousands of fossils, bones, musical instruments, and one of the greatest collections of taxidermy to be found in London, including a giant stuffed walrus. It even includes the peculiar Japanese 'Merman,' a 19th-century oddity that looks like a hybrid monkey-fish. The 16-acre gardens are home to foxes and prehistoric plant species, as well as a miniature golf course and Sunday farmers market. An astonishing continuation of one man's vision, Horniman certainly succeeded in his aim to "bring the world to Forest Hill". Let's just see if you can get through your visit without making any jokes about his name. *(100, London Road, Forest Hill, SE23; +44 208 699 1872; entrance to the museum and gardens are free, tickets are required for the Butterfly House, Aquarium and certain exhibits; gardens open Mon-Sat 7.15am-8.50pm, Sunsay & bank holidays from 8am-8.50pm; Horniman.ac.uk)*

Horniman Museum

What You Can Find Wandering Britain's Oldest Hospital

Relatively unknown but open to the public, St Bartholomew's Hospital is the kind of place you might trundle past on your daily commute without ever realising what's inside the 900-year-old institution. So let's fix that. The first thing that awaits is **St Bartholomew's Pathology Museum**, a three-floored cabinet of curiosity joined by a beautiful spiral staircase under a glass Victorian atrium, filled with jars of medical specimens, skeletal abnormalities and diseased organs preserved centuries ago. Equal parts macabre and majestic, come grimace at such oddities as the liver of a Victorian lady deformed by the prolonged tightening of her corsets, the fractured cervical vertebra of a prisoner executed by hanging, or the skull of John Bellingham, murderer of the only British Prime Minister to be assassinated. Part of the world-famous St Barts, the hospital where surgeon John Abernethy pioneered the idea of a medical school, where Sir James Paget founded scientific medical pathology, and where Sherlock Holmes first met Dr Watson, it was also once the epicentre of the 19th-century body snatching trade, where "resurrection men" would bring their stolen cadavers, freshly exhumed from Britain's graveyards, for medical students to study. The museum is still used by medical students today, which means getting inside as an outsider is going to involve a little extra effort, but not much. Visiting either involves emailing for an appointment or attending one of their unique and brilliantly imagined events: from talks on the history of bound feet or the poisons highlighted by Agatha Christie to practical classes in hands-on taxidermy. Evening events are typically filled with music and cocktails surrounded by 5,000 impeccably preserved medical specimens. Once you have an invite, finding the museum within the maze that is St Barts hospital is an adventure in itself, but we like a challenge don't we? *(3rd Floor, Robin Brook Centre, St Bartholomew's Hospital, West Smithfield, EC1A; see Qmul.ac.uk/pathologymuseum for further information)*

Don't leave the premises without taking a moment to enjoy the other architectural gems of the historic St Barts; its courtyards, fountains and gardens, but definitely do not miss the magnificent **Hogarth Stair**. Painted by 18th-century artist William Hogarth, his great big murals which wrap around the grand staircase make for a seriously cinematic finale to your visit. If you show up on Fridays at 2 pm at the Henry VIII Gate entrance (under the city's only public statue of the Tudor monarch), you can often find a very knowledgeable guide waiting to lead you up the staircase and into the dramatic Great Hall. You might also recognise the hospital's church, London's oldest surviving parish, which featured in films like *Four Weddings and a Funeral*, and *Shakespeare in Love*. Lastly, outside the Henry VIII gate, you can see the execution spot of the famed Scottish knight, William Wallace, or "Braveheart", as most of us know him. It's all very much worth a poke around this undervalued gem in the City. *(St. Bartholomew's Hospital, West Smithfield, EC1A, +44 203 465 5800; bartsheritage.org.uk)*

Eerie & Esoteric Meanderings

Into the twilight zone...

Vampire Hunting amongst Egyptian Tombs

Battling the ivy is a never-ending and full-time job for the groundskeepers at **Highgate Cemetery**. Despite their continued efforts to uncover forgotten graves swallowed by nature, it still looks like a lost world. Established in the 19th century to alleviate overcrowding in churchyards, Highgate is the most magnificent of London's "magnificent seven" cemeteries. Built like a fortress, the new private cemetery promised to keep out the problematic grave robbers of the 19th century behind its grand gates and fortified tombs. It became the most prestigious place to be seen as a Victorian, dead or alive; a fashionable and desirable way to spend an afternoon (or the afterlife). No expense was spared in erecting elaborate Egyptian-inspired tombs and Greek revival mausoleums for a family plot. Hidden in the heart of the West cemetery, an ethereal Egyptian gateway flanked by a pair of massive obelisks and overgrown with ivy, appears like a scene out of an Indiana Jones movie. Behind this gateway lies the alleys known as the Egyptian Avenue and the Circle of Lebanon, once perfectly pristine and manicured, dubbed the "Park Lake" and "Mayfair" of the Gothic necropolis. Exploring them today feels as if you've stumbled upon the ruins of some ancient civilization in North London.

Egyptian gateway in Highgate Cemetery

Terrace catacombs of Highgate Cemetery

From the start, Highgate cemetery had a flawed business model. Rights of burial were primarily sold in perpetuity rather than for a limited period, which means the dead in this cemetery own their plots forever. And of course, you can't ask the dead for maintenance fees. Generations later, families died out or moved away, leaving hundreds of graves abandoned, and in 1960, the London Cemetery Company was finally declared bankrupt. Shareholders left the keys to the local council, who closed its doors and let nature take over. The 1960s saw an intense period of vandalism for Highgate, reaching its peak when two so-called vampire hunters caused a media sensation, claiming a vampire was luring women to the cemetery. A mob descended upon the cemetery and staked and burned numerous corpses. The alleged vampire was never found. In the cemetery's catacombs, where tombs were ripped open by vandals, the exposed coffins can still be glimpsed in the darkness. In 1975, the Friends of Highgate Cemetery Trust came together to rescue the historic site from further ruin, later opening it back up to the public, but the West side of the cemetery is still a wild and precarious place for lone wanderers, open for guided visits only (booking

Terrace catacombs of Highgate Cemetery

Circle of Lebanon,
Highgate Cemetery

online is advised). Passionate volunteers lead small groups through the Grade I listed park throughout the week, highlighting the most curious graves and little-known stories behind them. The East cemetery, where Karl Marx is buried, is free to roam solo with your ticket, and well worth it too. If you're interested in volunteering for Highgate Cemetery; welcoming visitors, tending the landscape, helping out with events; you can get in touch via telephone – it's probably the best way to get an all-access backstage pass to one of London's most otherworldly places. *(Highgate Cemetery, Swain's Lane, London N6; +44 020 8347 2474 for volunteering; open everyday, see Highgatecemetery.org for details & tour bookings)*

Cemeteries might seem like a strange place for a stroll, but let's be honest – they're almost always more interesting than the local park. When inner city churchyards began overflowing with unhealthy graves, there was a Victorian movement to beautify cemeteries in outlying areas. Taking its cue from Paris' Père Lachaise cemetery, the creation of the "Magnificent Seven" gave Victorians a new social playground, as macabre as it might sound, turning cemeteries into popular destinations for a pleasant walk as much as places to pay one's respects. The slightly older sisters of Highgate are **Kensal Green Cemetery**, which opened in 1833, and **West Norwood Cemetery**; both blessed with lush grounds, winding paths and shady trees providing a pleasant backdrop for eye-catching Gothic Revival mausoleums, whose beautiful stone work wouldn't look out of place in a cathedral. But for all the beauty above ground, the cemeteries also have eerie secrets below. The old catacombs are no longer used, but these forgotten burial vaults; warrens of damp, brick corridors; are still stacked with ancient, lead-lined coffins. Kensal Green and West Norwood's catacombs still have their old *catafalques*, the hydraulic lifts used to bring the dead underground from the chapels above. Normally closed off to the public, the two cemeteries benefit from first-class volunteer groups that offer guided visits, occasionally into the catacombs themselves, as well as events, and historical walks above ground. *(Kensal Green: Harrow Road, Kensal Green, W10; open Mon-Fri 9am-5pm, Sun 10am-5pm; Kensalgreen.co.uk for information about upcoming tours. West Norwood: Norwood Road, West Norwood, SE27; Mon-Fri 8am-4pm, Sat-Sun 1am-4pm; Fownc.org)*

Hyde Park's Secret Cemetery for Victorian Fur Babies

In the continued pursuit and love of all things miniature, macabre, occult and overlooked, it may be of interest, particularly for an animal lover, to take a detour through London's royal park in search of the **Hyde Park Pet Cemetery**, a humble Victorian graveyard where hundreds of tiny sinking tombstones are carved with messages of varying degrees of melodrama and unabashed sincerity.

Hyde Park Pet Cemetery

The modest plot in London's Hyde Park was founded in 1881 by Mr Winbridge, a former gatekeeper. It was in the back garden of his three-bedroom gatehouse that the first pet was interred here – a Maltese terrier, remembered with a short but sweet headstone reading "Poor Cherry. Died April 28 1881." The story goes that Cherry and his owners had often strode through the park as a gleesome threesome, making friends with Mr Winbridge over the years. When Cherry went to dog heaven, it was only natural for a grave to be laid in the park behind the gatekeeper's lodge, which led to nearby residents requesting the same treatment. The majority of the plots are occupied by the pet dogs of well-to-do neighbours of the royal park, including the former Duke of Cambridge, though there lies the occasional cat, numerous birds and, notably, three small monkeys. For over twenty years, the gatekeeper would moonlight as the funeral celebrant, presiding over the burials of some 300 beloved pets. The last service to take place at this leafy site was in 1903. At its most beautiful, when the tiny marble headstones are surrounded by bluebells in Spring, visits to the cemetery can be arranged as part of a 'Hidden Stories of Hyde Park' walking tour every month for £12, or you can try to catch a glimpse of it when the leaves have fallen through the railings of Victoria Lodge. *(Victoria Lodge, Hyde Park, Bayswater Road, SW7; find dates and reserve your place at Shop.royalparks.org.uk/event)*

One Stop Shop for the Contemporary Occultist

Crystals? Check. Tarot Cards? You bet. Esoteric books? Take your pick from over 1500 titles. At **The Astrology Shop**, your occultist starter pack is ready and waiting. Since 1989, this mystical haunt in the West End has been providing witches-in-training, curious celebrities, and established astrologists with everything they need to grab this life, and the next, by the crystal balls. Shopkeeper Barry has over 20 years' experience in the cosmic fields; he's here to help you navigate the different energies and realms of the shop. Aside from esoteric accoutrements, staff specialise in on-the-spot personalised horoscope readings. A shy southern belle named Britney Spears came in for one at the beginning of her career. Just one warning: it's like heading to the supermarket when hungry; you'll pop in for some incense sticks and come out with a lunar calendar, burning sage and a lovestrology report. Whoops! Welcome to the Dark Side, it smells great. *(78 Neal St, Covent Garden, WC2H; +44 020 7813 3051; Open daily 11am-6pm; Londonastrology.com)*

A Night at the Conjurors Clubhouse

Magicians are by nature, a secretive lot. The explanations of their mind-bending tricks and mysterious sleights of hand are closely guarded, the secret art is only passed down from one generation of magicians to the next. And one of the highest echelons of this magic fraternity is **The Magic Circle**. Formed in 1905, admission to its inner sanctum is reserved only for the most skilled and handpicked magicians. Not for nothing is their motto, *Indocilis Privvata Loqui* – 'not apt to disclose secrets'. But it is possible to catch a glimpse into this hidden world by attending one of their brilliant close-up magic shows in the small theatre at their headquarters, which includes a look round the Magic Circle Museum. The air of mystery begins immediately: head down a small cobblestone street in Euston, to reach an anonymous blue door, marked only with a brass plaque featuring the signs of the zodiac. The museum and wall space is filled with striking vintage posters of past magicians, silk hat men, sawn-in-two ladies and a treasure trove of their most cherished props and tricks. Escape the everyday, and descend into the enchanting world of illusion. *(Centre for the Magic Arts, 12, Stephenson Way, Euston, NW1; +44 20 7387 2222; admittance is strictly by invitation or advance ticket for an event; Themagiccircle.co.uk)*

The Bookshop That Birthed Modern Witchcraft in Its Basement

Virginia Woolf isn't the only literary lady in Bloomsbury that you should know about. Meet Bali Breskin, she's a witch and a bookseller, both traits she got from her momma, Geraldine. Together they run the city's oldest independent occult bookshop. **The Atlantis Bookshop** was established in 1922 by magicians, for magicians, and remains that way today. Over the years, past and present big names in circles of sorcery have passed through the turquoise door with the broomstick outside, including Aleister Crowley and Gerald Gardner, otherwise known as the 'King of the Witches'. Gardner founded 'Wicca', the pagan roots of

The Atlantis Bookshop

witchcraft, and was a great friend of the Breskin family in his formative years. He would regularly use the basement of the shop to hold coven meetings in the 1950s. As well as selling a vast and eclectic range of new age books and magic ware, the shop remains an esoteric epicentre, for witches of the West End and beyond. The mother-daughter dream team offer tarot readings by appointment, afternoon teas with a medium, and hold modern day coven meetings just like back in the day, only this time they are passed off as conferences and spiritual book signings. *(49A Museum St, Bloomsbury, WC1A; +44 020 7405 2120; Mon-Sat 10.30am-6pm; Theatlantisbookshop.com)*

The Most Breathtakingly-Beautiful Disappointment

Freemasonry is famous for its principles of discretion, but these days, the largest worldwide secret society is ... well, less of a secret. True, the Freemason rituals and ceremonies are traditionally kept secret, but for the very simple reason that they don't want to ruin the novelty of the experience for its members, new and old. You and I on the other hand, can walk right up to

Freemason's Hall

its headquarters in central London and freely wander around the United Grand Lodge of England or get a tour of the place any day of the week. The **Freemason's Hall** in Holborn also happens to be one of London's greatest Art Deco treasures. Freemasons have been on the site since 1775, but their current British HQ opened in 1933 when the Art Deco movement happily collided with the esoteric aesthetics of Freemasonry, resulting in a match made in quirky design heaven. A terribly impressive and underrated London landmark, you'll walk around this gilded palace of marble open-mouthed at the detail on colourful mosaics and gilt thrones. The excellent guided or digital audio tours take in the magnificent Grand Temple, an active lodge, meeting place and museum, resembling a gentleman's cabinet of curiosities from the Age of Enlightenment, which is also free to visit on your own. Find Sir Winston's Churchill's Masonic apron, the golden throne used by the Prince of Wales and in the library (which is free to use) innumerable books on every facet of Freemasonry, all preserved under a rendering of the 'All-Seeing Eye'.

The largely-misunderstood fraternal organisation began for fairly practical reasons: back when medieval stonemasons went looking for work on some of the great projects around Europe, they needed something that would prove their level of skill and ability to prospective employers, without spending days sculpting a sample of finely carved stone. So they took with them handshakes and passwords, universally accepted amongst the guilds of skilled builders. It was during the Age of Enlightenment (and enlightened thinking) that the group began broadening its horizons; gathering to discuss issues of philosophy, religion, and life in organised settings, as well as accepting honorary elite members who weren't necessarily gifted with a chisel. They certainly rubbed the Catholic church the wrong way with their adjacent ceremonies and initiation rituals, further bolstering their numbers with the intrigue of mystery forbidden by the Pope himself. Today, it doesn't take more than a few seconds for Google to debunk the best conspiracies about the world's largest alleged secret society, but that doesn't mean there isn't wonder to be found lingering in the Freemason's Hall. Pick up some Freemason socks, cufflinks or even a felt square & compass Christmas tree ornament from the gift shop and do your part to keep the conspiracy alive. *(60 Great Queen Street, WC2B; +44 020 7395 9257; open to the public Mon-Sat 9.30am-5pm, free entry to museum, audio tours are £5, guided tours £12.50, private and bespoke tours available; Museumfreemasonry.org.uk / Ugle.org.uk/freemasons-hall)*

The Victorian Dinosaur Park that Survived National Ridicule

Long before dinosaurs were your Natural History Museum's biggest attraction, a collection of charmingly inaccurate sculptures still standing today in a South London park, were once considered the absolute authority on prehistoric

reptiles. As the study of dinosaurs progressed and the mistakes became more obvious, they turned into a national embarrassment for the scientific community and yet today they are classed as "Grade I Listed Buildings", holding the same status as St Paul's Cathedral and Buckingham Palace.

The **Crystal Palace Dinosaurs** were the first dinosaur sculptures in the world, unveiled in 1854, before the publication of Charles Darwin's *Origin of Species*, at a time when the theory of evolution was still a blasphemous joke. In a rush to name and claim a specimen before a rival did, many mistakes and inaccuracies were made by early palaeontologists. Scientists and academics resorted to underhand tactics to be recognised for their work in the 'game of bones'. But who can we thank for the construction of London's most fantastical beasts? That would be Richard Owen; a celebrity of Victorian society who coined the very word 'dinosaur' in 1842 and identified many new species.

Above: Crystal Palace Dinosaurs color print by G. Baxter, 1864
Right: Crystal Palace Dinosaurs today

On the eve of their reveal, a boozy eight-course dinner party attended by scientists, investors and other celebrities, was hosted inside a giant mould of the Iguanodon you can still see amongst the sculptures today. The finished herd of prehistoric monsters was unveiled to the public in 1854 and for nearly fifty years afterwards, over a million people per year went to see them.
As discoveries progressed in palaeontology and scientists gained greater understanding of how dinosaurs moved and lived, the sculptures began to look dated, almost abstract and very quickly became the source of ridicule. Tourism to the site dropped dramatically and the sculptures had already fallen into disrepair by the time a devastating fire broke out on the other side of the park and burnt Crystal Palace to the ground in 1936. Over time, the dinosaurs were obscured by foliage, and as the Second World War occupied the attention of London, the park without its crystal palace was largely neglected until 1952, when a restoration of both sculptures and the grounds was carried out. They now have a registered charity dedicated to their long-term preservation which proudly claims that the site now attracts as many visitors per year as it did when the dinosaurs first raised their heads – metaphorically, of course. The sculptures are located on the Dinosaur Park islands within the Lower Lakes in the south section of the park. While you're there, wander over to see what remains of the lost Crystal Palace. You can find the ruins of the water towers that once flanked the Victorian masterpiece on either side, the moss-covered balustrades which give you an idea of the palace's impressive length, and some ghostly stone sphinxes guarding the staircases that lead nowhere. *(Crystal Palace Park, Thicket Rd, Bromley SE19; nearest Park entrance to the dinosaurs: Penge Gate; open everyday from 7.30pm-5pm)*

Scientology's Secret London Townhouse

Come for the controversy, stay for the culture. Scientology is a treasure trove of conspiracy theories, however its London HQ is suspiciously standard. Unlike the imposing 'Big Blue' Church of Scientology in Hollywood, **Fitzroy House** sits in one of London's most beautiful regency squares. Sure, it looks lovely as 18th century townhouses do, but it doesn't stand out against its neighbours, which makes what goes on behind the heavy black door all the more intriguing. Step inside to find a shrine to L. Ron Hubbard, the sci-fi author and founder of Scientology, who made 37 Fitzroy Street his base for writing much of his best-known work. On the ground floor, he established the Hubbard Communication Centre, which was used to spread the word of his burgeoning religion around the world. To explore this 1950s time capsule full of photographs, Adler typewriters, manuscripts and reel-to-reel tape recorders, you'll need to book an appointment for a free guided tour. It's a good chance to ask some thinly-veiled questions over a complimentary cuppa. *(37 Fitzroy St, Fitzrovia, W1T; +44 020 7255 2422; By appointment everyday 11am-5pm; Fitzroyhouse.org)*

Hiding in Plain Sight

Nobody ever thinks to look there

Phone Home from the Original Red Phone Booth

They're bright red kryptonite for tourists who can rarely resist a photo opportunity with London's iconic phone booth, but few take their admiration further to find out just how they came about. The **first London telephone boxes**, or *kiosks*, were known as *K1*s. Introduced by the UK's Post Office in 1921, they were considered to be pretty disagreeable eyesores by the general public at the time, who voiced notable objections to their installation across the city. So in 1923, the public was called upon to create their own design for the kiosks, but still, they were unsatisfied with the results. A second competition was organised, this time narrowing the search down to submissions from established architects only, which gave us the telephone box as we know it today. The winning design was drawn up by Sir Giles Gilbert Scott who was inspired by a mausoleum he admired in St Pancras Old Church Gardens, designed by none other than Sir John Soane (pg 141) in memory of his departed wife Eliza. The grandiose 19th century stone tomb, which can still be visited today, has an unmistakable likeness to the modern phone booth's shape. The first *K2* boxes were installed in 1924, and one of them still stands, in working condition no less, just a few feet from Sir Giles Gilbert Scott's original timber prototype, both landmarked as the smallest listed buildings in London. So here's a challenge: go find these hidden relics of British telecommunication and phone home from London's first iconic red phone booth. You'll find the kiosks tucked away to the right of the entrance to the Royal Academy. The only question is: who will you call?
(K2 Prototype at the Royal Academy of Arts, Burlington House, Piccadilly, Mayfair, W1J; +44 207 300 8090; Royalacademy.org.uk)

George Basevi's painting of Sir John Soane's Tomb

© Sir John Soane's Museum

Above: 5 Broad Court, Covent Garden

Right: Red phone boxes at the entrance to the Royal Academy

In the market for an iconic Red Phone box?

Less than 10,000 red telephone kiosks remain on Britain's streets today and only about 30,000 calls a day are now made from them. Many of them were sadly melted down in the 1970s and 80s, but in recent years, British Telecom allowed local councils, organisations and charities to rescue and repurpose disused phone boxes into something useful for the community under their "adopt-a-kiosk" scheme. More than 5,000 have been adopted and converted into all kinds of novel uses, from tiny art galleries and miniature libraries (find one on Lewisham Way at the corner of Tyrwhitt Road, SE4) to take away cafés, smartphone repair stations and even the short-lived "world's smallest nightclub". Individual buyers have also been snapping them up from approved restorers. The telephone "cemetery" of rusting kiosks outside Tony Inglis' workshop, Unicorn Restorations, in Red Hill, Surrey, is an intriguing site (Unicornrestorations.com). Clients hail as far as Australia, where they might end up as a garden folly. In Florida and Dubai, you can find them in shopping malls. A fully restored booth will set you back around £8,500 but you can often find one in need of some TLC for around £2,000 on good old eBay.

Treasure Hunting on the Thames

One of the worst possible jobs you could have in Victorian London was to be a mudlark, but for many a modern-day pack-rat, it's considered to be the most rewarding way to spend a Sunday morning. Historically, mudlarks were impoverished youngsters between the ages of eight and fifteen or forgotten elders with strong bones who scavenged the muddy shores of the River Thames at low tide for anything of value to make a living. Throughout early modern times, the Thames was essentially a massive garbage dump where people and its industries threw away their unwanted items. Conditions back then were squalid; excrement and waste would come ashore from raw sewage, not to mention the odd corpse. Coal, rope, old iron and copper nails were some of the best finds they could hope for, which they sold to rag shops, earning about three pence per day (relatively speaking, £0.40 in modern currency). So why would anyone consider doing any of this for pleasure today? Treasure of course!

While the pitiful profession died out at the turn of the century, it became popular with hobbyists again some time in the 1970s. London Mudlark Facebook communities are hives of activity, where postings of fascinating finds will make your inner archaeologist drool: old clay pipes, coins, colourful pottery shards, thimbles, combs, and wig curlers are just a few of the items people have uncovered on the foreshore. Since the Thames' mud is anaerobic (without oxygen), most of these items are preserved as if they were tossed into its waters a few days ago. Best-selling author on the subject (*Mudlarking: Lost and Found on the River Thames*, 2019) and head of the 'London Mudlark'

Mudlarking on the Thames

Facebook page, Lara Maiklem, has been posting her loot online since 2012. Her finds include a complete medieval shoe, a 16th-century posy ring with the words "I live in hope" engraved on the inside, Roman gambling tokens and Tudor gold. Clay pipe stems (think of them as 17th-19th century cigarette butts) and pottery shards of the Delft, Georgian, Victorian and Tudor variety are the most commonly found objects on the foreshore. Want to have a go? Lara says "mudlarking is 10% practice, 10% knowing where to look, 10% knowing what to look for and 60% luck." To go it alone, you'll need a permit. The Port of London Authority expects all mudlarks to have one (Pla.co.uk/Environment/Thames-foreshore-permits) and to report anything over 300 years-old to the Museum of London.

If you don't have a permit, you can still experience mudlarking with the **Thames Explorer Trust** (*Thames-explorer.org.uk/guided-tours*) or the **Thames Discovery Programme** (*Thamesdiscovery.org/events-home*) with an expert guide, who will help you find and identify artefacts located on the surface of the foreshore. For mudlarks of all ages and experience, useful items to have on hand include rubber gloves, a good pair of rubber boots, plastic bags with a top closure, and some hand sanitizer for obvious reasons. Happy treasure hunting.

Mudlarking on the Thames

The Miniscule Mystery of a 19th-Century Banksy

London is home to some of the UK's grandest and most recognisable public monuments and statues, but tucked away on tiny Philpot Lane, not far from Tower Bridge, is **London's Smallest Statue.** A minuscule representation of two mice fighting over what looks like a piece of cheese, local lore has it that it commemorates two workmen from the 1860s who were working on the building and fought over a missing sandwich, falling to their deaths from the scaffolding, only for it to be reported that the fateful lunch was stolen by two mice. No records show just when and who put the nibbling mice there, but the whimsical little statue remains virtually unnoticed.

(23 Eastcheap, EC3M. The mice can be found on the left hand side of the building, currently a branch of Joe & the Juice, on the corner of Philpot Lane & Eastcheap)

Spot London's Wartime Stretcher Fences

World War II completely reshaped London's urban landscape in some very obvious ways, and some not so obvious ways. Walk along a quaint London street in Peckham or Brixton; take a stroll by Deptford, Oval, or East London, and you may catch a glimpse of some unusual residential fences that stand out from the rest. Here's why: in the early 1940s, there was an organised campaign to uproot London's wrought-iron railings to assist in the war effort (recycled iron is a key component in the steel industry), leaving entire blocks of residential housing without their ornamental Victorian ironwork, notably in working-class districts. When the London Blitz was finally over, authorities were left with an enormous stockpile of cast-iron stretcher beds; some 600,000 had been manufactured to carry injured people during the bomb raids, but now couldn't be melted down. Flip them sideways however, and you've got yourself a free fence! For London's fenceless homes and housing estates, the air raid stretchers fit the bill perfectly. Over time, many of the repurposed wartime relics were inevitably replaced with more traditional railings, but today there are groups like the Stretcher Railing Society who work to preserve the remaining stretcher fences, which they see as a unique and tangible artefact of wartime history. Less than a ten minute walk from The Watchhouse (your starting point for exploring Bermondsey, see pg 37), find one of the best examples of surviving stretcher fences surrounding the Tabard Garden Estate on the corner of Potier Street and Tabart Street. *(Nearest Tube station: Borough; SE1)*

Camouflaged in Bright British Green: The Roadside Cabby Cafés

Have you noticed the green wooden huts that look like garden sheds on the side of the road around town? Historically reserved for licensed taxi drivers only, they're a bit of an enigma to the average Londoner, like a secret clubhouse of sorts, hiding in plain sight. Originally established as a charity in the late 19th century to provide drivers of horse-drawn hansom cabs a convenient place to rest, seek shelter from the weather and purchase affordable hot meals and refreshments (strictly non-alcoholic, which was important for obvious reasons), many of these Victorian shelters are now historical landmarks. When the iconic motorised Hackney Black Cab replaced the horse-drawn cabs, the huts continued to provide the same service. However, their numbers have been dwindling for decades. Down to just thirteen cab shelters, dozens were damaged during the Blitz while others slowly fell into disuse. On the Chelsea Embankment however, a long-shuttered cab shelter recently found new life again as a charming al fresco café. Serving honest breakfasts, toasties, and Italian sarnies through the little green window, **Café Pier** is best visited when the tables and chairs are out during spring or summer with those unbeatable terrace views of Albert Bridge. One of London's prettiest bridges with some interesting little historic huts of its own, constructed in the 1870s, Albert

Stretcher Fences around the Tabard Garden Estate.

A metal stretcher during an ARP exercise in 1940

Bridge originally operated as a toll bridge for pedestrians and carriages. That quickly proved unpopular but the octagonal toll booths are still there; the only surviving bridge toll booths in London. *(Café Pier is located at Albert Bridge Gardens, 32 Cheyne Walk, Chelsea Embankment, SW3; find details of opening times on Instagram @cafepier_chelsea)*

A cab shelter which offers takeaway to the public on Kensington Road

The Chelsea Embankment cab shelter which opens as a café & terrace in the summer

The City's Mysterious Bridges to Nowhere

To catch a glimpse of a futuristic vision for London that was, simply look up, and spare a thought for the forsaken concrete pedway. Incomplete concrete fragments of a grand plan, the pedway was to be the key piece of an urban planner's utopia; a radical system of pedestrian footbridges designed to offer a safer and more enjoyable way to walk around the city, raised above the ever increasing numbers of traffic below. A "parallel pedestrian universe" as it was described, the thirty-mile network envisioned between Tower Hill and Fleet Street was very much a product of its time. Born out of the devastation of the Blitz in a forever-changed London, the pedways share all the concrete hallmarks of Brutalist architecture, but suffered varying states of completion between the 1950s and 80s. Life on the elevated walkways turned out to be rather less glamorous and practical than planners had envisioned. The network of pedestrian bridges that would supposedly connect the city, weaving through office buildings and over carriageways, was never properly mapped out from the start, which resulted in more of a pointless series of dimly-lit deviations

Pedways of the Barbican

than anything else. The costly and complicated network was shelved for good amidst a rising conservation movement. Ultimately, car-free bird's eye views weren't enough to get Londoners to climb up the pedway stairs. Creatures of habit, we overwhelmingly favoured the wind-sheltered streets over exposed walkways in the air.

Throughout the City of London, you'll find traces of 1960s and '70s pedway archaeology. At the northern end of London Bridge, spot an unmarked staircase to nowhere at the corner of an austere concrete building where Swan Lane meets Upper Thames Street. The top of the stairs once led to a footbridge, but now abruptly stops like a closed portal to an unknown dimension. Be on the lookout for what might appear to be unused or concealed balconies; they could very well be a dead piece of pedway leading to nowhere. You might also spot bricked-up or stunted abutments sticking out of buildings, originally intended to carry the weight of walkways that were never connected. The most complete surviving system of pedway architecture can be found in and around the Barbican, an enclave of elevated urban living (see pg 159). Start at the Barbican Tube station, take the stairs to the John Trundle High Walk and attempt to navigate your way to the Barbican centre using the pedways of a utopian London that almost was. Chris Bevan Lee's 2013 documentary short '*The Pedway: Elevating London*' is a brilliant and highly recommended look at the obsolete system (conveniently available on Youtube) .

A Victorian Time Capsule on the Thames, via Ancient Egypt

Egyptomania really began to kick off with the Napoleonic era, when ancient Egyptian treasures were uncovered, excavated from the desert, and brought to Europe, filling museums with looted Egyptian artefacts. The phenomenon gained further momentum in Britain during its occupation of Egypt from 1882 until 1956, when more British academics and archaeologists worked in Egypt, uncovering new treasures to bring back to London town. Sphinxes, scarabs and obelisks simply became part of the scenery, which might explain why most people now pass by **Cleopatra's Needle** on the Victoria Embankment without realising that it is by far London's oldest outdoor artefact. And not only that, but buried in the plinth of the Ancient Egyptian obelisk is a time capsule, sealed up when the sixty-nine foot monument was erected in 1878. The time capsule contains a peculiar assortment of Victorian items, including twelve photographs of the most beautiful society women of the day, a gentleman's lounge suit, boxes of hairpins and cigars, children's toys, a razor, a Bradshaw's railway guide, alongside a portrait of Queen Victoria, British coins and ten daily newspapers. Cleopatra's Needle itself has a twin, found in New York's Central Park, also with its own time capsule. The ancient monuments were carved around 1460 BC on the orders of Pharaoh Thutmose III, and were lost for centuries, until they were unearthed and displayed at the Cleopatra Caesarium in Alexandria, from where they get their name. The 3,500 year old obelisk was presented to Britain by the Sultan of Egypt, but it took 60 years to figure out how to move it, and by 1877, a perilous voyage saw the 224-ton monument finally installed by the banks of the Thames. Scour the riverbanks for other traces of England's Egyptomania such as sphinx heads and camels on the embankment's benches.
(Cleopatra's Needle, Victoria Embankment, WC2N, located between Embankment Station and Waterloo Bridge, and just steps away from Gordon's Wine Bar, see p57)

A thriving corner of Marxism in London

In 1933, with book burning at its height in Nazi Germany, left-wing activists sought to commemorate the 50th anniversary of the death of Karl Marx and protest what was happening in Germany the best way they knew how: by opening a library. Taking over a respectable looking Georgian house on Clerkenwell Green, the **Marx Memorial Library** soon became a vast archive of Marxist, communist and socialist books, pamphlets and artwork, all combined with a meeting place and study centre. The building chosen actually couldn't have been more perfect. In 1905, the exiled Vladimir Lenin published his *Iskra* newspaper here, which was smuggled back into Russia. A few doors down at the Crown Tavern, Lenin was thought to have met a young Joseph Stalin for drinks. The Marx Library harkens back to a time in the 1930s when Communism was still a lofty ideal, standing up to fascism and capitalism when Soviet intelligence was still cultivating the Cambridge Five spy ring, and Britons were volunteering

for the International Brigade to fight in the Spanish Civil War. But the library is far from an historic relic, and still holds lectures and exhibits, whilst making its unrivalled archive available for research; a place where, as Marx ended his Communist Manifesto, "Working Men of All Countries, Unite!"
(37a, Clerkenwell Green, EC1R; +44 020 7253 1485; Mon-Thurs 12pm-5pm, guided tours Tues and Thurs 11am; marx-memorial-library.org.uk)

Pelicans and Political Pawns in the Park

Bounded on all sides with British history, from Pall Mall to Horse Guards Parade and Buckingham Palace itself, it's hard to find a more prestigious public park than St James's. But one of its most charming draws is something a little more exotic: the **Pelicans of St James's**. The park has always been home to fanciful creatures; once upon a time you could even find camels, crocodiles and an elephant in the royal grounds. Returning from France, where he was impressed with the gardens of Versailles, Charles II decided to redesign the park, creating avenues of trees, a canal, and landscaped lawns. In 1664, the Russian ambassador added to the imported wildlife by gifting a pair of pelicans. The exotic birds soon became a mainstay of St James's Park, beginning the tradition of the gifting more pelicans from foreign ambassadors (three of the current birds recently came from the Prague Zoo). However, during the Cold War, the birds became the centre of a bizarre diplomatic incident. Legend has it that the US Ambassador, having noticed the Russian pelicans basking on the rocks by Duck Island Cottage, decided not to be outdone, and ordered some American pelicans as gifts. The US birds swiftly fell ill, and the Americans suspected the Soviets of foul play. This was the era of Cold War spy craft after all, with poison tipped umbrellas and lipstick pistols. With tensions on a knife edge, the poisoning of the rival pelicans was not so outlandish. The explanation was far more pedestrian: with ornithology perhaps not the ambassador's strong suit, the US contingent had imported saltwater pelicans from America, who ailed on the fresh water lake of St James's. Alas, the American pelicans were taken to a zoo,

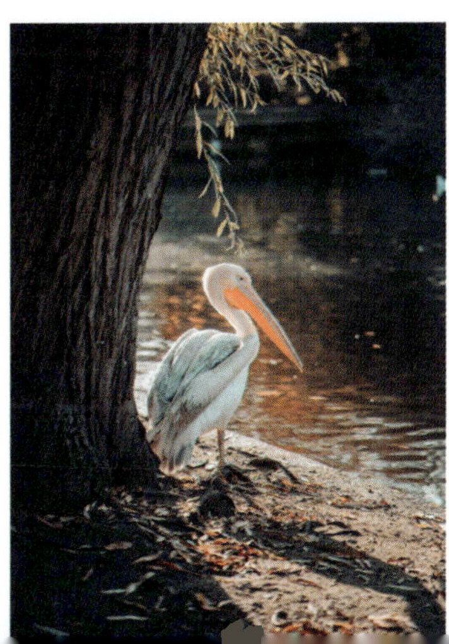

The Pelicans at St James's Park

presumably to the delight of the Soviet embassy. Spy stories aside, St James's park remains an oasis in the middle of the city, where you can rent a deck chair for £1.80 an hour and watch the half dozen pelicans being fed fresh fish everyday between 2.30pm and 3pm next to Duck Island. *(Duck Island Cottage, St, James's Park, 69 Horse Guards Rd, SW1A; the park is open 5am to midnight, all year round; Royalparks.org.uk)*

A Polly Pocket Police Station

Hiding in the shadow of one of London's tallest and most recognisable landmarks, is one of its smallest curiosities. In the Southeast corner of Trafalgar Square under the watchful gaze of Lord Nelson is a small granite turret, known as **London's Smallest Police Station.** If we're going to be nit-picky, it was mostly used as a surreptitious sentry box, with narrow, castle-like slits in the walls for officers to keep an eye out for law breakers. Trafalgar Square has long been a traditional meeting place for protestors, and following the General Strike Riots of 1926, the Met built the tiny observation post to keep tabs on the public. Less distinctive than the traditional blue call boxes, it was equipped with a direct phone line to Cannon Row police station, and a beacon light on top, which would flash a warning to nearby policemen whenever an officer picked up the telephone. The outpost has fallen out of use with the advent of wireless radios; look through the windows today and you're more likely to find mops and other cleaning supplies than a Bobby sheltering from the cold. Outside, you'll find a noticeboard with a quaint list of offences you shan't commit in Trafalgar Square: no boating in the fountains and feeding the ubiquitous pigeons.Check it out on your way to a jazz session at the Café in the Crypt (pg 316), another secret hiding in plain sight at London's busiest tourist hub. *(The pillar box is in the south east corner of Trafalgar Square, Charing Cross, WC2N)*

Britain's Smallest Police station

Here Be Dragons!

There are dragons guarding the City of London, if you just know where to look. With a slightly sinister appearance, painted silver with red tongues and wings, and clutching a St George's shield in their talons, these are the old **Dragon Boundary Markers**, that can be found at the entrances to the City. This is the ancient City of London, often called the Square Mile, or simply The City, that was originally founded by the Romans, and hasn't changed much in size since the Middle Ages. It was around then, that the City adopted the crest featuring a shield supported by two *rampant dragons argent.* The fierce-looking silver dragons stand on plinths and all face outwards, perhaps warning visitors of the dangers lurking within. The most spectacular can be found at Temple Bar, marking the boundary of the Cities of Westminster and London, but most of the other dragons were copied from the two you can find guarding Victoria Embankment, by Temple Place. Standing proud by the banks of the Thames, they originally adorned the entrance of the old Coal Exchange until it was torn down. The silver dragons were saved, copied and installed by the old entrances to the City such as London Bridge, Blackfriars, Aldgate and Farringdon. The old City of London remains an historic enclave, still the smallest county in the UK, and a creative way to explore its secrets is by keeping an eye out for the dragons who guard it.

Dragons of London

The Hidden Street Beneath Your Feet

The small traffic island on Charing Cross Road outside the Coach and Horses Pub looks common enough, until you crouch down and look through the grating. There you'll find something unexpected: two old street signs for **Little Compton Street**. They are all that remain of a forgotten street long since destroyed. Little Compton Street was one of the many tiny streets, lanes, alleyways and courtyards that once wove through the slums of London, but when Charing Cross Road was built in 1877 as a modern artery connecting Trafalgar Square and Tottenham Court Road, Little Compton Street was taken off the city's maps. Not much is known about the tiny street, except that No. 5 used to be the Hibernia Pub, where Rimbaud and Verlaine would often meet during their brief stay in London. How the two street signs came to survive under the traffic island is a mystery; whether they were simply buried over, or were perhaps saved and used as signposts for the utility tunnels, is unknown, but they remain a beguiling glimpse into old London history, hidden away beneath one of its busiest streets.
(The traffic island is in the middle of Charing Cross Road, opposite the Coach and Horses pub on Old Compton Street)

Turn a London stroll into a treasure hunt

From the quiet room where Sylvia Plath wrote *The Bell Jar* to the 1960s flat where Jimi Hendrix wrote some of his most famous guitar riffs, London's iconic Blue Plaques celebrate hundreds of remarkable people who have made the city their home. In fact, Hendrix considered number 23 Brook Street his first real home of his own, and it remains the musician's only officially recognised residence in the world (the apartment has since been recreated just as he would have left it, see page 113). Keeping a look out for the blue plaques is an enlightening and free way to discover the rich history of London as an open-air museum of architecture, revealing where notable people were born, once lived or might have achieved something remarkable. A large part of the charm of the distinctive plaques is the understated way they often modestly sum up a historic figure's life achievements; such as Van Gogh the 'painter', who visited London as a young man and lived at 87 Hackford Road in South Lambeth, or Luke Howard the 'Namer of Clouds', who lived at 7 Bruce Grove and whose classifications of nimbus, cirrus and the like, meteorologists still use today. And who knew that Vladimir Ilyich Lenin, the founder of the USSR, once lived in Tavistock Square, or that Ho Chi Minh once worked at the Carlton Hotel, Haymarket? The English Heritage website is an excellent resource for finding the blue plaques, and their free smartphone app suggests self-guided tours, such as a literary walk through Kensington, stopping by the former homes of James Joyce, T.S. Eliot, Agatha Christie and Siegfried Sassoon. *(English-heritage.org.uk/visit/blue-plaques)*

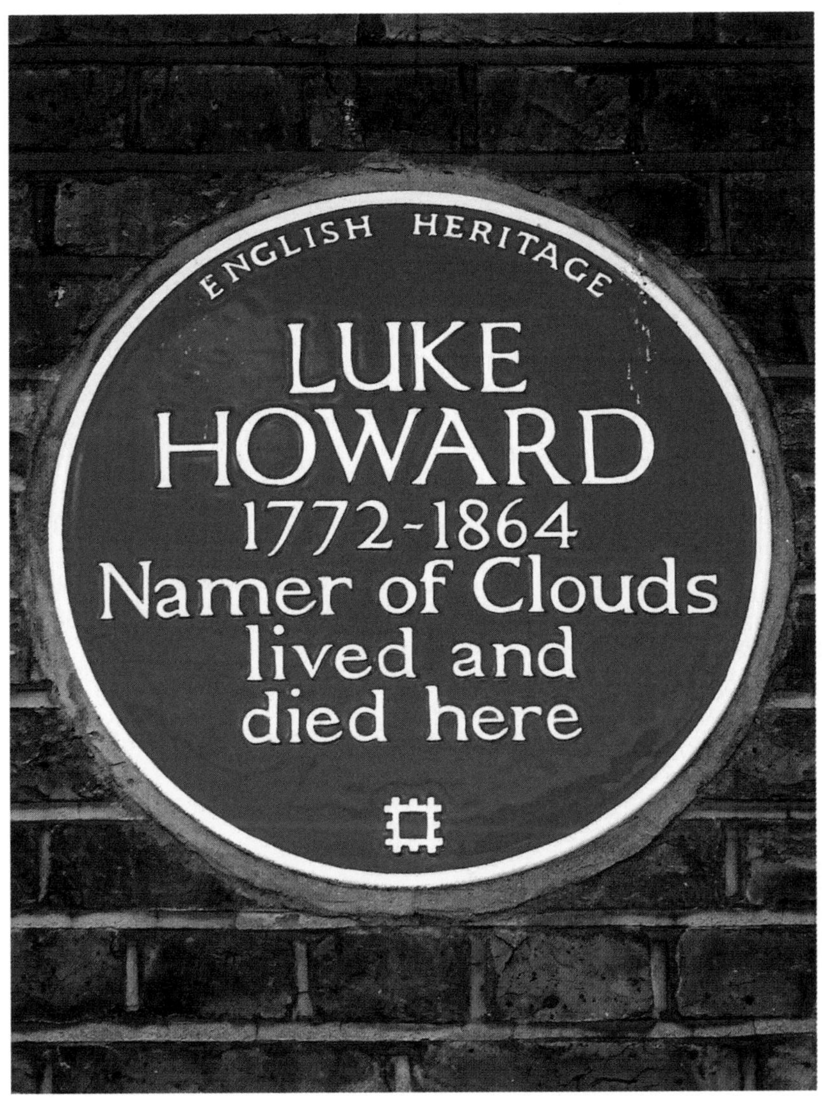

Luke Howard blue plaque on Bruce Grove

Mayfield Lavender Farm

09
The Lazy Escapist

Some of London's most beautiful parks and greenspaces were originally carved out by the elite trying to escape the plague or some other medieval pestilence. Pandemics have a habit of radically altering our perception of urban life, while reshaping our cities in the process. New models of healthy living, bucolic environments and quality of life become paramount. There's no arguing that the British do quaint country life better than anyone, but when you're in the mood for a trip out of town, first check what's on the city's doorstep. You won't believe how far your Oyster card will take you. London as we know it today, is a collection of medieval villages that simply kept expanding and populating the fields between them. Stop and smell the roses, and you'll realise this city is constantly reminding us of its quaint countryside past every chance it gets.

London Village Life

Pretend it's not a city

A Day Well Spent Where the World Begins and Ends

Greenwich is so charming that it's worth finding any excuse to make your way downriver and stay awhile. But if one place can claim to be the beginning and end of the Earth, it is a park in Greenwich. There you'll find an octagonal building atop a hill, and within its courtyard, a stainless steel strip set into the cobblestones, known the world over as the Prime Meridian. This marks an imaginary line running from the North to the South Poles at 0' longitude, dividing the world into its Eastern and Western Hemispheres. The Prime Meridian is part of the **Royal Observatory Greenwich**, established in 1675, setting the standard for astronomical excellence. Earning its reputation as the "centre of time and space", the Royal Observatory has long been at the forefront of accurate astronomy, from pioneering the naval navigation that would see the Royal Navy rule the waves, to establishing Greenwich Mean Time, the system by which most of the world sets their clocks. Winding spiral staircases lead visitors from one gallery housing ancient clocks, to a dome lined with giant old telescopes; literally a gateway to the stars. One Astronomer Royal, James Bradley, charted at least 60,000 stars from here between 1750 and 1762, observations that were so accurate they were still being used by modern

Greenwich Observatory

astronomers well into the 20th century. One can imagine him here on a clear night with the shutters open, observing a celestial feast. And don't forget the Planetarium next door. The observatory also offers various astronomy courses onsite for beginner, intermediate and advanced levels, from exploring the basics of how to use telescopes and identifying targets to a closer examination of stars and galaxy formations. Look out for the nifty green laser on the old Royal Observatory shining northwards in the direction of the Pole. *(Blackheath Ave, SE10; +44 20 8312 6608; open everyday 10am-5pm; rmg.co.uk/whats-on/astronomy-courses-royal-observatory)*

Turpin Lane, Greenwich

The Greenwich Royal Observatory might be your first priority, but if you're off to a reasonably early start, you'll have some time to browse the picturesque little shops at **Greenwich Market** on Turpin Lane, and even stop in at the fabulous little **Fan Museum** (see pg 145), all within a few minutes walk of each other. But of course it would be rude not to pay a visit to the **Queen's House**. The Queen in question is James I's wife, Anne of Denmark, for whom this classical masterpiece was built in the 17th century. Not just any royal abode, this was the first classical building in Britain, designed by England's first great architect, Inigo Jones, who's credited with introducing architecture from the Italian Renaissance and Classical Rome to the British landscape. It's dubiously claimed that the King commissioned the home as an apology for swearing at his wife when she accidentally shot his favourite dog during a hunt. The house comes complete with the grandest of gestures, Britain's first self-supporting or "floating" spiral staircase, fondly known as the Tulip Stairs. A sight to behold, look down and you'll see the geometric tiles softened by centuries of footsteps, look up and you'll see the twirling white staircase with its floral blue rails encircling the ceiling's glass roof where the sunlight beams through. Visitors were once afraid to use the novel staircase because they couldn't believe it wouldn't collapse. The house museum is totally free to wander around and imagine the lives of its inhabitants over the many years while admiring masters such as Hogarth, Gainsborough and Turner, but also sculpture, furniture, clocks, porcelain, and gold crockery. It makes an easy double date with the **Maritime Museum** next door and a visit aboard the **Cutty Sark**, a famous and beautifully

Queen's House

preserved 19th century British clipper ship. Speaking of maritime history, with its rich naval heritage, making your way to Greenwich by boat seems somehow fitting. One of the most pleasant ways to travel to Greenwich is by riverboat down the Thames. Thames Clippers' catamarans operated by Uber Boat (*Thamesclippers.com*) depart every 20 minutes throughout the day and take just under half an hour from the London Eye Pier to reach Greenwich Pier, a short walking distance to the Queen's House. *(Romney Rd, Greenwich, SE10; open every day 10am to 5pm; Rmg.co.uk/queens-house)*

When it's time for a well deserved riverside supper at the **Trafalgar Tavern**, on colder days, sit by the large bay windows overlooking the Thames, lapping right up to the tavern wall, while enjoying a traditional Greenwich Whitebait dinner. Opened in 1837, and named for the famous naval battle thirty-two years before, the Trafalgar is elegantly decorated with images of Admiral Lord Nelson, whose statue dominates the beer garden overlooking the Thames. It's hardly the worst place to enjoy a well-deserved pint with the sunset after a day spent discovering Greenwich, before sailing back to Central London. *(Park Row, Greenwich, SE10; +44 020 3887 9886; trafalgartavern.co.uk).*
One last thing to tempt you before catching a boat home: how about some live music at Oliver's Jazz Bar? (see pg 114).

Like life in a lively little market town

Ruddy-cheeked greengrocers, cheesemongers and bakers setting up gazebos in a South London car park on a Saturday morning is the sign of a good day. Like elves in Santa's grotto on Christmas Eve, while you sleep in, early bird traders and food trucks transform a college car park into a fabulous rural farmers market with a city setup; in short, the ultimate weekend feeding station. The shy younger sister of Borough Market (see p201), **Brockley Market** is much smaller, lesser-known and that little bit edgier. Come for breakfast, stay for lunch with plenty of places to perch and people-watch while sampling artisan pies, craft beer and all the market must-eats. Because it's out of the city centre, traders and locals know each other on a first-name basis; just eavesdropping will make you feel at the centre of the community and in on all the local gossip and recipe swapping. *(Lewisham College Carpark, Brockley SE4; Sat 10am-2pm; Brockleymarket.com)*

Farming in East London

The perfect Sunday morning in Hackney starts early at **Columbia Road Flower Market**, East London's floral extravaganza (see page 256) before wandering over to meet some farmyard friends. Animals in residence at the **Hackney City Farm** include pigs, sheep, goats, chickens and a horse. Young volunteers are welcome to help out with feedings and animal care. There's a lovely onsite café too and they have drop-in pottery classes for adults and children (no booking necessary) as well as some other workshops on offer. Bear in mind you are never far from urban farms in London – there are no less than twelve of them – offering family-friendly barnyard activities. *(1a Goldsmiths Row, London E2; +44 20 7729 6381; Tues to Sun, 10am–4 pm; Hackneycityfarm.co.uk)*

Lean more into London village life in Hampstead, pg 30 and Vauxhall's Bonnington Square, pg 270.

Hackney City Farm

I have this thing for Greenhouses

Botanical Brunching with the Girlies

When a busy girl gang needs to hold a long overdue catch-up summit, make it somewhere memorable and meaningful – like a greenhouse. Queens and princesses were instructed in botanical illustration, and in the 18th century, plant collecting became a highly desirable pastime, encouraged by fashionable ladies' periodicals. The greenhouse even became her beauty boudoir where she might pick out accessories for a growing fad in hair styles that incorporated anything from fruits, shells and artificial birds into her coiffure. A new stereotype of the sexually-liberated bad girl botanist was born in the turbulent revolutionary climate of the 1790s and an innocent pastime for genteel ladies was suddenly brewing an indulgent and "dangerous" feminist movement, making a patriarchal society very uncomfortable. Religious leaders warned that botanising girls who showed interest in exploring the sexual parts of the flower, were "indulging in acts of wanton titillation" – (just the sort of thing to fuel any female libertine's fire). The study of botany came to be considered so obscene that books on the subject were censored for women; branded unsuitable for her delicate sensibilities. Greenhouses: an enlightened woman's secret haven of discovery, expression and temptation – who knew?!

And with that in mind, the dining room at the back of **Bourne & Hollingsworth Buildings** is a botanical retreat; a veritable greenhouse with tropically-upholstered armchairs and a British weekend brunch menu that includes bottomless bellinis. You can also privatise the greenhouse for dinner parties and head downstairs after supper to the secret cocktail club room beneath the Clerkenwell clubhouse, appropriately named **Below & Hidden**. Decked out in bohemian kilims, you'll feel like you're partying in someone's very bohemian den of iniquity, with a DJ who'll keep you dancing past midnight. *(42 Northampton Rd, Clerkenwell, London EC1R; +44 20 3174 1156; open Wed & Thurs 4pm-12am, Fri 4pm-1am, Sat 10am-1am, Sun 10am-6pm; Bandhbuildings.com)*

Across town in Soho, an instantly-impressive greenspace to meet a friend for a long lunch is the **NoMad London** hotel's Edwardian greenhouse-inspired restaurant. Flooded with natural light in what was once the rather grim environs of Bow Street Magistrates' Court, Oscar Wilde, many an Edwardian suffragette, notorious London gangsters the Kray Twins, and even designer (and political activist) Vivienne Westwood were all booked here at some point in its 125-year history. Stay for pork rillettes served in a glass jar and order a tomato martini – surprisingly delicious, it looks far less clumsy than it sounds. *(28 Bow St, Soho, WC2E; +44 20 3906 1600; open everyday; Thenomadhotel.com/london/dining)*

Bourne & Hollingsworth Buildings

Equally ideal for giggling with a gossipy gal pal, glide up the white spiral staircase of **Mr Fogg's House of Botanicals** to the sumptuous soft furnishings of a cosy 'treehouse' in the city. Embrace the adventure and escapism of this verdant Victorian sunroom belonging to the eccentric (and imaginary) explorer Phileas Fogg, who's been busy collecting enviable souvenirs while travelling 'around the world in 80 days'. His suitcase of exotic ornaments and antiquarian artwork explodes at this dandy drinking spot spread over two foliage-filled floors in Fitzrovia. Cocktails channel the Victorian tradition of floriography; a secret language associated with flower-giving or arranging to express emotions that could, or perhaps should, not be spoken. Tipples of your choice are served in quaint teacups and nibbles are brought out in birdcages. *(48 Newman St, Fitzrovia, W1T; +44 020 7590 5256; Wed-Thurs 5pm-1am, Fri-Sat 3pm-1am, Sun 12pm-1am; Mr-foggs.com/house-of-botanicals)*

Flower Power by the Railway Tracks

In the shadows of Battersea Power Station (p103) lies a slither of green paradise, pumping out plants, pots, compost and cacti to London's green-fingered gardeners. Skinny but sprawling, a veritable hidden meadow squeezed in alongside railway tracks is a garden path worth being led up. A secret jungle within the concrete surroundings, **Battersea Flower Station** isn't your average garden centre. Grab some Coca Cola scented Geraniums for your window box (no kidding, they actually smell of Cola), or ask the team of gardeners for other hand-potted suggestions – they are some of the nicest people in London, ready to offer all their plant wisdom for free. Whether you're a certified botanist or just long overdue a 'stop and smell the roses' moment, this magical secret garden and its greenhouses await. *(320 Battersea Park Rd, Battersea, SW11; +44 020 7978 4253; Wed-Thurs 10am-5.30pm Fri-Sat 10am-6pm & Sun 11am-5pm; Batterseaflowerstation.co.uk)*

A Masterclass in Fairytale Greenhouse Living

The Anglo-Italian Boglione family arrived in the village-like borough of Richmond in the 1990s and moved into an elegant Queen Anne home overlooking a local plant nursery. When it came up for sale years later, the matriarch of the family jumped at the chance to create her own whimsical restaurant inside the greenhouses, calling it **Petersham Nurseries**. With the help of the Boglione daughters, they filled the nurseries with handpicked *objets trouvés,* unusual houseplants and kitchen & garden treasures – all shoppable before or after (or why not during) a lazy lunch under the canopy of bougainvillaea, vines and fragrant jasmine. A family and women-led business to this day, Petersham is effortlessly eccentric and enchanting in a way that can't be replicated. There is no flooring, for one – you'll be dining on *hoggin* (a mix of clay, gravel and sand), which feels unexpectedly warm and inviting. The rustic

English garden aesthetic is juxtaposed with antiques, art, textiles and furniture seemingly plucked from a Florentine farmhouse or summer pavilion in Jaipur, creating a romantic and endlessly inspiring escape for visitors from central London. Richmond, a charming 18th-century country town along the Thames at the end of the Tube (District line), is certainly worth a day to explore (seek out the artists of Paved Court or the Isabella Plantation on pg 390). But Petersham Nurseries is a destination unto itself, playing host to a range of weekly events including pasta masterclasses, workshops on creating your own bee nursery, tablescaping, festive wreath-making and more. For afternoon tea or a quick and light lunch, take a seat in the teahouse, but for a sit-down meal by candlelight, book a table in the main restaurant which serves seasonal dishes inspired by the garden that started it all. *(Church Lane, Off Petersham Rd, Richmond, TW10; see website for events and opening hours, Petershamnurseries.com)*

Petersham Nurseries

The Forgotten Power of the Parlour Palm (and a good Martini)

Once upon a time, social status had a lot to do with a common houseplant. The parlour palm, which referred to any number of varieties of palms, ferns, and other hardy perennials that were native to South America, Asia, and Africa, was one of the most significant status features in Victorian decor. From the late 1850s, its very presence became a symbol of wealth and intelligence in England, where a passion for raising exotic plants, particularly ferns and orchids practically became the national sport. Plants not only became part of the decor, they were part of the entertainment. Botany was a popular subject to be debated amongst high society and those who knew most about it were the toast of the room. So naturally, the parlour palm – or even better, a small rainforest of parlour palms – became the ultimate flex of the Victorian Age.

The Winter Garden, a cocktail bar hidden above London's oldest restaurant, **Rules**, is a stunning example of exotic indoor plant and parlour palm use from turn-of-the-century England. In what used to be the private dining room of King Edward VII (where he courted his mistress Lillie Langtry under the glass atrium), enjoy a perfectly-made Martini on a wicker chair amidst a potted parade of parlour palms. An exquisite cocktail menu you'd expect to find in a swish Manhattan hotel bar is overseen by Brian Silva, once of the Boston Colonnade Hotel, who offers cocktail masterclasses on Wednesday and Thursday afternoons (for groups of up to 4 people, £95 pp).

If drinks turn into dinner, culinary institutions don't come more respectable than Rules. The Covent Garden restaurant has been owned by just three families since it opened in 1798. Sumptuous clubby decor, exemplary old-world service, and a menu of 'classic game cookery,' puddings and pies, drawn mostly from the restaurant's private estate in the High Pennines, give Rules its traditional air. It seems not much has changed since the days when Charles Dickens through to Graham Greene once dined here.
(35, Maiden Lane, Covent Garden, WC2E; +44 020 7836 5314; Sun-Wed 12pm-10.45pm, Fri-Sat 12pm-11:45am; book dinner or cocktail classes via rules.co.uk)

Find more greenhouse greatness at the Barbican (see pg 161) and Kew Gardens (pg 299).

Fake a Vacation

London, is that really you?

Provence for a day

If you can't make it to the south of France in the summer, unbeknownst to most Londoners, you can still frolic amongst lavender fields, south of the city. In 2002, an old Victorian lavender field became **Mayfield Lavender Farm**, where you can now freely roam the endless rows of purple blooms with the company of fluttering butterflies and the hum of busy honeybees. Did you know the scent of lavender is so strong that it can last over 3,000 years? Remarkably, a sprig of lavender discovered in the sealed tomb of Tutankhamen still retained its distinctive fragrance. You can stock up on freshly cut lavender from the shop, but do also take a break at the café and sip al fresco lavender lemonade as the farm's bright red tractor named Looby Loo rolls by in the fields. Kids will *love* it. The farm is also home to its own idyllic theatre; a 250-seat open air auditorium that hosts classic plays and musicals with the most magical purple-hued backdrop. Open from June to August, but it's best to keep an eye on their Instagram or Facebook pages to check when the fields are in full bloom. *(1 Carshalton Rd, Banstead, SM7; +44 750 387 7707; £4 entry for adults and under 16s go free; public transport directions available via the website; Mayfieldlavender.com)*

Mayfield Lavender Farm

Where to Make a Splash in the City

Pond, pool or puddle, the urge to submerge yourself in the nearest body of water to cool off, may arise on a sticky London summer's day. Lidos; outdoor public swimming pools (derived from the Italian word "lido," which itself means "shore" or "beach"); became popular in the UK during the early 20th century as part of a movement towards improving public health and increasing leisure time among the urban population. However, London's lidos have a choppy history. Once a symbol of a golden new age of leisure in the 1930s, these outdoor swimming pools fell into decline in the latter half of the 20th century as foreign travel became cheaper and easier. Many of London's lovely lidos disappeared forever in favour of beach holidays abroad. In recent times, thanks to community campaigns, the tide is turning. More are reconnecting with the joys of urban swimming and there's a renewed appreciation for the elegant Art Deco designs that home these sparkling city waters.

Sitting hidden behind a row of willow trees in a South London park is the largest freshwater pool in the UK. Despite its enormous size, it's a sanctuary of seclusion for swimmers in the know. Surrounded by green space and tweeting birds, once you are through the gate, the city and its stresses suddenly disappear. The first toe was dipped into **Tooting Bec Lido** in 1906, making it one of the oldest lidos in Europe. It's a prime place to get in some serious lengths or sunbathe on a poolside lounger while marvelling at the perfectly Pantone changing cubicles. The lido is open to the public from May to September; the South London Swimming Club has exclusive use in the winter months. *(Tooting Bec Rd, Tooting Bec, SW16; +44 020 8835 0768; Placesleisure.org/tooting-bec-lido)*

Tooting Bec Lido

Commissioned in 1938, the heyday of Art Deco, **Parliament Hill Lido** is known for its splashing good looks. Saved from the wrecking ball on many occasions, North London natives are proud of their local heritage and protective of their privilege to swim in style 365 days a year. The modernist buildings surrounding the pool are satisfyingly symmetrical with narrow windows, elegant brick elevations and curved walls. Refurbishment has been sensitive, to enhance, not erode its original beauty. In 2005, a first-of-its-kind silver liner was added to the poolside which makes the water shimmer ethereally against a blue sky. The pool is not heated so it can get particularly chilly in the winter but you can dive into the onsite sauna followed by a hot chocolate in the café to warm up. *(Parliament Hill Fields, Gospel Oak, NW5; +44 020 7485 5757; Parliamenthilllido.org)*

Hidden in the hills of leafy Hampstead are a series of 30 ponds which were dug as reservoirs in the 17th and 18th centuries. Today, three of these **Hampstead Heath Ponds** have been specially designated for open water swimming – one for men, another for women and also a co-ed pool. For just £4, hardened pond dippers can float in the silky serene green water and front crawl alongside fuzzy ducklings. It's all rather poetic, not to mention breathtakingly cold too. You have been warned. *(Hampstead Heath, Hampstead, NW3; +44 020 7485 5757; Cityoflondon.gov.uk/swimming-at-hampstead-heath)*

Finally, fancy yourself as a bit of a pro? If you're more into perfecting your backstroke than floating about aimlessly, try East London's **Royal Docks**. Visitors are welcome if they stay in their lane, but experienced water waders really come into their own here. Once a hub for commercial shipping in the early 20th century, this gigantic open space now offers competitive triathlon training events, attended by Olympians. There's no getting lost amongst the reeds and losing track of time, swimmers are safety tagged which also logs and times distances. The water is tested regularly, wetsuits are available for hire and qualified coaches are onsite to help you beat your personal best. As with all of these swimming spots, opening times and prices change with the seasons so check ahead online first. *(Dock Rd, Royal Docks London, E16; Loveopenwater.co.uk/swimming-london-royal-docks)*

Holland Park's Kyoto Garden

Secrets in the Park

London is a city of parks. In fact, London is technically considered to be the world's largest urban forest by the United Nations. Yes, an actual forest. According to the UN's definition, a forest is any land that's at least 20 percent covered by trees. London has well over 8 million trees that cover 21 percent of the capital, not to mention over 40 percent of the city's public land is made up of green space. And of course, every forest (and London park) has its secrets. Our first stop: Japan, by way of central London. If someone were to show you a photograph of the **Kyoto Garden** without context, you might place it on some sacred Japanese mountain before identifying it as the secret garden hiding away behind some bushes in Kensington's Holland Park. Easily missed if you don't know about it, this unexpected Shangri-La was created in 1992 as an honourable gift from the Japanese government. And in traditional Japanese garden style, each detail is most carefully considered, the bonsai meticulously styled. Let your thoughts drift to the soothing sounds of the waterfall, tip toe on the stepping stones over the koi carp fish gliding through the pond and wait for the peacocks to emerge gracefully from beneath the maple tree. Zen indeed.

The bombed library at Cope Castle (1940). Now Holland House in Holland Park

While discovering the rest of Holland Park, bear in mind it was once a private estate in disrepair with an incredible Jacobean mansion in the middle, known as Cope Castle. Badly damaged during a German firebombing in 1940, only part of the east wing and the ground floor survived the war. The castle lay in ruins for many years before it was cleaned up, designated a listed monument and renamed Holland House. The former summer ballroom, where Lord Byron met his lover, Lady Caroline Lamb, is now an elegant, long-standing Italian restaurant in the park called **The Belvedere** *(Belvedererestaurant.co.uk).* In summertime, the Holland Park Theatre hosts its popular opera evenings *(Operahollandpark.com)* with the old mansion serving as a dramatic backdrop for the open-air stage. *(Holland park, Holland Park Ave, Kensington, W11; open everyday from 7.30am until a half an hour before dusk)*

Now, over to South London to explore the remains of a fashionable 18th century spa escape. There used to be a natural spring bubbling away in the midst of Streatham Common, and a spa house was built in the 18th century where people would come and stay to take the healing waters. The manor house has since been demolished, but **The Rookery Gardens** remained, and was re-landscaped and opened to the public in 1913. Today, under the loving care of the Friends of Streatham Common charity, it's an enchanting formal garden made up of walkways, rock gardens, cedar trees, ornamental ponds and fountains. Whether the waters still possess healing powers or not, the Rookery provides a welcome, soothing balm to city life. Make sure to drop by the charming Rookery Café, also found on the Common. *(Streatham Common, Covington Way, SW16; free entry, open 7.30am–fifteen minutes before sunset; sccoop.org.uk for details about the Friends of Streatham Common Co-op)*

Finally, to **Richmond Park**, where during a blight of the plague, King Charles I set up residence, becoming so taken with the wide open grasslands and lush forests that he introduced hundreds of wild deer to hunt (as one does). One of the grandest of the eight Royal Parks, Richmond's 2,500 acres range from wild open grasslands, where herds of royal deer still roam, to verdant forests filled with ancient trees. But the jewel of Richmond Park is actually the one area created in the early 19th century to keep the deer *out* and grow trees for timber. The enclosed and hidden floral paradise of **Isabella Plantation** wasn't actually opened up to the public until 1953. Wander in a haze amidst the giant clouds of azaleas, rhododendrons and camellias that surround manmade ponds, waterfalls and streams. It's most spectacular in late April and early May. Take a picnic, it will be an unforgettable one.

These little sanctuaries might not get as much hype as the Hyde Parks and Primrose Hills of this city, but they can remain our secret escapes. *(Richmond Park, Kingston-upon-Thames, TW10; Isabella Plantation open 7.30am–5.15pm, Royalparks.org.uk/parks/richmond-park for details)*

Isabella Plantation

The Tiny Island on the Thames that Hosted The Rolling Stones, David Bowie, and the UK's Largest Hippie Commune

Take a walk along the towpath where the Thames curves around Richmond village, past the gently bobbing boats moored at Twickenham, until you see a footbridge leading to an island in the middle of the river. That's **Eel Pie Island**, aka "Rock 'n' Roll Island"; the birthplace of a youth movement where music history was made. Its tiny expanse is home to just 120 residents, but don't be fooled by its size – this little island has a wild story. The island got its unusual name from the traditional eel pies that were once sold by its residents to passing river traders, and although the local delicacy died out, the name remained. It's rumoured that King Henry VIII used the island during the 1500s as a courting ground for his many mistresses. From 1830 onwards, a smart three-storey resort, Eel Pie Island Hotel, attracted summertime weekenders with its popular dancehall and live music events, but things got really interesting during the 1950s. The Roaring Twenties had been and gone, the glamour had faded, and the neglected hotel's old 19th century ballroom and dusty bar began playing host to some groundbreaking gigs.

Eel Pie Island Museum artefacts

First it was the jazz sessions, but then came a new sound of rock and British R&B reverberating from the dancehall, gradually transforming Eel Pie Island into an unexpected musical mecca. The weekly line-ups included a flood of up-and-coming, but still then-unknown bands, who went on to become some of the biggest names in rock 'n' roll history. Music legends who crossed the island's only footbridge include Pink Floyd, David Bowie, Eric Clapton, The Who, Black

Sabbath, Rod Stewart and The Rolling Stones, who were paid around £45 to perform at the club, christened "Eelpiland".

With bands like these playing almost every week, it becomes quite obvious why music historians claim that Eel Pie Island launched the UK's first underground music scene. The bohemian owner, Arthur Chisnell, who purchased the hotel in 1956, was an avid social researcher, philanthropist and a bit of a hero to London youngsters. During the week he hosted debates at the hotel for various student concerns, and was often known to use the club's profits to help hard-up teenagers who found their way to the island. As part of his social experiments, he issued Eel Pie Island "passports" instead of venue tickets to the growing crowds of art students and beatniks. During the first year of Chisnell's tenure, visitors could only access the island via a set of precarious rope pulleys – it was not until 1957 that the first bridge was built.

Eel Pie Island Museum

The gigs were infamously raucous and the liquor (amongst other substances) flowed freely. Crowded, loud, smoky, sweaty, and flooded with free spirits and music lovers, it was an escapist's paradise. But when the club failed to raise the funds required for much-needed repairs on the near-derelict venue, it was forced to close, and eventually occupied by a group of anarchist squatters, before a fire destroyed it in 1970. By then, the island had grown into a haven for society's waifs and strays, becoming the UK's largest hippie commune at that time.

The beatniks and the hotel may be gone, but Eel Pie Island has lost none of its bohemian flair. Today, it's technically a private island, home to a colourful array of inventors, artists, craftsmen and boat builders who proudly decorate their eccentric cottages, artist studios and meandering lanes. To visit, you'll need to plan ahead; the footbridge is only open to the public for two weekends a year (see Eelpieislandartists.co.uk for the dates). The summer and Christmas open days are special and festive occasions when resident artists open up their studios and offer tea (as well as stronger refreshments), along with a rare opportunity to hear their stories about island life along the Thames. Secret gardens, unexplored paths, and music history beckons. Back on the mainland, don't miss the **Eel Pie Island Museum**, a lovingly curated volunteer-run museum and a must for fans of jazz, blues and 60-70s rock. *(1-3 Richmond Rd, Twickenham TW1; Thurs-Sun 12-6pm; Eelpiemuseum.co.uk)*

A Victorian Botanist's Enchanting Asylum

On a glorious Spring day, or a crisp Autumn weekend, do yourself a favour and hop on an overground train from Liverpool Street station to **Myddelton House Gardens**. In less than an hour, you'll find yourself unwinding in botanical bliss, marvelling at the elegance of the tulip terrace, roaming the alpine meadow and soaking up the smell of fresh peaches in the glasshouse. Once the home of the eccentric horticulturist Edward Augustus Bowles, this is no ordinary back garden. The treasure of the lot, which Bowles called his "lunatic asylum" of plants, is a dizzying variety of flowers and trees he brought back from his world travels which, despite the British climate, somehow flourished at Myddelton. He dedicated his whole life to perfecting his garden, but Bowles was also just as passionate about rescuing things other people didn't want – specifically, architectural relics. Keep an eye out for discarded pieces of London Bridge (its medieval incarnation), the gothic edifice that was once Enfield's Market Cross, and a pair of 290-year-old lead ostriches, adopted from a nearby stately home. Lying around like archeological ruins are romantic moss-covered balustrades, headless statues and mysterious boulders of unknown origin whose history you can ponder over. This is a place to let both mind and feet wander. Save some time to stop in for tea at the house and visit the Bowles Museum. *(Myddelton House Gardens, Enfield EN2, London; +44 300 003 0610; open everyday 10am-4pm; Eabowlessociety.org.uk)*

Myddelton House Garden

A Storybook Getaway at the End of the Tube

Under the branches that brushed the hunting caps of medieval kings and queens who once trotted through **Epping Forest**, the history is palpable. A beautiful natural sanctuary on London's doorstep, there are still some 55,000 ancient trees growing here, twisted and shaped by time. Various meandering trails lead you through 8,000 acres of lush woodlands, open meadows and picturesque streams. You will absolutely forget you're in London.

Henry VIII and the first Queen Elizabeth kept a hunting lodge near the gates; a perfectly-preserved timber frame Tudor grandstand, now open to visitors as a small museum and visitors centre, full of interesting stories about the history of the forest. Come for the Sunday walks amidst a dense canopy of towering oak, beech, and hornbeam trees, and stay for a picnic, a horse ride, and the bird & deer watching. Look out for the longhorn cows roaming the forest too.

Finding such an enchanting escape should be harder to reach, but at the edge of North East London, you need only to jump on the Central line and ride it until the last few stops – Loughton or Theydon Bois station are both a very short walk to the entrance of the park. If you start in Theydon Bois, enter the park via Coppice Row, going up the hill and past the cemetery, arriving at a large grove, Theydon Plain. Walk across it until you intersect a path that shows up on Google Maps as "Forest Rd", which twists into the forest and leads you through some of the loveliest woodland, and eventually, up to a hill where you can see

Epping Forest

the whole village of Epping. And don't worry, there's a charming little pub to visit before heading home: make sure to drop by **The Bull** (*thebulltheydonbois.co.uk*) in Theydon for a late lunch or an afternoon pint. *(Epping Forest Visitor Centre, Paul's Nursery Road, Loughton, Essex, IG10; Queen Elizabeth's Hunting Lodge open Tuesday to Sunday, 11am – 1pm & 2pm – 4pm; VisitEppingforest.org).*

The Beaches Through the Trees

At the first sight of sun, Brits are known to strip off and pile on whatever slither of green land is available to them, which doesn't always make for the most relaxing of sunbathing sessions. But if you're looking for a spot to built some sandcastles, **Ruislip Lido** is a 60-acre lake with sandy beaches *and* a miniature railway going around it. Needless to say, a great destination with the kids. The signs say no swimming, but you'll notice swimmers blatantly ignoring council wishes and happily paddling around in summer. Whether you choose to dip your toes in or not, it's perfect for picnicking with kids around a pirate ship. *(Reservoir Road, Ruislip, HA4; Parking is limited but the H13 and 331 buses stop close by Ruislip Lido and the woods)*

Ruislip Lido

If you're up for venturing off the beaten track (which of course you are) and down a few muddy banks (still with us?), a rural riviera awaits (got you – sold). **Hackney Marshes** is the forgotten green giant of East London. This medieval marshland is the spiritual home of Sunday league football, but it's more than just a place for a kickabout on one of the 82 full-sized pitches. Head to the banks of the River Lea, peer through the elderflower trees and there you have it, the secret Hackney "beach". Wildlife conservationists discourage swimming and ask that visitors leave no trace, but if you promise not to leave your footprint so to speak, it's an idyllic spot to lay a blanket, catch some rays and sketch the kingfishers on the water. First-class foragers are also in luck with an abundance of pickable produce in the bushes. A leisurely afternoon in the English countryside is just a tube ride away. *(Homerton Rd, Hackney, E9; +44 020 8986 8615; 24-hour access; Hackney.gov.uk/hackney-marshes)*

Weekend Whiskaways

Out of town in 2 hours

Tea with the Mermaids

Even die-hard Londoners need a break from the Big Smoke sometimes. Country air is good for the soul. So is fresh sea breeze and sand between your toes. For the best of both worlds, hop on a train out of the city and in just over an hour, you'll find yourself in a delightful little chocolate box town on the south coast. **Rye** is as picture-postcard ready as English towns come. Ticking all the boxes, it's full of vintage tea rooms, haunted medieval inns and higgledy-piggledy cobblestone lanes, including one called Mermaid Street, which really is as magical as it sounds. Fuelled by artisan hot chocolate from Knoops (*Knoops.co.uk*), this sleepy storybook town is made for wandering. Browse secondhand books in the Tiny Book Store, stroll around The Strand's many nautical antique dealers and stop for a lobster lunch at the Globe Inn Marsh (*Ramblinns.com*). A short bus ride away is Camber Sands, a long golden beach with windswept sand dunes and the perfect place to fly a kite. Spend a night in the gorgeous sixteenth century Rye Windmill B&B (*Ryewindmill.co.uk*). Trains run every 30 minutes from St Pancras with a change at Ashford International, before arriving at Rye (*East Sussex, TN31*).

Mermaid Street

REAL CIDER FLYER
ROMNEY 90

GIGANTIC!
READY-TO-EAT
COOKED
DUNGENESS
CRAB
PACKING TO TRAVEL!
24 HOUR PACK
$5.00
48 HOUR PACK
$10.00

Dungeness

Lost in the British Desert (Yup, England has a Desert)

Welcome to the Wild, Wild West of... Kent? Quite obviously, Britain is not the place for sweltering Saharan sun, but it does rather shockingly have an officially designated desert, of sorts. Must be seen to be believed, the **Dungeness** estate is otherworldly and outlandish. A post-apocalyptic wasteland isn't exactly a description that would make anyone jump in their car and rush out of London, but this ghostly stretch of headland on the Kentish coast is exactly that, at first glance. A far cry from the modern metropolis, reachable in under two hours by car, Dungeness has one of the largest shingle beaches in Europe, which remains largely deserted and is getting bigger by the day as the seas continue to recede further back. Numerous lighthouses have had to be re-built over the centuries to keep up with the shoreline.

It is home to a remarkable range of rare wildlife and over 600 different plant species (a third of all those found in Britain), as well as, seemingly at odds to its conservation status, two nuclear power stations. Then, there is the "village" – or shall we say, ghost village. Strewn across the shingles are abandoned boats, railway tracks, derelict huts and fishing nets lending to the "end of civilisation" aura, but walk a little further and the spookiness dissipates when you stumble upon the friendly chaps at the Snack Shack serving up fresh crab rolls (*Dungenesssnackshack.net*). See, ghost towns aren't all that scary.

Dungeness

A beacon of light and a reminder that this is kind of a trip to the seaside, is the tall and mighty Old Lighthouse. First illuminated at the turn of the 20th century and saving ships from their peril during the wars, it's now decommissioned and open to the public from Easter to October. The internal spiral staircase leads to a super birds-eye view of the stark surrounding landscape. Bring your binoculars as from up here, the few remnants of life in the English desert can be seen in a hamlet of 1920s railways coaches converted into cottages. Although primarily occupied by off-grid fishermen and coastguards, the social seclusion and eerie silence of these weathered shacks would make for a pretty inspiring writer's retreat. Consider staying at Ness Cottage, which was used for many years as an artists retreat (*Nesscottage.net*). Just next door is the iconic coal-black, yellow-windowed Prospect Cottage, surrounded by driftwood sculptures and wildflowers miraculously sprouting from the barren beach. It was here that art house film director Derek Jarman lived out his final years, gardening, painting, and battling AIDS. The idyllic hideaway has since become a shrine, to which many film fans and art students make a windswept pilgrimage. For Jarman, Dungeness was an escape from England; a peaceful place to feel small and take in the surreal immensity of the sky and shingle against the background hum of the power stations. For anyone in need of just that too, take a solitary stroll along the 'Ness. Like the mysterious mythical monster by the same name, once seen, it will never be forgotten.
(Driving is recommended. For public transport, trains run every 30 minutes from St Pancras to Ashford International, from there take a bus to Dungeness, TN29)

Time has quite literally warped the village

Italy might have the leaning Tower of Pisa, but England has the crooked houses of **Lavenham.** A two-hour drive from London up the M11, the colourful half-timbered houses of this picture-perfect village look like they've been stretched and squeezed, then left untouched since medieval times. And actually, that's quite an accurate description of what happened. In the 15th and 16th centuries, Lavenham was one of the richest villages in the country because of its thriving wool trade. During this period of economic and population growth, the villagers rapidly built handsome houses using new timber, or "green wood", which notoriously warps and bends as it dries – but that was something to worry about later. They built the highest village church tower in Britain just to show off. And in 1487, when Henry VII visited, some of the merchant families were even fined for their excessive displays of wealth. However, as fast as the village gained its fortune, it was lost.

With the arrival of Dutch refugees and their cloth production that was cheaper, lighter and more on trend, Lavenham's industry perished, along with their plans to straighten up the village's wonky architecture. Somehow though, half

Crooked Houses of Lavenham

a millennium later, most of the crooked houses are still standing. Scenes for the Harry Potter films were secretly shot here, and Stanley Kubrick set parts of *Barry Lyndon* in the Guildhall. John Lennon and Yoko Ono also filmed their psychedelic *Apotheosis* movie on the market square.

Go beyond the facades and nose around one of Lavenham's crooked houses, a 600 year-old bright orange one that once belonged to a wool merchant. The latest custodians, Alex and Oli, a dashing couple who met during the pandemic and moved into their dream home shortly after, host theatrical one-hour time travelling experiences through their historic abode. Ask to see their showroom of antiques for sale or even better, plan your visit around one of their black tie immersive dinner parties. *(House visits £45 per person, dinners £150 a head; Bookings at crookedhouselavenham.com).*

Stop in at one of Lavenham's many vintage tearooms for a brew and you'll find some very cosy rooms at The Swan *(Theswanatlavenham.co.uk)*. The little oddities and did-you-knows of the village are endless – pass by Molet House where poet Jane Taylor wrote *Twinkle, Twinkle, Little Star* and spend the day getting lost down the little lanes.
(Hop on the train at Liverpool Street and take the train to Sudbury, bear in mind you will probably have to change at Marks Tey, then take the 753 Chambers bus to The Swan)

Cottagecore in the Cotswolds

If you're longing for a weekend escape à la Jane Austen and Beatrix Potter, make it a weekend in the Cotswolds. For that cinematic natural beauty, the charming market towns, and honey-coloured limestone cottagecore; it's all best visited by borrowing a set of wheels, but there are trains from London's Paddington Station to quaintly-named hubs like Moreton-in-Marsh. Where to hang up your Barbour and stay for the night? In the tiny, peaceful village of Ebrington, a two-hour car ride from London, **The Ebrington Arms** (*Theebringtonarms.co.uk*) was once the shop, the bakery, the butcher and the boozer combined, and it's still the only trading post in the village. The picturesque inn has been around since 1640; one of those places where you can imagine the old highwaymen stopping in for a night's rest by the crackling fire. Before retiring to your bedroom, you can meet most of the village locals, who gather for a pint after sundown.

Sezincote House

Bourton-on-the-Water

Come morning, pay a visit to the surprising **Sezincote House & Garden**, a "Mughal Indian palace" set amidst the Cotswold Hills. Still privately-owned, but open from May to September, the early 19th century estate was built by a wealthy surveyor for the British East India Company and is heavily influenced by Indian architecture. *(Sezincote.co.uk)*

Hop from one market town to another, starting with **Stow-on-the-Wold**, pausing for crumpets and cream at **Lucy's Tea Room** *(Lucystearoomstow.com)*, before carrying onto **Bourton-on-the-Water** to marvel at the only Grade-II listed miniature village in the country. A one-ninth scale replica of the fairytale Cotswold village of Bourton-on-the-Water, the **Model Village** was built by the

Bourton-on-the-Water's Model Village

local innkeeper and his wife in the 1930s, and contains every single building, from the town post office to the local Chinese takeaway, all built in Cotswold stone (*Theoldnewinn.co.uk/model-village*). There's even a miniature village *within* the miniature village, *within* the miniature village! Stick with the theme and do lunch in town at **The Mousetrap**; a small 19th century stone cottage inn, as quaint as the name suggests. *(Themousetrapinn.co.uk)*

Stow-on-the-Wold

Looping back to basecamp, swing by **Snowshill Manor and Garden**, a 16th century time capsule home of an eccentric English collector, packed with extraordinary treasures (*Nationaltrust.org.uk*). Next stop, not Rapunzel's tower but the Cotswolds highest castle. **Broadway Tower** is another local folly, open all year round, built "just for fun" by the land's aristocratic owner in 1798. They say it served as a lookout tower for his servants to know if he was coming home, but it was later used as a unique vantage point to track enemy planes over England during the world wars. A nuclear bunker was also constructed on the property during the Cold War and you can visit that too. *(Broadwaytower.co.uk)*

Also high on your to-do list: visit as many charming village pubs as you possibly can inside of 48 hours. Near Ebrington, warm your feet by the fire at two different pubs by the same name; The Horse & Groom in **Bourton-on-the-Hill** and **Upper Oddington**. And if you can't find a room at the Ebrington Arms, try **The Porch House** in Stow-on-the-Wold, a more convenient market-town choice for visitors without a car (*Porch-house.co.uk)*.

Ebrington Arms

Above: Broadway Tower
Below: Bourton-on-the-Water

WAY
OUT

10
Leading by Minority

Searching for London unknown? Glad we're on the same page. Multicultural communities are what makes London, but it's humbling to realise just how much of their story is missing from the city's mainstream narrative. The determination and ingenuity of marginalised communities to overcome adversity should be seen as nothing new, but keeping their legacies out of major museums and removed from the traditional London experience feels very, very outdated. Peel back the glossy exterior and get to know the parts that aren't primped and preened for mainstream tourism. You may come to find that you'll feel more at home and more in touch with yourself, than anywhere else.

"In London everyone is different, and that means anyone can fit in."
– Paddington Bear

The Multicultural Metropolis

Brixton Beats and South London Soul

Stay on the Tube until the end of the line; there's a top tip for not being a tourist in London. Pick one and give it a go. Final destinations are actually just the beginning. You could say those ticket barriers are an entrance gate to a wonderful new world yet to be discovered. Terminus neighbourhoods are arguably much more liveable places than central London. They're home to protective communities that fight to keep their quarter affordable and characterful, with plenty of independent shops and eateries where the barista knows your name. Best of all, with a strong connection to local history, different cultures have been able to shape their pocket of London into whatever they want it to be, for the benefit of us all.

If you take the Victoria Line southbound to the end of the line, as you walk up the steps to ground level, you'll be met with the smell of incense and the sound of Jamaican steel drums (say hello to busker Mikey for us). Welcome to **Brixton**. Directly across from the station, you'll find a mural to David Bowie, the local patron saint of South London, whose birthplace and childhood home is just around the corner at **40 Stansfield Road**.

Brixton Mural

Music flows through the streets of Brixton. Rock down to **Electric Avenue** as the catchy Eddy Grant song encourages, less than a minute from the Tube station, just before you get to **Reliance Arcade**, an Art Deco covered market fronted by

Brixton Market

a giant luminous neon rainbow. This historic market street, built in the 1880s, was the first in the world to be lit by electricity and remains just as vibrant today. Inside, you'll find tiny hair salons full of chatter, a Chinese herbalist, vinyl records shops blasting music and a ramshackle cobbler. It's a place for the Afro-Caribbean community to meet and mingle, a vibrant vein pumping blood to the heart of Brixton, all under one rainbow glazed roof. Grab a salt fish patty to go and upon exiting the arcade on Electric Lane, look up at the façade behind you to see a rare surviving example of British Egyptian-inspired architecture. In 18th century England, Egyptomania was en vogue following the discovery of Tutankhamun's tomb and European travellers became fascinated with Egyptian culture, bringing back tales of ancient remains to London. *(455 Brixton Rd, Brixton, SW9; Mon 8am-6pm, Tues-Sun 8am-11.30pm)*

Markets are the mainstay of Brixton's economy and its multicultural identity. Just off Electric Avenue, the outdoor stalls merge into a covered arcade called **Brixton Village** which leads on to the adjoining **Market Row.** Decorated with world flags and jubilant colours, here you can grab some yams and okra and shop traditional West African garms. There's also a bunch of international restaurants where you can sit and bask in the hustle and bustle of your surroundings. Longstanding local favourites include **Senzala**, a Brazilian creperie, **Mamalan** for the best baos out of Beijing, and **Fish**, **Wings and Tings**, a cheerful Caribbean joint serving top notch fried plantain and goat roti. Over on Station Road, the food fest continues at **Pop Brixton**, a community project turned marketplace set in colourful shipping containers. Popular with hipster types, especially after dark, it's a stellar spot for open mic nights and lively fiestas.

Brixton's diversity in its market offerings is no coincidence. The area's local history is not just worn on its sleeves everyday but built into the fabric of its future. In the 1940s and '50s, the grandparent generation of today's Brixtonians, many from the West Indies, came to the UK on a ship called Empire Windrush to help rebuild the war-torn country and in turn, received British citizenship. Brixton, specifically Coldharbour Lane near the markets, became an immediate temporary home to the Windrush Generation, as they are known, and many later settled here permanently. During the recession in the '70s and riots in the '80s, the Afro-Caribbean community faced intense prejudices and racist attacks. The fight of course isn't finished, and **Windrush Square**, an open green space has been named in honour of this generation's undervalued contribution to the neighbourhood and the country as a whole. You might encounter some local anti-gentrification protest groups meeting on the square, but you'll always find elderly Jamaican men chatting in patois, listening to reggae on a boombox and serving up jerk chicken to passersby. At 1 Windrush Square, these stories of the city's past are memorialised in the **Black Cultural Archives**, the only repository of Black culture and history in the UK. The vaults can be visited, and the centre often hosts insightful exhibitions and popping poetry nights. Spread the word: the brightest, boldest gem in the capital's multicultural crown needs protecting too.

Continue uncovering more of London's Black history and culture at 575 Wandsworth Road on pg 134, Kenwood House on pg 172 and The Little Yellow Door on pg 238.

Brixton Windmill

Brixton market

Little India

Bustling with colourful bazaars, street food vendors, restaurants and shops selling traditional ornaments, silks and spices, immerse yourself in a taste of India by enjoying a day exploring **Southall**. West London's South Asian district first attracted immigrants from Punjab in the 1950s, and swiftly blossomed into the vibrant corner of the city that's become known as 'Little India' or 'Little Punjab'. Today well over half of Southall's population traces their roots to South Asia, and you'll find thriving Sikh *Gurdwaras* alongside magnificent Hindu temples (the Gurdwara Sri Guru Singh Sabha is one of the largest Sikh temples outside of India). The Southall railway station sign is even written in Punjabi as well as English, and the famed Glassy Junction pub once accepted rupees in payment for pints (today the pub is home to the vegetarian restaurant *Saravanaa Bhavan).* Make sure to stop into the Palace Shopping Centre, an indoor market housed in what remains of an Art Deco cinema. Spoiled for choice when it comes to food, Roxy's is one of the longest running Punjabi restaurants in Southall, whilst Jalebi Junction is the perfect pitstop to pick up sweet jalebi to nibble on when walking around London's Little India.
(Take the Elizabeth line train to Southall from Paddington)

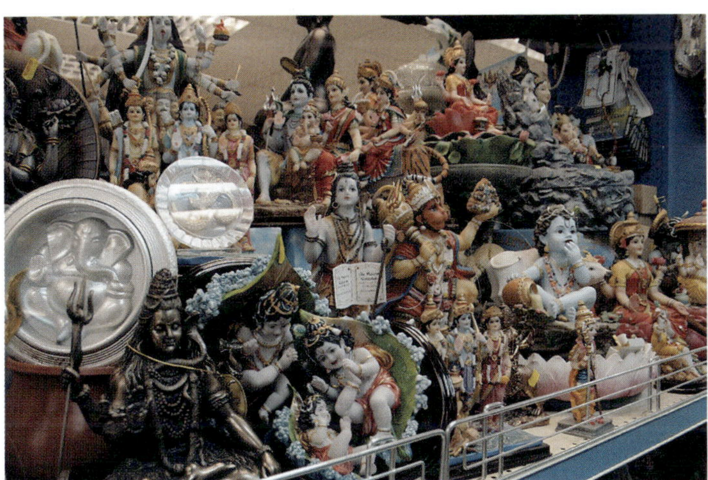

Southall

The 1960s Protest Party that became a Londoner's Rite of Passage

Notting Hill has seen seismic change over the years, most noticeably after the success of a certain eponymous 90s rom-com starring Hugh Grant and Julia Roberts, which put it on the world map and sent the gentle upward curve of house prices surging vertically. One of London's most expensive neighbourhoods today was once described in Jo Gannon's 1970 counterculture documentary, as "the world's most integrated ghetto" – something hard to imagine walking around its streets now. They say Notting Hill lost its soul, which in many ways, can ring true, but there are still pockets and people holding on to what it once was. And of course, once a year at the end of summer, there is the **Notting Hill Carnival** that sweeps through West London's streets. Picture a kaleidoscope of sequins and feathers on parade in celebration of Black culture and multicultural music. Curbside barbecues, rum cocktails on tap and the buoyant sounds of steel bands, calypso, soca, reggae, dub and ska. Even the buttoned-up Bobbies can't resist swaying to the beats of makeshift sound systems at every corner.

Notting Hill Carnival

Shall we start with some insider carnival tips? Don't cling to Portobello Road, which tends to be lined with the priciest food stands. Make a beeline for the family-run jerk chicken stalls set up on smaller side streets like **Jay Dee's Catering** on Lancaster Road, where you can find unbeatable Jamaican fare all year round. If you're looking for the front line of the dance party, the streets around All Saints Road typically host the most popular stages for underground music fans. Stop in for some Caribbean punch at **The Little Yellow Door** (see pg 238), the former site of the historic Mangrove café where the first contract for the Notting Hill Carnival was written up and signed. Around the corner on Colville Square, one of the carnival's most famed sound systems to look out for is "Rampage", known for giving a platform to UK talent right before they explode. The Mastermind Roadshow at the top of Ladbroke Grove also showcases the best of new soul, R&B and Hip Hop talent. When you're in need of a time out, head for one of the closest community gardens such as Tavistock Gardens, opposite the Red Lemon Pub, to chill out with good neighbourly vibes.

Dapper young Windrush man 1962

As you would for any busy festival, leave your troubles and valuables at home – but bring cash! Most ATMs in the area will run out of money, and fast. After all, Notting Hill Carnival attracts a staggering two million people every year – numbers that must have been unfathomable for the creators of its earlier versions. Indeed, Europe's largest street party wasn't always the sprawling celebration it is today.

The first carnivals were created by equal rights activists in the sixties as a means to ease tensions between the local White population and a growing Caribbean community arriving from far-flung islands. It was in post-war Britain that the first generation of Caribbean migrants were invited to join the ranks of working-class Britons, Jews, Irish, Greeks and Spaniards in the cramped tenements of West London to assist with labour shortages. Notting Hill quickly became home to the largest population of Caribbean people in Britain, bursting with multicultural vibrancy and diverse characters, but the community was soon scarred by social neglect, slum landlords and racial tension. Notting Hill was also a stronghold for the Union Movement, a far-right movement that rallied to "keep Britain White". Attacks and riots were rife. In an attempt to show solidarity within the community, local activists organised an indoor Mardi Gras-style carnival in 1959 with a lineup of Black jazz stars at St. Pancras Town Hall. The concept was resurrected in the 1960s by other community members who convinced a well-known Trinidadian musician and other Caribbean artists to participate in their street party. Horse-drawn carts were borrowed from traders in Portobello Road to make floats and the first official Notting Hill Carnival was born. Despite its popularity today, the lack of government funding and political pressures make its future relatively uncertain. So far though, the carnival remains top of the London events calendar, representing unprecedented resilience and the cultural diversity that make most locals proud to call themselves Londoners. *(The Notting Hill Carnival takes place the last weekend of August; festivities start from 9am until late; Nhcarnival.org)*

To discover more of multicultural Notting Hill, go in search of the Portobello Road of Yesteryear on pg 296.

Making Friends over All-You-Can-Eat Curry

The YMCA Indian Student Hostel has been providing a home away from home for Indian students in London since 1920. This may be known by some Londoners who walk past the building on the way to work, thinking it's not for them, but the secret lies within. Go through the rather pedestrian-looking entrance, then take the door on the right. The **Indian YMCA Restaurant** like the student hostel, is a welcoming and unpretentious place for strangers to come together and break naan. The self-service buffet and utilitarian layout

resembles a school canteen, complete with the classic net curtains and plastic trays. Students from the hostel who miss their mother's cooking share tables with local office workers who appreciate a good & affordable lunch. The friendly chefs are at hand to explain the rotating curry menu and will always encourage you to try something new. Finding a good meal for under a tenner in central London can be a challenge these days, but here you'll leave with change and a mango lassi for later.
(41 Fitzroy Square, Bloomsbury, W1T; +44 020 7387 0411; Open every day for breakfast, lunch & dinner; Indianymca.org/our-restaurant)

A Persian Grotto in Kensal Green

Looking to try a new cuisine and slip into another world for an evening? **Behesht**, meaning 'paradise' in Persian, is decorated with floor to ceiling Persian carpets, copper pots hanging overhead, carved wooden musical instruments and kaleidoscopic tiling in a tapestried tribute to Iran's romantic past. It's beautiful and bonkers, just like the two parrots that greet you upon arrival and the babbling fish pool in the foyer. The menu is comforting and warmly spiced, offering a wide range of starters ideal for sharing. Crunchy *tag digh*, *shirazi salad* and creamy *bourani* make a good combo for those new to Persian flavours before moving on to a traditional stew, known as *khoresht*. Not to be missed is the Persian bread, charred on the mighty mosaic tandoor. As there's no alcohol on the menu, the final bill is refreshingly low for a generous feast.
(1082-6 Harrow Rd, Kensal Green; NW10; +44 020 8964 4477; Everyday 12-11pm; Behesht.co.uk)

A Vegetarian's Culinary Cruise Through Kerala Backwaters

When it comes to curry and the colour pink, some like it hot. Easy to spot and smell a mile off, Stoke Newington's enticing South Indian eatery boasts a flamingo pink exterior and a just as fabulous fuchsia theme through the front door. Mouth-watering as well as eye-catching, **Rasa** dishes up wholesome vegan and vegetarian regional fare at very friendly prices. Indian cuisine is so much more than the British curry house staple that is a chicken tikka masala. Awaken your tastebuds to the explosive yet comforting flavours of the Malabar Coast. The long crispy dosas and punchy homemade pickles are out of this world, and great value too, as is the award-winning authentic vegan feast which you'll find local Tamil families tucking into on a Friday night. Portion sizes are generous and a cosy casual atmosphere invites sharing with friends. Be sure to leave a little room for *payasam*, a traditional sweet and spicy dessert so moreish you'll want one all to yourself.
(5 Stoke Newington Church St, N16; +44 20 7249 0344; Tues-Sun 5.30-10.30pm; Rasarestaurants.com)

Letting Loose in the Queer Metropolis

Welcome to the Cabaret Pub, Old Chum

As the legend goes, on one crazy night in the late 80s, Princess Diana enjoyed an undercover night out disguised as a man at **The Royal Vauxhall Tavern** accompanied by Freddie Mercury and Kenny Everett. The 19th century pub turned cabaret is one of London's oldest gay bars and was the UK's first building to be listed in recognition of its importance to LGBTQ history. First becoming a safe haven for local gay men after World War II, the venue began hosting makeshift drag shows by clearing one of the kidney-shaped bars to double as a stage for performers. Some of Britain's biggest acts rose to fame at the RVT, including Lily Savage (the late great Paul O'Grady), who was arrested there during a raid in 1987 at the height of the HIV/AIDS epidemic. The historic LGBTQ venue today, a glammed-up pub with a central stage, is thankfully once again a safe space, free of discrimination and host to a famous Sunday cabaret show as well as weekly quiz nights, club nights, talent contests and music concerts. Hold onto your wig, clutch your pearls, bring your stilettos and come join the party. *(372 Kennington Ln, London SE11; +44 20 7820 1222; open everyday; find the program at Vauxhalltavern.com)*

> ***"Time is on the side of the outcast. Those who once inhabited the suburbs of human contempt find that without changing their address they eventually live in the metropolis."***
>
> **– Quentin Crisp**

The "about bloody time" Museum

Writer, dandy, philosopher, creature of the night; Quentin Crisp was so many things, but above all he was steadfastly himself. Looking every bit the genderless dandy, decades before Bowie was on the scene, Quentin was one of London's most colourful residents and its first openly-gay celebrity. His 1968 book, *The Naked Civil Servant,* is a pain-riddled but quippy coming-of-age memoir on his pursuit of acceptance as a genderqueer man – a steep challenge before the gay rights movement. As a British eccentric in the 1920s and 30s, Quentin Crisp was a veritable Oscar Wilde reincarnate. At the onset of WWII, Crisp was declared as "suffering from sexual perversion" and turned away from service. During the London's 1941 Blitz, whilst everyone else was hiding in bomb shelters in the dark, Crisp, who'd stocked up on makeup and five pounds of henna to dye his hair, pranced through the city streets picking up American soldiers. He used effeminate fashion as means for exploring his gender identity, but also to cause a stir in a society and time in history where it was dangerous to be an openly gay person. Unearthing forgotten Quentin Crisp interviews on Youtube is a sure way to fall down the rabbit hole, but if you listen carefully, things get a little complicated. He often gave conflicting statements about gay liberation; sometimes he was even dismissive of the struggle for lesbian and gay equal rights, and seemingly contradicted himself from one interview to the next. If only he had lived to see a place like **Queer Britain**, the UK's first LGBTQ+ museum. They don't teach us about queer history in schools, but in the heart of London at King's Cross, the milestone community space celebrates the stories and contributions of LGBTQ+ individuals that for too long, have gone unseen and untold. Beyond a museum of artefacts and collections, it's a welcoming and free community space where education is a cornerstone of Queer Britain's work, engaging visitors of all ages and backgrounds through panel discussions, workshops, screenings, and more. Yes, quite sure Quentin Crisp would have really liked it here. *(2 Granary Square, Coal Drops Yard, King's Cross, N1C; Wed-Sun 12-6pm; Queerbritain.org.uk)*

Queer Britain museum

Drag Queens Serving Looks and Pulling Pints

"The gays throw the best parties" say drag queens turned pub landlords Jonny Woo and John Sizzle. And they ain't wrong. A glorious gay ol' time is guaranteed with these two and their eccentric extended family. **The Glory Pub** in Haggerston is a much-loved drag mecca and local linchpin for East London's LGBT crowd. To some degree, their events seem to fit the box of classic pub entertainment; live music, quizzes, cabaret, and bingo, but crank up the camp, mix it with a genuine community feel and you've got yourself something special and legendary. London's longest-serving Club Kid, Princess Julia, is part of the furniture here, with her Sunday salon and regular DJ sets. Princess Julia is a queer icon, credited with launching the New Romantic subculture in the 1980s, and is still found partying at this canalside pub into her 60s. In the company of drag queens and party princesses, what could possibly go wrong? You're in for a royally raucous night of pure unadulterated glory. Plastic tiaras at the ready. *(281 Kingsland Rd, Haggerston, E2; +44 020 7684 0794; Tues-Fri 5pm-12am, Sat 5pm-2am & Sun 6pm-11pm; Theglory.co)*

Queer Pop Paradise

Belinda Carlisle's gay anthem was right, Heaven *is* a place on Earth. And it's under a train station, who'd have thought it? Head to the pearly gates beneath Charring Cross for an out-of-this-world night out at **Heaven**, the city's largest LGBTQ+ nightclub. Having brought London's gay scene out of the dingy, dark and dangerous cellar bars and into the light of the mainstream, it's still going strong. After four decades of dancing, Heaven remains a haven for the gay community to be their true selves to the soundtrack of acid house, europop and camp disco classics. In the 80s, it was a magnet for celebrities like Freddie Mercury and Boy George. Thanks to this reputation and its bulging size, it's still the place to see international superstars let their hair down. Lady Gaga performed here stark naked and Cher debuted her iconic hit 'Believe' to packed crowds in 1998. As well as live music and regular drag shows on the two massive dance floors, there are smaller rooms and bars to float between if you need to take five. Each one has a different atmosphere and contrasting but still wickedly good tunes. So off you pop, dance towards the rainbow light, the angel-winged go-go dancers are calling...
(Charing Cross Arches, Villiers Street, WC2N; +44 0844 847 2351; Mon 11pm-5am, Fri 11pm-4am, Sat 10.30pm-5am, Sun 9pm-5am; Heaven-live.co.uk)

Go big or go home at Europe's largest and legendary fetish ball

At **Torture Garden**, the world's largest mixed (all sexualities welcome) fetish club, head-turning outfits are a must. Think fantasy fetish, leather and body art. Due to the size and range of activities, from dirty dancefloors and fashion shows to S&M dungeons, it's an eye-opening buffet of sexual delight ideal for kink-curious newcomers. *(Usually hosted monthly at Scala nightclub; see Torturegarden.com for event details)*

A Grassroots Movement of Kinksters

Transport yourself to the throbbing heart of Berlin's fetish club culture by taking a trip underground with **Klub Verboten**'s rampant ravers. Geared toward an LGBTQ+ crowd, expect hardcore bondage and deep techno. An address of a secret warehouse will be revealed to members on the night. Pay heed to the dress code of harnesses, chains, and PVC. As Britain's answer to Berghain, it pays to look gag-worthy. *(klubverboten.com)*

For more fun after dark with the queer community, check out the Hornecker Centre on pg 115, the Colour Factory on pg 274 and the Bethnal Green Working Men's Club on pg 244.

Girl Power

The Secret Girl Gang Clubhouse of Wrestling

The first rule of feminist fight club is to 'tell everyone about feminist fight club', says owner Emily Read. The second rule of fight club is 'support your local girl gang'. **EVE Wrestling** is a kickass pro-wrestling collective taking the 'man' out of WrestleMania and throwing the spotlight on the women smashing gender stereotypes into smithereens. Sure, competitors beat the living daylights out of each other, but it's a safe space out of the ring, meaning any hate speech or homophobia will get you drop-kicked out the door. Currently held in an enormous pub in East London's Walthamstow, an EVE wrestling match is a powerfully punk experience; savage body slams, dramatic WWE-style entrances, and explosive interactions with the crowd. The lashes may be fake, but the blood is real. So many women come for the cabaret and leave with self-defence stunts up their sleeves as well as an uplifting lesson in how to command a ring, or room, with a fiery don't-you-dare-mess-with-this presence. This was the aim when Emily founded EVE in 2009. After getting thwacked across the chops with sexism in the male-dominated wrestling industry, she set out on a mission to elevate women from a bikini-clad scorecard-holding sideshow to the main event. She reclaimed the toxic insults of 'fight like a girl' and plastered it on ringside banners as an empowering message to use your female force. It's more than entertainment, it's a fearlessly femme grassroots movement, putting society in a headlock and showing them who's boss. *(Big Penny Social, 1 Priestley Way, London E17; see website for events schedule; Evewrestling.com)*

Dedicated to Vaginas

It may be on the smaller side of London's cultural attractions, but the **Vagina Museum** is not trying to be 'tucked away' or 'off the beaten path', even though it very much *is*, hiding down an alleyway in East London's Bethnal Green. Vaginas and vulvas are the most stigmatised part of the female body, and people are still literally dying of embarrassment because we fail to talk enough about them. The world's first brick and mortar museum of its kind wants to change that. If you've got a vagina, or love someone who does, this is a place for open discussion, to view vagina-related imagery that isn't pornography and 'muff-bust' the most common vagina myths while learning a whole lot more truths. The gift shop is full of fascinating books, the café is a hoot, and every Friday evening, the museum is host to some kind of vagina-themed event, whether it be a book club, feminist lecture or body confidence-building workshop. *(Museum 275, Vagina, 276 Poyser St, Bethnal Green E2; Wed-Sun 10am-6pm; Vaginamuseum.co.uk)*

Girl on Top

At **Killing Kittens**, females come first. Set up by the Princess of Wales' former bestie, Emma Sayle, these parties are inclusive of everyone – but women call the shots, meaning men must wait to be approached. Sexually-charged drinks receptions are extravagant and exclusive, and members undergo a strict vetting process. Dress smart and sexy, and for added anonymity, masks are compulsory, meaning you never know who you might be rubbing (shoulders) with. Secret locations vary from elegant penthouses to country estates. House rules: leave your inhibitions (and Instagram) at the door. Respect the dress code and most importantly, each other's boundaries. It's a good idea to go with a friend or partner the first time, and although alcohol is a tempting social lubricant, especially if it's your first time, go easy. You don't want tomorrow's hangover to turn into a foggy game of kinky Cluedo, trying to remember which room you were in, with whom, and what weapon-like sex toy. (*Killingkittens.com*)

An Ode to the Forgotten Souls of London's Medieval Sex Workers

Down an unremarkable side street in Southwark near Borough Market, is a fenced lot filled with broken concrete slabs, patches of overgrown grass and the odd piece of abandoned construction equipment. Lengths of ribbon, handwritten messages and tokens weave a tight pattern through the bars of the rusty gates of **Crossbones Graveyard & Garden of Remembrance**; all tributes to the 15,000 'outcast dead' of London. In the early 1990s, Transportation for London sent heavy equipment to the area to excavate part of the Underground's Jubilee line extension. Neighbours and historians warned that any digging would disturb human remains and local regulators insisted on an archeological survey before digging commenced. It didn't take long for the Museum of London's archeological team to uncover the first bodies buried a few inches below the surface. The team dug further and found bones, boots, trousers, shirts, infant burial shrouds and coffins stacked nine or ten deep, side-to-side. Archeologists had six weeks to excavate the site and only enough time to remove 158 skeletons before construction commenced. The museum team reluctantly packed up their equipment and left behind the estimated remains of 15,000 people, dating back to the 16th century.

A majority of the dead were women, the unborn, or children under the age of six. Their remains showed signs of scurvy, rickets, broken bones, smallpox and syphilis. Almost all showed signs of malnutrition; not surprising as London life was harsh, particularly if you lived south of the river Thames. It was a crowded, dirty, miserable place known for various "liberties" forbidden in other parts of the city; bear-baiting, theatre performance and prostitution. The Bishop of Winchester who governed this area, known as Liberty of the Clink, collected taxes from local businesses and licensed the local prostitutes and brothels. Anyone unable to pay a fee or tax was thrown into the Bishop of Winchester's

Crossbones Graveyard

underground prison, the Clink. The sex workers, known as Winchester Geese, were destitute, desperate women and girls. Someone who contracted syphilis was often referred to as being "bitten by a Winchester Goose" and the resulting syphilitic pustules were called "goose bumps".

The Geese worked the streets, or "stews" (brothels), to feed themselves and their families, paying fees and taxes to the Bishop of Winchester until they died, at which time they were summarily denied the rites and comforts of a proper burial. The bodies of the women, their children, the destitute and the unwanted, were considered unsuitable for a religious burial and sent off to unmarked graves and unconsecrated ground in a desolate corner of Southwark, known as Cross Bones Graveyard. Being buried in unconsecrated ground not only implied an afterlife in purgatory, but their remains almost certainly became easy prey for the body snatchers that served nearby St Guy's Hospital. Even in death, the Winchester Geese and other unfortunates had no prospect of peace.

The cemetery closed in the late 1800s and the lot sat undeveloped until Transportation for London initiated the Jubilee Line extension. News of the site's tragic history and impending desecration prompted some sympathetic locals to post a plaque on a nearby wall that read, "*To fix in time, this site the Cross Bones Graveyard, where the Whores and the Paupers of the Southwark Liberty, in graves unconsecrated, lay resting... where now, at Millennial turning, the Whores and the Paupers and our Friends return incarnate, in ritual, with tribute and offerings, to honour, to remember.*" The plaque was removed. Another appeared in its place and was also removed until an official council-funded brass plaque was finally erected in 2006. A small, wild garden was planted and the "Friends of Cross Bones Graveyard" was formed. Small notes and memorials are still left on the cemetery gates; names, dates, prayers, candles and occasionally, bottles of gin. You may leave your own tribute on the gates of Cross Bones Graveyard or join the monthly remembrance service at 7pm on the 23rd of every month to remember the outcast dead of London. *(Union St, Southwark, SE1; learn more at Crossbones.org.uk before you go).*

Every Little Helps

Not Your Average Walking Tour

Arguably no one knows London better than the person who has faced sleeping on its streets. If you're interested in a walking tour, there are hundreds of companies to choose from, but there's only one like **Unseen Tours**, offering an entirely unique perspective, led by marginalised people who have been affected by homelessness. For Londoners and visitors alike, it's an opportunity to rediscover London's most storied neighbourhoods; from Soho to London Bridge; with a true local. Challenging the mainstream narrative, tag along with Pete for an entertaining but eye-opening ramble around Brick Lane or join Ben in King's Cross to have a conversation about how London's historic architecture blends and battles with the constant modern development. All the guides have their own stories to tell with a compass for the city's quirkiest corners. A majority share of ticket revenue goes directly into your guide's pocket and anything left is reinvested back into the volunteer network that engages with vulnerable men and women living on the streets of London. *(Unseentours.org.uk)*

Unseen Tour guides

Pay Less for a Cracking Breakfast, So Others Can Eat for Free

In a city where £20 won't get you more than a boiled egg, toast, and a mug of tea for brunch, a spot like **Eggs & Bread** is a beautiful thing. Everything is on the house, "no matter if you're a City Broker or simply broke". This simple café boasts the smallest menu on the street; tea, coffee, delicious porridge, toast and of course, eggs. Everything is self-service, just pop as many eggs as you like into the nifty little holder and lower into the boiler. When you're done, clean up after yourself and next to the dishwashing station, you'll notice a discreet contribution box. The idea is, that if you can afford to donate a little something, it will help provide a nutritious breakfast for the next person who may be less able to pay. To further support the morning breakfast service, there's a weekly Supper Club every Tuesday serving up a three course meal, with prosecco and wine, all for £24. Heart-warming and belly-filling. *(191 Wood St, Walthamstow, E17; Mon-Fri 7-11am & Sat-Sun 8am-12pm; Eggsandbread.co.uk)*

Helping youngsters get a leg-up in life at Brixton's Horse Club

Looking for happiness? Furry four-legged friends are known to help, but more than enough research suggests that to boost one's own mental health, volunteering is a great way to relieve anxiety or depression – a happy side effect of lending a hand to someone or a community in need. **Ebony Horse Club** is a unique little charity in the heart of Brixton changing the lives of inner city kids living in South London's most disadvantaged communities. Bordering a series of towering council housing flats, the stables are home to a team of horses that help offer kids a different path. Riding lessons are offered to youths at a subsidised rate of £7/hour, or free for those who cannot afford it. The club's president is none other than Queen Consort Camilla, but you don't need royal connections to volunteer to work directly with young riders. If you are interested in giving your time, email info@ebonyhorseclub.org for a volunteer application form. *(Ebonyhorseclub.org.uk)*

You might also be inspired by the charitable endeavours of the Pearlies of London on pg 73 and Redemption Roasters, the world's first behind bars coffee company on pg 265.

Ebony Horse Club

Nice day for a revolution...

The Clubhouse where the Frontline Journalists Hangout

If you know who Christiane Amanpour, Bob Woodward or Marie Colvin are, chances are, you know a bit about the profession of journalism, maybe even aspire to be a journalist, or at least follow international affairs closely enough. There are many more folks, however; cameramen, photographers, foreign correspondents; whose names we don't know, who risk their lives daily in the course of their work. **The Frontline Club** is the place to meet them. For the adventurous at heart (but risk-averse everywhere else), members and non-members can live vicariously through them by attending the club's diverse program of inspiring talks, debates, documentary screenings, book launches, training courses and other gatherings. Housed in a three-storey old Victorian coach house in Paddington, you might mingle with war correspondents

The Frontline Club

at a book signing, catch a panel discussion about how Tik Tok is changing journalism or attend a one day training course on first aid & resilience training (useful) for conflict zones (you never know). Every city has a journo hangout, but Frontline is unique in its endeavours to shine a light on the *un*reported world' to bring to light injustices in conflict and support various initiatives that ensure safety for journalists and their freedom of speech around the world. The club is also home to a restaurant open to the public on the ground floor, and a club room and bedrooms for members. And no, you don't have to be a journalist to join, but the idea is, if members do end up on the frontline, there's a clubhouse back in London to call home, where war stories, revolutions and under-reported causes aren't already yesterday's news. *(13 Norfolk Pl, Tyburnia, Paddington W2; +44 20 7046 7050; Frontlineclub.com)*

Revisit the West London Street that Seceded from Britain

More than 50 years on, whispers still linger of **Frestonia** in a once-lawless corner of London's Notting Hill, a "wild west" micronation that issued its own passports, and had its own national flag, government and constitution. The name "Frestonia" was derived from Freston Road, a street lined with terraced Victorian cottages which had been allowed to deteriorate so badly by the dawn of the 1970s, its residents were forced to vacate to the equally-grim local council estates of Trellick and Grenfell Towers. The eccentric vagrant community that had replaced them by 1974 however, proved rather more difficult to evict. In protest against the drastic redevelopment plans for the area that threatened to displace countless West Londoners, the squatters declared Freston Road and the diagonally adjoining Bramley Road, an independent state on October 31st of 1977.

For a brief but memorable decade, the lone republic of Frestonia, inhabited by over 100 squatters; a mix of artists, writers, musicians, activists and some troubled transients; functioned under ideals of anarchy and independence. An official Frestonian postage stamp was recognised by the Royal Post Office service to deliver the micronation's mail and the community also published its own newspaper. Ministers of State were appointed and the community set about establishing its own national culture, implementing independent food co-ops, childcare services and legal advice agencies. International journalists who flocked to Freston Road to cover the squatters' story were issued with foreign visitors badges.

The movement gained support from various notable figures in the arts and entertainment industry, as well as members of Parliament. Margaret Thatcher's longest-serving Cabinet minister, Sir Geoffrey Howe, sympathised with the Frestonians, publicly stating, "I can hardly fail to be moved by your aspirations." The British playwright, Heathcote Williams, Frestonia's then-appointed Ambassador to the United Kingdom, even succeeded in gaining the British court's recognition of his micronation's independence – albeit on a technicality. In a legal dispute denying the unauthorised performance of his play, *The Immortalist*, the courts ruled in Heathcote's favour to allow the work to debut at the microstate's "National Theatre", thus historically declaring that Frestonia was, for this purpose, independent of the UK.

The theatre, a red brick Victorian warehouse that hosted the republic's cultural events as well as its own government, played a key role in Frestonia's existence and still stands handsomely at the corner of Freston Road and Olaf Street. British punk rock band "The Clash" were welcomed by Frestonians to record their album there in 1982. Today, it's home to several artist studios as well as the

Welcome to Frestonia by Tony Sleep

Frestonian Gallery, a contemporary white-walled art space founded in 2017 that seeks to channel the Frestonian spirit by representing artists of diverse backgrounds and generations. *(2 Olaf Street, W11; +44 203 904 1865; Tues-Fri 11am-6pm, Sat midday - 4pm; Frestoniangallery.com)*

Although Frestonia was never genuinely recognized as a sovereign nation, its leading activists did apply for full membership of the United Nations and were working on forming an independent currency. But Frestonia was not without its problems. Many citizens suffered from addiction and survived largely on the kindness of their neighbours. Everyone knew who was on drugs and who was capable of fixing your roof, as one former resident, photographer Tony Sleep, put it. Although Frestonians endured living conditions that were declared unfit for human occupancy, more capable residents worked to create a home for themselves and kept the party going for nearly a decade as one large, semi-dysfunctional, yet fascinating communal family.

In 1980, the Greater London Council (GLC) intervened and negotiated with the Frestonians, offering alternative accommodation and financial compensation, ultimately leading to the fast decline of the young nation-state. When independence was lost, making way for the Notting Hill Housing Trust to begin redevelopment, many of the guiding forces behind Frestonia moved on and motivation for the upkeep of the rogue nation quickly deteriorated. While the majority of today's local residents of Freston road are hardly the anarchist type and hold no connection to the former republic, there is the lingering sense of a close-knit community, in part, thanks to some of the descendents of the original squatters that stuck around. You might even encounter an old Frestonian enjoying their beans on toast at the friendly **Embassy Café** just around the back of Freston Road. With a name that subtly nods to the area's historical ambitions for sovereignty, this long-running greasy spoon (albeit not entirely immune to the pressures of regeneration) is a comforting little reminder of some wild West London history. *(1 Mortimer Square, London W11; +44 20 7243 1676; open Mon-Sat 6.30am-3pm)*

The nest room at The Rookery

Where to Stay

Cheaper & Cheerful

The Goodenough Hotel: Fun fact – when I needed to hide away in London, parts of this book were written from one of the cosy single attic rooms of this Bloomsbury hotel. Ideal for solo trips with well thought-out and tastefully decorated rooms at reasonable prices, it is, in my opinion, more than good enough. Centrally located but situated on a peaceful residential square, you can easily walk to several museums found in this book just a few minutes away, as well as find useful bus routes to connect you to the rest of the city. One possible snag: there's no elevator and quite a few stairs to the top of your townhouse, but the friendly staff will be more than happy to assist. *(Thegoodenough.co.uk)*

Bermonds Locke: Located in brilliant Bermondsey (see pg 37), this one is highly recommended for slightly longer stays. An edgy and design-conscious apartment-style hotel with bright and spacious rooms that come with a kitchenette, washing machine, dishwasher and other equipment, but perhaps best of all, a co-working space with a charming outdoor patio and in-house bakery – oh, and a workout studio if that's of interest. The longer you stay, the better the rate. *(Lockeliving.com/en/london/bermonds-locke)*

The Windmill, Clapham: This charming pub and inn south of the river understands families (and dogs are well accommodated for too). Luxurious bedding, plenty of space, clawfoot bathtubs and nice bathroom products, you can't really ask more out of a room. Staff are all smiles and the lovely Clapham Common park is on your doorstep. The local pub is a favourite with dog walkers; not really the place you need to worry about noise levels. Clapham itself is an idyllic and very family-friendly residential area of London. The eclectic small shops of nearby Abbeville road are a delight to browse and if you have to tear yourself away, you've got two Tube stations on either end of the road that will get you to Oxford Circus in 15 minutes. *(Windmillclapham.co.uk/hotel-bedrooms)*

Mama Shelter: For all the amenities of a creative and contemporary four star hotel with unbeatable prices, this successful European hotel chain has got you covered. Quirky and comfortable, with a vast lobby for lounging on couches by the fireplace where food is served all day, you've got the choice of stylish single, double and motel-style duo double bed rooms. Hanging out in between Shoreditch and Hackney, a stone's throw from the charming shops of Columbia Road, you'll be ideally situated to make East London your playground, and with the Young V&A just down the road, as well as Hackney City Farm, keeping the kids entertained takes little effort (see pg378). Jump on a double decker bus right outside the hotel and you'll whizz right over to the West End and Soho in half an hour. *(Mamashelter.com/london-shoreditch)*

Mad Hatter Hotel: Dwarfed by surrounding skyscrapers but steps from the southern banks of the Thames for breezy river walks, this beautiful saloon-style pub and 30-room hotel was once a gentleman's hat factory. The Tate is a 3 minutes walk and you can be feasting at Borough Market in less than 15 minutes on foot. Rooms might be a tad dated but a good size, immaculate, and super comfy. The staff are so welcoming and breakfast is made with love; eat your heart out with those dippy eggs and soldiers, with or without the marmite. *(Madhatterhotel.co.uk)*

The Fox & Anchor: Down a quiet street in the beating heart of old Victorian working London, this historic pub is known for its phenomenal Sunday roasts, but it also has six classically decorated bedrooms upstairs. The stairs are narrow and steep and you may not be able to rely on bar staff to immediately carry your bags up, so if you're a fit, easy-going and mostly independent explorer, this could be the one for you. Enjoy a soak in the roll-top copper tub after an early morning plunge into Smithfield Market, the historic meat market around the corner (see pg 106); a unique behind the scenes look at London. The Barbican's cultural offerings are also nearby, as well as the City of London's ancient sites. *(Foxandanchor.com)*

The Old Ship Inn: The cute, tidy and very well-priced rooms here are surprisingly quiet given the lively pub downstairs and you'll have private access to the hotel side without needing to walk through the bar. This hidden Hackney gem of an alehouse is ideal if you plan on really getting to know East London and immersing yourself in the constantly evolving hipster heart of the city. *(Urbanpubsandbars.com/venues/the-old-ship)*

Upgrade within reason

Hazlitt Hotels: Imagine the sort of place Mr. Darcy and Elizabeth Bennet might stay on a trip up to London; a discreet boutique bolthole, masterfully restored to its Georgian glory. Prepare to be a little agasp when checking into one of the three historic properties of the Hazlitt Hotel group. For a romantic portal into the past, choose between **Hazlitt's** nestled in Soho, **The Rookery** tucked away down a narrow lane near St. Paul's Cathedral, and **Batty Langley's** on a cinematic cobblestone road in Shoreditch. Furnished with the finest antiques, blessed with fireside reading nooks and honesty bars, these are hotels that are designed to feel like a home, where knowledgeable staff are kindred spirits of the 'Don't be a Tourist' ethos. *(Hazlittshotel.com / Rookeryhotel.com / Battylangleys.com)*

Artist Residence: If you don't have any time to visit an art gallery while in London, you won't leave feeling like you've skipped out on culture staying at this lovely boutique townhouse tucked away in quiet Pimlico. Each bedroom is uniquely and tastefully decorated like a Warholian London pied-à-terre, filled with art and objects to inspire a creative guest. The short walk to Chelsea's Sloane Square is a treat, but if you're planning on staying in, the hotel serves breakfast, lunch and dinner in house and drinks all day. *(Artistresidence.co.uk/our-hotels/london)*

The Cubitt House: From the group behind some of the most elegant English gastropubs in the city, you can expect all the good taste and comfort to carry through upstairs where country inn chic welcomes the weary traveller. Three of the Cubitt House pubs have a collection of rooms with enviable fabrics and furnishings that look like they've been pulled straight from a Farrow & Ball moodboard. **The Grazing Goat** is supremely located in between Hyde Park and Oxford Circus on a quiet little street that feels like a village of small boutiques. **The Princess Royal** is every first-timer visitor's dream in the heart of Notting Hill, and **The Orange** is a stone's throw from the famous King's Road, surrounded by antiques shops and posh Chelsea restaurants and delis. *(Cubitthouse.co.uk/our-hotels)*

Boundary: In addition to being one of our romantic picks for al fresco rooftop date (pg 68), this edgy Shoreditch sanctuary around the corner from bustling Brick Lane has bright and spacious bedrooms, each individually inspired by a 20th century icon of the arts. If you're willing to splurge, there's even a suite personally designed by Sir David Tang. Try the memorable spiced cauliflower schnitzel at the all-day brasserie and don't miss dinner and drinks on the roof overlooking East London with the olive trees. *(Boundary.london/bar-brasserie)*

Airbnb Alternatives

The Landmark Trust: Hiding in the shadows of the mainstream travel industry since 1965, The Landmark Trust has been saving historic properties that would otherwise be lost or spoiled, carefully restoring them and renting them out as self-catering holiday homes. The majority of the charity's properties are located in rural England – browsing through the site to discover all the spectacular historic buildings where you can actually spend the night is entertainment in itself – but there are a handful of unique properties in London to consider. Stay at 43 Cloth Fair, the only remaining house in the City of London built before the Great Fire of London of 1666. Or make yourself at home on Princelet Street in an 18th century museum-worthy townhouse that once belonged to wealthy Huguenot merchants. As a party of six, the rental will cost the equivalent of £60 a night per person. To get first dibs on exclusive early-booking opportunities for new restorations, discover how to become a patron. *(Landmarktrust.org.uk)*

London Perfect Apartments: Purveyors of the most beautiful pads in West London, trust this family-run rental company to host you in a cosy Georgian townhouse apartment with a garden on the loveliest street lined with cherry blossom trees, or a Notting Hill nest with a dreamy roof terrace. An ideal option for families, all the amenities have been thought of – you won't want for anything. *(Londonperfect.com)*

Splurge-Smart Sanctuaries

The Stafford: If you'd like to play neighbours with the royal family living at St. James's Palace, this stately five star hotel surrounds a historic stable which has been turned into a beautiful courtyard for guests to enjoy al fresco cocktails from the American bar. There's a mini museum of wine in the basement that once served as a WWII shelter and now offers wine tastings and candlelit dinner parties in the 17th century cellars. Expect rooms with four poster beds, sumptuous fabrics and marble bathrooms. *(Thestaffordlondon.com)*

The Gore: In 1968, The Rolling Stones hosted their album launch party at the hotel bar, but it's more traditional English luxury than rock & roll digs at this Kensington mansion behind the Royal Albert Hall. Think antique carved beds, Tudor architectural accents in immaculate and high-ceilinged rooms, one of which Judy Garland stayed in. The restaurant has an award-winning master chef in the kitchen and a decadent afternoon tea is offered on velvet chesterfield sofas by the fire. Comfort cuts no corners here. *(Collezione.starhotels.com/en/our-hotels/the-gore-london)*

 **Find more hotels listed in the index.**

TELEPHONE
TELEPHONE

The
‘What’s Near(ish) Me?’
Index

Central London

City of London

St. Pauls, Barbican, Tower Hill

Drinking and Dining

Seeing and Doing

Borough of Islington (North)

Clerkenwell, Farringdon, Angel, Highbury & Islington, Holloway

Drinking and Dining

Seeing and Doing

Sleeping

Borough of Camden (North West)

Holborn, Bloomsbury, Camden Town, Belsize Park, Hamspstead

Eating and Drinking

Seeing and Doing

Sleeping

City of Westminster (West)

Soho, Covent Garden, Mayfair, Marylebone, Regent's Park, King's Cross, Hyde Park, Westminster, Pimlico

Drinking and Dining

Seeing and Doing

Sleeping

Kensington and Chelsea (West)

Drinking and Dining

Seeing and Doing

Sleeping

Hammersmith and Fulham (West)

Drinking and Dining

Seeing and Doing

Lambeth to Wandsworth (South West)

Vauxhall, Brixton, Clapham, Streatham, Battersea, Putney, Tooting

Drinking and Dining

Seeing and Doing

Sleeping

Borough of Southwark (South)

Bermondsey, Peckham, Rotherhithe, Camberwell, Dulwich Village

Drinking and Dining

Seeing and Doing

Sleeping

Borough of Tower Hamlets (East)

Shoreditch, Spitalfields, Bethnal Green, Whitechapel, Canary Wharf

Drinking and Dining

Seeing and Doing

Sleeping

Hackney (North East)

Shoreditch, Dalston, Hackney

Drinking and Dining

Seeing and Doing

Sleeping

Borough of Lewisham (South East)

Drinking and Dining

Seeing and Doing

Outer Boroughs

Ealing (West)

Seeing and Doing

Harrow (North West)

Seeing and Doing

Hillingdon (West)

Seeing and Doing

Richmond upon Thames (South West)

Drinking and Dining

Seeing and Doing

Hounslow (South West)

Seeing and Doing

Haringey (North)

Drinking and Dining

Seeing and Doing

Bromley (South East)

Seeing and Doing

Merton (South West)

Drinking and Dining

Seeing and Doing

A Little Further Out...

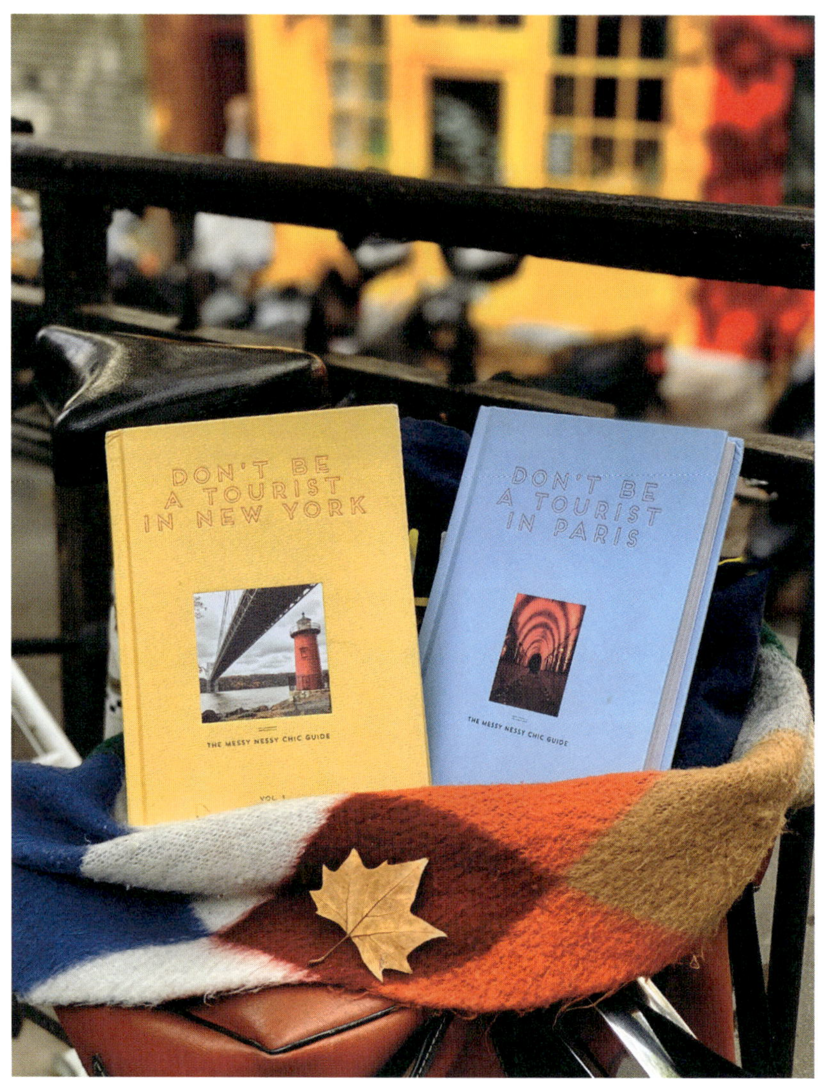
DON'T BE
A TOURIST
IN NEW YORK
THE MESSY NESSY CHIC GUIDE
DON'T BE
A TOURIST
IN PARIS
THE MESSY NESSY CHIC GUIDE

Also in this collection:

DON'T BE A TOURIST IN NEW YORK

and

Bookstores please contact:
DBTBooks@messynessychic.com

DISCOVER OUR EBOOK COLLECTION ON SHOP.MESSYNESSYCHIC.COM

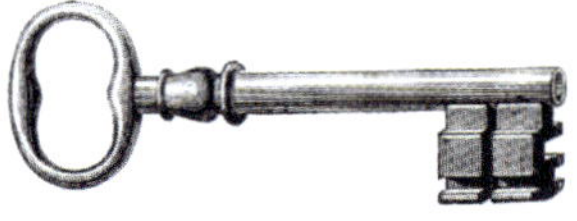

DON'T BE A TOURIST
MINI GUIDE TO
Amsterdam
A MESSY NESSY MINI GUIDE

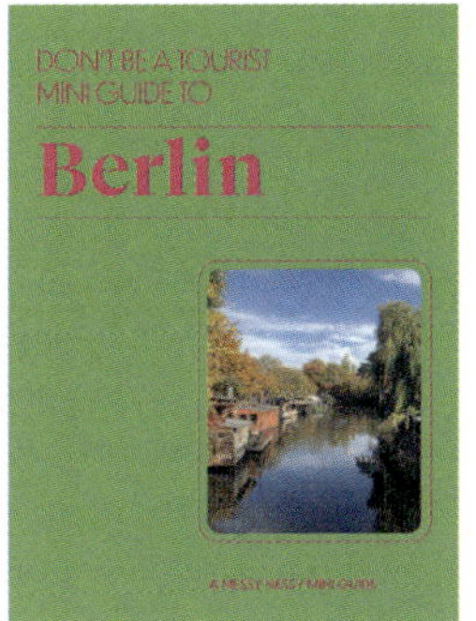
DON'T BE A TOURIST
MINI GUIDE TO
Berlin
A MESSY NESSY MINI GUIDE

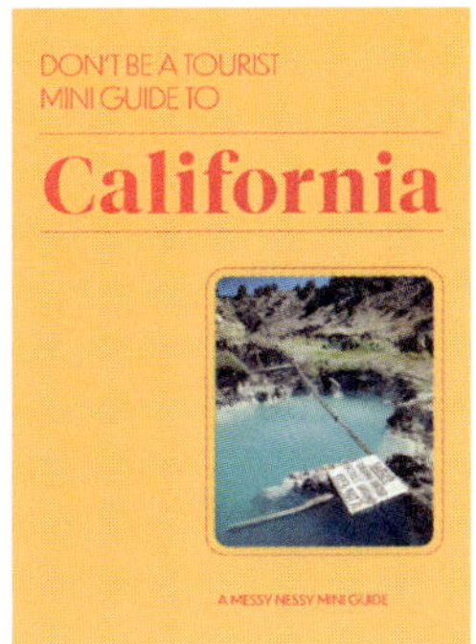
DON'T BE A TOURIST
MINI GUIDE TO
California
A MESSY NESSY MINI GUIDE

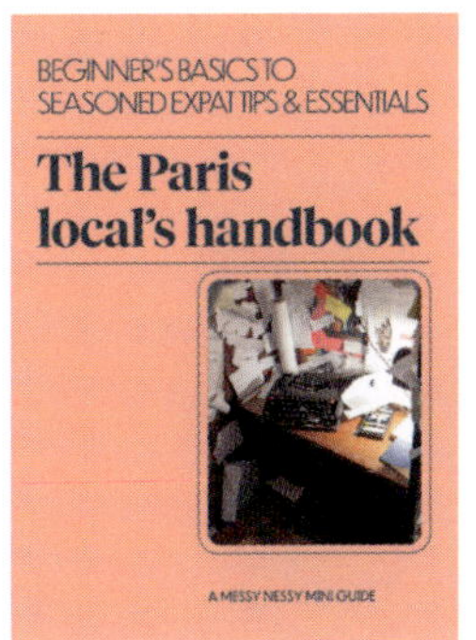
BEGINNER'S BASICS TO
SEASONED EXPAT TIPS & ESSENTIALS
The Paris
local's handbook
A MESSY NESSY MINI GUIDE

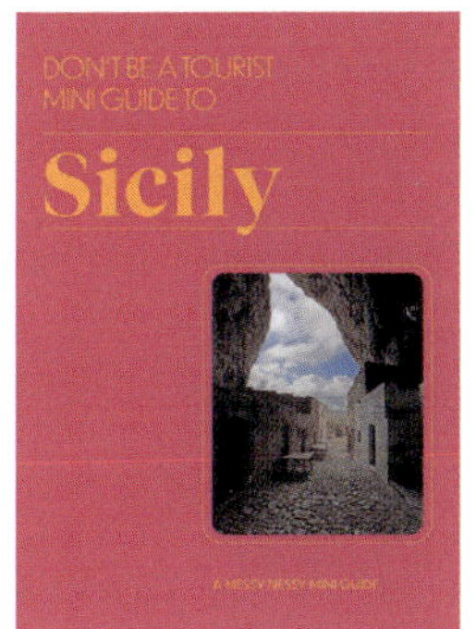
DON'T BE A TOURIST
MINI GUIDE TO
Sicily
A MESSY NESSY MINI GUIDE

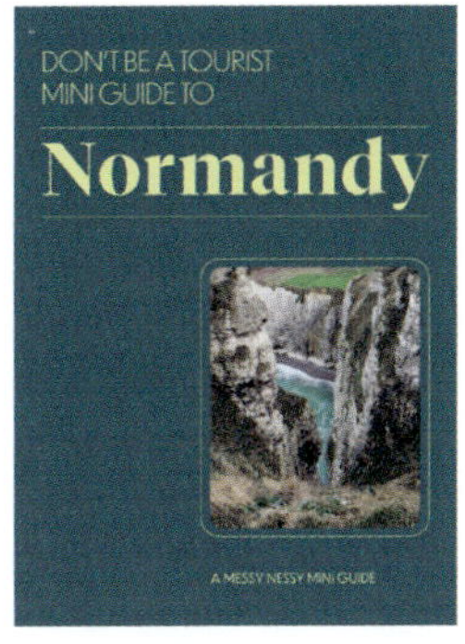
DON'T BE A TOURIST
MINI GUIDE TO
Normandy
A MESSY NESSY MINI GUIDE

DON'T BE A TOURIST
MINI GUIDE TO
Portugal
A MESSY NESSY MINI GUIDE

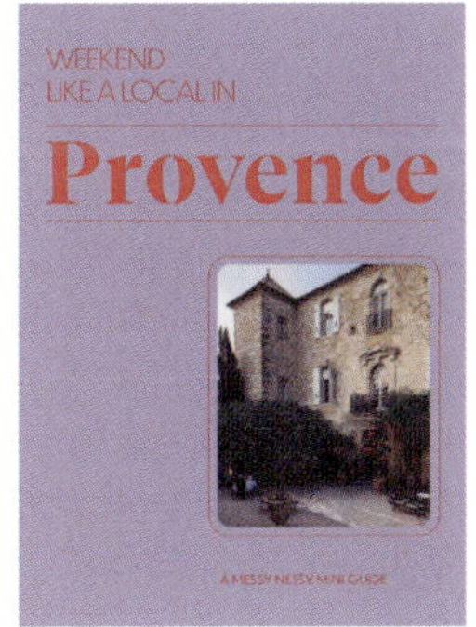
WEEKEND
LIKE A LOCAL IN
Provence
A MESSY NESSY MINI GUIDE

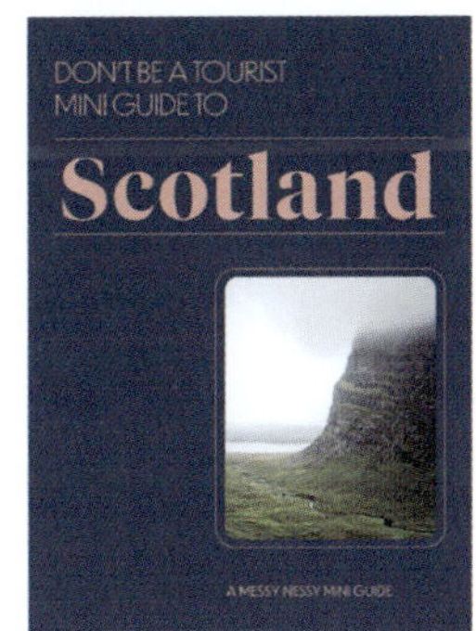
DON'T BE A TOURIST
MINI GUIDE TO
Scotland
A MESSY NESSY MINI GUIDE

Rambling Notes of a Traveller

Thank you

This book took a heck of a lot longer than planned to finish. One might say it took a lifetime. From the moment I began that first chapter to writing this final page, we had lost the Queen of England (not to mention another British queen, Dame Vivien Westwood), a global pandemic came and went, and I became a mother to my two children. That is to say that quite some time had passed. And so I want to start by thanking some people for their patience. My contributors, Molly Russell and Luke J Spencer, who never once questioned our slow but steady progress in bringing this book to life. Molly, I'm so grateful that you found me when you did, with your effortless writer's wit and mysterious ability to read my mind. I hope we get to work together for years to come. Luke, my trusty gentleman explorer for nearly a decade now: I and the internet owe you so much for your tireless curiosity and for all the fascinating little facts you've uncovered by walking into the overlooked places, talking to the unnoticed outsiders and asking the right questions. Scott Walker, I miss you and I'll always treasure your tips and advice. Lizzie Atanassova and Rooksana Hossenally, thank you for helping me lay the foundations in those early stages. My behind-the-scenes fairies, whose reassuring presence has been a godsend: Yasmeen Roundtree and Louisa Mahoney for keeping the fire lit at the MessyNessy HQ and Kate Prior, for coming back on board with your fine tooth comb and making sure we got it done right. Oksana Kravtsova, once again, you deserve a medal for your speed, patience and willingness to piece the pages together at the 11th hour. Thank you to the team at ACC Art Books for taking on my little publishing house at the beginning with just one book about Paris to our name and guiding us through the industry.

To my rock, my lifeboat and my everything, my husband Alex, thank you for always moving me forward and for all the thankless tasks you take on to make these books a reality. And to the joys of my life, Oscar and Maxine, I hope Mummy will make you proud – you've kept me laughing and bursting with love throughout. The next one is for you. To my parents, for raising me in London, putting up with me through those turbulent years and showing me the kind of places that last forever, I love you. Friends (and my dream girls), cheerleaders and devoted Messy Nessy Chic readers: the comfort and support you have brought me over the years has been my secret tonic. Thank you all for being the reason that I still continue to explore, learn and grow.

DON'T BE A TOURIST IN LONDON

A book by

Vanessa Grall

with writers and explorers

Molly Russell and Luke J Spencer

Art Direction & Design

Vanessa Grall & Alexandre Tavernier

Layout & Composition

Oksana Kravtsova

Editorial Assistance

Kate Prior

Yasmeen Roundtree

Elizabeth Atanassova

Rooksana Hossenally

Also in this collection

DON'T BE A TOURIST IN PARIS

DON'T BE A TOURIST IN NEW YORK

PUBLISHED BY MESSY NESSY CHIC

A DIVISION OF 13 THINGS LTD .

Unit 3, 1st Floor, 6/7 St. Mary at Hill

London, EC3R 8EE, United Kingdom

contact@messynessychic.com

First published 2024

British Library Cataloguing in Publication Data.

A catalogue record for this book is available from the British Library.

Printed in China on responsibly sourced paper.

ISBN: 978-1-9164309-4-5

Photography Credits

In addition to the photography by Vanessa Grall © MessyNessyChic, the following photographers / organisations contributed to the imagery of this book:

© British Library: Cook's Handbook for London map, 1887, Thos. Cook & Son Edition.
© Chuca Cimas: Page 96 (bottom left). Pg121 (right). Pg275 (left). Pg358 (bottom), Pg383.
© Johnny Stephens: Page 42. Pg44. Pg104
© Maggie Jones: Page 21. Pg47. Pg77. Pg86. Pg96 (very top left). Pg109. Pg121(left). Pg136. Pg153 (all three). Pg154 (right). Pg155. Pg156. Pg170. Pg203 (left). Pg204. Pg207. Pg225. Pg270. Pg271 (left). Pg302 (middle right). Pg325. Pg255 (bottom). Pg390 (right). Pg392 (top).
© Matt Brown: Page 208. Pg211. Pg215. Pg345. Pg364
© Ungry Young Man: Page 38 (top left). Pg40. Pg180. Pg182. Pg247
© Jim Linwood: Page 18. Pg69 (bottom). Pg171. Pg269 (left). Pg392 (bottom)
© Molly Russell: Page 138. Pg148. Pg151. Pg209. Pg352.

Pg26 © The Black Dog Pub Company. Pg45 © Sam Mellish. Pg48 © Richard Fib. Pg56 © Tap & Bottle. Pg57 © Paul Marc Mitchell. Pg58 © Rubedo.
Pg60, Pg318 © Midnight Apothecary. Pg61 © David Jensen. Pg62 © Eloise Isaac. Pg63 © Timothy Soar. Pg65 © Novelty Automation. Pg69 (top) © Alain Rouiller. Pg70 © Elle Pickering. Pg72 © Jack de Nijs. Pg74 © Julian Osley.
Pg76, 320 © Little Nan's Bar. Pg83 © Berry Brothers & Rudd. Pg85 © Alexander Baxevanis. Pg87 © Luigi Rosa. Pg88 © Andrew Stawarz.
Pg89, 277, 369 © It's No Game. Pg90 © Ewan Munro. Pg92 © Anders Thirsgaard Rasmussen. Pg96 (middle right) © Konstantina Zag. Pg96 (bottom centre) © Jim Osley. Pg96 (bottom right) © Garry Knight. Pg100 © George Rex. Pg103 © Amanda Slater. Pg104 © Johnny Stephens. Pg105 © Rayray. Pg106 © Alex Askew. Pg107 © Kleon3. Pg110 © Sue Barr. Pg113 © Michael Bowles. Pg120 © Stig Nygaard. Pg123 © David Mapletoft. Pg125 -127 © Sue Barr. Pg137 © English Heritage. Pg140 © John Carey. Pg141 - 142 © Gareth Gardner courtesy of Sir John Soane's Museum. Pg144 © Peter Dazeley. Pg145 © Visit Greenwich.
Pg146 © The Old Cinema. Pg149 © Sunbury Antiques. Pg150 © Lucy Naughton. Pg158 © Banalities. Pg160 © Damo1977. Pg165 © Nicolas Lysandrou.
Pg166 © Gary Campbell Hall. Pg174 © Phil Dunlop. Pg175 © The William Heath Robinson Trust. Pg179 © Manuel Harlan. Pg181 © EdwardX.
Pg184 © Tuur Tisseghem. Pg186 © Alexandra Kirr. Pg189 © Francesca Grima. Pg190 © Sanshiro Kubota. Pg192 -193 © Euan Myles. Pg196 © Hotel Kaesong. Pg196 (bottom) & Pg197 © Brad Hostetler. Pg201 © Darren Ee.

Pg203 © Max van den Oetelaar. Pg205 © Learning Lark. Pg212 © UK Parliament. P218 © Guy Parker. Pg219 © Miss Dilettante. Pg222 © Kyle Bushnell. Pg223 © Ann Lee. Pg224 © Mjfstudio. Pg226 © Bixentro. Pg231 © Bertie Watson. P237 © Tent at the End of the Universe. Pg238 -P239 © Little Yellow Door. Pg242 (both images) © Big Mamma Group. Pg243 © Jerome Galland. Pg245 © Moth Club. Pg248 (top right) © Notting Hill Arts Club. Pg248 (top left) © Charles Thompson. Pg250 © Aurélien Guichard. Pg254 © Annie Williams. Pg255 © Eilidh Wag. Pg256 © Aurelien Guichard. Pg263 © Vladislav Kolev. Pg264 (top) © Vladislav Kolev. Pg264 (bottom) © Louis Amore. Pg265 © Judy Valentine. Pg266 © Jeremy T. Hetzel. Pg267 © Jeremy T. Hetzel. Pg271(right) © Italo Deli. Pg272 © Thomas Rowlandson (Vauxhall Pleasure Gardens in about 1779). Pg274 © Cristian Bortes. Pg 279 © The Magic garden. Pg281 © James Morris. Pg283 © Ellora Prior & Celia Topping. Pg293 © B Bakery London bus. Pg296 © Adam Foster. Pg300 © Gemma Evans. Pg301, Pg302 (bottom left, right) © Edward Howell. Pg302 (top left) © Benn Mcguinness. P302 (bottom right) © Elissar Haidar. Pg203 (top right) © Max Letek. Pg303 © Benjamin Pollock's Toyshop. Pg304 © Postal Museum. Pg306 © Stan Middleton. Pg307 (left) © Alexander Baxevanis. Pg307 (right) © nzsteam. Pg308 © Andy Leigh. Pg311 © MinaLima. Pg312 © Kempton Steam Museum. Pg314 © Eloise Isaac. Pg317 © Paul Wilkinson. Pg326 (top) © Nicolas Lysandrou. Pg326 (bottom), 327 © Transport for London. Pg328 © Alejandro Olaya Torres. Pg329 © Rachelle Haun. Pg331 © Chris Howlett. Pg332 © WC Bars. Pg333 © Paul Farmer. Pg338 © Holborn Viaduct. Pg339, 342 © Loz Pycock. Pg343 © Andrew Moore. Pg344 © Keith Bowden. Pg346 © John Armagh. Pg350 © Leonard Bentley. Pg355 (top) © Wellcome Collection. Pg358 (top) © Marko Pekic. Pg360-361 © Alexander Savin. Pg365 © Charlie Egan. Pg368 © Betsy Weber. Pg371 © English Heritage. P372,385 © Abhishek-Banik. Pg375 © Surreal Name Given. Pg390 (left) © Laura Nolte. P394 © Acabashi. Pg395 © Martin V Morris. Pg396 © Sy. Pg398 (top left) © Peter Trimming. Pg398 (top right) © WoodleyWonderworks. Pg398 (left centre) © Polly Peterson. Pg398 (bottom left) © Mark Wordy. Pg398 (right centre) © Ian Clark. Pg398 (bottom right) © Mark Wordy. Pg401 © Karen Roe. Pg414 (right) © Clare Whiting. Pg415 © Jo.Sau. Pg416 © Nomad Tales. Pg417 © Howard Grey. Pg426 © Dilettantiquity. Pg428 © Unseen Tours. Pg430 © Mohamed Nanabhay. Pg432 © Tony Sleep. P434 © Hazlitt Group.